Lecture Notes in Computer Science　　　3284

Commenced Publication in 1973
Founding and Former Series Editors:
Gerhard Goos, Juris Hartmanis, and Jan van Leeuwen

Editorial Board

T0223563

Ahmed Karmouch   Larry Korba
Edmundo R.M. Madeira (Eds.)

Mobility Aware Technologies and Applications

First International Workshop, MATA 2004
Florianópolis, Brazil, October 20-22, 2004
Proceedings

 Springer

Volume Editors

Ahmed Karmouch
University of Ottawa, School of Information Technology and Engineering
161 Louis Pasteur St., Ottawa, ON K1N 6N5, Canada
E-mail: karmouch@site.uottawa.ca

Larry Korba
National Research Council of Canada, Institute for Information Technology
1200 Montreal Road, Ottawa, ON K1A 0R5, Canada
E-mail: larry.korba@nrc-cnrc.gc.ca

Edmundo R.M. Madeira
University of Campinas, Institute of Computing
Avenida Albert Einstein, 1251, 13084–971, Campinas, SP, Brazil
E-mail: edmundo@ic.unicamp.br

Library of Congress Control Number: 2004113942

CR Subject Classification (1998): C.2, H.4, H.5, H.3

ISSN 0302-9743
ISBN 3-540-23423-3 Springer Berlin Heidelberg New York

Springer is a part of Springer Science+Business Media

springeronline.com

© Springer-Verlag Berlin Heidelberg 2004
Printed in Germany

Typesetting: Camera-ready by author, data conversion by Olgun Computergrafik
Printed on acid-free paper   SPIN: 11331667   06/3142   5 4 3 2 1 0

Preface

It is becoming quite clear that there will be important technological advances in mobile and wireless connectivity, known as third-/fourth-generation (3G and 4G) mobile telecommunications systems. As a result we will be surrounded by ever-growing multidomain (technical and administrative) heterogeneous communications in both wired and wireless networks. This resulting environment deals with communication in multizoned networks, where people, devices, appliances and servers are connected to each other via different kinds of networks. Networks will be pervasive, ubiquitous, multiservice, multioperator and multiaccess. The mobility trend will also be spurred forward by the growing availability of mobile-enabled handheld devices.

Mobile systems are expected to provide mobile users with cost-effective, secure, yet ubiquitous service access anywhere and anytime. Users will then continue to enjoy the new-found freedom mobile access provides and will have increasingly high expectations of mobility-aware applications that should be capable of seamlessly supporting the mobile lifestyle.

The papers in this volume discuss issues from models, platforms, and architectures for mobility-aware systems to security, mobile agent technologies, sensitive communications, context awareness, mobile applications and management. They cover both practical experience and novel research ideas and concepts.

We would like to express our appreciation and thanks to the authors for their contributions to preparing and revising the papers as well as the technical program committee and the reviewers who helped put together an excellent technical program for the workshop. Special thanks are due to Hamid Harroud and Mohamed Khedr who kindly contributed their time and effort to help with the organization of the review process and the technical program.

October 2004   Ahmed Karmouch

Program Committee

T. Araragi, NTT, Japan
P. Bellavista, Bologna, Italy
F. Bellifemine, TILab, Italy
R. Boutaba, University of Waterloo, Canada
P. Brezillon, LIP6, France
B. Burg, HP Labs, USA
J. Celestino Júnior, FUC, Brazil
J-P. Courtiat, LAAS, France
J. Delgado, UPF Barcelona, Spain
O. Duarte, UFRJ, Brazil
M. Endler, PUC-Rio, Brazil
W. Enkelmann, Daimler Chrysler AG, Germany
B. Falchuk, Telecordia, USA
A. Galis, UCL, UK
M.-F. Gervais, LIP6, France
R. Glitho, Ericsson, Canada
Y. Gourhant, FT R&D, France
S. Guan, NUS, Singapore
S. Honiden, NII, Japan
E. Horlait, LIP6, France
R. Impey, NRC, Canada
Y. Ismailov, Ericsson, Sweden
A. Loureiro, UFMG, Brazil
M. Luck, University of Southampton, UK
T. Magedanz, FhG FOKUS/TU Berlin, Germany
J. Martins, UNIFACS, Brazil
F. McCabe, Fujitsu, USA
J. Odell, Odell.com, USA
S. Pierre, EP. Montreal, Canada
S. Poslad, Queen Mary, UK
F. Ramparany, France Telecom, France
V. Roth, FhG IGD, Germany
A. Seneviratne, UNSW, Australia
R. Stadler, ETH Zürich, Switzerland
L. Strick, FhG FOKUS, Germany
I. Venieris, NTUA, Greece
S.T. Vuong, UBC, Canada
J.-F. Wagen, University of Applied Sciences of Western Switzerland
M. Zhengkum, Nanjing University of Posts and Telecommunications, China

Table of Contents

Performance and QoS

Mobility Aware Systems and Services

Agent Technology and Applications

Mobility Prediction for Mobile Agent-Based Service Continuity in the Wireless Internet

Paolo Bellavista, Antonio Corradi, and Carlo Giannelli

Dipartimento di Elettronica, Informatica e Sistemistica
Università di Bologna
Viale Risorgimento, 2, 40136 Bologna, Italy
{pbellavista,acorradi,cgiannelli}@deis.unibo.it

Abstract. New challenging deployment scenarios are integrating mobile devices with limited and heterogeneous capabilities that roam among wireless access localities during service provisioning. This calls for novel middleware solutions not only to support different forms of mobility and connectivity in wired-wireless integrated networks, but also to perform personalized service reconfiguration/adaptation depending on client characteristics and in response to changes of wireless access locality. The paper proposes the adoption of Mobile Agent (MA) proxies working at the wired-wireless network edges to support the personalized access of limited wireless clients to their needed resources on the fixed network. In particular, the paper focuses on how to predict device mobility between IEEE 802.11 cells in a portable lightweight way, with no need of external global positioning systems. In fact, we claim that mobility prediction is crucial to maintain service continuity: MA-based proxies can migrate in advance to the wireless cells where mobile clients are going to reconnect to, in order to anticipate the local rearrangement of personalized sessions. The paper proposes and evaluates different mobility prediction solutions based on either client-side received signal strength or Ekahau positioning, all integrated in the SOMA platform. Both simulation and experimental results show that SOMA can predict the next visited cell with a very limited overhead and enough in advance to maintain service continuity for a large class of wireless Internet services.

1 Introduction

The increasing availability of public wireless access points to the Internet and the widespread popularity of wireless-enabled portable devices stimulate the provisioning of distributed services to a wide variety of mobile client terminals, with very heterogeneous and often limited resources. Even though devices and networking capabilities are increasing and increasing, the design of mobile applications will continue to be constrained by several factors, from limited display size to high connectivity costs, from bandwidth fluctuations to local resource availability, also abruptly changing due to client mobility among wireless cells during service provisioning.

Let us focus on the common deployment scenario where wireless solutions extend accessibility to the traditional Internet via access points working as bridges between fixed hosts and wireless devices [1]. An exemplar case is the usage of IEEE 802.11 access points to support connectivity of WiFi-equipped terminals to a wired local area network [2]. In the following, we will indicate these integrated networks with fixed

A. Karmouch, L. Korba, and E. Madeira (Eds.): MATA 2004, LNCS 3284, pp. 1–12, 2004.

Internet hosts, wireless terminals, and wireless access points in between, as the wireless Internet.

Service provisioning over the wireless Internet must consider the specific characteristics of client portable devices, primarily their limits on local resources and their high heterogeneity. Limited processing power, memory and file system make portable devices unsuitable for traditional services designed for fixed networks and require both assisting wireless terminals in the service access and downscaling contents to obey resource constraints. In addition, portable devices exhibit extreme heterogeneity of hardware capabilities, operating systems, installed software, and network technologies. This heterogeneity makes hard to provide all needed service versions with statically tailored contents and calls for on-the-fly adaptation of service provisioning.

We claim the need of middleware solutions to dynamically adapt service results to the specific properties of client devices and to the runtime resource availability of the provisioning environment [3-6]. Middleware components should follow client roaming in different wireless localities and assist them locally during their service sessions. Moreover, client limited memory suggests deploying middleware components over the fixed network, where and when needed, while portable devices should host only thin clients, loaded by need and automatically discarded after service.

By following the above solution guidelines, we have recently designed and implemented application-level middlewares, based on Secure and Open Mobile Agent (SOMA) proxies, to support the distribution of context-dependent news and video on demand to wireless devices with strict limits on on-board resources [5, 7, 8]. The primary design idea is to dynamically deploy SOMA proxies acting on the behalf of wireless clients over the fixed hosts in the network localities that currently offer client connectivity. In particular, this paper focuses on a crucial challenge for MA-based middlewares for the wireless Internet: how to predict the client movements among wireless cells, making unnecessary any external Global Positioning System (GPS). Mobility prediction permits to migrate personalized SOMA proxies in advance with regards to the client roaming. Thus, SOMA proxies have the time to proactively reorganize user sessions in the newly visited network localities, by rebinding to needed resources and local middleware components for service adaptation, with the ultimate goal of supporting session maintenance and continuous service provisioning [5].

We propose three different mobility prediction solutions, all exploiting a first-order Grey Model (GM) [9]. The first approach uses only the client-side monitoring data about Received Signal Strength Indication (RSSI) in a decentralized, lightweight, and portable way (we call it RSSI-GM for shortly). The other two solutions take advantage of the positioning data provided by the commercial Ekahau Positioning Engine (EPE) [10]. Ekahau Cell Probability (ECP) exploits the EPE-provided probabilities of being located in a cell, both currently and in the recent past, as the input for GM-based mobility prediction. Ekahau Distance (ED)-GM bases its prediction on the current/recent distances of client nodes from the borders of IEEE 802.11 cells of base stations in their visibility.

We have evaluated the performance of the three mobility prediction solutions both via a simulator, which can model nodes randomly roaming among IEEE 802.11 localities, and by exploiting a system prototype deployed over WiFi-enabled PDAs with MS Windows CE.NET. Both experimental results show that the simplest and completely decentralized RSSI-GM approach outperforms the others. In addition, notwithstanding the portable and application-level approach, RSSI-GM has demonstrated to be capable of predicting the next cell location enough time in advance to permit SOMA middleware to rearrange personalized sessions before the client connects to the new wireless locality. This permits to provide adapted services to limited wireless devices without any interruption in the case of client roaming.

2   Motivating Mobility Prediction in MA-Based Middlewares

Service provisioning in the wireless Internet usually calls for downscaling service contents to suit the specific limits of client devices. For instance, dynamic content negotiation and tailoring are crucial for multimodal services providing resource-consuming multimedia in Web pages. In addition, device mobility requires other support operations that are too expensive to be performed by severely limited devices, e.g., context-aware local/global resource retrieval and binding. On the one hand, local discovery operations may consume non-negligible client resources to explore the execution environment and to negotiate with available services. On the other hand, the global identification and retrieval of user-related properties, such as user/terminal profiles and security certificates stored in directories, may require long continuous connectivity, difficult to be handled directly by portable devices.

We claim that wireless Internet service provisioning can significantly benefit from distributed and active infrastructures of mobile middleware proxies working in the fixed network on behalf of portable devices [6]. Proxies can decide the best adaptation operations to perform on service results and can be in charge of any additional management operation, such as supporting connectivity and discovering the needed resources/service components. Moreover, proxies can act, locally to the client, as distributed cache repositories for successive service requests. In addition, if proxies are mobile, they can follow device movements during service provisioning by supporting session migration between the different network localities visited, and install automatically only where and when needed [6].

For all above reasons, the primary design choice in SOMA-based middlewares for the wireless Internet is to provide any wireless device with one SOMA-based companion entity, called *shadow proxy*, which run in a wired node (place) in the same wireless network locality that currently provides connectivity to the device [5, 8]. Wired/wireless terminals in a locality can be grouped into logical domains, as depicted in Figure 1; domains are disjointed, even if they include wireless access points with coverage areas that partially overlap.

Shadow proxies are in charge of determining the applicable context for their clients and of consequently retrieving and binding to the needed local/global resources. Proxies solve the issues related to receiving, caching, and coordinating the tailoring of service contents by taking context-dependent decisions based on profile metadata that describe device characteristics and user preferences [6].

In the following, the paper concentrates on the crucial issue of how to predict the client movements between SOMA localities in order to migrate in advance the proxies to the next domain of attachment of their associated clients. A detailed description of the implementation of the different SOMA middleware components that support the distribution of context-dependent news and video on demand to wireless devices is out of the scope of the paper, and can be found elsewhere [5, 8].

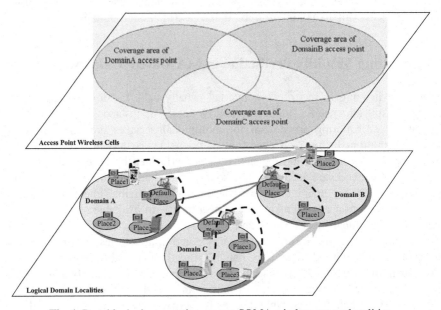

Fig. 1. Portable devices roaming among SOMA wireless access localities.

To better understand the need for mobility prediction, let us describe the service management operations that the SOMA-based middleware performs in response to a client change of locality. Let us suppose a user roams from DomainA to DomainB in Figure 1 while she is receiving her personalized location-aware service contents. Note that user movements also produce the user change of access point coverage area, since in location-aware services clients should typically associate with their closest base station. Depending on the (usually configurable) handoff strategy of the underlying communication layer, the user device is transparently de-associated from the origin wireless cell and associated to the destination one i) when the client no more receives the origin signal, ii) when the destination RSSI overcomes the origin RSSI (handoff hysteresis = 0), iii) or, more generally, when the destination RSSI overcomes the origin RSSI of a specified threshold t (handoff hysteresis = t), also to reduce bouncing effects.

Once notified of the communication handoff, the middleware should migrate the shadow proxy to the destination domain. There, the proxy should instantiate and configure the needed local middleware components and reconnect to the server (or to an equivalent local replica of it) before being capable of serving its client again. This can cause a temporary suspension of the service typically experienced by the client as a provisioning block or delay [8]. The goal of mobility prediction is to effectively perform the migration of a shadow proxy clone before the client communication handoff, so to establish the cloned proxy in the new destination domain, ready for the service session of its incoming client.

Let us notice that the addressed wireless Internet provisioning environment considers medium/short-range wireless technologies (IEEE 802.11b or Bluetooth) in open and extremely dynamic scenarios where the user mobility behaviors change very frequently and irregularly. Thus, the relevant results of research activities about handover prediction based on user movement patterns/history cannot apply [11].

3   The Proposed Mobility Prediction Solutions

In this paper, we propose and compare three alternative solutions for mobility prediction: RSSI-GM, ECP-GM, and ED-GM. The proposed solutions do not need any additional specific hardware; in particular, they do not require external GPSs, which are still rather expensive, battery-consuming, and therefore unsuitable for very resource-constrained wireless devices. Moreover, the mobility prediction solutions, which we have evaluated and implemented for IEEE 802.11 connectivity, are easily applicable also to wireless clients that exploit other forms of access point connectivity, e.g., Bluetooth clients towards Bluetooth infotainment points [12]. The only constraint is to have client-side awareness of RSSI, either directly exploited in RSSI-GM or indirectly used (via the EPE mediation) in both ECP-GM and ED-GM.

3.1   Received Signal Strength Indication-Grey Model

The RSSI-GM prediction solution requires a lightweight client stub running on any client device. It is the client stub that autonomously predicts the next cell visited by the hosting wireless device and that communicates the prediction to the shadow proxy place, thus triggering the clone migration. To this purpose, the client stub needs to access the monitoring data about the RSSI values of the IEEE 802.11 base stations in its visibility. The RSSI data is used as input for a simple Grey-based discrete model GM(1,1) for the prediction of future RSSI values [9]. Client stubs achieve platform- and vendor-independent visibility of RSSI data by integrating with portable and dynamically installable monitoring mechanisms, as extensively described in [13].

Given one reachable access point and the set of its actual RSSI values measured at the client side $R_0 = \{r_0(1), ..., r_0(n)\}$, where $r_0(i)$ is the RSSI value at the discrete time i, it is possible to calculate $R_1 = \{r_1(1), ..., r_1(n)\}$, where:

$$r_1(i) = \sum_{j=1}^{i} r_0(j)$$

Then, from the GM(1,1) discrete differential equation of the first order:

$$\frac{dr_1(i)}{di} + ar_1(i) = u$$

the client stub determines a and u, which are exploited to obtain the predicted RSSI value $pr(i)$ at discrete time i according to the GM(1,1) prediction function:

$$pr(i) = \left(r_i(1) - \frac{u}{a} \right) e^{-ak} + \frac{u}{a}$$

When the *pr(i)* for a base station *x* overcomes the *pr(i)* for the currently associated base station *y*, then the client stub communicates the mobility prediction to the shadow proxy place, thus triggering the proxy clone migration.

The above solution for client mobility prediction is completely local and lightweight; any client stub can estimate its future RSSI values simply by maintaining a finite series of previous RSSI data. In particular, the client stub catches the needed monitoring information and predicts the next cell in a completely autonomous way, with a very limited overhead. The client stub exploits the limited bandwidth wireless channel only occasionally to inform the shadow proxy place in the case of predicted change of logical domain.

3.2 Ekahau Cell Probability-Grey Model and Ekahau Distance-Grey Model

Similarly to RSSI-GM, both ECP-GM and ED-GM prediction solutions use GM(1,1) discrete models. However, they do not exploit RSSI data as the input values for the prediction models but, respectively, the estimated probability that a client device is located in a cell and the estimated device distances from the borders of IEEE 802.11 cells of access points in visibility. In these two solutions, it is directly the SOMA place hosting the shadow proxy execution that performs mobility prediction by communicating with EPE to obtain the needed information about cell probabilities and distances.

EPE is a widespread commercial solution for non-GPS-based positioning in IEEE 802.11 infrastructure-mode networks [10]. For any target device, EPE provides the probabilities that the device is located in a set of pre-defined logical areas, i.e., configurable disjointed portions of the wireless deployment scenario. Bayes-based probability estimation is performed by observing the current and recent RSSI values at the target device, by comparing them with a database of RSSI samples for the provisioning environment, and by considering a set of specified admitted mobility paths in that environment. This implies that system administrators must provide EPE with a map of the environment and the admitted paths of client movements in any specific deployment scenario. In addition, an initial "learning" phase is necessary for EPE to acquire the database of RSSI samples for the different points of the provisioning environment. The EPE system consists of a centralized server responsible for the whole processing to obtain the position estimations, and of lightweight clients that run on wireless clients and regularly send the observed RSSI values to the EPE server.

Given a target device, ECP-GM considers the finite set of probabilities provided by EPE and applies GM(1,1) to these probabilities. The proxy clone migration is triggered when the predicted probability of the current shadow proxy cell becomes minor than the predicted probability of another logical area. ED-GM, instead, exploits the position estimation provided by EPE to calculate the distances between the target device and the cell borders of visible base stations, and applies GM(1,1) to these distances. In this case, the proxy clone migration is triggered when the predicted distance from the borders of the current cell exceeds the predicted distance from the borders of another logical area.

Let us note that, differently from RSSI-GM, both ECP-GM and ED-GM are not completely decentralized prediction solutions. It is the Ekahau client running on the target device that monitors RSSI data and regularly sends them to EPE. In addition, the shadow proxy in charge of mobility prediction has to interwork with the centralized EPE, which feeds the proxy with current estimations about either cell probabilities or distances from the cell borders of visible base stations. In addition, since the Ekahau client is available only for MS Windows, ECP-GM and ED-GM are not portable on different operating systems, differently from RSSI-GM.

4 Simulation and In-the-Field Experimental Results

To evaluate the effectiveness and performance of the proposed prediction solutions, we have developed three alternative implementations of the mobility prediction module: all the solutions are integrated with the SOMA platform and present the same API. SOMA[1] is a Java-based mobile agent system intended to support service provisioning in pervasive and ubiquitous environments [5, 7]. We have extended SOMA with the mobility prediction module by adding a shadow proxy which is a new MA subclass that exploits the usual one. The SOMA platform (by either the client stub in RSSI-GM or the SOMA place in ECP-GM and ED-GM) automatically notifies the shadow proxy in the case of handoff prediction for the associated client devices. The prediction notification triggers the transparent cloning of the shadow proxy and the clone migration to the predicted cell. The original proxy executes at its previous place until the associated device eventually exits its wireless access locality and completes its handoff. Application developers can concentrate only on the service-specific application logic that implements this part of shadow proxy while SOMA automatically handles cloning, anticipated migration, and lifecycle management of shadow proxy instances.

We have measured some performance indicators for all three mobility prediction solutions in both a simulated environment (with a large number of mobile clients roaming among a large number of wireless localities) and our campus deployment scenario. Considered performance indicators are:

- effectiveness $E1_{\%} = \left(1 - \frac{NFSP}{NR}\right)*100$

  where $NFSP$ measures times the wireless devices do not find their shadow proxies already running at their destination domains at their arrivals, while NR is the total number of client handoffs;

- efficiency $E2_{\%} = \left(\frac{USP}{NM}\right)*100$

  where USP is the number of shadow proxies eventually used by the wireless clients and NM is the total number of migrated proxies;

---

[1] Additional information about the SOMA platform and its downloadable code are available at: http://lia.deis.unibo.it/Research/SOMA/

- advance time AT, i.e., the time interval between the shadow proxy arrival at the destination domain and the eventual client reconnection to that domain.

Effectiveness and efficiency are both significant performance indicators. In general, high effectiveness may be tied to low efficiency: an excessive migration of proxy clones to visible localities generates useless network traffic (migrated clones are automatically discarded if the associated clients do not reach them within a timeout).

We have measured the three indicators above in a challenging simulated environment where 16 access points are regularly placed in a 64m x 64m square. We have developed a simple lightweight simulator to analyze wireless device movement and to monitor RSSI. Already existing but more complex simulators cannot supply so easily and efficiently these feature. We have simulated two extreme trajectories: *trajectory1*, a straight path with constant random velocity between two random points, and *trajectory2,* with random variable velocity and with random direction with a Gaussian component of 30 degree standard deviation. In both trajectories the velocity is always between 0.2 and 2.5 m/s to mimic the behavior of walking mobile users. Typically, wireless device performs a cell roaming when the destination cell RSSI rises above actual cell RSSI of a fixed hysteresis threshold. In our simulated environment the hysteresis threshold value ranges from 0 to 2 db. On the average, each mobile client has the contemporaneous visibility of 6 access points, that represents a worst case scenario significantly more complex than the actually deployed wireless networks (where usually no more than 3 access points are visible from any point). We have evaluated scenarios with fewer access points for each wireless client device; in all the scenarios $E1_\%$, $E2_\%$, and AT have proven to be better than in the simulation case.

Table 1 shows the average performance for a set of about 600 experiments where wireless devices roam by following *trajectory1*. When handoffs are rarely predicted, that is when $E1_\%$ is really low, AT is not shown because it does not present a significant positive value, due to poor performance. RSSI-GM outperforms the other solutions for all three performance indicators. EPE performs positioning quite well, but it is less prompt in ascertaining device movements that affects negatively ECP-GM and ED-GM performance. When the hysteresis threshold increases, roaming is delayed and there is more time to predict wireless device roaming: consequently both $E1_\%$ and AT increase. In this case, RSSI-GM $E2_\%$ lowers because delayed roaming triggers more predictions, most of them unnecessary. In summary, RSSI-GM $E1_\%$ is good also with a null hysteresis, and a higher hysteresis does not make $E1_\%$ much better. As a consequence, $E2_\%$ decreases since NM increases and USP is almost constant. On the contrary ECP-GM and ECP-GM $E2_\%$ often rises, in particular when $E1_\%$ increases, because the number of useful predictions significantly increases, proportionally more than total number of predictions. In fact, NM increases but USP increases further.

Table 2 shows the average performance measured with client devices moving according to *trajectory2*. As expected, the Gaussian trajectory component makes handoff prediction more difficult; however, the performance exhibits only a slight occasional deterioration. Let us stress that simulated scenarios are worst case scenarios. In simulation we assume the visibility of several nearby access points and more unnecessary predictions occur than in a real scenario with fewer visible access points, where wireless devices rarely come close to several access points. Moreover, we have tested our system also with irregular access point dispositions, with negligible performance deterioration.

Table 1. RSSI-GM, ED-GM, and ECP-GM performance results in the case of trajectory1.

	$E1_\%$			$E2_\%$			AT (s)		
Threshold (db)	0	1	2	0	1	2	0	1	2
RSSI-GM	79.01	91.69	94.67	80.53	74.27	74.19	2.99	4.34	5.30
ECP-GM	9.67	14.89	19.61	30.07	33.24	37.32	---	---	---
ED-GM	21.93	34.99	43.01	40.63	43.79	47.21	---	0.79	2.56

Table 2. RSSI-GM, ED-GM, and ECP-GM performance results in the case of trajectory2.

	$E1_\%$			$E2_\%$			AT (s)		
Threshold (db)	0	1	2	0	1	2	0	1	2
RSSI-GM	75.35	91.00	93.01	78.61	76.31	72.86	2.88	4.12	4.80
ECP-GM	10.37	13.50	20.18	34.10	34.62	38.97	---	---	---
ED-GM	22.12	33.00	37.94	40.34	44.15	43.78	---	0.84	1.91

Apart from simulation, we have tested the three different mobility prediction modules over an actual deployment scenarios with 5 partially overlapping IEEE 802.11b wireless cells and 10 client devices (Compaq iPAQ h3850 with Windows CE.NET) randomly roaming in the campus environment. The deployed CISCO Aironet 1100 access points use a null signal strength hysteresis threshold for cell handoff triggering. The client-performed scan for visible access points requires only a very limited packet exchange, with negligible bandwidth occupation. The experimental results outperform the simulation-based, by also verifying the assumption that the simulated environment represents a worst case scenario. RSSI-GM shows better performance despite the strong signal fluctuations observed in the real environment because access points are not as close as in simulations. For the same reasons, also ECP-GM and ED-GM show better performance, even if still worse than RSSI-GM.

In summary, the RSSI-GM mobility prediction solution has proven to offer the best performance, both in the simulated environment and the actual deployment, at least when the goal is handoff prediction and not fine-grained positioning prediction. In particular, RSSI-GM achieves AT values that permit SOMA to move and reorganize the middleware support in the next visited locality for a wide set of Internet services. In addition, if compared with ECP-GM and ED-GM, RSSI-GM has also significant advantages in terms of simplicity since it does not need additional components as EPE. For a more detailed presentation of the RSSI-GM, ECP-GM and ED-GM experimental results in different simulated environments, please refer to http://lia.deis.unibo.it/Research/SOMA/MobilityPrediction/

5 Related Work

Several relevant research activities have recently investigated the issues involved in achieving full visibility of mobile device position, most of them with the goal of supporting the provisioning of location-dependent services, some of them to provide the basis for mobility prediction solutions.

A rough estimate of mobile device position can be obtained via different positioning techniques, which are based on RSSI, angle of arrival, time of arrival, or time difference of arrival [14]. It is possible to achieve higher accuracy in position estimation by exploiting either positioning-specific hardware or additional information about the deployment environment. On the one hand, Medusa and the widespread GPS require clients with additional receivers and typically impose larger energy consumption at the clients [15]. On the other hand, some positioning solutions exploit the knowledge of RSSI distribution and/or the movement history (and usual habits) of the target mobile devices, such as in RADAR [16] and Ekahau [10].

By focusing on mobility prediction, most proposals in the literature require the knowledge of both the current position and the speed of target devices. [17] predicts future location/speed by exploiting a dynamic Gauss-Markov model applied to the current and historical movement data. [18] bases its trajectory prediction on the spatial knowledge of the deployment environment, e.g., by considering road network databases, and on past trajectories followed. [19] focuses on mobile ad hoc networks and is aimed at predicting the dis/connection time of mobile devices by monitoring device position and speed; it exploits RSSI data only to identify when the devices are located in overlapping areas with multiple base stations in direct visibility.

Few research activities have addressed mobility prediction with no need of monitoring the location and speed of mobile devices, similarly to what proposed in SOMA. [20] predicts future RSSI values by using a retroactive adaptive filter to mitigate RSSI fluctuations; the device handoff is commanded when the difference between current and predicted RSSI values is greater than a specified threshold. [21] exploits a Grey model to decide when actually forcing the communication handoff by comparing RSSI predictions with average and current RSSI values. However, both [20] and [21] apply RSSI prediction to improve the communication handoff process, e.g., to reduce unnecessary bouncing handoffs due to signal fluctuations, and not to predict the movements of wireless clients with the goal of anticipating the support reorganization in the access locality to be visited.

A very few proposals have recently started to investigate the possibility to integrate mobility prediction with MA anticipated migration over the fixed Internet, with the goal of pre-setting up the next visited wireless access locality. Their main idea is to exploit the history of the past movements of target devices, by assuming a high probability of recurrent mobility patterns. In [22] the MA state is used to maintain the information about the cell paths covered by the MA-associated mobile devices; MAs entirely base their predictions on these historical data. [23] represents an evolution of this kind of approach, by exploiting a machine learning automaton applied to path historical data. To the best of our knowledge, SOMA (extended with RSSI-GM) is the first MA platform that integrates a lightweight and completely decentralized mobility prediction solution, which is exclusively based on the simple RSSI information and implemented in a completely portable way.

6 Conclusions and Ongoing Work

The wireless Internet deployment scenario strongly suggests dynamic middlewares to support the provisioning of personalized services that are reconfigured and tailored at the wireless access locality, to fit the specific characteristics of roaming client devices. The design guideline of exploiting MA-based middleware proxies that work over the fixed network on behalf of their resource-constrained clients is showing its suitability and effectiveness, especially when associated with mobility prediction solutions. These solutions can enable the proactive migration of middleware components to the access localities that are going to be visited by the roaming users.

Our work of design, implementation, and evaluation of different prediction solutions has achieved two main objectives. On the one hand, it has shown that predicting the next visited cell is possible with a limited overhead and enough time advance to preserve service continuity in a large class of wireless Internet services. On the other hand, it has pointed out that simple lightweight solutions such as the completely decentralized RSSI-GM can even outperform more complex approaches such as ECP-GM and ED-GM. As a consequence, we have decided to integrate the RSSI-GM prediction module in the next release of the SOMA platform.

The promising results obtained by the RSSI-GM integration in SOMA are stimulating further related research activity. We are working on achieving service continuity in our MA-based middleware for the dynamic tailoring of Video-on-Demand streams to mobile wireless devices [7, 8]. In particular, this requires combining mobility prediction with the identification, design, and implementation of optimal strategies to dimension client-side buffers for multimedia streams. Buffer size should depend not only on the device profiles that describe the memory characteristics of access terminals, but also on the estimation of service resume time after client handoff. A too small buffer endangers streaming continuity, thus thwarting the anticipated migration of MA-based proxies; otherwise, a too large buffer uselessly wastes the typically limited memory of client devices.

Acknowledgements

Work supported by the Ministero per l'Istruzione, l'Università, e la Ricerca (MIUR) with the FIRB WEB-MINDS Project "Wide-scale Broadband Middleware for Network Distributed Services" and by the Consiglio Nazionale delle Ricerche (CNR) with the Strategic IS-MANET Project "Middleware Support for Mobile Ad-hoc Networks and their Application".

References

1. M. S. Corson, J. P. Macker, V. D. Park, "Mobile and Wireless Internet Services: Putting the Pieces Together, *IEEE Communications Magazine*, Vol. 39, No. 6, June 2001.

2. W. Stallings, *Wireless Communications and Networks*, Pearson Education, Aug. 2001.
3. S. Saha, M. Jamtgaard, J. Villasenor, "Bringing the Wireless Internet to Mobile Devices", *IEEE Computer*, Vol. 34, No. 6, June 2001.
4. K. Curran, G. Parr, "A Middleware Architecture for Streaming Media over IP Networks to Mobile Devices", *IEEE Int. Conf. Wireless Communications and Networking (WCNC)*, Mar. 2003.
5. P. Bellavista, A. Corradi, R. Montanari, C. Stefanelli, "Context-aware Middleware for Resource Management in the Wireless Internet", *IEEE Trans. on Software Engineering*, Special Issue on "Wireless Internet", Vol. 29, No. 12, Dec. 2003.
6. P. Bellavista, A. Corradi, R. Montanari, C. Stefanelli, "Dynamic Binding in Mobile Applications: a Middleware Approach", *IEEE Internet Computing*, Vol. 7, No. 2, Mar.-Apr. 2003.
7. P. Bellavista, A. Corradi, C. Stefanelli, "Application-level QoS Control and Adaptation for Video on Demand", *IEEE Internet Computing*, Vol. 7, No. 6, Nov.-Dec. 2003.
8. P. Bellavista, A. Corradi, "How to Support Internet-based Distribution of Video on Demand to Portable Devices", *IEEE Int. Symp. on Computers and Communications (ISCC)*, July 2002.
9. J.L. Deng, "Introduction to Grey Theory", *The Journal of Grey System*, Vol. 1, No. 1, 1989.
10. Ekahau, Inc. – *The Ekahau Positioning Engine v2.1*, http://www.ekahau.com/products/positioningengine/
11. J. Chan, S. Zhou, A. Seneviratne, "A QoS Adaptive Mobility Prediction Scheme for Wireless Networks", *Global Telecommunications Conf. (GLOBECOM)*, Nov. 1998.
12. Teleca AB - *Bluetooth Local Infotainment Point (BLIP)*, http://www.teleca.com
13. P. Bellavista, A. Corradi, "Mobile Middleware Solutions for the Adaptive Management of Multimedia QoS to Wireless Portable Devices", *IEEE Int. Workshop Object-oriented Realtime Dependable Systems (WORDS)*, Oct. 2003.
14. J.J. Caffery, G.L. Stüber, "Overview of Radiolocation in CDMA Cellular Systems", *IEEE Communications Magazine*, Vol. 36, No. 4, Apr. 1998.
15. A. Savvides, C.-C. Han, M. Srivastava, "Dynamic Fine-Grained Localization in Ad-Hoc Networks of Sensors", *ACM Int. Conf. Mobile Computing and Networking (Mobicom)*, July 2001.
16. P. Bahl, V. Padmanabhan, "RADAR: An In-Building RF-based User Location and Tracking System", *IEEE Infocom Int. Conf.*, Mar. 2000.
17. B. Liang, Z.J. Haas, "Predictive Distance-Based Mobility Management for Multidimensional PCS Network", *IEEE/ACM Transactions on Networking*, Vol. 11, No. 5, Oct. 2003.
18. H.A. Karimi, X. Liu, "A Predictive Location Model for Location-based Services", *ACM Int. Workshop Advances in Geographic Information Systems (GIS)*, Nov. 2003.
19. S.-J. Lee, W. Su, M. Gerla, "Wireless Ad hoc Multicast Routing with Mobility Prediction", *ACM/Kluwer Mobile Networks and Applications*, Vol. 6, No. 4, Aug. 2001.
20. V. Kapoor, G. Edwards, R. Sankar, "Handoff Criteria for Personal Communication Networks", *IEEE Int. Conf. Communications (ICC)*, May 1994.
21. S.T. Sheu, C.C. Wu, "Using Grey Prediction Theory to Reduce Handoff Overhead in Cellular Communication Systems", *IEEE Int. Symp. Personal, Indoor and Mobile Radio Communications (PIMRC)*, Sep. 2000.
22. K. Al-Agha, T. Al-Meshhadany, L. Perato, "Resource Allocation Based on Handover Prediction in WCDMA", *IEEE Vehicular Technology Conf. (VTC)*, Sep. 2002.
23. S. Hadjiefthymiades, V. Matthaiou, L.F. Merakos, "Supporting the WWW in Wireless Communications through Mobile Agents", *ACM/Kluwer Mobile Networks and Applications*, Vol. 7, No. 4, Aug. 2002.

Development Methodology
for Location-Aware Mobile Agent

Kazutaka Matsuzaki[1], Nobukazu Yoshioka[2], and Shinichi Honiden[1,2]

[1] University of Tokyo,
7-3-1 Hongo, Bunkyo-ku, Tokyo 113-0033, Japan
{matsuzaki,honiden}@nii.ac.jp
[2] National Institute of Informatics,
2-1-2 Hitotsubashi, Chiyoda-ku, Tokyo 101-8430, Japan
nobukazu@nii.ac.jp

Abstract. We describe a methodology which enables development of flexible
and reusable mobile agent applications for location aware indoor environments.
The methodology, which is named "Workflow-awareness model" (WFA), is based
on a concept where a pair of mobile agents cooperate to perform a given task to
realize separation of concerns for software maintenance. The paper outlines the
methodology, and shows how the concepts work in the prototype environment.
Usefulness of this methodology concerning its efficiency and software engineering aspects are analyzed.

1 Introduction

Recent progress of developments in wireless networks and mobile devices enables mobile users to use various kinds of services from their mobile devices through wireless
connections. RF tag technologies used in local positioning products that sense the real
world are emerging. Enterprises have performed many demonstration experiments to
add traceability features into physical distributions. RF tags are used in our study to
provide user tracking services inside a building as in [8]. The tag readers inside the
building will sense mobility of both mobile entities (users wearing an ID card or carrying a mobile phone with RF tags) and local facilities. Local facilities are supposed to
publish their functions as Web Services to indoor user [2]. In this mobility aware indoor
setting, a user may use a printer according to certain conditions such as accessibility,
QoS, proximity, security and so on from his mobile device through wireless connection.

There are various studies which concern mobility awareness. However, studies regarding development methodologies in this area are somewhat rare.

In the above settings, the user's mobile device has to interact many times with service providers and user tracking services, which is unfavorable since mobile wireless
connection is unstable and handling large size data with mobile devices is not prefer-
able. [16] uses mobile agents in the Internet environment to reduce a mobile devices
loading for the outdoor user. In our study, applications are built as mobile agents that
execute tasks over wired networks as proxies. Various kinds of agent application logics
have been considered regarding mobility aware environments. The logic of applications

A. Karmouch, L. Korba, and E. Madeira (Eds.): MATA 2004, LNCS 3284, pp. 13–26, 2004.

get modified, or even become corrupt, however, when they are adapted to changing situations such as tuning their performance, or testing whether they are capable of running in a given environment, etc.

The motive of this study is to realize an efficient application development method that can avoid such logic corruptions of applications. Functions of such application agents include application logic, service adjustment (discovery, negotiation, check alive), performance tuning techniques (e.g. interleaving access), testing and other supportive tasks. Code structures of such applications become monolithic and complex, which troubles application programmers.

In order to solve this challenge, we have proposed a "Workflow-awareness model" [3]. The model consists of several notions: Pairing, Workflow-awareness (WFA) and practical use of AspectJ. Pairing means that the application consists of two agents. One executes application logic and the other performs secondary tasks. WFA means that execution states of the application logic agent are monitored by the pairing agent. AspectJ is used to weave concerns into an agent for application logics to automate WFA and to alter behaviors of methods used in WFA. We made these notions into practice by creating prototype environment.

In Section 2, we discuss the assumptions of our target environments and the actual issues in developing the target application. Section 3 presents our methodology feature to overcome the issues. Section 4 illustrates the design and implementation and Section 5 evaluates the efficiency and reusability of our model. Section 6 surveys related works and Section 7 provides a summary and discusses future issues.

2   Background of This Research

2.1   Target Settings

Fig. 1 illustrates our target setting. Our target setting is inside a building where the locations of entities are managed. These entities include local facilities, e.g. printers, monitors, and user's belongings, e.g. mobile phones and ID cards. Many sensors inside the building track movements of these elements. Information from these sensors is

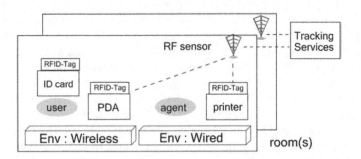

Fig. 1. Sketch of our target setting. A user and his PDA are in a wireless environment while his agent and local facilities like a printer are in a wired environment in a building. All the physical entities inside the building are managed by tracking services through RFID tag information.

managed in a central server in the building. This information is available to software with proper permission. Furthermore, local facilities publish their functions as Web Services to such software. A mobile user may use a printer according to certain conditions such as accessibility, QoS, security, proximity, etc. However, access to various services from mobile devices including PDAs is considered to be unstable since its connection is wireless and the user is moving continuously. This makes it difficult to realize functions that require many interactions between user and services and transferring large size data. We use mobile agent technology to support such users under the said settings. [16] has been studying the use of mobile agents to support the mobile user for a while. In their research, the mobile agent roams the Internet and follows the user's movement so that the user can use proper network services with context-awareness. We also apply similar mobile agents in our target settings. In this example, the mobile agent identifies the most suitable printer considering its proximity, QoS, accessibility, and security as a proxy, reducing risks and inconveniences for the wireless users. In our study, the main task of the agent is to integrate and search the most suitable services on behalf of the user using location information of entities inside the building. In this example, the agent task is just about finding a printer on behalf of the mobile user, but we believe that there are various kinds of application logics for the agent in these settings. We also think these application logics are important and view them as development targets.

2.2 Issues

Since many functions are required for such an agent, the agent application is sometimes hard to develop. These functions include application logic (process integration of applications, users and services), service selection (service matching, ordering search timings), adaptation to the mobile settings (user's movement monitoring, service availability checking) and security (authentication, encryption). Our concern is about the re-usability of the agent code. Many functions entangle in a code, which makes it hard for someone else to modify it. These issues are not soluble simply by using multi-thread programming. The threads of the agent will not be able to perform their tasks independently of other relevant threads at separated places. For example, one thread wants to keep working at remote host but the other thread wants to come back to the user's mobile device to search surrounding services via Bluetooth. Furthermore, tuning code for performance and testing the code are also necessary for actual deployment. Coding anticipating run-time situations at design time is quite challenging for application programmers and presents a totally new sphere of issues.

Thus some good application design to separate concerns that will not suffocate the procedure of each concern is required.

In the next section, we will present our model for overcoming such issues that apparently seem contradictory.

3   Workflow-Awareness Model

We have proposed a new model named Workflow-awareness model, which is based on three points, two main concepts and one implementation technique.

3.1 Pairing of Agents

As the first point, in order to solve the above-mentioned problems, we propose to deploy two types of mobile agents: Master Agent (MA) and Shadow Agent (SA). This is intended for separation of concerns in agent development [10]. A monolithic agent with traditional manner is divided into a MA and a SA depending on the kind of tasks.

- **Master Agent (MA)** has application logic fulfilled by communication among a user and services.
- **Shadow Agent (SA)** carries out supportive tasks well-timed for a MA execution states. A SA's tasks are dependent upon environments or situations where the MA is deployed, e.g. using to check availability of services, pre-process before using services, adapt to the changes of the environment, performance tune, encrypt, authenticate-cache, test the MA execution etc.

As for performance tuning, the SA works as a proxy of the MA for some tasks (interleaving execution, preemptive execution etc.). For example, preemptively searching services and future communication for some data [11]. These actions enabled by pairing are useful when the MA and the SA work at the separated hosts each other since they have remote communication abilities by ACL.

3.2 Workflow-Awareness (WFA)

Brief Description of WFA. The second point is Workflow-awareness (WFA). This is a kind of meta-level control of a MA by a SA. The MA is made with its own application logic, which is represented in a kind of finite state machine. The SA knows the MA's *Workflow*, object model of its whole state transition, through the execution by receiving the information of the MA's execution state. This enables the SA to invoke its tasks at proper timings depending on the application (MA) executing phases. For example, when the MA starts executing (n)th state, the SA also starts service matching required in the MA's ($n+1$)th candidate states.

Mechanism of WFA. Fig. 2 shows an interpretation process from a MA code to *Workflow*. A SA has this *Workflow* class object as a field value. This *Workflow* is kept reflecting the MA execution state so that the SA can use this information. The Workflow consists of multiple *WFStates*, which are made from each state of the MA. In our current implementation, these elements include: service matching information, migration destination information, service invocation information, and state transition information. We included these because they can be easily affected by the execution environment. It is not clear when they are required, even used or not, or succeed or not. In order to complete the application logic these elements are adequately handled.

A programmer codes a SA conscious of important events of a MA through WFA related APIs. In our current implementation, these APIs functions are: acquiring state transition information, sending control message to a MA in order to alter its execution, controlling over timings of service matching, and inspecting for a MA's field values for diagnostic. These APIs are implemented to send/receive ACL messages [7] bi-directly.

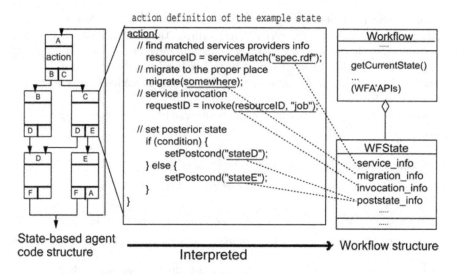

Fig. 2. Interpretation processes of an MA code. The agent code is made in a form of finite state machine. Each state of the MA is interpreted into WFState, which becomes a component of *Workflow*. *Workflow* elements (arguments of methods) are extracted into WFState.

```
1  class SAStateINIT extends ShadowState{
2      public void action(){
3          Workflow workflow = initWorkflow();
4          while (workflow.active()){
5              if (workflow.enterState("MAStateWaitTalking")){
6                  serviceMatch("printer_spec.rdf");
7              }
8              if (workflow.enterState("MAStateMiddle"){
9                  if (workflow.getMAFieldValue("mission_flg")
                                        .equals("false"))
10                     forceMigrate(aid, "myPC");
```

The important point of this code is that the MA's application logic would be preserved even when performance tunings (line 6-8) and testing (line 9-11) are done.

3.3   Practical Use of AspectJ

As an implementation technique, we applied the AspectJ by two points. The first is that we can automatically update *Workflow* so that it keeps reflecting of the MA's state without giving the programmer any additional tasks. The second is that AspectJ can make a SA work as a proxy of the MA, which is done by intercepting the method execution. As for the first point, we wove "workflow updates modules" at the compile time so that the *Workflow* in the SA can indicate real execution state information at execution phases. In relation to the SA *Workflow*, every time a message is received a change is occurred in the state machine of the *Workflow* And the second point, we also apply AspectJ to intercept and modify the execution of a MA. Normally a MA executes service matching with *serviceMatch* method. The behavior with this method is searching suitable services, e.g. sending a query to directory services or migrating somewhere to broadcast. But when the SA works preemptively, this method is rewritten so that the MA waits the information from the SA. This modification occurs only when assigned in the SA code.

Owing to this methodology, performance tuning can be done with keeping the MA's logics.

3.4   Scenario with WFA and Location-Awareness

We explain an example scenario which is realized by WFA and location-awareness.

Building Settings. We give some assumptions as for target building settings.

- Fragmented network group: There are many network groups, e.g. different organizations, in the building.
- Global-scope tracking services: Elements inside the building are tracked their position. And this information is served at the global scope of the building, which is available from every network group.
- Hierarchical service discovery: The building publishes public services of each network groups at the global scope, however, the private services of the network groups are not registered at the global scope. Discovering such private services depends on each network group administration policy.

Scenario. A mobile user visits the building. He is a guest of group A and launches agents to print a document. Application logic of the agents is as follows: (1) migrate to the fixed network inside the building. (2) use global discovery services. (3) use tracking services. (4) identify the positions of user and candidate printers. (5) wait for the request by the user. (6) show the list to the user when requested. (7) print the document.

Especially, the SA's tasks in this scenario are to catch the movements of the user and update the available and proximate printer list on behalf of the MA. And if the proximate printer to the user does not publish its service at the global scope, the agents have to migrate to the network group to search services. Aside this, authentication-cache of the services is done by the SA for the MA before ahead. It helps to reduce response time after the user issuing his request.

In other case, the SA re-identifies the suitable printer since it knows how the execution goes on by pre-fetching the predictable next steps of the MA. If some services used in the next state are related with some specific location, the SA might well to search printers around the location, too.

These kinds of fine tunings are hard to realize by a MA alone. The WFA offers a solution to such situations.

4   Design and Implementation

This section presents the design and prototype implementation of our Tracking Services (TS) and Workflow-awareness.

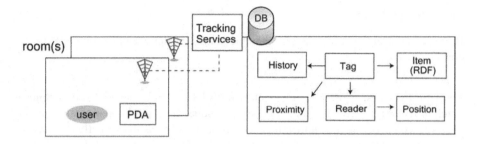

Fig. 3. Basic structure of Tracking Service (TS). TS manages RFID-tags information and provides relational information of RFID-tag IDs, Items (local facilities, user belongings), positions, readers, history and proximity.

4.1 Tracking Services (TS)

Fig. 3 illustrates TS deployed environment inside a building where RF tag readers are placed in each room. Information from these readers is integrated and managed by the global-scope TS of the building. The managed information includes the readers, local facilities and user's registered belongings. TS publish its services related to this information to authenticated client application. From a tag ID (strings), meta-information of the related item and its position can be obtained. TS also provides histories of a tag's position and neighboring item information depending on the access right of a client.

4.2 Workflow Awareness Framework

In our framework, agent programs are coded with state based programming style [1]. We explain the behavior of the framework about how to make SA and MA work cooperatively. Manipulation order of the two agents by our framework is as follows:

1. Extraction of *Workflow* elements from the MA: In order to generate *Workflow* for WFA, some elements are extracted (See. Section 3.2). Then construct the *Workflow* and manipulate it so that it is initialized as a field value of the SA.
2. Weaving workflow updates modules: On the MA side modules to automatically send messages at every state transition are woven. On the SA side, a receiver module is woven to run as a listener thread so that its *Workflow* is updated whenever receiving messages by the MA side module. As a result of this update operation, the SA will start the proper tasks at the given timing.
3. Weaving synchronization modules: Synchronization is needed between the MA and the SA to exchange information and to wait the other agent's task. These synchronization modules also make the two agents exchange ACL messages between them.
4. Modification to the MA behavior to make use of the SA.: The SA can work as a proxy of the MA. In this framework, this is done by intercepting method executions of the MA to prevent the MA from doing a duplicated task. The behavior of the MA's method execution concerned is modified to wait messages from the SA.

4.3   Current Status

The system presented in this paper was implemented in Sun's Java Developer Kit version 1.4.

Tracking Services. Current implementation of TS is build with RF Code's Spider which provides active RF-tags. Each tag has a unique identifier that periodically emits an RF-beacon that conveys an identifier. The system allows us to explicitly control the omni directional range of each of RF receivers to read tags within about15 meters. The RF readers are placed in each room and registered to the TS about belonging network groups and absolute positions. TS polls the readers to retrieve the active tag information. TS is composed in a form of the Web Services so that they can provide inter-operability and high level services to agents. A recognized item's position is roughly handled as the same of its reader position. Reader's position is represented in the format (latitude, altitude, floor).

WFA Framework. A prototype implementation of the WFA framework is done with Bee-gent 2.0, and AspectJ 1.1. Bee-gent is a multi-agent framework for bonding multiple services by interacting with services. Application programmer codes a SA with referring the MA task description. Both the MA and SA are mediation agents in Bee-gent, which are mobile agents that move from one site to another where they interact with services. Originally they promote inter-application coordination by communicating with services through ACL message passing.

For programmers, the WFA framework provides base classes for the MA and SA and some aspects for adding functions. These aspects have pointcut definitions and advices to automate WFA messaging, and delegation of method execution between the MA and SA.

5   Evaluation of the WFA

In this section we discuss effects of WFA concerning its contribution to efficiency and maintenance.

5.1   Effectiveness: Evaluation of WFA Overhead Time

As evaluation of the WFA effects on execution time, we measured and analyzed overhead time during the execution of a typical sequence. This is intended to see if WFA methodology works not only in theoretical but also in practice. Considerable elements causing overhead are communicative costs between the MA and SA and computational cost added by the SA. The details of communicative costs are synchronizations between the MA and the SA, message passing to update a *Workflow*, and other additional messaging to inform the MA of data fetched by the SA well ahead. For example, inform the pre-fetched data about available services. In order to calculate the overhead, we execute a simple sequence with and without WFA.

Sequence of the Experiment. Experiment settings are shown in Fig. 4. The sequence is composed of five phases: (1) a user walks into network group B from A with doing his own task (e.g. using PDA as a wireless IP phone). (2) His agent follows the movements and enters in the same network group. Then it waits for the user's task to finish. (3) The agent queries for services in the network group B. (4) The agent receives the information. (5) The agent uses services for the user.

In this sequence, the agent can know a physical position of the required services from tracking services inside the building, but cannot discover a logical address (WSDL) of a suitable services because of the building service providing policy (See Section 3.4). The agent has to migrate to a host in a target network group to discover proper services with a provided discovery method.

We define time consumption of user's task as Time_User (sec) and that of searching services as Time_ServiceMatch (sec). Since we need to measure the pure overhead by WFA, we suppose these values are set 0. The agent may send query for location information, but this can be also ignored with the same reason.

Results. Fig. 5 shows the execution sequences and results. In Case1 the MA solely does the job and in Case2 the MA and SA cooperate to complete tasks, i.e. using WFA. As for Case2, the SA creates idling time for the MA to wait for messaging and calculation. The overhead of this examination is considered as the difference (Total time of Case2) - (Total time of Case1). The brackets in the result table in Fig. 5 mean that they are derived from waiting for SA's calculation. They are added to the overhead when the MA needs not to do other job. Details of the action added in Case2 are processing and communication for synchronizations (sync), processing for service matching (serviceMatching) and processing and communication to inform the SA (inform). We appropriate the communication (messaging) time to the MA because the message passing is asynchronous and then the SA can do other task in background (Fig. 6).

WFA avoids causing negative effects when the service matching takes more than 2.136(sec) and the user talks more than 1.202(sec) in this settings in this example set-

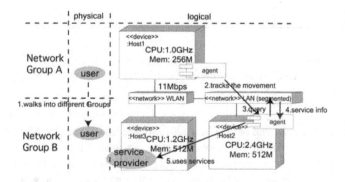

Fig. 4. Examination settings: Host 1 is a host where the agent exists when it receives request from the user. Host 2 is where the agent starts service discovery and Host 3 provides the target services. Host 2 and 3 are in the same network group.

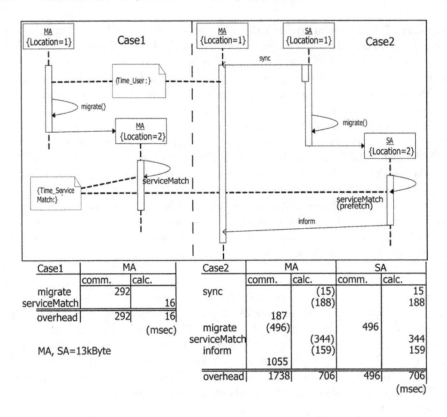

Case1	MA	
	comm.	calc.
migrate	292	
serviceMatch		16
overhead	292	16
		(msec)

MA, SA=13kByte

Case2	MA		SA	
	comm.	calc.	comm.	calc.
sync		(15)		15
		(188)		188
	187			
migrate		(496)	496	
serviceMatch		(344)		344
inform		(159)		159
	1055			
overhead	1738	706	496	706
				(msec)

Fig. 5. Sequence diagram and measurement data of Case1, 2.

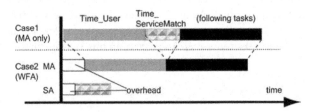

Fig. 6. General calculation for time consumption. WFA causes some overhead time with both MA and SA, however total execution times can be reduced.

ting. The items related to communication depend on network performance and the items related to processing depend on machine performance and situations. Since this experiment setting is rather small, the network latency measured becomes also small. The point is that order of the calculated data is not so large as to cancel the effects of preemptive or parallel execution by the agents. The time for application to search and check availability of the services supposed to be large with complicated condition settings and negotiations. And user must consume no less than minutes order that it is also feasible to use WFA.

Moreover, in a real environment, there must be some restrictions about MA's locations. For example, if a MA has gone to search some services then the user has been kept wait until the MA comes back. In another case, if the MA has been occupied with interactions between some services, the MA cannot even start searching. These situations make total execution time of Case1 much longer.

The measured values in the experiments do not give a general conclusion since they are affected deeply by network conditions, query targets and size of transported data. However it indicates that the overhead does not makes WFA always be useless.

5.2   Code Reusability

Maintenance ability of WFA is provided by switching SAs depending on the deployment environment without giving any modification to a MA. For example, if a programmer does not know whether or not application logic works well in a new environment, then a SA is made with a test code for tuning and checking the application (MA) behavior. WFA is also useful for debugging in a distributed environment application. Remarkable virtue is that original application logic (i.e. MA) is completely preserved even in debugging time. This separation of experimental code and actual deployment code is another objective. After testing, a SA for performance tuning will be deployed, or a MA is deployed as a standalone application without a SA. Preserving MA'fs application logic is preceded by deploying proper SAs depending on a situation.

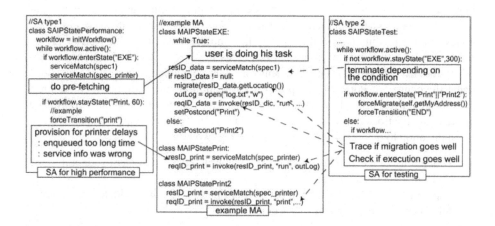

Fig. 7. Code structure model of MA and SAs using WFA.

Fig. 7 shows a code structure model of our proposal. Deploying SAs to adapt to situational diversities such as secure migrations and action timings saves from reducing a MA's application logic reusability. As we described in Section 4, additional behaviors related with *Workflow* are automatically supported, which does not put additional tasks on programmers. This methodology delegates programmer to control details behavior of agents, which is intended to reduce total coding burdens by preventing code corruptions and keeping good maintenance ability.

There are various kinds of techniques to improve an efficiency of an application in a distributed environment [11]. Our methodology allows such techniques used with keeping the original application logics. Restriction is that the MA and SA should be on networks somehow exchanging messages.

6   Related Work

This section discusses several studies that have influenced various aspects of this methodology, which is in conjunction with research areas.

As for pairing of the agents, [19] introduces a secure protocol using a cooperation agent recording the path history of each other. [13] uses a pair of agents for interleaving access to services. [13] deploys a delegate-agent for using web services so that efficiency and reliability are increased. In our methodology, the MA and SA each have their own programmed tasks and sometimes act in remote places, which enables a new function in addition to interleaving effects.

Several papers have explored meta-level architecture and reflection for mobile agents [6, 12, 4]. In [6], an agent reasons about the beliefs of another agent, as well as about the actions that other agents may take. This meta-reasoning is similar to WFA : however, it does not support the agent division of labor in different places. This support is desirable under mobile settings so as to efficiently complete tasks.

Several papers discuss mobile agents from an AOP point of view. [10] proposed to introduce the Role Model into an agent system for analysis, design, and implementation. [15] took another approach for separation of concerns for mobile agents by using policy control for binding. In this approach, a mobile agent, called a shadow proxy, roams a fixed network to bind needed resources in place of the applications on mobile terminals. [15] has good mechanisms for resource binding treatment. This is done under the control of Ponder [5], a policy specification language. In our methodology, mobile agent tasks not only work as a proxy resolver for resources but also coordinate between applications and services in wired and wireless networks, i.e. a main part of the application logic. Our priority is considered in two points:

– Availability of the agent execution state enabling the programmer to adapt it to the environment characteristics.
– Capability to handle complex jobs by coordination of a pair, which cannot be resolved only by forking a new process.

Most of the approaches intended to exploit logical mobility for supporting user's physical mobility provide middleware [17, 14, 16, 20]. These middleware supports logical mobility in infrastructure levels. [16] realizes the access control of resources from the context information of the middleware components (mobile proxies). Relevant access control rules, client location, user preferences, privacy requirements, terminal characteristics, and current state of hosting environments can be considered, which helps mobile clients obtain flexible access to the resources. [9] uses agent's *view* [18], a new concept in which an agent takes their perception as centric context. An agent has multiple views and uses declarative specifications to control each view. Properties of the individual data items, the agents that own them, the hosts on which the agents reside, and the physical and logical topology of the ad hoc network are taken into consideration. This view mechanism enables applications executing under mobile settings to react and adapt continuously and rapidly to changes in operating conditions. We would like to investigate a middleware design to fit our methodology reusing some functions of these existing approaches.

7   Conclusion and Future Work

In the present study, a mobile agent based development methodology for application in location aware settings has been proposed and evaluated with prototypes. This study offers a Workflow-awareness model based on paired agent cooperation for aiding programmers in handling run-time events efficiently while separation of concerns is kept. The methodology also applies AspectJ practically in its implementation. *Workflow* object contains the latest information on the agent execution state and the pair agent can decide on its action accordingly. This cooperation enables the effective behavior of agents at the service exploitation time. The direction of our future research is to provide modeling process for analyzing the task separations. We are also presently striving to design middleware that suits well with WFA methodology.

References

1. Bee-gent website, 1999. http://www2.toshiba.co.jp/beegent/.
2. Print service interface version 1.0 working draft, 2003.
3. *Ubiquitous Application Development using a Mobile Agent-based System*, 2003.
4. Walter Cazzola, Shigeru Chiba, and Thomas Ledoux. Reflection and Meta-Level Architectures : State of the art and future trends. In *Object-Oriented Technology (ECOOP 2000 Workshop Reader)*, Vol. 1964 of *Lecture Notes in Computer Science*, pp. 1–15. Springer-Verlag, 2000.
5. Nicodemos Damianou, Naranker Dulay, Emil Lupu, and Morris Sloman. The ponder policy specification language. *Lecture Notes in Computer Science*, Vol. 1995, pp. 18–38, 2001.
6. Jürgen Dix, V. S. Subrahmanian, and George Pick. Meta-Agent Programs. Technical Report 21–98, 1998.
7. FIPA. Fipa acl message structure specification, 2002.
8. Andy Harter and Andy Hopper. A distributed location system for the active office. *IEEE Network*, Vol. 8, No. 1, / 1994.
9. Roman G.C Julien, C. Egocentric context-aware programming in ad hoc mobile environments. In *International Symposium on the Foundations of Software Engineering*, pp. 23–30, 2002.
10. Elizabeth A. Kendall. Role modeling for agent system analysis, design, and implementation. *IEEE Concurrency*, Vol. 8, No. 2, pp. 34–41, 1999.
11. Doug Lea. *Concurrent Programming in Java: Design Principles and Patterns, Second edition*. Addison-Wesley, 1999.
12. Thomas Ledoux and Noury M. Bouraqadi-Saadani. Adaptability in mobile agent systems using reflection. In *RM'2000, Workshop on Reflective Middleware, Middleware'2000*, April 2000.
13. Zakaria Maamar, Quan Z. Sheng, and Boualem Benatallah. Interleaving web services composition and execution using software agents and delegation. In *AAMAS 2003 Workshop on Web Serices and Agent-Based Engineering*.

14. C. Mascolo, L. Capra, S. Zachariadis, and W. Emmerich. Xmiddle: A data-sharing middleware for mobile computing. *Wireless Personal Communications*, Vol. 21, No. 1, pp. 77–103, 2002.
15. Rebecca Montanari Paolo Bellavista, Antonio Corradi and Cesare Stefanelli. Dynamic binding in mobile applications : A middleware approach. *Internet Computing*, Vol. 7, No. 2, 2003.
16. Rebecca Montanari Paolo Bellavista and Daniela Tibaldi. Cosmos: A context-centric access control middleware for mobile environments. In *Mobile Agents for Telecommunication Applications, 5th International Workshop, MATA 2003*, Vol. 2881 of *Lecture Notes in Computer Science*, pp. 77–88, 2003.
17. Gian Pietro Picco, Amy L. Murphy, and Gruia-Catalin Roman. LIME: Linda meets mobility. In *International Conference on Software Engineering*, pp. 368–377, 1999.
18. Julien C. Roman, G.-C. and A. L Murphy. A declarative approach to agent-centered context-aware computing in ad hoc wireless environments. *Software Engineering for Large-Scale Multi-Agent Systems*, 2003.
19. Volker Roth. Secure recording of itineraries through co-operating agents. In *ECOOP Workshops*, pp. 297–298, 1998.
20. Stefanos Zachariadis and Cecilia Mascolo. Adaptable mobile applications through satin: Exploiting logical mobility in mobile computing middleware. *UK-UbiNet Workshop*, September 2003.

Distributed Shared Contexts

Rosa Alarcón[1], César Collazos[2], and Luis A. Guerrero[1]

[1] Department of Computer Science, Universidad de Chile,
P.O. Box 2777, Santiago, Chile
{ralarcon,luguerre}@dcc.uchile.cl
[2] Systems Department FIET, Universidad del Cauca,
Campus Tulcan, Popayán-Colombia
ccollazo@unicauca.edu.co

Abstract. Mobile solutions have gone beyond the role of personal tool to offer solutions in supporting coordinated work. Mobile workers shift constantly from individual to group work, access shared virtual environments from different devices and can create new elements when disconnected (annotations, appointments, etc.). However, current approaches focus either on individual or group work, as well as on the restrictions and affordances that mobile devices and mobility provides, but they do not address the huge heterogeneity, inconsistencies and complexity derived when both working modes are mixed. We are interested in the construction of virtual environments that can be accessed transparently anywhere, anytime on anything, but also exploit the advantages that mobility aware technologies provide. Context-based design facilitates the construction of such environments because they isolate and provide structure to the application layer facilitating adaptation to devices' characteristics, reducing the impact of devices heterogeneity and easing the shift among different working modes.

1 Introduction

When designing applications for mobile technology, the focus often relies on the restrictions and affordances that those devices provide, that is their need for dynamic reconfiguration, adaptivity, asynchronous interaction, context-awareness and lightweight middleware [1]. For instance, Personal Information Management (PIM) applications, which include calendars, to do's, notepads, e-mail alert among others; deal with issues like limited screen size, storage and memory and disconnected operations. Their main concern is data synchronization between the mobile device and the PIM system. Although first approaches conceived a PIM as a personal server running on user's desktop computer, current designs are based on Web servers and are integrated into enterprise's strategies. Now, personal information can be accessed from different devices (i.e. handhelds, data-enabled cellular phones, pagers, badges, etc.), and synchronization occurs not only between the PIM and each device, but also with organizations' databases, other networked applications and groupware.

Other approaches take advantage of different wireless networks like cellular, LAN, PAN (Personal Area Network) or BAN (Body Area Network) networks [2]. Although previous design restrictions applies in this kind of networks, users can update their versions more frequently and access huge databases on demand, or the information can be made available (pushed) to them proactively, based on their context. This area of research is know as context-aware computing [3], which are systems that examine and react to an individual's changing context. Typically "user context" is described in

A. Karmouch, L. Korba, and E. Madeira (Eds.): MATA 2004, LNCS 3284, pp. 27–36, 2004.

terms of the user's current location taking into account the *social* (at home, at the office, etc.[4], [5], [6]), *physical* (light, noise, etc.[7]) and *informational* (guided tours, tourist maps, etc. [8], [9]) characteristics associated to the user's current physical environment.

But mobile solutions have gone beyond the role of a personal tool to offer large-scale solutions in supporting coordinated work for teams, groups, and organizations. The adoption of mobile devices is most clearly seen in the professional world, for instance, IDC forecasts that the remote and mobile workforce will grow, in the US, to 47.1 million by the end of 2003 (37% of total workforce). Traditionally, work groups have been supported by collaborative systems that allow them sharing software artifacts, objects and self-representations enabling a virtual *shared environment*.

For instance, a mobile healthcare system supports workers' activity, but also information exchange, collaboration, coordination of activities and resources and decision-making [10]. Furthermore, based on the relevance of the events that occur in the shared environment and the current user context, group members can be contacted proactively (push) through different devices either fixed or mobile [11]. In both cases contextual information related to workgroup activities (i.e. activities' status, ongoing activities, changing artifacts, etc.) is presented to users so they can be aware of the status and progress of their work and can coordinate their future actions.

Mobile computing has become a useful and promising technology for supporting individuals, but as their potentiality is being acknowledged for professionals, it is creating new interaction paradigms for supporting work groups and organizations and adding also huge heterogeneity. However, it is very interesting that when designing context-aware systems, information must be adapted to user context; but when designing groupware systems, we are dealing with the provision of contextual information related to group activities, without taking into account users context when receiving the information; something similar occur with classic PIM systems.

Our aim is to support the development of shared applications that can be accessed anywhere, anytime on anything, but current approaches support either individuals or work groups and are designed separately or are considered merely extensions of each other, making it hard to design applications that can be easily adapted to different interaction modes (i.e. disconnected operations, mobile computing, nomadic computing, groupware applications, etc.).

In this paper, we propose a design based on multiple, possibly competing contexts (individual vs. shared) that represent users' activities, actions and status at a high level. The set of contexts are shared by people and agents, accessed from different devices and adapted to users' current context. By designing an application at a meta-level, the transition between different interaction modes is reduced but it is possible to provide richer contextual information. The strategy and the proposal draw from previous experiences in the subject, although our current approach is more general.

Section 2 discusses in detail the conceptual definition of context while section 3 presents the architecture proposed. Section 4 present an application based on the architecture of section 3. Finally, section 5 presents our conclusions.

2   Shared Contexts

Although the word "context" appears repeatedly in the area of context-aware computing there are not a consensual definition of its meaning. This is perfectly understandable as concept meaning is only valid in the scope of a determined context.

In broader terms context can be defined as "the interrelated conditions in which an event, action, etc. takes place"[1]. Because this definition is too general, researches have tried to determine which is the situation at hand and then, which conditions must be considered as part of its context (engineering point of view [12]).

2.1 Related Work

In linguistics and natural language research, context has been used as an interpretation medium for establishing the meaning of a sentence. For instance if we say: "I like to play with my sister", it is assumed that my sister and I are playing together and not that she is a toy. That is, social context narrows down the proper interpretation of an expression [13]. It is clear that a context can serve for restricting the solution's state space for problems related to automatic reasoning [12], or when huge amount of data is searched. For example, Web searching systems filter the information by estimating its relevance in determined contexts of interpretation such as pages' popularity (Altavista, Google), categories (Vivisimo), geographic zones (Lasoo), etc.

In the area of context-aware computing, context is usually related to the "computing" conditions in which users are immersed (network connectivity, communication bandwidth and nearby resources), their "personal and social" conditions (user's location, people nearby and social situation, for instance, Office Assistant [4], Conference Assistant [5], GeoNotes [6]), the "information" associated (guided tours, tourist maps, etc., for instance, CoolTown [8], Tourist Guide [9], Cyberguide[5]) or the "physical" conditions of users' surroundings (lighting, noise, etc., for instance, Tangible Bits [7]) [3]. Others, identifies *primary* (location, entity, activity and time) and *more complex* context derived from the primary ones [6].

Context is used for interpreting user's needs and intentions, and adapting the application (reconfiguration or information) or the environment itself (proximate selection, adaptable environments) according to them [3], [2]. Typically, context has been studied by considering the interaction between an individual and a context-aware or a knowledge-based system, but as professionals and organizations are adopting this technology, more work group applications for mobile platforms are being designed.

In groupware, an underlying mechanism, called "Awareness", renders the shared environments' state and changes to users [14], providing contextual information (where, when, what, who, how) so users *understand* how their actions fit in the group goals and can regulate their behavior [15], [16]. Contextual information is presented as visual, aural or physical gadgets (i.e. "new" icons in BSCW[2] systems). However, shared context is unstructured, implicit, created by users' actions and restricted by the application and this same approach is used when handheld devices are involved.

2.2 Distributed Shared Context

When users work together, they share a context that comprehends both, high level elements such as users' actions (and their consequences) and low level elements such as users' computing situation (and their restrictions). For instance, AwServer [11] is a multi-agent system that delivers contextual information about users' actions (high level of abstraction) trough different Internet-based channels *proactively*. Users are

---

[1] See Merriam-Webster Dictionary at http: // www.m-w.com
[2] For more information on BSCW see http: // bscw.fit.fraunhofer.de/

contacted through e-mail, private messaging systems and cellular phone or regular groupware widgets; depending on the relevance of the information, users' availability (i.e. from 8:00 to 19.00) and devices' characteristics (low level of abstraction).

Again, context serves as an interpretation medium to infer information relevance (on the context of work at a high level) and users' disposition to be interrupted (on the context of users' devices capability and social situation at a lower level). Additionally, by having a context designed at a high level, it significantly facilitates the construction of applications that extend and ground context's semantics [18]. However, we argue that in [11] devices are merely seen as different interfaces of a unique virtual space through which the system propagates contextual information but, although it supports adaptation (as applications can react to contextual information), the workload (actions) created in portable devices is neglected.

Actions and conditions related to mobile devices (and hence, context) could be very different from those related to more powerful, but fixed devices. So, although some coherence in the interfaces for both systems is required, this does not implies that mobile applications are necessarily a smaller subgroup of fixed applications or just a reduced interface. For instance, when a group works together in a shared editor, users go through phases of *self-organization* (of ideas, thoughts and critics) and then, once they have a clear picture of their contribution they go to a *sharing* phase where they can argue and negotiate [19]. Clearly, although users share the same objects (i.e. a paper), their activities and are slightly different in both cases, that is, the context that they share includes isolated tasks as well.

This way, context is spread or distributed among different devices (and perhaps applications). From this perspective, a context-based design approach can ease the construction of applications where transition among different interaction modes (i.e. working isolated vs. working together) is facilitated for end-users and developers.

3 Proposed Architecture

Context must be represented through structures, schemata, scripts, rules, etc. Those representations capture the static aspect of context at design time; dynamic aspects are created when people or agents interact. We have designed a FIPA [19] compliant multi-agent system called "DSC Server" (Distributed Shared Context) where a set of agents, named "Context Managers" (CM), maintains the distributed shared context.

DSC Server is an extension of [11]. Users' actions are interpreted through a *work context* that must be instantiated in order to reflect the task at hand (called a *local vocabulary*). Both contexts are represented as ontologies (concepts, predicates agent actions) [20] implemented as java classes of JADE (see [21] for further information).

Events in a groupware application (Gevent) are sent to a Context Manager agent (CM), which infers its relevance in the work context; then, a User Context Agent (UCA) propagates the event to the user interface (classic feedback) or another group member (user 2 in Fig.1). Grayed components of the figure are fully described in [11] and [17] and are not the main concern of this paper. CM agents move to portable devices, when working in isolation, events correspond to a Local context (Levent).

DSC is designed in two conceptual layers (local vocabulary): one describing the *structure of the document* where users work on, and the other the set of possible user *actions* and the application *status* (considered as a Finite State Machine) (Fig.2).

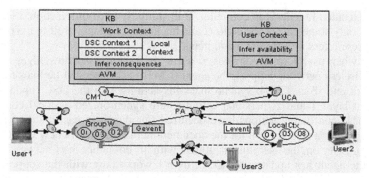

Fig. 1. System overview. Events occurred in a groupware application (*Gevent*) are propagated to *DESC* server through a *Proxy Agent* (PA). A *CM* agent is associated to each *user*. Local events (*Levent*) are propagated to the server as well

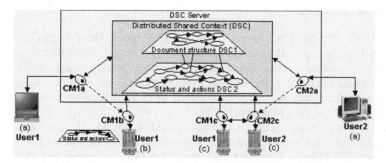

Fig. 2. System architecture. A *CM* agent is associated to each *user*. Agents maintain a *distributed shared context*, and support 3 *interaction modes*, which are classic groupware interaction (a), isolated work (b) and collaborative interaction based on mobile computing

3.1 Interaction Modes

Classic groupware interaction. In fig.2 (a), user 1 (represented by a laptop) and user 2 (represented by a desktop computer) work collaboratively in a classic groupware interaction (i.e. both users work together editing a document at the office). Every action performed in the application is sent to the agent associated to each user (CM1a and CM2a, respectively), which in turn updates the DSC.

Isolated work. When user 1 moves to his handheld (that is, stop working on his laptop and logs in-to his handheld), the agent moves to the handheld (CM1b) and, if there is not a wireless network available, the agent request the user to synchronize the application so that, a part of the context that is suited to the handheld is downloaded. Now, user 1 is able to work alone on his mobile device independently and other users can be aware that user 1 is on his moving and working alone (i.e. commenting a document when he is in the subway). See fig.2(b).

Wireless support. User 2 also moves to his handheld and walks around his office with wireless network support (fig. 2(c)). The agent moves also to his handheld (CM2c) and user 2 can continue his work. However, as we argued before, the possible actions that a user can perform in a handheld are different than those actions that could be executed in a desktop computer. But, similarly to (b) interaction, user 2 now can access only some part of the context and his interface adapts itself to the possibilities (i.e. present less or different menu items).

Finally when user 1 finally arrives to users' 1 office and acknowledges the existence of wireless network support, the agent (CM1b) asks user 1 if he likes to exploit the network and if so, CM1b synchronizes his actions with the DSC (updates DSC concepts at layer 1 and 2, personal activities are synchronized as local context for each user). If conflictive actions have occurred (another user has modified also the same paragraph), a new version for the document item is created (a new version of the paragraph). Later on, the user must negotiate with his co-author the final version.

Once the agent has updated the DSC, user 1 works now with the support of the wireless network (c). It is also possible that user 1 and 2 meet (resource discovery) and decide to work together on his handhelds (i.e. they could be at the cafeteria).

3.2 Agents' Structure

Users interact with the DSC Server through a CM agent. These agents restrict the global DSC according to the current restrictions and opportunities that devices provide, but also capture actions that users perform when working isolated. The set of actions and states that reflect the isolated working mode is called "Local context" and in addition to document structural units (DSC layer 1) is used to construct a local Knowledge Base for the CM agent (Fig.3).

Although it is possible for agents to reason based on this KB, up today we have not designed specialized reasoning tasks that support isolated work, but we plan to do so as future work in order to determine the impact of devices restriction (limited storage, battery, etc.). When synchronization is required only actions and concepts related to DSC1 are uploaded to the DSC server. We have implemented an interface mapping function as well; with this approach interfaces' elements like menu items are generated automatically according to the local context (the set of possible actions).

Contexts based design makes possible to integrate different devices (and their interfaces) straightforwardly. However, since contexts are represented as ontologies (concepts, predicates and agents actions), the main drawback is that it requires extra effort from developers, which can be demanded if they are not used to model domains in those terms. On the other hand, end users can switch from isolated to shared work smoothly as well as from different devices and applications: they can switch between a java editor, a web-based schedulers or a web-based project manager designed to share the application layer at a conceptual level, that is their context ontologies.

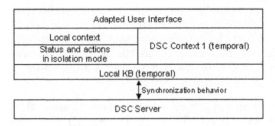

Fig. 3. Agents' behavior. A *CM* agent *adapts* the *user interface* according to the *local context* and *synchronizes* the local changes with the *Distributed Shared Context*

4 An Example Application

D-Write (Distributed Writing) is a collaborative writing tool based on DSC Server, designed to support three interaction scenarios: a user management component, a Web editing module and a PDA text-editing module. For implementing the Web and PDA version, it is only necessary to design the Distributed Shared Context (DSC) in both layers: Document structure (fig. 4(a)), and status and actions (fig. 4(b)).

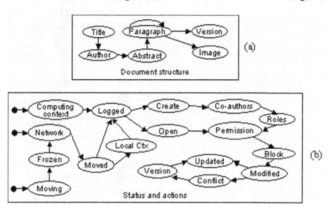

Fig. 4. Distributed Shared Context. Application context is described through *document structure* and the set of possible *states and actions* available for each device

In fig. 4(a), a D-Write document contains a title, an author, an abstract and a series of paragraphs, which can contain images and can have associated a version, those are represented as concepts and stored in a KB (JESS[3] facts). The minimal unit (atom) is a paragraph. For the sake of simplicity a partial view of the possible states is shown in Fig.4(b). In the figure, the nodes denote the states while the arcs the actions that cause a state change; again for simplicity arcs are not labeled in the figure.

As we can see, when users start the application (i.e. from a PDA or making a request to a Web site), the application recognizes its computing context, that is, whether it is running on a PDA or in a Web client. Depending on the computing context other procedures are available for the user; those are: authentication, document manipulation (create or open documents, determine co-authors and their roles and hence the set of permissions assigned to the user, modifying documents and handling conflicts and versioning), moving to another device and downloading a restricted context (a subset).

The user interface is adapted according to the devices type: functions available for the device are mapped from the context available for the device. For instance in fig. 5(a), we present the Web version and in fig. 5(b), the PDA version. Both interface designs are similar although the PDA module is smaller and specific. Entrance to the system is done through the main page. Here, basic data for connection to the server is initialized. Co-authors may create new documents or open previous ones (fig. 4(b)). Shared documents may have several versions, which can be navigated by a co-author, however, even though personal annotations keep versions as well, only its owner can

---

[3] JESS is the Java Expert System Shell. See http://herzberg.ca.sandia.gov/jess/ for more information.

access them and because they are stored in DSC Server, user could work isolated whenever they require it in any device (perhaps her notebook, at home).

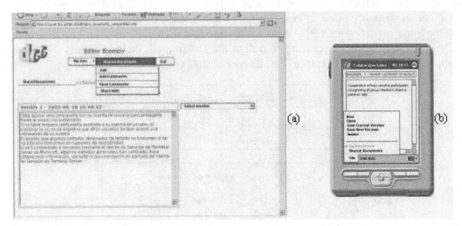

Fig. 5. D-Write editor allow users to edit a shared document from a Web browser and a PDA editing module. The PDA allows making personal *annotations* as well

5   Conclusions

The aim of this paper is to understand the distinction between personal and public artifacts and how a context-based design can facilitate the construction of environments that can be accessed anywhere, anytime on anything. By modeling the set of possible actions available for a particular device, we maximize its particular strengths and capabilities. By designing applications at a high level of abstraction, adaptation different modes of interaction and device's restrictions are eased. This recommendation mirrors Norman's advocating of information appliances [22].

In humans, awareness is a complex mental state through which individuals understands their immediate context and its changes and can regulate their actions and acquire new information [23]. Although not fully understood, it seams that we associate actions with multiple contexts at a time. For an observer, a user action conveys much information depending on the action itself, the context where it occurs and the observers' own experiences.

In [11] users' actions are interpreted on the context of work and practical inferences are made (responsibility, failure of expectations, etc.), however, when interactions are more flexible and are not restricted by work constraints (i.e. collaborative creation of a document, artistic work, etc.) the relations are relaxed so much that the inferences are not very interesting (perhaps because work context does not apply anymore). Because we are interested in more relaxed environments (such as learning environments), in this paper, we want to explore a more general approach.

The approach allows us to build applications that can be accessed from different devices, adapt to them and fully exploits their capabilities. However some questions arise. For instance, it can be argued that modeling every possible user action is not possible. This concern is closely related with the dynamic aspect of context: contexts change over time. It is possible that processing power required to keep KBs of different context could be a issue, up today we have not built more complex examples (like a shared scheduler or a project manager), but we are planning to do so, in order to get an insight on developers' extra effort required, as well as technology restrictions. On the plus side, as agents' mobility and synchronization tasks are encapsulated in the DSC-Server, an application can be accessed for different devices that we could not anticipated before.

Today, PDAs are perceived as highly personal devices containing specialized person information, while single display groupware are highly public devices containing specialized group information. To become an information appliance they need to share this information. The problem is how people move their personal artifacts (created on their PDAs) into the public domain (manipulated on the single display groupware) and back again. Our main goal is to understand how people distinguish between these personal and public artifacts, its consequences when designing CSCW tools and how to present context-based relevant information. Application design at a high level of abstraction eases to achieve these objectives.

Acknowledgements

This work was partially supported by the Chilean government funds MECESUP, under grant N° UCH019, and FONDECYT, under grant N° 1030959. We would like to thank the support of the Colombian program Colciencias.

References

1. Gaddah, A. and Kunz, T.: A survey of middleware paradigms for mobile computing, Technical Report SCE-03-16, Department of Systems and Computer Engineering, Carleton University, Ottawa, Canada, July 2003.
2. Chen, G. and Kotz, D.: A Survey of Context-Aware Mobile Computing Research. Technical Report Dartmouth Computer Science Technical Report TR2000-381, 2000.
3. Schilit, B. N., Adams, N. and Want, R.: Context-Aware Computing Application. Proc. of IEEE Workshop on Mobile Computing System and Application, IEEE Computer Society Press (1994) 85-90. December 1994.
4. Yan, H., Selker, T.: Context-aware office assistant. In: Proceedings of the 2000 Int. Conference on Intelligent User Interfaces, New Orleans. ACM Press. (2000) 276-279.
5. Persson, P.: Social Ubiquitous Computing. In CHI 2001 Building the Ubiquitous Computing User Experience, Position Paper.
6. Dey, A., Abowd, G., Salber, D.: A conceptual framework and a toolkit for supporting the rapid prototyping of context-aware applications. Human Computer Interaction Vol.16. Special Issue on Context-Aware Computing. (2001).
7. Ishii, H., Ullmer, B.: Tangible Bits: Towards seamless interfaces between people, bits and atoms. In Proceedings of the CHI '97 Conference on Human Factors in Computing Systems. New York, NY: ACM Press. (1997) 234-241.
8. Barton, J., Kindberg, T.: The Cooltown Experience. In CHI 2001 Building the Ubiquitous Computing User Experience, Position Paper.
9. Davies, N., Mitchell, K., Cheverest, K., Blair, G., Developing a Context Sensitive Tourist Guide. In: First Workshop on Human Computer Interaction with Mobile Devices.
10. Muñoz, M. A., Gonzalez, V. M., Rodríguez, M. and Favela, J.: Supporting Context-Aware Collaboration in a Hospital: An Ethnographic Informed Design. CRIWG 2003: 330-344.
11. Alarcón, R. and Fuller, D. A.: Intelligent Awareness in Support of Collaborative Virtual Work Groups. In Proc. of CRIWG'2002. Lecture Notes in Computer Science, Springer-Verlag, Berlin (2002) pp.168-188.

12. Brézillon, P. and Abu-Hakima, S.: Using knowledge in its context: Report on the IJCAI-93 Workshop. The AI Magazine, (1995) 16(1) pp. 87-91.
13. Leech, G.: Semantics: The Study of Meaning. Harmondsworth, UK: Penguin, (1981).
14. Sohlenkamp, M.: Supporting group awareness in Multi-User Environments through Perceptualization. GMD Research Series (1999) N°6 Zugl.: Padderborn, Univ. Diss.
15. Dourish, P. and Belloti, V.: Awareness and coordination in shared workspaces. In Proc. Of CSCW'92, (1992) pp.107-114.
16. Fussell, S., Kraut, R., Lerch, F., Scherlis, W., McNally, N. and Cadiz, J.: Coordination, overload and team performance: Effects of team communication strategies. In Proc. Of CSCW'98 (1998), pp. 275-284.
17. Alarcón, R. and Fuller, D. A.: Application Design Based on Work Ontology and an Agent Based Awareness Server. In Proc. of CRIWG'2003. Lecture Notes in Computer Science, Springer-Verlag, Berlin (2003) pp.: 314-329.
18. Burg, B.: Foundation for Intelligent Physical Agents. Official FIPA presentation, Lausanne, February 2002. See http://www.fipa.org for further details.
19. DeSanctis, G.: Shifting Foundations in Group Support System Research. In Group Support Systems – New Perspectives, L. Jessup, J. Valacich (eds.), MacMillan Pub. Co., New York, (1993), pp. 97-111.
20. Gruber, T. R.: Toward principles for the design of ontologies used for knowledge sharing. In Guarino, N. y Poli, R. (ed.), Formal Ontology in Conceptual Analysis and Knowledge Representation, Kluwer Academic Publishers, Deventer, The Netherlands.
21. JADE is the Java Agent DEvelopment Framework (http://jade.tilab.com/).
22. Neisser, U.: Cognition and Reality. Freeman, W. H. (ed), San Francisco (1976).
23. Norman, D. A.: The Invisible Computer. MIT Press (1998).

Support for Context-Aware Collaboration

Hana K. Rubinsztejn, Markus Endler, Vagner Sacramento,
Kleder Gonçalves, and Fernando Nascimento

Departamento de Informática, PUC-Rio
R. Marquês de São Vicente 225
22453-900, Rio de Janeiro
{hana,endler,vagner,kleder,ney}@inf.puc-rio.br

Abstract. This paper describes a middleware architecture with its location inference service (LIS), and an application for context-aware mobile collaboration which is based on this architecture. The architecture, named *Mobile Collaboration Architecture* - MoCA comprises client and server APIs, a set of core services for registering applications, monitoring and inferring the execution context of mobile devices, in particular their location. This architecture is suited for the development of new kinds of collaborative applications in which the context information (connectivity, location) plays a central role in defining both the group of collaborators, and the communication mode.

Keywords: Mobile Computing, Middleware, Context-awareness, Mobile Collaboration

1 Introduction

With the increasing popularity of mobile technologies, high-speed wireless communication is now available in many locations such as corporate offices, factories, shopping malls, university campi, airport halls, cafes and at homes. Moreover, with the widespread availability of cheaper and more powerful portable devices, there is also an increasing demand for services that support seamless communication and collaboration among mobile users. User mobility has also inspired the development of many *location-based* services, such as automated tourist guides or generic location-specific information services. We believe that user mobility and wireless communication capabilities also open a wide range of new and yet unexplored forms of collaboration, in which information about the user's context, for example, her position, plays a central role in defining both the group of collaborators, and the communication mode.

Concerning the first aspect, we believe that, unlike in traditional groupware, the group of collaborators tends to be dynamic and formed spontaneously, for example, motivated by a common interest, situation or environment shared among the peers. In particular, collaboration happens in form of spontaneous and occasional initiatives of requesting or giving assistance, sharing news or contributing to the building of public knowledge. Thus, participation is very often motivated by the implicit gain of reputation caused by providing help or a contribution [1].

A. Karmouch, L. Korba, and E. Madeira (Eds.): MATA 2004, LNCS 3284, pp. 37–47, 2004.
© Springer-Verlag Berlin Heidelberg 2004

In terms of the second aspect, we think that the user's context (e.g. her current location, quality of the connectivity, or her current activity/task) will be an important factor when determining the most appropriate communication mode for a given situation or task, i.e. whether synchronous or asynchronous communication is to be used in each situation. In particular, for mobile collaboration we are convinced that both modes of communication are equally important and that they will probably be used in an interleaved way.

Finally, due to the intrinsic weak and intermittent connectivity in mobile networks, there is need to re-define the notion of mutual *collaboration awareness*. For example, when a user is engaged in a synchronous collaboration session and for any reason suffers an involuntary and temporary disconnection, in most cases it is important that her new context (e.g. disconnected) is shared among the collaborating peers, so as to minimize the disruption of the group dynamics. Hence, we think that mobile collaboration tools should support some degree of context sharing.

In order to share our vision of new forms of context-aware collaboration, consider the following scenario:

Scenario: In the cafeteria during lunch, Alice realizes that she has probably forgotten her home keys in the lab. But since she has an important meeting afterward she cannot return there to check for the keys. So she calls the lab but because it is lunch hour, nobody picks up the phone. So she decides, using her wireless enabled PDA, to send a message to the lab's virtual note board, asking for any student or lab staff who happens to come into the lab to store away her keys in her drawer. As soon as Peter enters the lab and turns on his notebook, he is notified of a new message from Alice to the lab. Because he is a regular lab user, he is authorized to open it. He reads the message, finds and stores Alice's keys, and closes the message with an OK. When doing so, Alice is automatically notified that someone has read her message and probably attended her appeal. Although she does not know who it was, she knows that if necessary she could later check in the virtual note board who it was. So she decides to remotely remove her note. She then rushes to the meeting, where she arrives 20 minutes late. In the meeting, she realizes that the most important topic has already been discussed. Instead of asking (and disturbing) someone, through her PDA, she searches for any meeting-specific note being shared by any of the participants. Fortunately, Helen the secretary, is her friend, and Alice can immediately know what she has missed. Moreover, she can see that right now Helen is scribbles: "Late again, uh?".

This scenario shows the benefits of location-specific asynchronous and synchronous communication. The first is useful as a form of any-casting, while the latter may be useful in situations where sharing of documents is required among people which are co-located, and participating in the same event, such as a meeting, a presentation or a class.

The aforementioned discussion and scenario suggest that environments for developing mobile collaboration applications and services should incorporate new mechanisms facilitating the collection, the aggregation and the application-level access to different kinds of information about the individual and collective context of a user or group of users, including their location.

This paper describes a middleware architecture (MoCA) with its location inference service (LIS), and an application for context-aware mobile collaboration which is based on this architecture. The work is part of a wider project which aims at experimenting with new forms of mobile collaboration and implementing a flexible and extensible service-based environment for the development of collaborative applications for infra-structured mobile networks.

In the following session we present a general overview of MoCAand its main components. Our current work on context-aware collaborative applications is presented in Section 4. In section 5 we discuss some related work and make a comparison with the MoCA architecture. Finally, in section 6, we make some considerations with regard to the MoCA properties, and mention other ongoing work that in the scope of this project.

2   Overview of MoCA

The *Mobile Collaboration Architecture (MoCA)* consists of client and server APIs, basic services supporting collaborative applications and a framework for implementing application proxies (*ProxyFramework*).

In MoCA, each application has three parts: a server, a proxy and a client, where the two first execute on nodes of the wired network, while the client runs on a mobile device. A proxy intermediates all communication between the application server and one or more of its clients on mobile hosts.

Applications with requirements to scale to large numbers of clients may have several proxies executing on different networks. The proxy of an application may execute several tasks, such as adaptation of the transferred data, e.g. compression, protocol conversion, encryption, user authentication, processing of context information, handover management and others. Most of such tasks require quite a lot of processing effort, and hence, the proxy also serves as a means of distributing the application-specific processing among the server and its proxies.

The MoCA was designed for infra-structured wireless networks. The current prototype of this architecture works with an 802.11 wireless network based on the IP protocol stack, but the architecture could as well be implemented for a cellular data network protocol, such as GPRS.

MoCA offers client and server APIs and a *ProxyFramework*. The server and the client of a collaborative application should be implemented using the MoCA APIs, since they hide from the application developer most of the details concerning the use of the services provided by the architecture (see below). The *ProxyFramework* is a white-box framework for developing and customizing the proxies according to the specific needs of the application. It facilitates the programming of adaptations that should be triggered by context-change events.

In addition, the architecture offers the following core services which support the development of context-aware collaborative applications:

- *Monitor*: is a daemon executing on each mobile device and is in charge of collecting data concerning the device's execution state/environment, and sending this data to the CIS (*Context Information Service*) executing on one (or more) node(s) of the wired network. The collected data includes the quality of the wireless connection, remaining energy, CPU usage, free memory, current Access Point (AP), list of all APs and their signal strengths that are within the range of the mobile device.
- *Configuration Service (CS)*: this service is in charge of storing and managing configuration information for all mobile devices, so that these can use MoCA's core services, such as CIS and *Discovery Service (DS)*. The configuration information is stored in a persistent *hash table*, where each entry (indexed by the device's MAC address) holds the following data: the (IP:port) addresses of a CIS server and a *Discovery Server*, and the periodicity by which the *Monitor* must send the device's information to the CIS. The MAC address-specific indexing is essential for implementing a distributed CIS, where each server gets approximately the same context processing load.
- *Discovery Service (DS)*: is in charge of storing information, such as name, properties, addresses, etc., of any application (i.e. its servers and proxies) or any service registered with the MoCA middleware.
- *Context Information Service (CIS)*: This is a distributed service where each CIS server receives and processes devices' state information sent by the corresponding *Monitor*s. It also receives requests for notifications (aka subscriptions), specified by an *Interest Expression* in SQL syntax, from application Proxies or other services. The CIS generates and delivers these notifications whenever a change in a device's state is of interest to the subscriber.
- *Location Inference Service (LIS)*: infers the approximate *symbolic* location of a device by interacting with the CIS. Details of this service will be presented in Section 3.

For more information concerning the interaction among the MoCA services, the reader is referred to [2].

3   Location Inference Service

The *Location Inference Service (LIS)* is responsible for inferring the approximate location of a mobile device from the *raw* context information collected by the CIS for this device. It does this by comparing the device's current pattern of RF signals received (from all "audible" 802.11 Access Points) with the signal patterns previously measured at pre-defined *Reference Points* in a Building or Campus. Therefore, before being able to make any inference, the LIS database has to be populated with RF signal probes (device pointing in several directions) at each reference point, and inference parameters must be chosen according to the specific characteristics of the region. In fact, the number of reference points determines the reliability of the inference. LIS uses a hybrid and hierarchical location model where position can be given either by coordinates or by symbolic name. The LIS architecture is outlined in Figure 1.

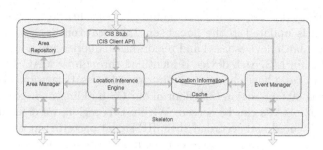

Fig. 1. LIS Architecture

The **CIS stub** requests to the CIS periodic notifications of the RF signal strengths sensed by a device from several APs (i.e. the RF pattern), collects and prepares this information for location inference.

The **Inference Engine** applies the *Multiple Nearest Neighbor* technique, as used in RADAR [3], to infer the approximate location of the device. This technique calculates the Euclidean *Signal Distance* d_k to a reference point k, based on the difference between each component $i \in [1, m]$ of the RF signal pattern (i.e. signal from each one of the m APs) collected for the device s'_i, and the corresponding component of the RF pattern s_{ki} of the reference point, which has been previously measured and recorded.

$$d_k = \sqrt{(s_{k1} - s'_1)^2 + (s_{k2} - s'_2)^2 + ... + (s_{km} - s'_m)^2}$$

Each coordinate of the (estimated) position of the device is then computed as the weighted mean value of the corresponding coordinate of only some reference points, which happen to have the lowest Signal Distances.

Since the RF signal is subject to much variation and interference, the inference can only be approximate. However, in order reduce the error, when comparing the RF patterns of a device and a reference point, we always use the mean value of several (e.g. $N = 20$) probes, and extreme values are previously discarded.

As part of LIS' configuration, a MoCA administrator can define geographic regions of arbitrary size and shape, assign them a *symbolic region* name, and use them to construct a hierarchical topology (i.e. composite regions with nested subregions) for his site. This information will be stored in the **Area Repository** in XML format. Accessing the **Area Manager**, the **Inference Engine** is able to map the coordinates of the inferred point to a symbolic region.

The result of an inference is the information of a device's coordinates, or if it is positioned inside any of the symbolic regions defined by the user. This information will then be recorded in the **Location Information Cache**. Because of the hierarchical topology, even if a device is not detected within an atomic symbolic region (e.g. a room), it will be detected in the enclosing region.

The **Event Manager** is responsible for processing queries and requests for notifications from applications which are interested in the location (or its change) of one or several devices, as well as sending the notifications whenever a device's location is updated in the `Location Information Cache`. LIS provides an interface for both device-based and region-based queries and notification subscriptions. Within LIS, each device is identified through its MAC Address.

Preliminary tests have shown that LIS can deliver satisfactory precision. We tested it on the 600 m² region (5th floor of our CS building), where signals from up to eight 802.11 APs can be sensed. Within this region, we defined reference points (i.e. measured and recorded their RF signal patterns) at approximately every 4 meters, mainly in corridors and common halls. The measurements were made at several, randomly chosen, test points in this region. For each test point, we made 20 measurements and computed the error (the Euclidean Distance, in meters) between its actual geographic position and the position inferred by LIS.

Table 1. Preliminary Precision Results

Percentage of Test Points	50%	70%	90%
Error (in meters)	1.56	1.74	2.84

Table 1 presents the errors (in meters) obtained with 50%, 70% and 90% of the test points. For example, for 70% of the tests, the error was at most 1.74 meters. And even for 90% of the tests, the error at most 3 meters.

The results obtained in our experiments are similar to the ones described in [3], which was expected since the algorithms are equivalent. As a next step we will experiment with other inference algorithms, such as the ones described in [4, 5] that use a probabilistic approach which seems to be more robust to variations of the RF signal strength. However, for the sort of location-aware applications we are developing, the achieved accuracy is fairly good and sufficient.

4   Application: Notes in the Air

In this section we present a Collaborative Application which we are developing as case study of MoCA.

NITA (from "Notes in the Air") is an application to post text messages (and files, in general) to a symbolic region. Hence, any client which is currently in (or enters) this region and has the proper authorization will automatically receive this message. There are several other projects with similar services combining messaging with spatial events. However, most of these services where implemented from scratch or without a general middleware support for context monitoring and inference.

In NITA, the sender of a message can set its destination (a symbolic region), the users authorized to read the message, and the time period the messages is to be readable. Moreover, it can search for available NITA servers, their regions, and visible users in each of the regions. A potential receiver can set her visibility flag (on/off), choose which types of messages she wants to receive, and choose between an immediate display of the message, or if it should be logged for future reading.

When a message is first read, its author receives an acknowledge message with a timestamp on it. It does not contain the reader's identity because such information would raise privacy problems, i.e., the author would know what time the reader was in a location. The acknowledge message is just used to inform the sender that her message was read at least once, and when.

When a user enters in a new symbolic region, the LIS service informs the NITA proxy about this change of user location. The latter forwards this information to the server application which calls the *removeUser()* method on the *Location object* related to the previous region and the *addUser()* method on the *Location object* representing the user's current region. Then, the *Location object* sends to the client application on the mobile device the list of IDs of all messages posted to the location it represents. A *new messages on the air* warning appears on user's screen, and the user can open a window to browse the list, showing subject and author of each message. If she decides to read one, the message's ID is sent to the application server, which retrieves the related message from the database and sends it to the client. Hence, only the desired messages are actually sent to the users. Besides, the user can choose whether to save or discard a message. On the former case, the message is saved on a previously configured URL, which can point to a local file system or to the user's remote account on the NITA server.

Besides this asynchronous kind of communication, NITA also provides a synchronous mode of communication. Each symbolic region has a chat room associated to it, allowing users to send/receive synchronous messages to/from people in the same location. This feature is interesting for regions with many people. For instance, a conference room, where users can communicate with each other without disturbing the speaker, or a bar, where shy people want to first have a virtual conversation before engaging in a meeting in the physical world.

Furthermore, the user does not need to be in the same place as her peers. When she first opens the application, she is automatically added to her current location and the chat room related to it. But she can browse and join other chat rooms and therefore be able to communicate with peers in other regions. In this case, her icon appears in a different way so the others know that she is not physically present in the region. It is also possible to send messages to a specific peer, as in normal peer-to-peer communication.

In addition to symbolic regions, a chat room can be created and associated to subjects. Hence, users can meet to talk about a topic of their interest, no matter where they are. This way, NITA works like a conventional wireless chat application.

Because NITA is essentially a message retrieval service driven by spatial events of the kind (*Device X detected in region Y*), and by communication events, it interacts closely with the location service LIS (cf. section 2), which provides derived/inferred context information.

The NITA proxy is in charge of querying the LIS service about its region structure and registering interest in location changes of the clients it represents. Moreover, it manages the client's profile, i.e., whether it should filter out some messages, log the messages or forward them to the client. Although many of these tasks could as well be performed by the NITA server, this decentralization is necessary for providing a scalable service.

5   Related Work

Much research related to middleware and programming environments for mobile and context-aware applications [6, 7] has been done, and many influenced our work. However,we will only discuss some architectures/environments with similar goals as MoCA. Furthermore, we will present also some applications which use the device location as the main context information, like NITA.

5.1   Middlewares

ActiveCampus [8] is a large project at UCSD which provides an infra-structure focusing on integration of location-based services for academic communities. It employs a centralized and extensible architecture with five layers (Data, Entity Modeling, Situation Modeling, Environment Proxy and Device) which supports a clear separation of the collection, the interpretation, the association with physical entities and the service-specific representation of context information. Currently, they implemented and deployed two applications: ActiveCampus Explorer, which uses students' locations to help engage them in campus life; and ActiveClass, a client-server application for enhancing participation in the classroom setting via PDAs. Like in MoCA, location is inferred by measuring the RF signals from 802.11 Access Points.

Aura[9] is a project at Carnegie Mellon University which is developing a system architecture, algorithms, interfaces and evaluation techniques needed for pervasive computing environments. The architecture components comprise Coda - a nomadic file system, Odyssey - for resource monitoring and adaptation, Spectra - remote execution mechanism and Prism - a new task layer above applications that is responsible for capturing and managing user intent to provide support for proactivity and self-tuning. Aura also offers a bandwidth advisor service (for IEEE 802.11 wireless networks) with two components for monitoring and prediction, and a user location service based on signal strength and 802.11 access point information, similar to LIS.

STEAM [10] is an event-based middleware for collaborative applications where location plays a central role. It is a system specially designed for ad-hoc mobile networks, and hence inherently distributed. It supports filtering of event notifications both based on subject and on proximity.

In MoCA we take a similar approach as in ActiveCampus, where context information (of any mobile user) may not only trigger user-transparent adaptations, but may also affect the specific functions available (and behavior) of the application at each point of time and space. Through its core services and the *ProxyFramework*, MoCA makes available to the application developer a wide range of context information, e.g. the user device's (approximate) location, the quality of the connectivity, the device characteristics, and available resources, which she can use according to the specific needs of the application.

Compared to ActiveCampus' architecture, MoCA proposes a decentralized context-information service (CIS), which can be used by other services for deriving some higher-level and application-specific context information. Moreover, MoCA also supports service integration, extensibility and evolution through the Discovery Service and well-defined interfaces between the core services.

5.2   Applications

There are several location-aware applications described in literature. comMotion[11, 12] and Stick-e Notes[13] post messages (to-do lists, news from the Internet, etc) to a place, using a GPS device to get the user's location information. As in NITA, information is delivered according to physical location and/or user identity. Cyberguide[14] is a mobile context-aware tour guide that offers information to users according to their position or orientation. The information is retrieved by anyone who is in a specific area, and cannot be filtered according to user identity.

In many applications, the positioning information is only used by the beholder of the device and is not shared. This way, it doesn't contribute to other purposes, i.e., knowing the location of a peer might suggest places of potential interest, as mentioned in Conference Assistant[15], where users attending a conference indicate their level of interest in a particular presentation to the application. Some privacy issues arise from this feature, and therefore some applications, like Cricket[16], chose not to provide it, avoiding a common database that holds such information, as used in NITA. But we believe that with some precaution, like using buddy-lists and configuration of a set of properties, privacy can be assured.

According to the limits imposed by their positioning technology, all applications can be used either indoors (Cricket) or outdoors (comMotion, Stick-e Notes) but not both. Currently, NITA is also restricted to indoor use (because of LIS), but we designed NITA to be independent of the location technology. Furthermore, all the above-mentioned applications support either synchronous or asynchronous communication, but not both, as NITA does.

6   Conclusions

We believe that collaboration among mobile users requires new and different middleware services. These should use context information about individuals and groups which can be used not only to enhance collaboration awareness, but also to enable new forms of collaboration.

Compared with other middlewares and environments for mobile collaboration, MoCA offers a generic and extensible infrastructure for the development of both new services for collecting and/or processing context information, and collaborative applications that make use of this information to determine the form, the contents and/or the peers involved in the collaboration. By developing the LIS service, we have shown how MoCA can be extended to incorporate new services that infers an abstract context, as for example, the device location from "raw" context data, such as 802.11 RF signals.

So far, we have implemented the *Monitor* for WinXP and Linux[1], the *Configuration Service*, and prototypes of the *Context Information Service* and the *Location Inference Service*. Although, preliminary tests have shown that LIS can deliver satisfactory precision, we are still experimenting with different inference algorithms, as well as assessing the accuracy of the inference in other areas on the campus.

Application NITA is still being developed, but we can already notice the benefits of using MoCA's services, especially LIS, the APIs and the *ProxyFramework*. Their use reduced considerably the complexity of the application development since the application just needs to register for notification of context changes. We have already developed one other context-aware application using MoCA, named W-Chat which is a chat tool providing collaborative peers with information about mutual (wireless) connectivity. Moreover, we are also planning to use MoCA and LIS for the development of location-aware information services for the university campus.

References

1. Rheingold, H.: Smart Mobs: The Next Social Revolution. Perseus Publishing (2002) ISBN: 0738206083.
2. Sacramento, V., Endler, M., Rubinsztejn, H., Lima, L., Gonçalves, K., Bueno, G.: An Architecture supporting the development of Collaborative Applications for Mobile Users. In: 2nd. Intern. Workshop on Distributed and Mobile Collaboration (DMC2004), IEEE WETICE-2004, Modena, Italy (2004)
3. Bahl, P., Padmanabhan, V.N.: RADAR: An in-building RF-based user location and tracking system. In: INFOCOM (2). (2000) 775–784
4. Ladd, A.M., Bekris, K.E., Rudys, A., Kavraki, L.E., Wallach, D.S., Marceau, G.: Robotics-based location sensing using wireless ethernet. In: Proceedings of the 8th annual international conference on Mobile computing and networking, ACM Press (2002) 227–238
5. Roos, T., Myllymaki, P., Tirri, H., Misikangas, P., Sievanen, J.: A probabilistic approach to wlan user location estimation. International Journal of Wireless Information Networks **9** (2002) 155–164
6. Chen, G., Kotz, D.: A survey of context-aware mobile computing research. Technical Report TR2000-381, Dept. of Computer Science, Dartmouth College (2000)
7. Mascolo, C., Capra, L., Emmerich, W.: Middleware for Mobile Computing (A Survey). In: Advanced Lectures in Networking. Volume LNCS 2497. Springer Verlag (2002) 20–52

---

[1] These implementations are mostly independent of the 802.11b chip set. And we are currently working on a WinCE version.

8. W. G. Griswold, R. Boyer, S.W.B., Truong, T.M.: A component architecture for an extensible, highly integrated context-aware computing infrastructure. In: Proc. of the 25th International Conference on Software Engineering (ICSE 2003), Portland, Oregon. (2003)
9. Garlan, D., Siewiorek, D., Smailagic, A., Steenkiste, P.: Project Aura: Toward Distraction-Free Pervasive Computing. IEEE Pervasive Computing (2002) 22–31
10. Meier, R., Cahil, V.: Exploiting proximity in event-based middleware for collaborative mobile applications. In: 4th IFIP International Conference on Distributed Applications and Interoperable Systems (DAIS'03), Paris, France. (2003)
11. Marmasse, N.: comMotion: a context-aware communication system. In: CHI '99 extended abstracts on Human factors in computing systems, MIT Media Laboratory, ACM Press (1999) 320–321
12. Marmasse, N., Schmandt, C.: Location-Aware Information Delivery with ComMotion. In: HUC - Handheld and Ubiquitous Computing. Volume 1927 of Lecture Notes in Computer Science., Springer (2000) 157–171
13. Pascoe, J., Ryan, N.: Stick-e notes.
(http://www.cs.ukc.ac.uk/research/infosys/mobicomp/Fieldwork/Sticke)
14. Long, S., Kooper, R., Abowd, G., Atkeson, C.: Rapid prototyping of mobile context-aware applications: The cyberguide case study. In: 2nd ACM International Conference on Mobile Computing and Networking (MobiCom'96). (1996)
15. Dey, A.K., Salber, D., Abowd, G.D., Futakawa, M.: The conference assistant: Combining context-awareness with wearable computing. In: ISWC - 3rd International Symposium on Wearable Computers . (1999) 21–28
16. Priyantha, N., Chakraborty, A., Balakrishnan, H.: The Cricket Location-Support System. In: 6th ACM/IEEE MobiCom, Boston, MA (2000) 32–43

Building Policy-Based Context Aware Applications for Mobile Environments

Hamid Harroud, Mohamed Khedr, and Ahmed Karmouch

Multimedia & Mobile Agent Research Laboratory,
School of Information Technology & Engineering (SITE), University of Ottawa,
161 Louis Pasteur St. Ottawa, ON, Canada K1N 6N5, Canada
{hharroud,mkhedr,karmouch}@site.uottawa.ca,
http://deneb.genie.uottawa.ca

Abstract. Advances in portable devices and wireless technology eased the seamless service provisioning to mobile users in pervasive environments. However, the limited capabilities of portable devices, network heterogeneity, and the spontaneous interactions due to users and devices mobility placed significant burdens on applications deployed in these environments. This paper describes an innovative approach for supporting mobile users with context-aware services wherever they go and with whatever devices they use. This approach is based on a novel framework that provides necessary features and services to facilitate building context-aware mobile applications. The framework uses semantically modeled policies to adapt the application behavior dynamically based on the situation of its users. The framework negotiates contexts and sets levels of agreements needed to translate automatically these contexts to a set of semantic policies.

1 Introduction

Portable computing devices and wireless networking technologies have contributed to the growing acceptance of mobile computing applications and increased the possibility of seamless and pervasive services suited to mobile users. However, due to the limitation in devices' capabilities, networks heterogeneity and dynamism of users, considerable burdens are placed on developers building mobile applications. These burdens are the results of relieving end-users from being constantly aware of the detailed interactions taking place in their computing environment. Two goals are required to reduce these burdens significantly. First, users and applications should have the ability to state declaratively contexts and services that they are interested in and suit their situation. Second, the environment should be able to support automated adaptability using policies that govern the behaviour and interactions among users and applications.

This paper describes the approach we have taken to address these two goals. The approach is based on a multi-agent framework that relieves developers from building software components that are common across various mobile applications and allows them to focus on the specific objectives of the applications they are developing. In addition, the framework enables the rapid development and adaptive deployment of mobile applications using semantic policies and context level agreements. This adap-

A. Karmouch, L. Korba, and E. Madeira (Eds.): MATA 2004, LNCS 3284, pp. 48–61, 2004.
© Springer-Verlag Berlin Heidelberg 2004

tation is based on generating semantic policies as an outcome of a negotiation process and the runtime execution of these policies.

The interest of the research community in using agent technology to support mobile computing [1, 2, 3] is motivated by agent's intrinsic properties such as autonomy, mobility and decision-making. To exploit these properties in our framework, we attached policies to agents' behaviors. These policies define the actions that agents can perform, resources that they can use and information that they can access. In addition, these policies are tightly bound to the context in which they are evaluated and used. Based on the agent's state, tasks and the operating-environment conditions, a policy will be triggered forcing the agent to adapt accordingly.

Managing context at the framework level greatly simplifies the development of context-aware applications. This is achieved by providing a set of APIs for manipulating context, for generating policies, and for negotiating context that will facilitate the discovery of relevant context in the environment and the delivery of the appropriate information to mobile users' applications and devices. In order for the framework to successfully use, exchange, and manage context information, we propose to translate the effective contextual information that is used by mobile applications into a set of policies. Generated context policies are represented semantically to help achieve the common understanding of policies across different domains and to allow inference over these policies with the intention of automating the process of generating implicit policies.

This paper is organized as follows. The following section presents our motivations and related work. Section 3 describes the developed agents constituting the building blocks of our semantic, policy-based framework. Section 4 discusses the context ontology model and the process of semantically generating policies according to the modeled context. Context negotiation for setting context levels among agents is also described in this section. Section 5 highlights our prototype implementation and discusses the framework performance evaluation. We conclude the paper in section 6 with the summary and future work.

2 Motivations and Related Work

Recent research projects are exploring the use of context information to facilitate the development of mobile computing applications [1,4,5]. The Colomba framework [1] separates service logic from binding management. This permits developers to reuse service components independently of each other. Colomba uses context and location awareness to support the dynamic binding management. Research proposed in [5, 4] had developed middlewares for supporting smart spaces in which context is maintained by a set of registries in the environment.

Our framework complements these research projects by using context-sensitive policies. These policies address the automated provisioning of services to users using context negotiation and ontologies. With context negotiation and semantically modeled context, applications and services are easily developed and deployed in various mobile situations using our framework.

3 The Policy-Based Agents Framework

We designed and developed a multi-agent framework with features derived from the need to provide developers with a set of generic agents capable of building complex context-aware applications. Developers should be able to incorporate and extend the framework rather than developing their own software components to support context-awareness in mobile computing. The framework should also provide some basic services such as naming, discovery, and event handling as well as optional services that can be plugged to the framework such as security and repository facilities.

Agents are provided with a set of policies that govern their overall behaviour in the environment and in specify their privileges and constraints. Each policy includes conditions that permit or prohibit an agent (called the subject) to perform actions on target components. Conditions may concern the subject, the target or a particular state or event of the operating environment. The introduction of specific policies inside each agent provides it with more pro-activeness in facing new situations at visited sites, especially with the possibility of discontinous interconnection. We separated between the coding parts of the agent and the monitoring policies so that the agent strategies and its overall behavior can dynamically adapt to the agent's context.

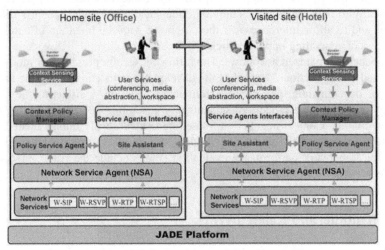

Fig. 1. The agent-based framework architecture

A simplified architecture of the framework is depicted in fig. 1. It shows the main agents of the framework that cooperate to prepare and configure an execution environment for mobile user as they moves from one location to another (from his/her office to a temporary location such as a hotel). The framework starts with the Network Service Agent (NSA). NSA provides a simple interface to network services, and exposes these interfaces to users and domains to access and use based on their context. Network services include tracking the location of mobile users, providing context-based quality of service and managing multimedia sessions. NSA removes the need for users or applications to deal with network services directly, thereby allowing them to focus on the real tasks at hand. The adaptation necessary to cope with changes in network conditions and the environment context is initiated by the NSA, rather than by users themselves. W-SIP is an example of a network service that is integrated in the framework. W-SIP is a wrapper agent that interfaces the Session Initiation Protocol (SIP). W-SIP is used to project users' availability and presence automatically to users subscribed with the framework. In the same manner, other network services are plugged-in the framework by wrapping them through agents [6].

On top of NSA is the Context Policy Manager (CPM). CPM is responsible for monitoring context information and managing the environment resources based on this context. This includes memory usage, processing time, bandwidth allocation, and resources consumption. Any changes that may occur to these monitored components will be sent by the CPM to the policy service agent to generate and trigger policies.

The Policy Service Agent (PSA) manages policies of the domain under its administration in order to control the behavior and decision-making of the system agents. The PSA is responsible for monitoring events and conditions likely to trigger policies, as we will discuss in section 4.1. To enforce a particular policy, the PSA invokes a set of actions to be executed. For instance, the PSA may prohibit an authorization to a participant seeking access to a particular service or resource at a specific site.

The Site Assistant (SAT) is in charge of preparing and setting up a temporary working environment to a user at the visited site. During setup phase, the SAT at the visited site establishes a negotiation process with the SAT at the home site to determine the visiting user profile and the authorized services as we explain in section 4.2. A site represents a location that a mobile user is visiting such as a hotel, or a business company. It may also represent a meeting room or an office within an organization.

Services such as the audio/video conferencing and the media abstraction service are offered to mobile users through Service Agent (SA) interfaces. Each service is associated with a SA. A wide range of services can be provided to mobile users by defining their corresponding SA.

4 Semantic Modeling of Context and Policies

Current context-aware research projects model context according to the tasks that the application layer performs rather than the application's functional intentions [1, 4, 5]. These models are ad hoc in nature. The problem lays in their extensibility and interoperability with other systems. This ad hoc modeling also limits the use of context across different domains due to the lack of a common understanding of the meaning of context information. Ontologies represent a new paradigm for modeling and representing the context needed in pervasive computing. During the ontology design, we faced the question of what contextual information to model. This was largely due to the overwhelming variety of possible context in pervasive environments. We concluded that to formalize all context information is unrealistic. Instead, it is more appropriate to model context in the form of **levels of expressiveness**, shown in figure 2a, where the highest level is an abstraction of all concepts of context and as we go down the levels, context is expressed in more details and refined to a more concrete representation.

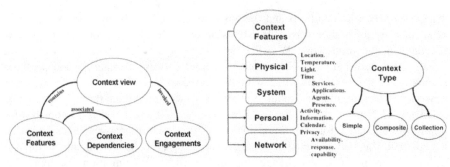

Fig. 2a. The upper context ontology

Fig. 2b. The defined context features and their context types

The highest level of abstraction in our context ontology is the *ContextView*. This provides a point of reference for declaring context information. *ContextView* represents the different types of context that belong to a given entity. An entity could be a user, a service or even the environment itself. At least one instance of the *ContextView* will exist for each entity in the environment. The properties *contains*, and *invokes* are properties of the *ContextView*. The classes *ContextFeatures* and *ContextEngagements* are the respective ranges of those properties. These classes are considered to be the second level of expressiveness in the ontology. Each instance of the *ContextView* will contain a subclass of the *ContextFeatures* that is *associated* with one or more *ContextDependencies* classes and is *invokedby* a *ContextEngagements* class.

The *ContextFeatures*, shown in figure 2b, consists of the classes related to the physical environment (such as location), classes related to the system (such as services), classes related to persons (such as ongoing activities and identity), and classes related to the underlying network (such as availability and bandwidth). Each of these classes is categorized as simple, composite of other context information, or collection of similar context information. More information about our context ontology is presented in [7].

4.1 Semantic Policies

To control the autonomous access of services and resources in different sites and to grant users with dynamic access to services, policies have to be defined and understood by both machines and humans and to be domain interoperable. In addition, policies have to be easily managed and manipulated according to the surroundings' context. We therefore modeled policy information using OWL, Ontology Web Language, to integrate it easily with our ontologies for modeling context and the agent framework. The semantic policies in our framework encapsulate the rules, governing the access to and the interaction with entities, with meta-data information and enforcement roles. The designed policy ontology aims at facilitating the processes of editing, manipulating, exchanging, and executing policies rather than developing a complete powerful policy system. This is because we believe that policy management system must be separated into policy-dependant part, represented by the ontology, and a policy-independent part represented by the system using these policies.

Our policy ontology has the following classes and properties:

- Policy (issuedBy*, appliesTo*, appliesWhen*, name*, appliesWhere*, priority*, equivalentTo*, composedOfPolicies*, policyRule*, enforcementType*, requiresOtherPolicies*)
  - o Authorization ()
  - o ContextSpecificPolicy (category*, description*)
  - o Obligation ()
- PolicyEnforcement ()
  - • instance Inform
  - • instance Negative
  - • instance Negotiable
  - • instance Positive
  - • instance Restricted
- PolicySimilar (degreeOfCertain*, similarIn*, similarTo*)
- Rule (hasAntecedent*, hasConsequent*, hasInferenceType*)

The PolicyEnforcement() class allows the corresponding agent to deduce action(s) to be performed as policy enforcement. For instance, the *Negative* value enforces not to do the rule, where the *Negotiable* value may initiate a negotiation process in case of conflicts or inconsistencies in the applied situation [7].

A policy can be either an authorization policy that permits or prohibits actions on target entity or an obligation policy that acts as the trigger for actions to be performed when conditions are applicable [6]. In addition, we have defined a generic policy class, *ContextSpecificPolicy*, which can be used by application developers to specify other types of policy that do not fall into these two categories. If the generic policy class is used, the developer will specify its category and gives a description to it to avoid repeated definition of policies that might exist in the system.

Each policy has properties that state meta-information associated with the policy such as the entity that issued the policy, entities to which it applies and the location and time of enforcing the policy. In addition, the developer may state if this policy is equivalent to another policy and states the degree of equivalency using the *Similar* class. This class, defined in our fuzzy ontology [8], allows agents to invoke other policies in case of uncertainty and vagueness in the captured context and thus increases its robustness and performance.

Table 1 shows an example of a semantic policy that is used in our ad hoc group meeting application, which we implemented using our agent-based framework. The policy states that the PSA is obliged to grant user *Khedr* the ability to use the video service and to be authenticated using the CPM agent located at MMARL lab if the current activity is *meetingA*, and the video source is *VideoServer1*. The policy is only valid to individuals who are member of the MMARL-Group and applies only during the time interval from 12:00PM to 14:00 PM on Monday, 24 of May. The user will be automatically authenticated, as he will be detected and recognized by the CPM agent while entering the MMARL lab space.

This approach of semantically modeling policies enriched our agent framework with the ability of common understanding of policies as well as the ability to process, derive and trigger new policies. For instance, using our inference algorithm found in [9], this policy can be applied to location B502, which is not stated in the policy. This new generated policy is also valid because B502, as a location, is inferred to be equivalent to MMARL location. Policies that apply to MMARL are therefore applicable to B502 and are automatically assigned to this location with no human intervention.

Table 1. An example of a semantic polic

Policy	Antecedent 1	Antecedent 2	Antecedent 3
<Obligation rdf:ID= "VideoStreaming"> <appliesWhen> <ConTime:FormalType rdf:ID="ClockMeeting"> <ConTime:hasTimevalue> 12:00PM,14:00PM </ConTime:hasTimevalue> </ConTime:FormalType> </appliesWhen> <appliesWhen> <ConTime:StandardTime rdf:ID="CalanderMeeting"> <ConTime:hasTimevalue> Monday,May 24, 2004 </ConTime:hasTimevalue> </ConTime:StandardTime> </appliesWhen> <appliesTo> <Confoaf:Group rdf:ID= "MMARL-Group"> <Confoaf:name> MondayGroupMeeting </Confoaf:name> </Confoaf:Group> </appliesTo> <enforcementType> <PolicyEnforcement rdf:ID="Positive"/> </enforcementType> <appliesWhere rdf:resource= "&Loc;MMARL/> </Obligation>	<ConRule:Antecedent rdf:ID="polAntc1"> <ConRule:EntityA> <Voc:Variable rdf:ID="VideoSource"/> </ConRule:EntityA> <ConRule:EntityB> <ConDev:Server rdf:ID="VideoServer1"/> </ConRule:EntityB> <ConRule:relation> <Voc:Property rdf:ID="is"/> </ConRule:relation> </ConRule:Antecedent>	<ConRule:Antecedent rdf:ID="polant2"> <ConRule:EntityA> <Voc:Variable rdf:ID= "DestinationUser"/> </ConRule:EntityA> <ConRule:relation rdf:resource="#is"/> <ConRule:entityB> <Confoaf:Person rdf:ID="Khedr "/> </ConRule:entityB> </ConRule:Antecedent>	<ConRule:Antecedent rdf:ID="polant3"> <ConRule:EntityA> <Voc:Variable rdf:ID="Activity"/> </ConRule:EntityA> <ConRule:relation rdf:resource="#is"/> <ConRule:EntityB rdf:resource="&Time; meetingA"/> </ConRule:Antecedent>

Consequent 1		Consequent 2	
<ConRule:Consequent rdf:ID="polcons1"> <ConRule:EntityA> <Voc:Variable rdf:ID= "ProvideService "/> </ConRule:EntityA> <ConRule:relation rdf:resource="#is"/> <ConRule:EntityB> < ConProf:ServiceCategory rdf:ID= "VideoPrinter"/> </ConRule:EntityB> </ConRule:Consequent>		<ConRule:Consequent rdf:ID="polcon2"> <ConRule:EntityA> <Voc:Variable rdf:ID= "AuthenticateVia"/> </ConRule:EntityA> <ConRule:relation rdf:resource="#is"/> <ConRule:EntityB> <Confoaf:SoftwareAgent rdf:ID="CPM-MMARL"/> </ConRule:EntityB> </ConRule:Consequent>	

Policy states :

   If (VideoSource is VideoServer1) &(DestinationUser is Khedr) &(Activity is meetingA)
   Then (ProvideService is Video) & (AuthenticateVia is CPM-MMARL)

Policy Type: Obligation
Policy Enforcement: Positive
Policy applies to: MMARL-Group.
Policy applies where : MMARL
Policy applies when : Monday, May 24, 2004 from 12:00 PM to 14:00 PM

4.2 Context Negotiation and Policy Enforcement

Managing context information at the framework level permits multiple domains and applications to exchange contextual information and form a large-scale pervasive environment. However, this raises issues of filtering, aggregating, and invoking context that matters to a specific application from the global captured context. To overcome this problem, the framework uses a Context Level Negotiation Protocol (CLNP) [7]. The CLNP is a multi-attribute negotiation protocol that allows automated context identification and agreement depending on applications and users requirements. The outcome of the CLNP negotiation is used by the PSA to register and execute contextual information and services implicitly, and to decide the way by which the requested information will be delivered and monitored. The protocol allows applications and users to send a context negotiation request to the PSA. The PSA in return maps the request to context specification parameters and issues a negotiation request to the CPM.

The negotiation between the PSA and the CPM continues until an agreement is reached based on a utility function calculation, which has the following characteristics:

- A lower bound on x (the normalized negotiated context parameter). Below this value, user satisfaction is negligible and is approximated to zero.
- An upper bound on x. Above this value, any gain in user satisfaction is negligible and is approximated to one.
- Between these two bounds, satisfaction factor is a monotonically increasing function of x.
- A controlling parameter "p" for projecting the user satisfaction.

The logarithmic function matches these requirements. The utility function can therefore be represented as a logarithmic function in the form of

$$U(x) = a \cdot \ln(b \cdot x + c) \qquad\qquad 1$$

$$a = \frac{1}{p - A_o} \qquad\qquad 2$$

$$b = \frac{e^{1/a} - 1}{R - A} \qquad\qquad 3$$

$$c = \frac{R - Ae^{1/a}}{R - A} \qquad\qquad 4$$

Where U(x) = utility function.

    x = context parameter values in negotiation.
    p = user sensitivity parameter.
    A_o = expected context sensitivity.
    A = minimum context parameter value.
    R = maximum context parameter value.

The utility function depends on the sensitivity parameter p. For every value of p, agents project their interest in a context specification according to the utility function shape. For example for p values smaller than A_o, the user is more sensitive to larger values of the context parameter than to smaller values, such as location information in outdoor applications. For p values larger than A_o the user is more sensitive to smaller context values than to higher values, such as delay in emergency notification time.

The CPM decides the working utility curve according to the negotiation process. The optimal utility curve is accomplished by applying the following decision equations on the initial context parameter value A_L requested by the users.

$$U(A_L)_{x=A_L} = a.\ln(b.A_L + c)$$

$$If \quad U(A_L) \ll U(R) \quad for \quad A_L < R, \& \quad A_L > \left[\frac{A+R}{2}\right] \qquad 5$$

then $P < A_o$, agent is more sensitive to large context values and P is chosen from equation 2 to satisfy equation 5

$$If \quad U(A_L) \gg U(A) \quad for \quad A_L > A, \& \quad A_L < \left[\frac{A+R}{2}\right] \qquad 6$$

then $P > A_o$, agent is more sensitive to small context values and P is chosen from equation 2 to satisfy equation 6

After deciding the utility function curve for each context parameter, the CPM assigns a weighted priority value for each context parameter that indicates its importance (as perceived by the user) in the overall negotiation. The CPM and the PSA use the priority values to differentiate between levels of context representation and delivery to the user.

The weighted priority value takes the form

$$W_i = \frac{A_{Li} - A}{R - A} \qquad i = 1...N \qquad \text{N= total number of context parameters.}$$

The total satisfaction value will be equal to $\sum_i U(x_i).W_i$. The CPM then decides if an agreement has been reached using this value, or if the negotiation should continue.

5   Implementation and Framework Evaluation

We designed and implemented a prototype system to evaluate our proposed policy-based framework using JADE agent platform. The prototype tests the applicability, scalability and context effectiveness when used with the semantically modeled policies that govern system behaviour and entities activities. To demonstrate the applicability of the framework, the prototype was used to implement and manage various mobile computing scenarios such as ad hoc group meetings and multimedia service provisioning applications.

Figure 3 illustrates the ad hoc group meetings scenario. Users are spontaneously connected to one another, and may share all the resources and services in the room.

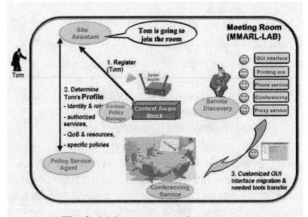

Fig. 3. Ad-hoc group meeting prototype

These resources and services are either provided by the room authority, or brought in by users. Different context-aware services were implemented and integrated to the prototype. This includes a conferencing service, a service discovery, and a scheduling service. The developed services prove our premise that semantically modeling context and policies reduce the burden of building context-aware applications and at the same time increase their reusability as the behaviour of the service components, modeled through policies, are separated from their concrete implementation. Figure 4 exemplifies this premise.

The graph in figure 4 is a visual representation of the user *Khedr's* context, and the printing services in the surroundings. The black rectangles represent classes defined in the developed context ontologies while the red rectangles are instances of these classes. Captions on the arrows represent the properties defined for these instances while arrows' directions point to values assigned to these properties. The figure also shows how the framework generates the code required to define these contexts and policies that govern the application behaviour.

The first part of the code addresses the registration process of the ontologies used in this situation and their namespaces and prefixes. The second part of the code is the actual modeling of the captured context using the developed ontologies. This includes user information, location information, and services in the environment.

The PSA then uses this information to generated policies on the fly for the detected entities. For example, the excerpt shows the *KhedrPrinterAccess* policy and the rule associated to this policy. The beauty of generating policies on the fly using context is demonstrated when the user starts to move and changes location. This is shown in the last part of the code. The new policy, *SamePlacePolicy*, is generated when the user changes his location to MMARL place. In addition, the code shows how the framework managed to relate policies together and state their similarities using our fuzzy ontology [9].

Table 2 illustrates an example of the generated policies on the fly and the process of exchanging context information in agent communication language, ACL, messages.

The first column in table 2 is an excerpt of a REQUEST ACL message sent from the user agent of *Khedr* to the PSA in the environment. The message states that the user is requesting a printer with a printing specification found in the *PrinterSpecification.owl* file. The message also shows that the agent supports the CLNP protocol for negotiation and CLA as the ontology.

The second and third columns in the table are a sample of the semantic policies used by the PSA in the system. The policy states "If (Requester belongsTo MMARL-Group) Then (GrantAccessToService belongsTo A606)" with negative access policy enforcement. This means that any user belonging to the MMARL-Group will not be given a grant to access services that are belonging to the location A606.

Using this policy as well as other generated policies, the PSA decides that the service matching the printer specifications that was sent in the request message would be printer HP_N1 and not HP_N2. This is because the generated policy shown in table 2 prohibits MMARL-Group, which *Khedr* is a member of, from accessing services in A606 as shown in figure 4.

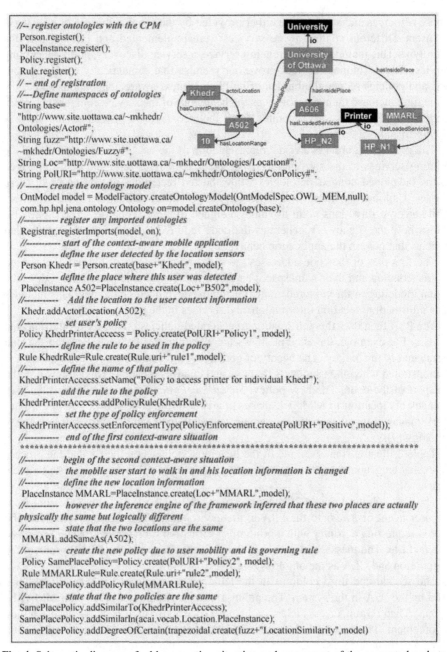

```
//-- register ontologies with the CPM
Person.register();
PlaceInstance.register();
Policy.register();
Rule.register();
// -- end of registration
//---Define namespaces of ontologies
String base=
"http://www.site.uottawa.ca/~mkhedr/
Ontologies/Actor#";
String fuzz="http://www.site.uottawa.ca/
~mkhedr/Ontologies/Fuzzy#";
String Loc="http://www.site.uottawa.ca/~mkhedr/Ontologies/Location#";
String PolURI="http://www.site.uottawa.ca/~mkhedr/Ontologies/ConPolicy#";
// ------ create the ontology model
OntModel model = ModelFactory.createOntologyModel(OntModelSpec.OWL_MEM,null);
com.hp.hpl.jena.ontology.Ontology on=model.createOntology(base);
//----------- register any imported ontologies
Registrar.registerImports(model, on);
//----------- start of the context-aware mobile application
//----------- define the user detected by the location sensors
Person Khedr = Person.create(base+"Khedr", model);
//----------- define the place where this user was detected
PlaceInstance A502=PlaceInstance.create(Loc+"B502",model);
//----------- Add the location to the user context information
Khedr.addActorLocation(A502);
//----------- set user's policy
Policy KhedrPrinterAccecss = Policy.create(PolURI+"Policy1", model);
//----------- define the rule to be used in the policy
Rule KhedrRule=Rule.create(Rule.uri+"rule1",model);
//----------- define the name of that policy
KhedrPrinterAccecss.setName("Policy to access printer for individual Khedr");
//----------- add the rule to the policy
KhedrPrinterAccecss.addPolicyRule(KhedrRule);
//----------- set the type of policy enforcement
KhedrPrinterAccecss.setEnforcementType(PolicyEnforcement.create(PolURI+"Positive",model));
//----------- end of the first context-aware situation
*****************************************************************************
//----------- begin of the second context-aware situation
//----------- the mobile user start to walk in and his location information is changed
//----------- define the new location information
PlaceInstance MMARL=PlaceInstance.create(Loc+"MMARL",model);
//----------- however the inference engine of the framework inferred that these two places are actually
physically the same but logically different
//----------- state that the two locations are the same
MMARL.addSameAs(A502);
//----------- create the new policy due to user mobility and its governing rule
Policy SamePlacePolicy=Policy.create(PolURI+"Policy2", model);
Rule MMARLRule=Rule.create(Rule.uri+"rule2",model);
SamePlacePolicy.addPolicyRule(MMARLRule);
//----------- state that the two policies are the same
SamePlacePolicy.addSimilarTo(KhedrPrinterAccecss);
SamePlacePolicy.addSimilarIn(acai.vocab.Location.PlaceInstance);
SamePlacePolicy.addDegreeOfCertain(trapezoidal.create(fuzz+"LocationSimilarity",model))
```

Fig. 4. Schematic diagram of ad hoc meeting situation and an excerpt of the generated code to model context and policies semantically

This policy is enforced even that **A606** and **MMARL** locations are within the range of "10 meter" specified by the *hasLocationRange* property as shown in figure 4. This is because the policy has an enforcement type equal to negative and not negotiable.

To evaluate the scalability and context effectiveness, we conducted experiments that measure the average delay taken to achieve negotiation of context information as an indication of the system scalability while we present the percentage of time taken to complete a service request-lookup-match-response cycle using our agent framework as an indication of the policy effectiveness in our framework.

Table 2. A graph of the context of user *Khedr* and policies applied to the environment

Agent ACL message	Policy definition and rule antecedent part	Rule consequent part
(REQUEST :sender (agent-identifier :name Khedr@skdanah:1099/JADE :addresses (sequence http://skdanah:7778/acc)) :receiver (set (agent-identifier :name PSA@skdanah:1099/JADE :addresses (sequence http://skdanah:7778/acc))) :content "Printer file:./PrinterSpecification.owl" :ontology CLA :protocol CLNP)	<Authorization rdf:ID="policy2"> <policyRule> <ConRule:Rule rdf:ID="GrantAccess"> <ConRule:hasAntecedent> <ConRule:Body> <ConRule:and> <ConRule:Antecedent> <ConRule:EntityA> <Voc:Variable rdf:ID="Requester"/> </ConRule:EntityA> <ConRule:entityB rdf:resource="#MMARL-Group"/> <ConRule:relation> <Voc:Property rdf:ID="belongsTo"/> </ConRule:relation> </ConRule:Antecedent> </ConRule:and> </ConRule:Body> </ConRule:hasAntecedent>	<ConRule:hasConsequent> <ConRule:Head> <ConRule:and> <ConRule:Consequent> <ConRule:entityB> <Loc:Room rdf:ID="A606"/> </ConRule:entityB> <ConRule:relation rdf:resource="#belongsTo"/> <ConRule:EntityA rdf:resource= "# GrantAccessToService"/> </ConRule:Consequent> </ConRule:and> </ConRule:Head> </ConRule:hasConsequent> </ConRule:Rule> </policyRule> <appliesTo rdf:resource= "#MMARL-Group"/> <enforcementType> <PolicyEnforcement rdf:ID="Negative"/> </enforcementType> </Authorization>

Policy states :
    If   (Requester belongsTo MMARL-Group)
        Then (GrantAccessToService belongsTo A606)
Policy Type: Authorization
Policy Enforcement: Negative
		Result = Printer HP_N1

Figure 5-a shows the average negotiation time taken to reach an agreement, using the context negotiation protocol described in section 4.2, when varying the number of requests while fixing the number of context providers. The figure shows that the delay is linearly proportional with the number of request, except for the last value, which is a good indication of the system scalability. The reason for the increase in delay in the last value is attributed to the fact that the number of request is 3 times the number of context providers and thus it took much longer time to settle an agreement between the context providers and the user. However this also indicates that the system may gracefully degrade in performance when it is highly overloaded.

Figure 5-b illustrates the percentage of time taken for a complete cycle of service provisioning in case of high overloading. The figure shows that the time taken to process policies is nearly 36% of the total life cycle time while 36% is used for exchanging messages between agents and 28% for repository and information access. This indicates that the overhead of introducing policies to context-aware applications in extreme overloading is not quite annoying compared to the gain achieved in the framework awareness and the rapid deployment of services for mobile users.

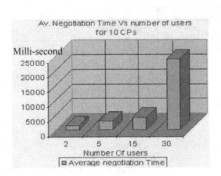
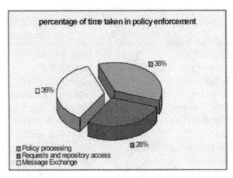

Fig. 5a. Average negotiation time

Fig. 5b. Percentage of time taken in polixy enforcement

6   Conclusion and Future Work

In this paper, we described a novel framework that supports the rapid building of context-aware applications for mobile computing environments. The framework accomplishes this with its ability to define, use, and enforce semantic policies that govern the behaviour of each application components. By supporting mobility in its different forms and taking into consideration the context, users do not have to explicitly specify and configure their working environment each time they move from one site to another.

Our next focus is on extending the context policy manager with a fuzzy inference engine in generating policies that will provide a necessary robustness against uncertain situations in the environment and maintain its performance even in vague or corrupted context information.

References

1. P. Bellavista, et al, "Dynamic Binding in Mobile Application: a Middleware Approach," IEEE Internet Computing, Vol. 7, No. 2, March-April 2003.
2. E. Kovacs, et al, "Integrating Mobile Agents into the Mobile Middleware," Proc. Mobile Agents Int'l Workshop, Springer-Verlag, Berlin, 1998, pp. 124-135.

3. S. Lippers, A. Park, "An Agent-Based Middleware: A solution for Terminal and User Mobility," Computer Networks, Sept. 1999, pp. 2053-2062.
4. M. Román, et. al, "A Middleware Infrastructure for Active Spaces," IEEE Pervasive Computing, pp. 74-83, Vol.1, No.4, October-December 2002.
5. S. Yau, et. al, "Reconfigurable Context-Sensitive Middleware for Pervasive Computing," IEEE Pervasive Computing, pp. 33-40, Vol.1, No 3, July-September 2002.
6. Hamid Harroud, et al, "Policy-driven Personalized Multimedia Services for Mobile Users," IEEE Transactions on Mobile computing, Vol.2, N° 1, October-March 2003.
7. M. Khedr, A. Karmouch, "A Semantic Approach for Negotiating Context Information in Context Aware Systems," IEEE Intelligent Systems Magazine, to appear.
8. http://www.schemaweb.info/schema/SchemaDetails.aspx?id=159.
9. M. Khedr, A. Karmouch "ACAI: Agent-Based Context-aware Infrastructure for Spontaneous Applications," Journal of Network & Computer Applications, to appear.

Contextware Research Challenges in Ambient Networks

Ahmed Karmouch[1], Alex Galis[2], Raffaele Giaffreda[3], Theo Kanter[4],
Annika Jonsson[4], Anders M. Karlsson[5], Roch Glitho[6], Mikhail Smirnov[7],
Michael Kleis[7], Christoph Reichert[7], Alvin Tan[2], Mohamed Khedr[1], Nancy Samaan[1],
Laamanen Heimo[5], May El Barachi[6], and John Dang[3]

[1] University of Ottawa, Canada
karmouch@site.uottawa.ca
[2] University College London, UK
a.galis@ee.ucl.ac.uk
[3] British Telecommunications PLC, UK
raffaele.giaffreda@bt.com
[4] Ericsson Research, Sweden
theo.kanter@ericsson.com
[5] TeliaSonera
anders.m.karlsson@teliasonera.com
[6] Concordia University, Canada
roch.glitho@ericsson.com
[7] Fraunhofer Institute FOKUS, Germany
smirnow@fokus.fraunhofer.de

Abstract. Network-centric context information is used to make networks more receptive to the users' needs by personalizing the communication process and making it more sensitive to changes that may occur in the surroundings. As such, it is a natural step that context awareness should be suitably incorporated within traditional networks in order to create an 'ambient network'. This approach is aimed at enabling the co-operation of heterogeneous networks on demand, transparently to the potential users, and without the need for preconfiguration or offline negotiation between network operators. This paper discusses the approach taken by authors to incorporate context-awareness into ambient networking concepts. It discusses how network-related context information should be utilized in ambient networks for the end user to fully experience the pervasiveness of a network and the research challenges arising from this utilization. The paper also evaluates the benefits of employing context information and contextware concepts in ambient networks.

1 Introduction

The concept of ambient networks (AN) aims to enable the co-operation and composition of heterogeneous networks on demand, transparently to the potential users, and without the need for pre-configuration or offline negotiation between network operators [11, 12, 14]. An AN achieves this aim by seamlessly incorporating context information into service provisioning [13], network composition, and service adaptation. Context information is any information that can be used to characterize the situation and/or operational state of an entity under different circumstances. An entity

A. Karmouch, L. Korba, and E. Madeira (Eds.): MATA 2004, LNCS 3284, pp. 62–77, 2004.

can be a person, place, physical object, or computational object that is considered relevant to the interaction between a user and an application, including the users and applications themselves [1]. A key characteristic of ANs is their extreme dynamism, as the information that is used to characterize the situation of an entity changes constantly and rapidly. Therefore, network-related context information is necessary to manage the interactions between heterogonous networks and to form an ambient network. Consequently, ANs focus on network-related contexts, and as such, the relevant entities sources of context are network nodes or networks.

In ANs, user, application, and service specific context information is not considered in isolation, but may trigger the selection of the appropriate subset of context information, according to various situations, through the Ambient Service Interface (ASI). The 'contextware' concept is introduced, which is a set of functional elements of an ambient network architecture directly involved in the provision of context aware communications. Contextware offers an opportunity to increase system productivity in a substantial way, as well as to provide an efficient approach for personalizing network services. Contextware networking enables new types of application and service in ambient environments. This will be able to optimally exploit the availability of multiple networks and devices, relative to the purpose of the communication, hence the user's context.

This paper investigates different ambient networking scenarios where contextware communication and context information management may bring significant improvements in performance, and enable new services to be offered to mobile users.

Although the advantages of extending networks with contextware are obvious, the complexity of designing and deploying such services is also high and requires the introduction of appropriate concepts, tools, and infrastructures. Therefore, several research challenges in employing context information and contextware concepts in ambient networks are still under research.

The rest of the paper is organized as follows. Section 2 discusses ambient networking in detail. Section 3 illustrates contextware functionality in the ambient network architecture and evaluates the benefits and research challenges of employing context information and contextware concepts in ambient networks. A scenario employing contextware concepts in the ambient network project is described in section 4. Finally, Section 5 concludes the paper.

2 Ambient Networking

Ambient Networks aim to compose different network types so as to provide seamless ubiquitous connectivity in various forms. This composition will ultimately enable users and operators to jointly exploit the available wireless and fixed network resources for a broad range of services. Context-based network composition will enable rapid adaptation of network topology as required for mobile networks. Such instantly composed networks can be used for both service provisioning and management operations support. Thus, an AN's motivation is similar to the goal of pervasive computing i.e., the user seeks to obtain the seamless connectivity even when there is abrupt disconnection and to obtain the personalized access to Internet services [2]. Currently, nodes (or devices) are enabled to change their point of attachment to the Internet without having to change their IP address [3]. While IP addresses possibly represent the most important aspect of context data for ANs, there are other parameters that need to be considered as well. For example, the attributes of human users', devices', and networks' characteristics are also significant aspects of context data.

The main characteristics of ANs [14] are:

- All-IP Network: ANs are based on all-IP based mobile networks and can be regarded as the outcome of a continued adoption of Internet design principles.
- Heterogeneity: ANs are based on a federation of multiple networks of different operators and technologies.
- Mobility: In dynamically composed network architectures, mobility of user group clusters would support effective local communication. An AN mobility solution will have to work well across business and administrative boundaries, which requires solutions for the security issues of inter-domain operation.
- Composability: It can be dynamically composed of several other networks to form a new AN. Cooperating ANs could potentially belong to separate administrative or economic entities. Hence, ANs provide network services in a cooperative as well as competitive way. Co-operation across different ANs is facilitated by the Ambient Network Interface (see Figure1).
- Provisioning of well-defined control interfaces to other ANs and to service platforms or applications.
- Explicit Control Space: Provisioning (at least a subset of) the Ambient Control Space functions. When ANs and their control functions are composed, care must be taken that each individual function controls the same resources as before. By composing two ANs, resources shall not become common assets, but rather assets that can be traded.
- Accessing the services of an AN is via the Ambient Service Interfaces.
- Context Sensitive Communications: Communication between actors in the ambient networking domain that is sensitive to changes in the context situation. This enables the actors to respond to changing context situations or even to orchestrate such responses.

One of the main research challenges in ANs is to seamlessly integrate context information in order to provide novel services and service adaptations, instantly compose networks, and support mobility and heterogeneity. Generally, context information is made of autonomous objects that can also be used by a number of application services, but that exists independently of the application services. A context may either refer to the aspects of the physical world or to the conditions and activities in the virtual world. An object-oriented view of context information and operations would involve various types of context information represented as generic classes. In different situations, context objects (i.e., instances of these classes) are instantiated according to the appropriate service requirements. The focus is on network-related context information as an AN is extremely dynamic and the information that is used to characterize the situation of an entity is continuously changing. It is therefore necessary to keep track of this information and to manage it. The relevant entities of network- related context information include network nodes and network parameters. Examples of context information include the location of a node in the network topology [1, 4], its own resources, network resources available to it, and its other states (for example, mobility, security, etc.).

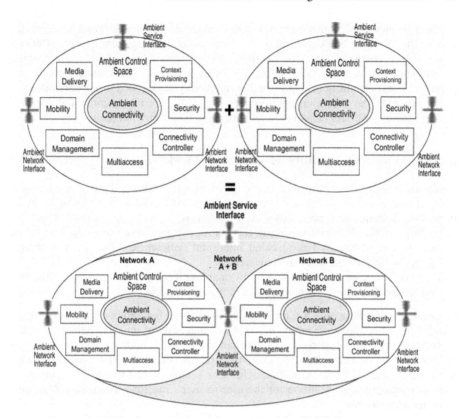

Fig. 1. Ambient Network Composition and Control Space

Network-related context information is necessary to manage the interactions between heterogeneous networks forming an AN and to adapt the network topology resulting from the network composition. If multiple ANs are available for peering, selecting the right AN(s) to connect to will be crucial for the performance of the resulting composed system. In this case, protocols adapt themselves based on the context information.

2.1 Contextware

The term "contextware" introduced in this paper is a set of functional elements of an AN architecture directly involved in the provisioning of context-aware communications. It refers to the network-level software system that is sensitive to an entity's context, where the communication channels are established between contextware components based on and triggered by specific context control data. It responds (proactively and/or reactively) to changes in its environment. Contextware communications would be activated by actions such as connectivity service redeployment, network/ domain (self) reconfiguration, network/domain (self) optimization, etc. on the occurrence of a context-triggered event.

Autonomic management and communication of context information, unique to an end-user, at the network-level reduces the amount of human interaction and attention required to input and manage service-centric data. As human attention is generally seen as the 'ultimate bottleneck' in networking and computing, contextware offers an opportunity to increase system productivity in a substantial way, as well as to provide an efficient approach for personalizing network services. The network could just provide a transport utility or a more active role could be assigned to the network such that it becomes the execution environment itself [9]. Therefore, context-aware networking functions could be added to an existing network environment.

2.2 Key Contextware Features of Ambient Networks

While the Internet reaches an impressive scale of inter-connected devices, its ability to adapt to new functional requirements has slowed with time. In addition to the ever-increasing demands of mobile applications, network services currently face relative inflexibility in the IP infrastructure. In this sense, the pervasive use of the Internet to support such applications has revealed important deficiencies. One such structural deficiency is the absence of context awareness.

These deficiencies are absent in ANs by enabling its contextware features. The following are the main contextware features of the AN concept.

Dynamic Structuring of AN. Conceptually, an AN is a federation of internetworking architectures that capitalize on the inherent heterogeneity of the environment in order to improve the users' experience, rather than adopting the traditional compromise of the lowest common denominator. This AN structure integrates and enables the network capabilities of different technologies to a seamless, end-to-end, or domain-to-domain communication solution for the user-to-user / machine-to-machine / user-to-machine interactions.

The dynamic AN structures, including All-IP based network, network composition, network heterogeneity, and network mobility are all meaningless without their contexts, and contextware provides this context which renders them exploitable. Self-composition, reconfiguration, and self-management across domains are all key features of ANs, and all these require context information.

Contextware Communication. An AN supports interactions between actors using context sensitive communications i.e. communications between actors in the ambient networking domain that is sensitive to the changes of the context situation. This type of communication would involve:

- *Context negotiation*: This represents the process by which the network's contexts can be identified and 'traded', thus facilitating the overall management process in ANs.
- *Context interpretation*: This represents the method of transforming raw context information to network related information for further processing and use.
- *Context level agreement*: This represents the mechanism of reaching an agreement for exchange of context information between context services and context sources [15].
- *Quality of Context*: This represents the parameters and the measurement of the process of composing/aggregation of context data for a particular purpose.

Contextware communications would be triggered by actions such as connectivity service redeployment, network/domain (self) reconfiguration, network/domain (self) optimization, etc. on the occurrence of a context event.

Context Control Space. The context control space is a key concept to the definition of contextware. The context control space represents the contextware control and management functionality [14]. The AN context control space hosts a number of provisioning contextware functions. Also, whenever there is a context trigger, the context control space is responsible for sending control messages that can be used for adaptation of services on the fly via the Ambient Service Interface [11].

Provisioning of Networking Functions and Network Services. Contextwarenetworking functions could be provided by means of telecommunication and IP network providers. A key point here is the role assigned to the network. The network could just provide a transport utility; wherein the contextware networking functions would be deployed in specialized and possibly distributed servers. Another option is to assign a more active role to the network, such that it becomes the execution environment itself. This is a more distributed approach, which seems to be more scalable and it is based on self-composition and self-management principles. With both options, contextware-networking functions could be added to an existing network environment.

Autonomic management and communication of context information in network services greatly reduces the amount of human interaction required to input and manage context data or, in general, service and network data. Contextware networking provides an efficient and convenient approach to personalize network services.

- *Monitoring of Contextware-Networking Functions and Services.* Contextware also provides a unique possibility to query the network and learn about the communication behavior patterns. This enables network operators and service providers to further optimize service behavior or service delivery behavior, and add or re-dimension communication infrastructure where needed.
- *Leveraging Contextware in Services and Applications.* Applications and services can delegate service delivery to Contextware networking functions via Application Programming Interfaces (APIs) that are available through the ASI. Adding Contextware networking functions enables the planning of service delivery and optimized utilization of available infrastructure. Also, the above mentioned APIs can be used by services and applications to learn about communication conditions over e.g. space and time, for adaptive service behavior in mobile devices.

3   Contextware in Ambient Networks

One of the main focuses in ambient environments is seamless integration of context information for service provisioning, network composition, and service adaptation. The contextware functionality would enable such services. Contextware networking enables novel applications and services in ambient environments. These applications can help users to react positively to unexpected events such as emergency situations, acquire value-added services, receive messages in the most useful and suitable manner, or obtain compensation when planned activities are changed or delayed. The key contextware features of ANs were described in section 2.2.

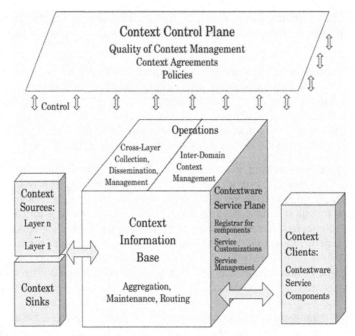

Fig. 2. Contextware Reference Model

3.1 Main Concepts and Systems

The research motivation in this paper is driven by five key concepts that propose requirements for the existence of ANs. The Figure 2 shown below exemplifies the main concepts into a contextware reference model.

The five main concepts that will guide towards the realization of "contextware" functionality within an AN architecture are,

- Context Information Base
- Cross-Layer Collection, Dissemination and Management of Context Information
- Context Control Plane
- Context Level Agreement
- Quality of Context

These five key concepts satisfy the requirements for the support of contextware communications in ANs. These concepts are described next in the following subsections.

Context Information Base. The Context Information Base (CIB) illustrates one of the main contextware components and represents a distributed repository from which up-to-date context information can be extracted i.e., the CIB repository contains all the relevant context data and computation that belong to the entities that are subjected to contextware. The task of collecting, processing, and distributing context information to and from the AN entities poses the requirement for a generic component, rather than application- or device-specific components, in the AN. The CIB is the generic component that is used for interaction with application, device, and service specific components in the AN. The objectives of the CIB are,

- to encompass the physical and logical source and sink for context data,
- to provide efficient context handling mechanisms for context formalisms, context data update, maintenance, and composition rules, context aggregation and context distribution.

The CIB further collects, disseminates, process, and manages context information from different layers since, for example, without a context source at the data link layer it would be not possible to collect information about the status of the network interfaces. These context sources at different layers (for example, sensors detecting user location, bandwidth monitors, etc.) must have interactions with the context control plane (via the CIB) notifying changes to the executing applications as soon as they happen. The CIB may also save the history of context information or further processed context information in order to provide support for predictions about possible future states or actions.

For example, consider two ambient networks AN1 and AN2, where an agreement exists between both the ANs to cooperate in order to provide an end-to-end service to a specific user. The CIBs of both the ANs are the context sources and sinks for the exchange of context data via the Ambient Control Interface (ACI). The ACI facilitates the interaction between the CIB and context control space. The ACI functions enable inter-domain context negotiation across domains. If AN2 denotes the AN of a provider, the role of the CIB during the peering process is described as follows.

1. The service specific information in the CIB of AN1 is distributed across all the AN domains involved (i.e., AN2, transit ANs, and the AN hosting the provider of the service).
2. The context control plane takes account of the users' context data and enables inter-domain negotiation.
3. Context data collection and dissemination by utilization of the CIBs of the involved ANs ensure continuity of the service the user has subscribed to.

From a service provider's view, the CIB is the central source of end user context profiles. In the case of mobile end users, an archive of the users' previous movements can be cached in the CIB.

Cross-Layer Collection, Dissemination and Management of Context Information. Up-to-date and valid context information is the key requirement for successful utilization of context information in services offered by ANs. For example, service adaptation based on outdated context information could cause various problems. This in turn demands just-in-time collection, dissemination, and management of context information. This concept captures the mechanisms and protocols needed for providing efficient contextware functionality i.e., it represents the 'behind the scenes' work of the CIB, as the nature of the managed information is diverse and distributed. Therefore, the CIB must be kept up-to-date as much as possible.

Examples of efficient mechanisms for collecting and distributing context information are the push mechanism, pull mechanism, tuple shared space, and persistence mechanism. Context information sources at different layers (for example, sensors detecting user location, QoS monitors, etc.) must have interactions with the Context Control Plane (CCP) in order to allow notifications of changes as soon as they happen. The CIB stores the context information received from different sources residing at different layers.

Context Control Plane. The Context Control Plane (CCP) is another key con-·textware concept. In contrast to the previous concepts, the idea behind the CCP is satisfying more the 'how do we make use of context information' issue. The CCP represents the contextware control and management functionality delivering information to contextware clients. It involves a distributed signaling and set-up system for predeployment actions in implementing context-aware services on the network. Also, whenever there is a context trigger, the CCP is responsible for sending control messages that can be used for adaptation of services on the fly via ASI [11]. The AN context control plane hosts a number of provisioning contextware functions including:

- Totality of context policies and agreements for an AN domain.
- Context agreement and policy lifecycle management functions as well as conflic-tresolution mechanisms for policies and agreements.
- Control of context information to enable flexibility and self-aware capabilities.
- ACI functions, which enable inter-domain context negotiation across domains. These facilitate connections of AN context control functions with functions from other domains.
- Context registration and registrar functions, which advertise the presence of context control space functions in adjacent domains in order to allow dynamic composition of control functions.
- Aggregation functions, which support a simple plug-and-play and unplug-and-play context composition between AN domains. They are designed to support user mobility, service mobility, and network mobility.
- Inter-context-networking heterogeneity functions, which enable an inter-context networking architecture that makes heterogeneity explicit so that it may be exploited.
- Homogeneous model of services and applications, which provides a homogenous view of any application or service and could make use of the functions of the context control space.

Context Level Agreement. The vast quantity and diverse quality of context information, as well as the fact that not all contexts are of interest to the user and the network, requires introduction of context level agreement (CLA) concept, by which context specifications can be negotiated with an ontology-based model [15].

The concept has the following main advantages:

- CLA provides a declarative method to help users to specify their context requirements and context providers to offer dynamic customized context-based service information.
- CLA protects context providers against unexpected degradation in performance. Since they are aware of the users' requirements, they can better manage their resources.
- CLA can be used across domains to provide an assurance of seamless contextbased services in a large environment.

- CLA provides an easy mechanism for context providers to intelligently supply and monitor contextual resources. They can obtain and analyze user data without unnecessary distractions for the user.

Broadly, we define three types of CLA as follows.

1. Passive context: Each user's context specifications are simple and need little or no complex operation from the context provider.
2. Active context: Users are more interactive; their context specifications are a result of complex operations from the context provider, such as filtering, merging, composing, and monitoring. Negotiation at this level is designed to achieve common understanding of the context's meaning and format.
3. Spontaneous context: Context management and inference that are able to cope with the uncertainty and vagueness inherent at higher context levels are essential. The negotiation at this level is designed so that a personalized group of context providers can manage the requirements of the users' context like information persistence, methods of delivering contextual information, access to remote context information, and inference on each user's context.

For CLA to be dynamic, automated, and extensible, key issues are to provide (a) a framework for negotiating context specification and (b) an ontology that provides standard and extensible constructs of context and negotiation performatives.

Quality of Context. Context information, by its nature can be uncertain, incomplete, or unavailable at certain times. The Quality of Context (QoC) concept is meant to capture this specific aspect, which might eventually influence the way control functions are enforced. The QoC refers to the usefulness and quality of the context information and processes in relation to a specific operation. Therefore, the QoC is essentially any information that describes the quality of information. Certain parameters that determine this 'usefulness' include precision, probability of correctness, trustworthiness, resolution, and validity period [5]. Also, the QoC for particular context information could vary from different viewpoints such as, the viewpoint of the network provider, service provider, context owner, context provider, contextware service provider, network user, and contextware service user.

3.2 Key Research Challenges

Several research challenges arise from introducing context-awareness within networks. The five concepts discussed in the previous section are coupled with research challenges that broadly contribute to the need to address context-sensitive communications.

Mobile computing followed by pervasive computing and ending with ambient computing are opening the door for a new era where human and computing resources are integrated into one world. This hybrid environment introduces challenging issues ranging from the network level up to the application level in conjunction with social and personal matters. A solution to most of these challenges lies in knowledge and ambient interaction. Knowledge is achieved through context, while ambient interaction is achieved using 'context sensitive communications'. This being the case, and considering the characteristics of ambient computing environments (mainly heterogeneity, mobility, and dynamics), we need new techniques to achieve reliable, when needed, non-intrusive communication. One way to achieve this is by making the applications contextware and the network context sensitive. This is termed as contextsensitive communications [6] and this type of communication supersedes client-server communication [7].

Context-sensitive communication is a type of communication [8], where the communication channel is established between devices based on some specific contexts. The new challenges that arise in order to provide context-sensitive communications include (i) systematic adaptation and customized representation of context, (ii) context association in a real-time behaviour, and (iii) spontaneous processing and dissemination of acquired context [5]. Therefore, the basic requirement to provide contextsensitive communications is that the underlying system itself should be contextsensitive. An example of context sensitive communication is proposed in [8] for certain systems, in order to deal with the above listed challenges and facilitate interoperability independently of device and network type, while an agent based middleware is proposed in [6].

Except for proximity preference, there is no clear ongoing research into how entities can communicate with each other using contextual information as the basis of communication. This deficiency in current research is due to the focus of context on proximity only and thus prevents current contextware systems from considering other contextual information when initiating communication and interaction between entities. Furthermore, there is no obvious reliable means of disseminating context information between entities (i.e., users, services) or between system components.

Further challenges arise from the requirement that an infrastructure can rearrange its topology, thus implying that new knowledge may be added to contextware from hitherto unrelated ANs. The challenge is to find solutions that support (ad-hoc) extensions of context ontologies and models. This could be achieved through employing standardization and publication of namespaces and extension rules, as well as means for conflict resolution and arbitrating the semantics of knowledge, possibly assisted by a third party. This is especially challenging, since context objects include behavior. The challenge is to find minimal and sufficient standards for describing contexts, which are inherently open-ended.

We envision a new method of communication that is capable of providing nonintrusive automated connectivity and information exchange in contextware environments. The communications in this ambient environment are sensitive to the changes and are capable of creating, modifying, and adapting sessions and maintaining persistency of the contextual preferences of the sessions. We have identified five characteristics that a general context sensitive communication protocol (CSCP) [5] must handle and this includes Mobility, Management, Technology transparency, Association, and Personalization. These characteristics elevate context from an ambiguous concept to an essential active component in ambient computing.

4 A Contextware Scenario in the Ambient Network Project

The AN scenario discussed in this section, which necessitates contextware communication and context information management is expected to bring significant improvements in the performance and scalability of services rendered to mobile users in ANs. The scenario strongly emphasizes contextware functionality and offers a possibility to further explain and elaborate the conceptual views. It makes the usability of (and need for) contextware more concrete from a user's and network's perspective.

The recurring theme throughout the scenario is a series of triggering events, which require a 'context lookup' and a subsequent action generated by the context control plane. Also, a CIB is created in an ad-hoc fashion on behalf of the user and joining data from different sources in different domains through policy-based rules [10] enforced by the CCP. To highlight the issues faced by the implementation of contextaware systems, 'proactive' and 'reactive' behaviors are also illustrated as means to update, disseminate, and manage appropriate information stored in the CIB. A user-centric approach is taken throughout the scenario. This scenario is set in 2015, in a world where secured Internet connectivity as well as enhanced mobile services can be obtained from any location using any device. The motivation for the 'active pipe' service offering was the strong 'pull' factor from mobile Internet consumers. A large majority of end users are well-equipped with a set of smart mobile devices enhanced with location sensors (e.g., GPS), and public transportation systems (e.g., trains and taxis) are also equipped with WLANs. This scenario is based on the 'active pipe' service domain.

4.1 Scenario Outline

The following scenario highlights the contextware functionality.

Scene 1 – At the client's office: Sara, a consultant, visits her client's site. She uses her laptop to access her files in her head office via the client's local Ethernet LAN and can conveniently do her research using data from the database in her office. The connection is a VPN, thus she can securely access confidential information without fear of her connectivity being tapped. She also occasionally listens to BBC news sessions in her laptop.

With reference to Figure 3 shown below, both domains A and B agree to cooperate in order to provide end-to-end services to their end users using ANs. Sara moves into domain A, and the context data of her laptop triggers the network composability between both domains A and B via the ANI (orange arrows). The relevant preliminary context data is passed on to the CIB using an algorithm to distribute it efficiently. The CIBs also disseminate context information amongst themselves. The illustrated concepts include the CIB and cross-layer collection, dissemination and management of context information. The administrators of both domains then configure the network nodes via the ASI (blue arrows) according to Sara's context data i.e., userLocation, userID and serviceType. Initially, a VPN connection is set up and Sara's access point is via the programmable router A-1.

Scene 2 – Leaving the client's office: It is now almost 6.00 p.m. and her children are back from the crèche. She needs to prepare their dinner and has to head for home although her work is not done yet and the deadline is tomorrow. Her PDA informs her that she is running out of time and automatically orders a taxi to get her to the train station, as well as a reserved seat on the train home. The taxi service was ordered using the cellular carrier and advertisement of nearby taxi companies. Her laptop is switched off and the BBC session is transferred to her PDA.

Scene 3 – Train journey: Sara takes the 6.20 pm train for her 40-minute journey home. Because there is a WiFi hotspot in the train, she takes out her laptop and reestablishes the 'virtual pipe' she had when she was at the client's site. She is happy to get an extra half-an-hour's worth of quality work done. She now chooses to receive

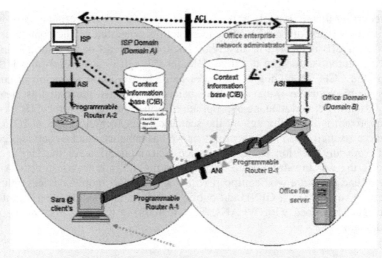

Fig. 3. The first instance where Sara moves into the client domain

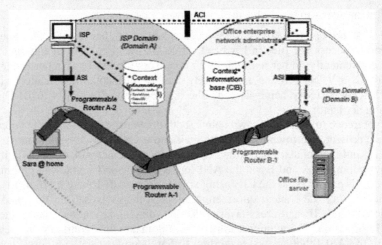

Fig. 4. The final instance where Sara moves back to her home domain

BBC news on her mobile phone until her devices are integrated with her home network. Simultaneously, multimedia from BBC news is routed to Sara's media server at home via the broadband infrastructure, anticipating her arrival.

Scene 4 – At home: Sara is now in the kitchen, popping the stuffed turkey into the oven. Again, she conveniently plugs her laptop into her wireless broadband connection. She duly continues her work as before and constantly reminds herself of the turkey in the oven, while occasionally casting an eye on the selected multimedia BBC news that is playing.

When Sara finally moves from her client's premises to her house, her access point is now via the programmable router A-2 (shown in Figure 4). When she turns ON her laptop, her location context is sent to her ISP, who further computes this information as appropriate. The ISP further uses control-plane signaling for inter-domain negotiation with the office administrators, where the CCP concept is illustrated together with inter-domain context management. Similarly, the CIB is being looked up to ensure that the ISP has the requisite SLA with the office. Sara is successful in obtaining pervasive and private connectivity, without any breaks in her service.

4.2 Scenario Analysis

In this communication scenario, the consultant Sara is interacting with her remote Intranet and the public Internet from her client's premises AN1, while on the move AN2, and from her home AN3 in a seamless manner. In order to collect and organize all the relevant files she wants to have in her personal laptop, Sara switches ON her laptop to start the job while at her customer's premises, which is the triggering event in this scenario. Location sensors identify her presence via the RFID tag she wears and update her profile accordingly. Location and composition of context via pre-existing policies allows the CCP to infer that there is a need to initiate a 'network action' i.e., establish a VPN to Sara's Intranet. The proactive behavior in this particular scene of the scenario would be to update the location regularly, while the reactive behavior would be to check her location only when an application that needs information about her location is about to be launched.

A 'context lookup' and a set of policies may dictate the messages initiated by the CCP and can be more or less onerous depending on the nature of the triggering event. For example, the triggering event could be 'I want to use this application' or 'I am likely to use this application'. Based on the triggering event, the user could move from GPRS to WLAN and again to GPRS. Therefore, the triggering events can be all those that are likely to affect the way an application runs. While performing her first task, Sara also opens a live BBC session. As soon as this triggering event happens, context lookup precedes the application-launch and extracts (based on 'application specific' rules) from Sara's CIB, the devices that are available to her to perform this second task and the features of the access networks those devices are attached to. This particular task illustrates a context composition example. Also, as the access rights and resources available to visitors varies from those available to employees, her profile of 'usable devices/resources' must be updated.

In order to consider the dynamics that may be associated with similar communication tasks, the scenario illustrates that the user is moving from one location to another and so she must handover connectivity through various providers. Thus, the scenario evolves around the two tasks that Sara is carrying out. One is 'organizing files', that requires connectivity to a public and a private network, and the other is a multimedia 'BBC session' that is continuously adapted to her mobility patterns or as her environment changes. Both these tasks require the use of context information, which is collected, composed, and disseminated on behalf of Sara to/from different sources/sinks, together with the complexity of having to cross different provider domains. In particular, the 'mobility scenes' of the scenario must address sharing partial information across provider domains in order to collaboratively create a whole picture that benefits the user.

This scenario could be viewed from different perspectives such as the end user perspective, operator perspective, service provider perspective, and network perspective. An end user perspective is followed in the above discussed scenario. If this scenario is viewed from a network perspective, the following are analyzed. A part of the attractiveness of ANs is the ability of an end user to use any device to obtain seamless service across any type of network. These aspects present the most challenging issues in providing pervasive computing experience for end users [9]. The scenario presented in the active pipe service domain summarizes the following.

- The CIB is distributed across all the involved domains.
- The CCP that takes account of Sara's contexts enables inter-domain negotiation.
- Context data collection and dissemination ensure continuity of the service.
- Sara's movement across domains warrants inter-provider interaction.

In essence, it is reiterated that in order for Sara to experience ubiquitous Internet access, context awareness (in particular, Sara's locations and identity context) is a prerequisite to realize the goals of ambient networking.

5 Conclusions

Ambient networks aim to merge different network types so as to provide seamless connectivity in various forms. Since context is implicitly a necessity to make any network an ambient one, without context-awareness, we cannot create an ambient network. For an end user to experience the pervasiveness of a network, the enabling technology must always know the user's context, which implies that the context information must be propagated at the network level to improve the services/products offered by the service provider.

If multiple ANs are available for peering, selecting the right ANs to connect to will be crucial for the performance of the resulting composed system. In this case, protocols adapt themselves based on context information as follows: the context information base of each AN holds the context information that defines the peering preferences and capabilities of the AN; network information about available ANs for peering can be obtained from a context source using the concept of cross-layer collection; using inter-domain context management, the required exchange of context information between ANs is established; after the selection of the most suitable ANs for peering, the context-control plane initiates and controls the peering process. Furthermore, context management is important to enhance the user experience during communications. Context information can be used to make networks more receptive to users' needs and enhance the users' experience by making the communication easier and richer. For instance, a streaming service for a mobile user can be optimized by making use of context information such as the capabilities of the available end-devices and the current network connectivity of the user.

In conclusion, exploiting network-related context information can make ambient networks simpler, more efficient, and more powerful. This simplifies the management of the networking infrastructure for network operators, while also providing end-users with value-added services and an enhanced communication experience. Several research challenges arise in view of introducing context-awareness within networks and currently, only few of them have concrete solutions to enable context-sensitive communications. This vision of simplified and yet powerful networks is the essence of Ambient Networks.

Acknowledgement

This paper describes work undertaken in the context of the Ambient Networks – Information Society Technologies (IST) 507134 project. The IST program is partially funded by the Commission of the European Union. The views and conclusions contained herein are those of the authors and should not be interpreted as necessarily representing the Ambient Networks project.

References

1. Dey, A. K., Understanding and using context, Journal of Personal and Ubiquitous Computing, Volume 5 (1), pp. 4-7, 2001
2. Kleinrock, Leonard, Nomadicity: Anytime, anywhere in a disconnected world, Mobile Networks and Applications 1, (1996) 351-357. C. Perkins, Ed., IP Mobility Support for IPv4, RFC3344, August 2002
3. Schilit, B.N., Theimer, M.M., Disseminating active map information to mobile hosts, IEEE Network, Volume: 8, Issue: 5, pp. 22 – 32, September 1994
4. Buchholz, T, Kupper, A, Schiffers, S. – Quality of Context Information: What is it is and why we need it – In proceedings of the 10th HP-OVUA Workshop, volume 2003, Geneva, July 2003
5. Khedr, M. and Karmouch, A. "Exploiting SIP and agents for smart context level agreements", 2003 IEEE Pacific Rim Conference on Communications, Computers and Signal Processing, Victoria, BC, Canada, Aug 2003
6. Yau, S. S. and Karim, F. "A Lightweight Middleware Protocol for Ad Hoc Distributed Object Computing in Ubiquitous Computing Environments", Proc. 6th IEEE Intl. Symposium on Object-Oriented Real-Time Distributed Computing (ISORC 2003), pp.172-179, May 2003
7. Yau, S. S. and Karim, F. "An Adaptive Middleware for Context-Sensitive Communications for Real-Time Applications in Ubiquitous Computing Environments", t Real-Time Systems, The International Journal of Time-Critical Computing Systems, Kluwer Academic Publishers, Dordrecht, The Netherlands, vol. 26, no. 1, pp. 29-61, Jan 2004
8. Crowcroft, J., Hand, S., Mortier, R., Roscoe, T., Warfield, A., Plutarch: An argument for network pluralism, ACM SIGCOMM 2003 Workshops, August 2003
9. Galis, A., Denazis, S., Brou, C., Klein, C. (ed) – " Programmable Networks for IP Service Deployment" ISBN 1-58053-745-6; pp450, May 2004; Artech House Books; www.artechhouse.com
10. Yang, K., Galis, A., Policy-driven mobile agents for context-aware service in next generation networks, IFIP 5th International Conference on Mobile Agents for Telecommunications, Marrakesch, October 2003, ISBN 3-540-20298-6 - Lecture Notes in Computer Science, Springer-Verlag
11. Niebert, N., Flinck, H. Hancock, R. Karl, H. Prehofer, C. "Ambient Networks – Research for Communication Networks Beyond 3G"- 13th IST Mobile and Wireless Communications- Summit 2004, 27-30 June 2004, Lyon, www.mobilesummit2004.org
12. WWI-AN Ambient Networks Project WWW Server - www.ambient-networks.org
13. R6-1 Report: "Network Context Management, Concepts, Scenarios and Analysis of the State of the Art "– Ambient Networks project internal report – March 2004 https://bscw.ambient-networks.org/bscw/bscw.cgi/0/11562
14. Norbert Niebert, et.al, "Ambient Networks: An Architecture for Communication Networks Beyond 3G", *IEEE wireless magazine*, April 2004
15. M. Khedr, A. Karmouch, "A Semantic Approach for Negotiating Context Information in Context Aware Systems", *IEEE Intelligent Systems Magazine*, to appear

Awareness on Mobile Groupware Systems

Manuele Kirsch-Pinheiro[*], Jérôme Gensel, and Hervé Martin

Laboratoire LSR – IMAG
BP 72 – 38402 Saint Martin d'Hères Cedex, France
{Manuele.Kirsch-Pinheiro,Jerome.Gensel,Herve.Martin}@imag.fr

Abstract. Mobile Groupware Systems employ devices such as PDAs and cellular phones to explore the opportunities that mobile technologies grant for cooperative work. However, due to the physical constraints related to these devices,
such systems must adapt the content of information to user's context. This adaptation usually takes into account user's location and device. As for the users
of Groupware Systems, mobile users need to be aware of what is going on inside the group in order to better perform their own activities. This refers to the
notion of awareness support, which stands for the knowledge a user has about
the group itself and her/his colleagues' activities. In this paper, we propose a
context-based awareness mechanism for mobile Groupware Systems. This
mechanism takes into account both the user's physical and organizational context in order to filter the awareness information and to deliver relevant information to mobile users.

Keywords: Context-aware computing, adaptability, awareness support, mobile
computing, computer supported cooperative work.

1 Introduction

Groupware Systems are usually conceptualized as software systems that allow computer supported cooperative work. For some years, Groupware Systems, such as
BSCW[1], have been using the Web in order to provide a world wide access to their
users. With the massive introduction of web-enable mobile devices, such as laptops,
PDAs and cellular phones, users of this kind of devices can access the system virtu-
ally everywhere. The use of such mobile devices leads to a new generation of Groupware System, called here *mobile Groupware System*, which are Groupware Systems
intensely accessed through mobile devices.

However, the use of mobile devices introduces several technical challenges. Specially, systems should carefully select and adapt the information to be displayed (as
well as the supplied services) to the physical constraints of these devices (limited
display size, power and memory capacity…). Obviously, a system cannot deliver the
same (amount of) information to a mobile device that it delivers to a fixed device (a
desktop, for example). It has to select a reduced set of information to be delivered and
to adapt the presentation of this content to the target device (for instance, to transform
XHTML files into WML files, or to debase the quality of a video sequence). Moreover, since the user of such devices may move and change of device, this adaptation
process should take into account her/his current context (where she/he is, which device she/he is using, etc), in order to better cater the information for this mobile user,
i.e. to determine which information is relevant, which media types can be used, etc.

---

[*] Author receives grants from CAPES-Brazil (BEX 2296/02-0).
[1] http://bscw.gmd.de/

A. Karmouch, L. Korba, and E. Madeira (Eds.): MATA 2004, LNCS 3284, pp. 78–87, 2004.
© Springer-Verlag Berlin Heidelberg 2004

Therefore, the ability to detect the context characterizes the so-called *context-aware systems*, whose premises include that the computing device should be aware of the user's circumstances and should be able to interpret any interaction in an appropriate manner [13].

Context-aware systems usually adopt a notion of context limited to the physical aspects, such as the user's location or device (see [2] as an illustration). However, a mobile user is often involved in some cooperative process. And, as any other user of a classical cooperative environment, a mobile user should be aware of what is going on inside the group in order to build a sense of community [15]. This means that mobile Groupware Systems should provide their users with an awareness support adapted to their mobile situation. Awareness support in Groupware Systems refers to the knowledge a user has and to her/his understanding of the group itself and her/his colleagues' activities, providing so a shared context for individual activities in the group (e.g. [5] and [11]). This notion of awareness is often neglected by context-aware systems, which ignore the organizational context of the cooperative work. This organizational context is related to the activities, the status and the composition of the group, a knowledge usually supplied by awareness support in Groupware Systems.

However, a selection of the information is necessary for mobile users because awareness support may generate too large amounts of information, and because the constraints of these mobile devices impede the presentation of all available information. We believe that mobile Groupware Systems should take into account both the physical and the organizational context of the user in order to filter the available awareness information and to reduce it to a restricted set of relevant pieces of information that can be physically handled by the mobile device.

In this paper, we propose a context-based awareness mechanism which uses a description of the current user's context. This description integrates, on the one hand, the concepts related to the notion of awareness (definitions of group and role, activities and work process, etc.) and, on the other hand, the concepts related to the user's physical context (location, device…). We use an object-oriented representation in which the concepts are represented by the means of classes and associations. We aim at managing asynchronous Groupware Systems, such as systems managing group calendar, messages and shared repository (a shared workspace). We assume that those systems are composed by many components (for access control policy, for communication facilities, etc.) which are connected and communicate with each other (and possibly with other instances on remote sites). We consider awareness mechanism as one of such components, and we propose a filtering process that exploits the context representation mentioned above to better select the awareness information delivered to mobile users.

This paper is organized as follows: first, we introduce some work related to adaptation (Section 2). Second, we discuss the notion of awareness (Section 3). Then, we present our proposed description of the mobile user's (Section 4), and describe the filtering mechanism based on this description (Section 5), before we conclude (Section 6).

2 Context and Adaptation for Mobile Users

The development of software applications for mobile devices involves several technical challenges, which makes adaptation crucial for the usability of such systems [7].

In this context, many researches deal with the adaptation of multimedia and web-based information content to mobile devices. These works usually take into account the technical capabilities of the client device, and adapt the content of the information to be delivered, by transforming the original content so that it can be handled and displayed by the device (see, for example, [17] and [10]).

Additionally, some works adapt the content by filtering it according to the physical context of the client device. The notion of context which is used includes aspects concerning the device itself and also aspects such as the user's location and time (see, for example, [2], [13] and [12]).

Our approach also relies on the selection of the content delivered to the user considering her/his current context. However, we differ from other works on context-aware computing by considering the user's context from two points of view organizational and physical. In fact, the organizational context, as much as the physical context, plays a critical role in shaping an action, and also in providing people with the means to interpret and understand action [4].

The coupling of this two types of context allows to evaluate what is relevant for a mobile user, and thus, to select the available information for her/him. On the one hand, users of mobile Groupware Systems are involved in a cooperative process and are particularly interested in information related to this process. They are more particularly interested in events related to their work context, *i.e.* events that can lead them to take better decisions and/or to increase their capacity to decide [3]. On the other hand, by using mobile devices, users have to cope with several restrictions inherent to the limited capacity of their devices (particularly the reduced display capacity). In our approach, we try to represent and explore the organizational and physical context in order to filter the awareness information in a suitable way for mobile users.

3   Adaptation Needs for Awareness Support

The term *awareness* has a large meaning in the Computer Supported Cooperative Work (CSCW) community and is actually used in very different situations [11][18]. Generally, awareness refers to actors' taking heed of the context of their joint effort, to a person being or becoming aware of something [18]. However, this definition is too vast to be used for a Groupware System, so we adopt a more concise one, which defines awareness as "an understanding of the activities of others, which provides a context for your own activity. This context is used to ensure that individual contributions are relevant to the group's activity as a whole and to evaluate individual actions with respect to the group goals and progress" [5].

There is, in the CSCW community, a consensus about the importance of the awareness support for cooperative work (see, for example, [18] and [6]). Awareness represents the knowledge about a group involved in a collaborative process, its activities, status and evolution [8]. Relying on an awareness support, users can coordinate and evaluate their own contributions considering the whole group evolution. Such an awareness support can be seen as an implicit coordination mechanism [16]. Indeed, if the members of a team are kept aware of their project status and activities, then they are able to communicate (exchange information) with each other and to coordinate themselves. Then, this knowledge refers to the organizational context in which the cooperative work takes place.

However, as stated by Espinosa et al. [6], the functionalities of an awareness tool have to meet the informational requirements of the tasks performed by the users. Otherwise, awareness support can turn out to a distraction.

For users who access Groupware Systems through a web-enabled mobile device, the delivered information should also comply with the material constraints of their device as well as their changing location. Consequently, information delivered to a mobile user should be limited to the one which is relevant for the work he/she performs, but also it should cope with her/his location and be formatted according to the capabilities of the client device. This is why information has to be adapted to the organizational and physical context of a mobile user interacting with a Groupware System. In order to adapt the awareness information to such mobile users, a Groupware System has to rely on an adequate representation of the notion of context which it can consequently use for adaptation purposes. In the next section, we describe the representation of the notion of context we propose to be exploited by the awareness mechanism.

4 An Object-Oriented Context Representation

In order to create a useful representation of the user's context at a given moment, we restrict this representation only to aspects that we consider as essential for an awareness mechanism embedded in a mobile Groupware System. A special emphasis is put here on how it is used by mobile users. However, this representation could also be used by other components of the Groupware System, those in charge of the presentation of information, for example.

There are, in the CSCW literature, several propositions of user's context representation. For instance, Leiva-Lobos and Covarrubias [9] consider a threefold context for cooperating users: spatial, temporal and cultural. The spatial context contains shared artifacts found in both the physical and the electronic space. The temporal context refers to the history of past cooperative activities and to the expected or future ones. The cultural context gathers users' shared view and practices (*i.e.* the community practices). Similarly, Allarcón and Fuller [1] describe the work context using the following entities: the content (*i.e.* tools, shared objects, etc.), the process (*i.e.* activities and their calendar) and the users themselves. In addition, these authors define the notion of the user's electronic location as an entity of the user's context.

Synthesizing these works, we have identified five viewpoints which compose the notion of context we propose: *space, tool, time, community* and *process*. These viewpoints correspond to main concepts of the context representation. The space viewpoint refers to the concept of physical *location*. The tool viewpoint concerns the concepts of physical *device* and *application*. The time viewpoint points to the concept of a common *calendar* the group shares. The community viewpoint refers to the composition of the community of users, including the concepts of *group*, *role* and *user*. Finally, the process viewpoint concerns to the *process* (workflow) performed by the group, including the concepts of *activity* (task) and *shared object* (an object handled by the group).

We consider these concepts as the most relevant ones when defining a mobile user's context for a cooperative environment. Fig. 1 presents an object-oriented representation (using UML) of this notion of context. In this diagram, the concepts listed above (user, group, role, location, etc.) are represented by classes (*member, group, role...*) and the relations that hold between them by associations.

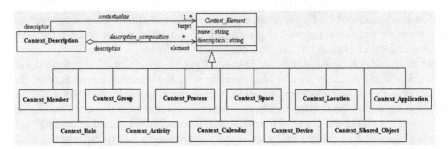

Fig. 1. The context description and the basic elements of the context representation[2].

The context description is seen as a composition of the elements mentioned above. It is then represented by a *context description* class, which is a composition of these *elements*. In addition, this description is linked to another element for which it describes a specific context. For instance, the context of a user (here, called *member*) who is currently accessing the system, or the context in which an application can be executed.

As shown on Fig. 2, the basic elements which form the context are related to each other, defining associations between the corresponding concepts. Thus, a *member* *belongs* to the group through the *roles* she/he plays in this *group*. We also consider that each group *defines* a *process* (or adopt a predefined one). This process *respects* a given *calendar* and is *composed* by a set of *activities* (or tasks, also composed by subtasks). A *role allows* the execution of one or more activities (which may be possibly executed by other roles). Each activity is *performed* by a member and *handles* a set of *shared objects* (composed by other objects) through a set of applications, which are *designed* for specific devices. A *member* is located in a certain *space*, which is

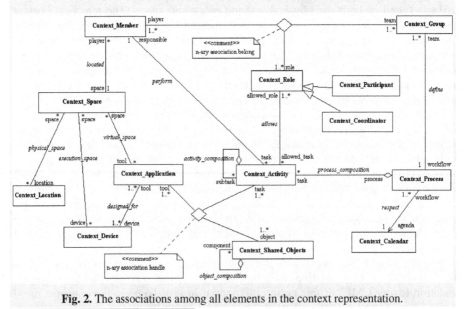

Fig. 2. The associations among all elements in the context representation.

---

[2] Please note that in the rest of the paper we omit the "Context_" prefix for readability.

composed by a *physical space* (the physical *location* of the member), by a *virtual space*, corresponding to the *application* that is accessed, and by an *execution space*, including the *device* employed.

The classes and associations of this context description form the schema of a knowledge base which allows to describe the context of a mobile user accessing a Groupware System. Then, the awareness mechanism can exploit this context representation to better cater information delivered to the user. At a given moment, the context information concerning a user is represented by instances of the classes and associations of this knowledge base. These instances are aggregated into a context *description* instance, which represents, completely or partially, the context related to a specific element. For instance, a *context description* instance may refer to the context of a user currently accessing the system, including instances describing this member, her/his roles, the activities she/he is performing, and possibly her/his location. It may as well partially describe the context, including only instances referring to the space (location, device, and application) and ignoring all information about the activities and the group process.

In order to build these instances, we assume that the Groupware System has a component which detects the current user's context and dynamically creates the corresponding context description. For mobile users, this component has to determine the physical location of the user (through GPS technology or estimation based on signal strength, e.g. [2] and [12]) and to discover what are the characteristics of the client device, and to identify the user and the activities she/he is performing. Frequently, this component is not able to determine all the elements of the context representation. For example, when the Groupware System integrates a workflow component, it can determine easily what activities (tasks) a user is working on. Otherwise, it is very difficult for the context detection component to determine them, and it may ask the user for some help (as suggested by [13]) or omit this information in the context description. This omission means that the system does not have enough knowledge to represent these elements, and then can make no assumption about them.

We have implemented this representation using the AROM system [14]. AROM is an object-based knowledge representation system, which adopts classes/objects and associations/tuples as main representation entities. This object-oriented representation can be easily adapted for different Groupware Systems using the specialization mechanisms proposed by the AROM system. For instance, the Groupware system designer may define new subclasses of any context elements (such as the "Participant" and "Coordinator" classes in Fig. 2), even for the root element of the proposed class hierarchy (the *element* class). In addition, the use of the AROM system allows to perform queries such as: "is a user currently using a given device?", or "is a user in a specific location?". This corresponds to ask if the instances representing such device or location belong to the current user's context description. In the next section, we describe how an awareness mechanism can take advantage of this context representation.

5   A Context-Based Filtering Process

We consider the awareness mechanism as a component of the mobile Groupware System. This component able to analyze users' activities, as well as those performed by other components (for instance, a workflow component), in order to collect information that could be relevant to the group members and enhance the group's perform-ance (for instance, the information about a deadline, a meeting, a document that is available, a colleague that is on-line, etc.).

In this work, we exploit the context representation presented above to perform the information, using an event-based awareness mechanism. In other words, we assume that all the awareness information is carried by events. We assume that events are defined by the Groupware developer and that each event contains useful information for the group members about a specific topic. Additionally, we define the concept of *general profile* (see Fig. 3), which represents the preferences and the constraints that the system should satisfy for a given element (group member, role, device...). For group members, this concept specializes in *preferences*, which describes the prefer-ences of the user concerning the awareness information delivery. For devices, it spe-cializes in *characteristics*, describing the capabilities of the referred device. These profiles may typically define conditions under which events (and, consequently, in-formation) should be delivered, as well as its quantity (maximum number of events or Kbytes supported). The *characteristics* profiles can be represented using the CC/PP[3] reference. The *preferences* profiles may indicate a priority order for the events, the time interval that is suitable for the user, and other conditions related to the context description (for instance, if the current device is a given one, or if a given activity has been performed).

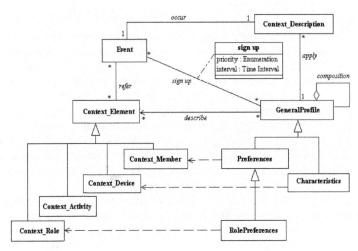

Fig. 3. The application of the context representation to the awareness mechanism[4].

As an illustration, let us introduce an example considering a mobile Groupware System which has shared repository and synchronous/asynchronous communication features. In such a system, a user may define a *preference* profile indicating events related to some modifications made on a report that she/he is writing, to the availabil-ity of the other group's members or to the group's deadlines. In addition, she/he may associate to this profile a time interval, specifying that she/he is interested only in

---

[3] http://www.w3.org/Mobile/CCPP/

[4] The prefix "Context_" is used to distinguish between the elements of the context representa-tion and those of the awareness mechanism.

events performed last week or which should occur during the next one (such as a deadline). In fact, we consider that each group member can define for herself/himself a set of profiles and the circumstances in which these profiles should be applied, as explained later in this section.

In order to perform the context-based filtering process, we associate each *context description* instances with each *event* instance, with a *general profile* instance, or with an active user. This reflects the fact that *i)* events are (or should be) produced in a certain context, *ii)* at least, one *context description* instance describing the circumstances in which a profile can be applied is associated with this profile, *iii)* once a mobile user accesses the system, she/he is doing so through a specific context, which is identified by the system and represented by a *context description* instance as well. The Fig. 3 presents the associations between events, profiles and the classes defined by the context representation (see Section 4).

The proposed filtering process is performed in two phases, using the *context description* instances associated with the group member and the general profiles in order to perform the selection of the suitable events for this member. In the first phase, the awareness mechanism selects the profiles (preferences or characteristics) that are applicable to the current member's context description. Then, in the second phase, it applies the selected profiles to filter the available events. We consider that each group member can define circumstances, through a *context description* instance, in which each profile can be applied.

The first phase, profile selection, is performed by comparing the content of the *context description* instances of both, user and profile: if the *context description* instance of the profile has the same content or is a subset of the current user's *context description* instance, then this profile can be applied. We consider that the *context description* instance and its associations with other instances define a graph, where the nodes represent the instances and the edges between them represent the tuples in which these instances are involved. Thus, a context C is a sub-context of a context C' whenever the graph corresponding to C is a subgraph of the graph corresponding to C'. For instance, a user may define a profile that is applicable only when she/he is working on an activity which concerns the referred report and when she/he is working on a desktop device. This means that this profile is not selected when she/he is working on her/his PDA, even if she/he is involved in one of these activities. This is because of the context description of this profile does not match the user's context description (it does not include the node referring to the PDA device, so it is not a subset of the user's context description). On the other hand, if the same user defines a second profile including, as context element, an instance referring to this PDA device (*i.e.* a profile for the situations in which she/he is using it), this profile is selected in this situation. In addition, individual elements of the user's context may have in turn their own profiles, which are also taken into account in the selection process (for instance, the device employed by the user may have a *characteristics* instance associated with it that will be considered).

Once all applicable profiles are selected, the second phase begins. Here, the awareness mechanism compares the conditions associated with these profiles to the information carried by the set of available events. Then, among the available events, the awareness mechanism selects only those which correspond to (*i.e.* match with) the conditions expressed by the profiles, that is the ones which are considered as relevant for the user's context. This matching can be achieved in different ways. We propose to perform it gradually, respecting the order in which they have been selected. This means that, for each profile, the filtering process selects the event instances corresponding to the event types signed up by the profile, and then it applies the conditions expressed on this profile.

For instance, let us consider a user who has two selected profiles: one including the event type corresponding to the colleague's availability (called "on-line" event type), and another including the event type related to a particular group's activity ("activity X" event type). Additionally, each profile expresses an extra condition: a time interval condition (colleagues available right now) for the former profile, and a context condition (the event must handle a given shared object) for the latter. Using these profiles, the filtering process will select only the instances of these two event types ("on-line" and "activity X") which correspond to the expressed conditions (the time condition for the instances of the first event type, and the context condition for the instances of the second one). The process will ignore other instances that do not correspond to these event types, neither to these conditions. Furthermore, the context condition is expressed as a context description instance. Its evaluation is performed by comparing it with the *context description* instance associated with each event instance (through an operation similar to the one used to select the profiles). The time condition evaluation exploits the *interval* attribute of the class-association *sign up* between the classes *Event* and *General Profile* (Fig. 3).

The result of such a filtering process should be a reduced set of events that will be delivered by the Groupware System to the mobile user (possibly, after the application of other adaptation components that should adapt the presentation of the selected information to the capabilities of the current device).

6   Conclusion

This paper presents a context-based filtering process for awareness mechanisms in mobile Groupware System, which relies on a context representation, described using an object-based knowledge model. This context representation differs from other works by combining two points of view (organizational and physical context), as well as by using an object-oriented representation. This representation has been implemented using the AROM system, and we are now performing preliminary tests, considering more particularly the subset relation between context description instances. We are also implementing the filtering process, using a framework for awareness support called BW [8]. We expect to perform more practical tests with mobile users through a test application, a cooperative game especially designed for this purpose. Through these tests, we expect to evaluate the effective impact of our proposition for mobile users and the usefulness of this mechanism by the users.

In addition, we expect that these practical tests will show more about the scalability of this proposition. Preliminary tests are promising since the AROM system seems able to handle large amounts of instances. Finally, considering the filtering process, its scalability and adaptability depend mainly on the profile definition. The process proposed in this paper presents some limitations (*e.g.* the user has to predefine the conditions of the profile application and the conditions for the events selection), and we intent to improve this definition on the future.

References

1. Alarcón, R., Fuller, D.: Intelligent awareness in support of collaborative virtual work groups. In Haake, J.M., Pino, J.A. (Eds.), CRIWG 2002, LNCS 2440. Springer-Verlag (2002) 168-188.
2. Burrell, J., Gray, G.K., Kubo, K., Farina, N.: Context-aware computing: a text case. In: Borriello, G., Holmquist, L.E. (Eds.), Ubicomp 2002, LNCS 2498. Springer-Verlag (2002) 1-15
3. David, J.M.N., Borges, M.R.S.: Improving the selectivity of awareness information in groupware applications. In: International Conference on Computer Supported Cooperative Work in Design (CSCWD'2001). IEEE Computer Society (2001) 41-46. http://equipe.nce.ufrj.br/mborges/publicacoes/CSCWD%202001.zip (Mar. 2001)
4. Dourish, P.: Seeking a foundation for context-aware computing. Human Computer Interaction, vol. 13, n° 2-4. Hillsdale (2001) 229-241
5. Dourish, P., Bellotti, V.: Awareness and Coordination in Shared Workspaces. Proceedings of ACM Conference on Computer-Supported Cooperative Work (CSCW'92). ACM Press (1992) 107-114
6. Espinosa, A., Cadiz, J., Rico-Gutierrez, L., Kraut, R., Scherlis, W., Lautenbacher, G.: Coming to the wrong decision quickly: why awareness tools must be matched with appropriate tasks. CHI Letters, CHI 2000, vol. 2, n° 1. ACM Press (2000) 392-399
7. Jing, J., Helal, A., Elmagarmid, A.: Client-server computing in mobile environment. ACM Computing Surveys, vol. 31, n° 2. ACM Press (1999) 117-157
8. Kirsch-Pinheiro, M., de Lima, J.V., Borges, M.R.S.: A Framework for Awareness support in Groupware Systems. Computers in Industry, vol. 52, n° 3, Elsevier (2003) 47-57
9. Leiva-Lobos, E.P., Covarrubias, E.: The 3-ontology: a framework to place cooperative awareness. In Haake, J.M., Pino, J.A. (Eds.), CRIWG 2002, LNCS 2440. Springer-Verlag, (2002) 189-199
10. Lemlouma, T.; Layaïda, N.: Context-aware adaptation for mobile devices. In: IEEE International Conference on Mobile Data Management (2004) http://opera.inrialpes.fr/people/Tayeb.Lemlouma/Papers/174_lemlouma_MDM2004.pdf (Mar. 2004)
11. Liechti, O.: Awareness and the WWW: an overview. In: ACM Conference on Computer-Supported Cooperative Work (CSCW'00) - Workshop on Awareness and the WWW. ACM Press (2000) http://www2.mic.atr.co.jp/dept2/awareness/fProgram.html (Dec., 2002)
12. Muñoz, M.A., Rodríguez, M., Favela, J., Martinez-Garcia, A.I., Gonzalez, V.M.: Context-aware mobile communication in hospitals. Computer, vol. 36, n° 9, IEEE Computer Society (2003) 38-46.
13. O'Hare, G., O'Grady, M.: Addressing mobile HCI needs through agents. In: Paternò, F. (Ed.), Mobile HCI 2002, LNCS 2411. Springer-Verlag. (2002) 311-314
14. Page, M., Gensel, J., Capponi, C., Bruley, C., Genoud, P., Ziébelin, D., Bardou, D., Dupierris, V.: A New Approach in Object-Based Knowledge Representation: the AROM System. In: 14th International Conference on Industrial & Engineering Applications of Artificial Intelligence & Expert Systems, (IEA/AIE2001), LNAI 2070, Springer-Verlag (2001) 113-118
15. Perry, M., O'Hara, K., Sellen, A., Brown, B., Harper, R.: Dealing with mobility: understanding access anytime, anywhere. ACM Transactions on Computer-Human Interaction, vol. 8, n. 4. ACM Press (2001) 323-347
16. Projet ECOO: Projet ECOO: environnements et coopération. Rapport d'activité, INRIA (2001). http://www.inria.fr/rapportsactivite/RA2001/ecoo/ecoo.pdf (Nov. 2002, in French)
17. Schilit, B.N., Trevor, J., Hilbert, D.M. and Koh, T.K.: Web interaction using very small Internet devices. Computer, vol. 35, n°10. IEEE Computer Society (2002) 37-45
18. Schmidt, K.: The problem with 'awareness': introductory remarks on 'Awareness in CSCW'. Computer Supported Cooperative Work, vol. 11, n° 3-4. Kluwer Academic Publishers (2002) 285-298

ICoMP: A Mobile Portal Model Based on Reflective Middleware and Mobile Agents

Marcos Vinicius Gialdi[1], Edmundo R.M. Madeira[1],
Paul Grace[2], and Gordon Blair[2]

[1] IC – Institute of Computing
UNICAMP – University of Campinas
13083-970 Campinas, SP, Brazil
{marcos.gialdi,edmundo}@ic.unicamp.br
[2] Distributed Multimedia Research Group, Computing Department
Lancaster University, Lancaster, UK
{gracep,gordon}@comp.lancs.ac.uk

Abstract. Mobile Computing enables information access anytime, anywhere. However, the needs of users and the constraints generated by the mobile environment raise the necessity to personalize access to services. This paper describes ICoMP (I-centric Communication Mobile Portal), which is a mobile portal that offers services based upon user profiles (these contain information including: preferences, available resources, location and environment context). Notably, ICoMP follows an I-Centric approach, whereby the system dynamically adapts to manage both user requirements and changes in the mobile environment. ICoMP's infrastructure extends a reflective middleware (ReMMoC) with both context support, and an agent platform (Grasshopper) to improve access to information and application services. In this paper, we evaluate our implementation of the ICoMP portal in terms of memory footprint cost and support for mobile applications.

Keywords: Mobile Portal, Adaptation, I-centric, Reflective Middleware, Mobile Agents

1 Introduction

Mobile devices, like portable computers and PDAs, have the capacity to communicate across wireless networks with telecommunication and Internet services. In a mobile environment, two mobility types can be characterized: personal and terminal. Personal mobility is the ability for users to access services using different devices and networks, wherever the users are. Terminal mobility is the capacity of a mobile terminal to change the network attachment point and retain the same network address. However, personal and terminal mobility introduces new constraints not found in the fixed network.

The requirements of users and the constraints generated by the mobile environment raise the necessity to personalize access to application services. In this direction, some works have already been proposed [1–3] that adapt the user

A. Karmouch, L. Korba, and E. Madeira (Eds.): MATA 2004, LNCS 3284, pp. 88–97, 2004.

session to a context of service offer based upon user preferences. However, mobile environments are also characterised by changing environmental conditions including variable network Quality of Service, limited end system resources and heterogeneous service platforms (e.g. mobile agents, Web Services or CORBA services). Reflective middleware has been identified as well suited to solving these challenges [5]. We believe that Mobile Portals can be better supported by reflective middleware. Here, mobile portal is related to the traditional concept of Internet portal accessed by mobile devices.

In this paper we describe the ICoMP (I-centric Communication Mobile Portal) infrastructure; this is a Mobile Portal that offers services based upon user profiles, and adapts to user requirements and changes in the mobile environment. ICoMP uses the I-Centric approach, where communication systems adapt to the communication space, enviroment and individual situation [4]. Underpinning ICoMP is ReMMoC [5], a reflective middleware that reacts to environmental changes to overcome service heterogeneity i.e. it interoparates with different middleware styles (RPC, publish-subscribe etc.). However, ReMMoC does not currently support mobile code, whose properties of asynchronous operation, retrieving context based information offline, and processing distribution are ideally suited to Mobile Portals. Therefore, ICoMP adds agent funtionality (the Grasshopper platform) to improve mobile client interoperability (interoperation with agent-based services).

The paper is organized as follow. Section 2 introduces the basic concepts related to ICoMP. Section 3 presents the architecture of the portal, implementation issues and an example mobile application scenario. Section 4 evaluates the ICoMP portal. Section 5 describes related work, and finally Section 6 concludes the paper.

2   Background

2.1   Context

Humans can deduce and interpret the context of a current situation and react in an appropriate way.

Context-aware means be able to use context information. A system is context-aware if it can extract, interact and use context information and adapt its functionalities to the current context. Then, the information and services can be presented to the users according to the current context; a service can be automatically executed when in a certain context and context information can be stored for a future query.

2.2   Mobile Agents

Mobile agents are processes (or active objects) that are capable of migrating between network hosts during their execution, carrying their execution state. Thus, they can offer a uniform paradigm to distributed objects, with synchronous and asynchronous message passing, object passing, mobile and stationary objects. Mobile agents offer an alternative communication paradigm that is well suited for building distributed mobile applications. Mobile devices can send mobile agents to the fixed network to execute user tasks (e.g. information retrieval) in an efficient way, that overcomes many of the problems associated with the domain of mobile computing.

Mobile agents are well suited to mobile portals; they can utilise information from user profiles to find the most appropriate information or service to present to the user. Mobile agents also make better use of available resources.

2.3 Reflective Middleware

One of the properties of middleware is its capacity to hide the details of distributed communication and platform heterogeneity. However, many application types (including mobile, multimedia and real-time) need to be able to inspect both the current behaviour of the middleware and the current environmental conditions, and then dynamically change the behaviour to obtain the best level of service. For example, a videoconference application can obtain the best quality of service by selecting the appropriate transport protocol for the network (e.g. wireless LAN, wired LAN, Internet). In other words, some applications benefit from middleware that hides low level details of distribution, but others can improve performance knowing the dynamic state of lower layers, and adapting the middleware to the applications needs.

Reflection is now an established solution to create middleware with these properties. The key to the approach is to offer a meta-object protocol (MOP), supporting access to a self-representation of the underlying platform. The self-representation is causally connected to the middleware platform, any changes made to the representation generates changes in the middleware implementation and vice-versa. The MOP provides operations to inspect the internal details of a platform (introspection), and in addition, the MOP typically provides operations to alter the underlying middleware (adaptation). Thus, it is possible to select network protocols, security policies, cryptography algorithms, and other mechanisms to get a better system performance in different contexts and situations.

3 The I-Centric Communication Mobile Portal

3.1 *Approach*

The design and implementation of ICoMP are based upon three complementary technologies: an I-Centric system, mobile agents and reflective middleware. In this section we describe how these are utilised to create our Mobile Portal model. Furthermore, we describe an example mobile scenario and discuss implementation issues.

Looking at the behaviour of human beings and their communication space, it is obvious that human beings interact to a set of contexts in their environment.

Personal communication space is defined by: individual needs and preferences, the people who human beings interact with, and the set of devices that each individual controls. In this way, a new approach is to build communication systems not based on specific technologies, but rather individual communication spaces. The I-Centric communication system is an approach to design communication systems that adapt to the individual communication space, environment and situation. I means individual, Centric means adaptable to the individual needs. The diversity of devices, telecommunication technologies, services, positioning and detection systems, and context-aware and location-aware applications can be seen as technologies that enable I-centric communications.

ICoMP is based upon ReMMoC (Reflective Middleware for Mobile Computing) [5], which uses reflection and component technology to resolve the problem of heterogeneous middleware technologies in the mobile environment. Mobile applications and services are typically implemented using different middleware platforms (e.g. RPC, message-oriented, event based paradigms) and advertised by different service discovery protocols (e.g. SLP, UPnP, Jini and Salutation). Using ReMMoC the mobile portal can interoperate with services irrespective of the technology they are implemented and advertised.

In the ICoMP model, mobile agents execute services like information search and user services such as buying movie tickets. Furthermore, mobile agents are used to retrieve information and services that aren't on the Portal. ReMMoC provides no support for code mobility, therefore ICoMP integrates a mobile agent platform (Grasshopper) into the portal to add these capabilities. Grasshopper is a mobile agent platform released by the IKV in 1998. Grasshopper is implemented in Java and based on the MASIF (Mobile Agents Standard Interface) standard, which defines an interoperability interface between mobile agent platforms.

3.2   Overall Architecture

The mobile devices that access the Portal services are characterized by different processing capacities, memory and screen sizes (cell phones, PDAs, notebooks, among others). Each type of device is treated in a different way when offering services to the user.

At the heart of the ICoMP model are profiles. The profile concept is modeled in two parts: a part of the profile information is stored on each mobile device the user is using, for example, the user agenda (when the device has storage space for this), and the other part is stored in the user home (user network). The user profile is specified by the following information: *Context, Name, Address, Occupation, Agenda, Favorites, History, Preferences. Context* contains information related to the environment, *Name, Address, Occupation* are personal informations, *Agenda* contains information about the user agenda, *Favorites* contains the user's favorite *sites, History* is the history of accessed *sites* and *Preferences* indicates the user preferences, like preferred kind of sports and movies.

Context is described by *Device, Protocol, Network* and *Location. Device* describes features of the device, *Protocol* specifices the available protocols, *Network* indicates the network technology and available bandwith, and *Location* indicates where the user is.

However, this information may not always be available. In this case, ICoMP specifies different levels related to the *Profile*, from a level with a minimal information set to a level with all profile information.

Components. The overall architecture of the ICoMP model, which is separated into individual components, is described in turn.

– *Profile* stores information related to the user profile. This is composed from part of the information stored at user home, part of the information stored on the device and the information that is provided by *Context Providers* like the *Context Toolkit*[1].
– *Context Providers* are systems that capture context information and make this information available.
– The *Reasoning Deducer* makes deductions that define which kinds of adaptation may be performed, based upon *Profile* and *Service Providers* infomations.
– The *Adapter* receives results from the Reasoning Deducer describing what types of adaptation and communication could be done, decides which one to do and then executes. These may be of the following types: offering services to the user, interoperating with the service providers or sending a new mobile agent. The Adapter is the "brain" of the model, it indicates what each component must do to execute the adaptation.
– *Service Providers* implement their application services based upon reflective middleware. Hence, these are the components that implement the service functionality offered by the Portal.
– *Mobile Agents* are responsable for offering mobile agent based services to the portal e.g. information retrieval.

Interfaces. The ICoMP component interfaces are:

– *Reasoning Deducer*:
  • IReasoningDeducer - this interface offers methods to get the profile information and make the deduction based on the profile information, indicating what kind of adaptation can be done.
– *Adapter*:
  • IAdapter - this interface offers methods to make the adaptation based on *ReasoningDeducer* results.
– *Mobile Agents*:
  • IMobileAgents - this interface must offer methods like to dispatch, return, clone, create, active agents, among others:
– *Reflective Middleware*(Service Providers) - the reflective middleware must have interfaces to identify all connections between the middleware components, allow the inspection of component interfaces and associate /desassociate interceptors to an interface.

Services. In a general way, the user can request services of the Mobile Portal, and the Portal can then offer these services to the user based upon profile information, characterizing the I-centric approach. Moreover, the user can bring her agents and launch them in this new environment or create new agents.

3.3 Example Scenario and Implementation Details

To illustrate how ICoMP operates we describe a typical application scenario. A user connects to a network, where a Mobile Portal offers services to her. This is performed based on the user profile, through the user preferences, available resources and the current context information. For example, when a user, who lives in London and has a profile indicating that she likes mood movies, goes to New York, when connecting to the NY network, the NY Mobile Portal itself adapts to the profile of this user, offering a cinema programme related to mood movies. If the user is using a cell phone, for example, the title, time and location can be seen. Using a PDA, the title, time, location and synopsis can be seen. Using a notebook, the title, time, location, synopsis and a trailer can be seen. Moreover, the user can dispatch mobile agents to buy tickets, search for opinions about a movie, among others. It is important to note that mobile agents are autonomous and can be programmed with some level of intelligence.

Based on the example above, we've implemented both the ICoMP model and an application service. It is important to note that we used this Movie Portal application to show the benefits of the ICoMP model. The implementation environment is based on the Windows operating system. The reflective middleware (ReMMoC) and mobile agents (Grasshopper) interfaces are commented below.

Interfaces. It is important to note that the Grasshopper and ReMMoC interfaces meet the ICoMP requirements. The Grasshopper interfaces offer methods to create, move and clone agents, among others. ReMMoC provides a simple binding interface to automatically interoperate with discovered services.

Components. Based upon our portal model described in the previous section, Figure 1 illustrates the implementation of individual components:

Profile: Stored as an XML schema. This schema results from informations provided by the *home profile, context provider* and part of the *profile* stored on the mobile device. In this case, the used informations are related to user preferences, favorites sites and accessed site history.

Context Providers: Systems that provide context information through an XML interface, like the Context Toolkit.

Reasonig Deducer: This is implemented in Prolog, in this case called Prolog Deducer. Prolog deduces what can be offered to the user based on facts that describe her preferences, favorite sites, history and what the service providers can offer.

Adapter: Uses the Prolog Deducer services through the interface IPrologDeducer to decide what type of adaptation will be done, interacts with the service

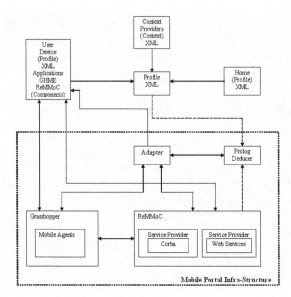

Fig. 1. Implementation Model

providers through the ReMMoC client middleware and uses mobile agent services through Grasshopper. Moreover, the Adapter can offer services to the user, indicating where the service is and providing the whole infrastructure in terms of interfaces and methods, allowing the user themselves to access the offered services. For example, the Adapter decides how to present a content to the user based on her available resources e.g. her mobile device.

Service Providers: These are implemented over heterogeneous middlewares and their services are advertised through different service discovery protocols. However, the Service Providers are accessed through the ReMMoC API, which offers a higher level abstraction to discover and interoperate with heterogeneous middleware implementations, hiding the technology from both the portal and user.

For instance, in our Cinema Portal, we can abstract the operations to access the Cinema services by describing this service using only the abstract part of the WSDL language. This description is stored on the mobile client along with the ReMMoC components that deal with heterogeneous technologies. Invocation of the ReMMoC API with an abstract WSDL operation will then interoperate with the corresponding service in the portal independently of how it is implemented.

In our prototype, the provided services are implemented using CORBA Orbacus and implemented in Java. The Service Providers offer informations about movie programming.

According to the specification above, an application can then use movie services. For example, a user can query the synopsis of a certain movie through her Pockect PC. In this case, to get this service, the application queries a WSDL file to obtain the information related to the operation.

Through ReMMoC, it is possible to interact with heterogenous implementations of services. In this example, the components are configured to deal with CORBA and SLP (*Service Location Protocol*) protocols. However, it is possible through reification, to automatically reconfigure the components to interact with other technologies. For example, the same Cinema service can be offered to the portal as a SOAP Service and advertised by UPnP (*Universal Plug and Play*).

Mobile Agent Platform: The mobile agents are implemented upon the Grasshopper platform. The mobile agents export their services through the IAgent and IMobileAgent interfaces. In our prototype, we have implemented the access to mobile agents through cell phones. In this case, the agents reside on the fixed network and are accessed through Servlets. Moreover, Grasshopper has a version for Windows CE that can be used.

The diagram illustrated in Figure 2 shows the sequence of method invocations describing the sequence of actions for the Portal offers services to the user and to the user access Portal services.

Based on the Movie Portal example, the Profile of the user is built through the method *getprofile*. Then, the method *makededuction* is called to deduce what kind of services can be offerred to the user. The method *makeadaptation* is called to decide what kind of adaptation must be done to offer services to the user. After this, the user calls the method *GetSynopsis* to access the Movie Portal service. Moreover, the user can call an agent to buy the movie tickets through the invocation of the method *CallAgent*. It is important to remember that through ReMMoC the user can access services independently of the middleware technology and using Grasshopper mobile agents it is possible to operate in a disconnected mode, sending an agent to buy tickets and disconneting.

Fig. 2. Sequence Diagram of the Movie Portal

4   Related Work

Some projects have investigated adaptation in a mobile environment:

MyCampus: A Semantic Web Environment for Context - Aware Mobile Services [3] is a semantic web environment for context-aware services.

CAMP: *A Context-Aware Mobile Portal* [2] is an architecture defined by combining Internet Portal technology with personal and terminal mobility with context-aware concepts, allowing the development and customization of services. The main idea is to provide users with several services that are automatically adaptable to the user context.

At Georgia Tech, a project was developed to create an architecture that supports the develpment of context-aware applications, this architecture is formed of a set of tools called the *Context Toolkit*[1].

Therefore, the ICoMP is a model for Mobile Portals like CAMP, enabling personal and terminal mobility. Like Context Toolkit, ICoMP supports the usage of context information to adapt to the user needs. Like My Campus, ICoMP offers services based on agents. However, ICoMP differs in that it utilises both a reflective middleware and a mobile agent platform to overcome heterogenous service implementation and support features like processing distribution, travelling on the network, among others.

5   Evaluation

This section provides an evaluation of the client-side ICoMP components in terms of the memory footprint sizes. Table 1 exemplifies the ReMMoC memory footprint size for StrongARM devices (e.g. pocket pcs). This demonstrates that the size of the core framework and example configurations are around 600 Kbytes, and are therefore suitable to operate on handheld devices.

Table 1. ReMMoC memory footprint size for StrongARM devices

Component	KBytes
Core ReMMoC Components	72.5
ReMMoC (Corba and SLP)	250.5
ReMMoC (SOAP and UPnP)	246.5
OpenCOM	27.5

For ICoMP, we have implemented an application that accesses agent services through cell phones. The memory footprint size depends on the application, because the mobile agent platform (Grasshopper) is in the fixed network. For example, the size of the application that sends agents to buy movie tickets is about 30KBytes.

On the other hand, Grasshopper has a version for WinCE, which is portable for devices based on MIPS, ARM and SH-3 processors. The memory footprint size is approximately 700 KBytes, and suitable for devices like Pocket PCs.

Therefore, it is important to note that all of the technologies that compose the ICOMP portal are well-suited to mobile devices in terms of memory footprint. However, using the ICoMP model it is possible to use service providers based on reflective middleware and mobile agents too. Using just Grasshopper for WinCE it is possible to access only agents.

Furthermore, ICoMP offers several user interactions e.g. accessing agents and services in heterogeneous environments through PDAS, cell phones and laptops as shown in our scenario. Agents are particulary good for asynchronous operations (disconnected operation), for example, in a Movie Portal the agents can search for opinions about movies and buy tickets to a movie session, among others. Beyond this, it is possible to implement agents with some level of intelligence to perform more complex tasks. Moreover, the simple abstration of

ReMMoC and Grasshopper APIs simplifies the development of both user and agent interactions in a mobile environment with heterogeneous implementations.

6   Conclusion

This paper presents a new approach to develop an infrastructure for Mobile Portals that enables adaptation that is more accurate to the user needs and changes in a mobile environment. ICoMP is originally distributed, consequently scalable. This Portal is original in the sense of integrating the two services access: to information and services offered by service providers, and to services offered by a mobile agent platform like dispatching and receiving agents. Moreover, the Adapter can be seen as "maestro" in a service orchestration.

Related to the implementation, it is important the fact that the model is componentized, and hence flexible. Therefore, it is possible to add new technologies, or remove techniques and services. This is especially important given the variable resources available of different types of mobile device. Moreover, the used technologies, like ReMMoC and Grasshopper, meet the requirements of mobile environments.

On the other hand, I-Centric, Reflective Middleware and Mobile agents are complementary technologies that can be used to solve the problem of offer and access services in a mobile environment.

As future work, we intend to develop other applications that use all the resources that ICoMP can offer. Beside this, the Mobile Portal infrastructure must be suitable to the standards that are emerging for adapting systems, like CC/PP, a standard to describe user preferences and devices capacity, and for ontology standards like (DAML + OIL) and RDF (*Resource Description Framework*).

References

1. Salber, D., Dey A.K., Abowd, G.D. *The Context Toolkit: Aiding the Development of Context-Enabled Applications. In Proceedings of the CHI 99 Conference on Human Factors in Computing Systems: The CHI is the Limit, pp. 434-441, Pitsburgh, PA, May 1999, ACM Press.*
2. Mandato, D., Kovacs, E., Hohl, F., Amir-Alikhani, H. *CAMP: A Context - Aware Mobile Portal*, IEEE Communicatios Magazine. pp. 90-97 January 2002.
3. Sadeh, N.M. *A Semantic Web Environment for Context - Aware Mobile Services*, Carniege Mellon University, 2002.
4. Arbanowski, St., van de Meer, S., Steglich, St., Popescu-Zeletin, R. *The Human Communication Space: Towards I-centric Communications.* v. 5, Personal and Ubiquitous Computing, Issue 1, 2001.
5. Grace, P., Blair, G., and Samuel, S. *"ReMMoC: A Reflective Middleware to Support Mobile Client Interoperability"*, In Proceedings of International Symposium on Distributed Objects and Applications (DOA), Sicily, Italy, November 2003.

Configuration Management
for Networked Reconfigurable Embedded Devices

Timothy O'Sullivan and Richard Studdert

University College Cork, Department of Computer Science, Cork, Ireland
{t.osullivan,r.studdert}@cs.ucc.ie

Abstract. Distribution of product updates to embedded devices can increase product lifetimes for consumers whilst increasing revenues and brand loyalty for vendors. Dynamic provisioning of application solutions to embedded devices are complex due to their heterogeneous nature. This paper proposes a configuration management architectural framework which incorporates a mobile agent based push methodology for networked reconfigurable embedded devices. FPGAs (Field Programmable Gate Arrays) are hardware components within embedded systems that can be dynamically reconfigured. Product updates are composed of both software and reconfigurable hardware code which can be tailored to the physical constraints of the device. Push technology is a distribution mechanism initiated by the vendor enabling delivery of product updates. The proposed infrastructure is built upon the solid foundations of agent-based design patterns. Agent technology provides an ideal environment for embedded systems management. Mobile agents completely encapsulate hardware-software based solutions providing a coherent abstraction for their distribution. The paper also outlines an initial demonstrator system.

1 Introduction

Current and future generations of high performance embedded devices (e.g. PDAs) demand a broad range of end-user applications. Embedded system designers are responding to these consumer pressures with the development of networked reconfigurable embedded devices capable of providing a range of high-performance, compute-intensive applications. Each application is composed of a hardware-software mix configured to deliver optimum performance for the user whilst also respecting the physical constraints of the device. FPGAs are hardware components playing a key role in the construction of these embedded devices. They are a reconfigurable hardware technology with the ability to perform computations in hardware to increase performance whilst retaining much of the flexibility of a software solution [1].

Increasingly intense competition combined with time-to-market pressures compels embedded device manufacturers to release early product versions to guarantee adequate market share. Full-product functionality is then achieved in the market-place through a configuration management technique of distributing hardware-software based updates and patches. Push technology is a distribution mechanism initiated by the vendor enabling delivery of product updates to embedded devices.

A. Karmouch, L. Korba, and E. Madeira (Eds.): MATA 2004, LNCS 3284, pp. 98–107, 2004.

Embedded systems are evolving and demand more proficient development methods and tools for their design, deployment and management [2]. A flexible, robust and proactive distribution framework is especially required to allow vendors confidently disseminate their updates and modifications to customers after initial product releases. All updates should interoperate seamlessly with the embedded device ensuring minimal disruption to the customer.

This paper builds upon our previous work [3] and proposes a configuration management architectural framework incorporating a mobile agent based push methodology for networked reconfigurable embedded devices. This innovative approach identifies agent technology as an ideal environment for embedded systems management. It asserts this approach is particularly suitable as a push-based distribution mechanism for embedded devices. A push strategy utilising agent technology allows for the coherent distribution of hardware-software application solutions to networked embedded devices. An agent-based middleware framework is efficient in its use of network bandwidth and is flexible in dealing with intermittent network connections. These characteristics are highly beneficial for mobile wireless embedded devices. Agent technology also encourages management decentralisation minimising the load on the network management centre and thus reducing points of failure within the network [4].

In the rest of this paper, an examination of related work in this area is presented (Section 2). The third section presents an overview of the configuration management distribution methodology proposed for networked reconfigurable embedded devices. This section highlights the architectural framework, explores the design patterns employed and describes the technologies utilised to realise the overall system. In section four an experimental prototype currently being constructed is depicted. Finally, section five concludes with remarks on future research.

2 Related Work

Push technology has been applied within various research communities as an architectural paradigm for data dissemination.

Telecommunications research has explored the push concept as a method for the provisioning of configuration settings to mobile phones [5]. The wireless application protocol (WAP) and the GSM short messaging system (SMS) are combined to provide the implementation framework. A beneficial scenario is highlighted whereby the hand-held devices belonging to selected personnel at a disaster site are automatically adapted for specifically directed emergency communications.

Parallel computing has also been exposed to the potential of push-based technology. In [6], a novel mobile agent-based push methodology is proposed within the supercomputing domain. This approach allows users to dispatch their jobs as agents who roam the network seeking servers on which they can execute their task. This is advantageous as it produces an adaptive and fault tolerant execution model.

Push-based technology also plays a key role within the configuration management community [7]. A push-based distribution strategy enabling software deployment utilising a mobile agent framework is presented. Key benefits of an agent-based approach to configuration management are flexibility, reliability and increased performance [8].

An embedded systems configuration management technique focusing on hardware upgrades is proposed in [9]. Their methodology targets remote FPGA devices. Object-oriented programming techniques are applied to an FPGA configuration bitstream. An object is created encapsulating any additional information it may require for its delivery, verification and use. The object is packaged into a payload which is pushed over a TCP/IP network to the embedded device. Through object-oriented design and analysis techniques, an additional layer of abstraction is achieved providing a more robust and reliable deployment methodology.

It is clear the concept of configuration management is increasing in importance within the embedded device co-design community. It is recognised that with shorter time-to-market windows and increasing demands for additional product functionality, there is a need to develop methods and tools to dynamically deploy hardware-software based application solutions to consumer embedded devices [2].

The approaches in [7, 8] show the combination of mobile agents and push-based distribution strategies are a highly appropriate implementation methodology for configuration management. This paper extends these approaches to target the unique properties of reconfigurable embedded devices to enable cohesive upgrades to their reconfigurable hardware and software based components.

3   Distribution Methodology

Embedded systems are increasingly networked and composed of reconfigurable hardware to enable both application diversity and greater performance. This paper proposes a configuration management architectural framework incorporating a mobile agent-based push methodology to target such embedded devices.

A mobile agent-based push framework allows for the coherent distribution of application solutions to embedded devices. An agent can completely encapsulate all necessary reconfigurable hardware and software code comprising an application solution.

An agent-based approach allows for an additional layer of abstraction in the modelling and conceptualisation of a system. An agent's ability to deal with intermittent network connections and its efficient use of network bandwidth makes agent technology a highly appropriate middleware for embedded device management. Additionally, an agent's characteristics of autonomy and mobility are encouraging attributes for push-based distribution.

An overview of the agent concept is presented in Section 3.1. The role of each agent within the configuration management architectural framework is outlined in Section 3.2. The infrastructure is built upon the solid foundation of agent-based design patterns which are highlighted in Section 3.3. A description of the agent development environment employed is presented in Section 3.4. An overview of reconfigurable hardware is given in Section 3.5 whilst details of the enabling technology allowing dynamic FPGA reconfiguration are outlined in Section 3.6.

3.1 Agent Concept

In the context of software engineering, an agent can be defined as [10]:

> An entity within a computer system environment that is capable of flexible, autonomous actions with the aim of complying with its design objectives.

A mobile agent adheres to the above definition as well as having the added capability of traversing networks. An agent platform is the physical infrastructure (consisting of machine(s), operating system, agent support software, etc) enabling agent deployment and execution [11]. Agent-oriented concepts and techniques are recognised as being well-suited to developing complex and distributed systems [12]. The networked heterogeneous devices our work is focused on fit aptly into this category of system. Jennings and Wooldridge [13] make a substantial and persuasive case for using an agent-oriented methodology to engineer these types of systems.

3.2 Agent Roles

The proposed structure of the configuration management architectural framework utilising a push-based mobile agent approach is outlined in Figure 1. The role of each agent is outlined as follows:

- **Provisioning Server Manager**
  Instances of this agent reside on each provisioning server. It operates as the   main point of contact between the system administrator and the push-based deployment network. It responds to distribution requests by the administrator by invoking a Distribution Master agent to communicate product updates or fixes to all relevant embedded devices.

- **Distribution Master**
  This agent is instantiated as needed and has responsibility for coordinating deployment of application solutions to all appropriate embedded devices. It coordinates with a profiles repository to discover all devices that qualify for a solution. The update is retrieved from a hardware-software application solutions repository. This agent creates a number of Application Courier slaves to deliver the update. The functionality of this agent is based on the master component of the master-slave design pattern [14].

- **Agent Management System (AMS)**
  This agent is responsible for maintaining knowledge about the location of each agent within the platform. This information is used by the Distribution Master to determine the destination of each Application Courier.

- **Application Courier**
  This agent is instantiated as needed and has responsibility for carrying application solutions to embedded devices. The agent encapsulates all necessary software and reconfigurable hardware code to execute an update on the embedded device. It provides a coherent approach to push-based distribution. The functionality of this agent is based on the slave component of the master-slave design pattern.

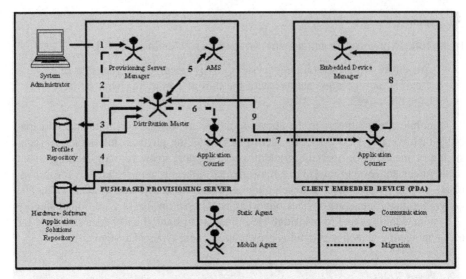

Fig. 1. Configuration Management Architectural Framework

- **Embedded Device Manager**
  This single instance agent is a permanent resident on the embedded device and has responsibility for gathering and maintaining information about the physical device and its owner. Application Courier agents interact locally with the Embedded Device Manager to ensure successful execution of an update process.

3.3 Agent-Based Design Patterns

Design patterns were originally conceived through the visionary work by Alexander in the field of architecture and urban planning [15]. In the context of software engineering, a design pattern can be defined [16]:

> As a particular recurring design problem that arises in specific design contexts and presents a well-proven generic scheme for its solution. The solution scheme is specified by describing its constituent components, their responsibilities and relationships, and the ways in which they collaborate.

Design patterns provide a strong foundation in constructing agent-based applications. The configuration management architectural framework proposed employs the master-slave design pattern [14].

The pattern is appropriate for frameworks replicating a particular service through delegating the same task to several independent suppliers. The pattern is mostly applied to industrial systems requiring fault tolerance however it is also a highly apt framework for the distribution of application solutions to networked embedded devices. The Distribution Master and Application Courier agents represent the master and slave components of the pattern respectively. The behaviour of the pattern within the framework is shown in Figure 2.

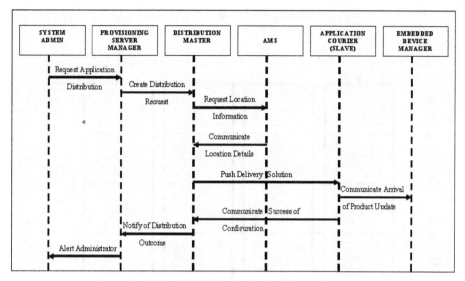

Fig. 2. Master-Slave Behavioural Pattern

3.4 Agent Development Environment

The proposed mobile agent-based push methodology for the distribution of hardware-software based application solutions utilises JADE as the active agent platform on all provisioning servers and JADE-LEAP as the active agent platform on all embedded devices.

JADE (Java Agent Development Framework) is a Java-based open source software development framework aimed at developing multi-agent systems and applications [17]. JADE-LEAP (Java Agent Development Framework-Lightweight Extensible Agent Platform) is an agent-based runtime environment that is targeted towards resource-constrained mobile embedded devices [18].

Both JADE and JADE-LEAP conform to FIPA (Foundation for Intelligent Physical Agents) standards for intelligent agents. FIPA is a standards organisation established to promote the development of agent technology [11].

3.5 Reconfigurable Hardware

The reconfigurable computing concept was first presented by Estrin in 1963 [19]. Field Programmable Gate Arrays (FPGAs) are an enabling technology for reconfiguration. FPGAs are used to accelerate algorithm execution by mapping compute-intensive calculations to the reconfigurable substrate [1]. A generic island-style FPGA routing architecture has a structure as shown in Figure 3.

The Configurable Logic Blocks (CLBs) are used to construct logic and they consist of look-up tables, flip-flops and multiplexers. The Input-Output Blocks (IOBs) provide a communication interface between the internal circuitry of the FPGA and the external environment. The programmable interconnect configures routing and is

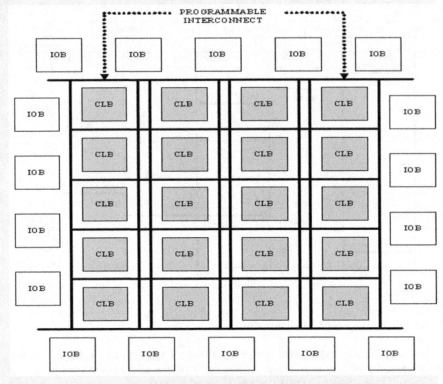

Fig. 3. Generic Island Style FPGA

used to connect the inputs and outputs of the CLBs and IOBs. A hardware design is implemented by manipulating these elements to represent the necessary circuitry.

3.6 JBits Technology

JBits is a Java-based application programming interface (API) developed by Xilinx [20] corporation allowing creation and dynamic modification of their FPGA circuitry [21].

The proposed approach to distributing hardware-software based application solutions involves an agent encapsulating JBits code allowing the agent to dynamically manipulate FPGA hardware on an embedded device. An outline of the architecture of an embedded device enabling both agent migration and also the execution of hardware-software based application solutions is shown in Figure 4.

The mobile agent represents a coherent approach to distributing heterogeneous solutions. The diagram above illustrates the middleware an embedded device needs to support in order to enable networked reconfiguration. An agent contains executable code which can be destined both for the reconfigurable logic and for the CPU of the embedded device. The agent platform is middleware technology allowing the agent to interact with the device.

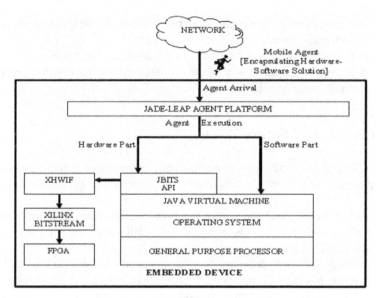

Fig. 4. Embedded Device Architecture

The Jbits API and XHWIF (Xilinx HardWare InterFace) enable the agent to communicate and configure the hardware portion of its code to the reconfigurable logic. The XHWIF is a device library residing on the embedded device which provides an interface between an FPGA and the Jbits API. Using the Jbits API and the XHWIF an agent can interact with the FPGA (to control execution, obtain feedback, perform partial reconfiguration, etc). The agent reconfigures the FPGA logic by invoking Jbits API commands to download a Xilinx bitstream to the FPGA.

The software portion of the Java-based agent code is interpreted and executed by a Java virtual machine (JVM) working in collaboration with an operating system residing on a general purpose processor in the embedded device.

4 Experimental Prototype

An experimental prototype is currently being developed to fully establish the potential of the proposed configuration management methodology.

The embedded device platform will consist of a Dell Axim X5 PDA running a Pocket PC 2003 operating system and executing the JADE-LEAP agent platform using a personal profile-based Java Virtual Machine. The hand-held device will be connected to a Xilinx XCV1000-6 FPGA enabling it to execute the reconfigurable hardware code portion of an application solution.

The provisioning server will consist of a high-end Pentium PC executing the JADE agent platform. It is envisaged wireless communication between the embedded device and the provisioning server will be over a Wi-Fi network. The objectives of this proof of concept demonstrator are to:

- Ensure the proposed infrastructure supports push-based configuration to heterogeneous embedded devices.
- Examine the performance and robustness of the deployed framework.
- Develop a range of application scenarios to demonstrate the benefits and effectiveness of the proposed solution.

5   Conclusions and Future Work

This paper proposes a configuration management architectural framework enabling dynamic provisioning of application solutions to networked reconfigurable embedded devices.

A push-based architectural framework has been outlined that incorporates mobile agent technology and FPGAs. This infrastructure is built upon the solid foundations of agent-based design patterns.

The proposed approach provides for the coherent distribution of hardware-software based applications to networked embedded devices. By integrating agent middleware technology, an effective embedded systems configuration management environment has been established.

This approach reduces the burden on embedded system development as it allows a high-level of abstraction in interpreting the conceptualisation and implementation of management techniques for distributed heterogeneous devices. From a network perspective, it encourages management decentralisation helping to minimise the load on the network management centre and thus improving system robustness.

This paper also includes an outline of an experimental prototype currently being constructed to verify the potential of the proposed configuration management approach. Further research includes:

- Exploring performance of agent-based approach to mobile wireless-based reconfigurable embedded devices.
- Further examination of the services and potential benefits offered to networked reconfigurable embedded devices by agent technology.
- The provision of dynamically partitioned application solutions comprising of software and reconfigurable hardware code that are optimised to each individual embedded device's needs and resources. This will entail extending the existing agent middleware framework to represent and communicate device characteristics and user preferences.

Acknowledgements

This work is funded by the Boole Centre for Research in Informatics.

References

1. Compton, K., and Hauck, S.: Reconfigurable Computing: A Survey of Systems and Software. ACM Computing Surveys, Vol. 34, No. 2, (June 2002) 171-210
2. Fleischmann, J., Buchenrieder, K., and Kress, R.: Java Driven Codesign and Prototyping of Networked Embedded Systems. In Design Automation Conference (DAC), (1999)
3. O'Sullivan, T., and Studdert, R.: Mobile Agent Technology and Networked Reconfigurable Embedded Devices. In Proceedings of International Conference on Pervasive Computing and Communications, (June 2004)
4. Raibulet, C., and Demartini, C.: Mobile Agent Technology for the Management of Distributed Systems – a Case Study. In TERENA Networking Conference, (2000)
5. Ladas, C., Edwards, R., and Peersman, G.: Use of Wireless Application Protocol Service Configuration Provision over the Short Messaging System for Nomadic Device Adaptation. In Proceeding of the 2nd Symposium on the Convergence of Telecommunications, Networking and Broadcasting, (June 2001)
6. Xu, C., and Wims, B.: A Mobile Agent Based Push Methodology for Global Parallel Computing. In Wiley Journal: Concurrency – Practice and Experience, vol. 12, (July 2000) 705-726
7. Hall, S., R., Heimbigner, D., and Wolf, L., A.: A Cooperative Approach to Support Software Deployment Using the Software Dock. In Proceedings of the 1999 International Conference on Software Engineering, (May 1998), 174-183
8. Berghoff, J., Drobnik, O., Lingnau, A., and Monch, C.: Agent-Based Configuration Management of Distributed Applications. In Proceedings of 3rd International Conference on Configurable Distributed Systems, (1996)
9. Casselman, S., and Schewel, J.: Net Aware BitStreams that Upgrade FPGA Hardware Remotely Over the Internet. In Proceedings of SPIE, vol. 4867, (July 2002)
10. Wooldridge, M: Agent-Based Software Engineering. In IEE Proceedings of Software Engineering 144, (1997) 26-37
11. FIPA (Foundation for Intelligent Physical Agents) "FIPA Agent Management Specification", available at http://www.fipa.org
12. Jennings, R., N.: An Agent-Based Approach for Building Complex Software Systems. Communications of the ACM, vol. 44, no. 4, (2001) 35-41
13. Jennings, R., N., and Wooldridge, M.: Agent-Oriented Software Engineering. Handbook of Agent Technology (ed. J. Bradshaw), AAAI/MIT Press, (2000)
14. Buschmann, F.: The Master-Slave Pattern, Pattern Languages of Program Design, Coplien, O., J., and Schmidt, D., (Eds.), Addison Wesley, (1995) 133-142
15. Alexander C.: The Timeless Way of Building, New York: Oxford University Press, (1979)
16. Buschmann, F., Meunier, R., Rohnert, H., Sommerlad, P., and Stal, M.: Pattern-Oriented Software Architecture: A System of Patterns, Wiley, Chichester, (1996)
17. Bellifemine, F., Poggi, A., and Rimassa, G.: JADE – FIPA-Compliant Agent Framework. In Proceedings of PAAM 1999, (1999) 97-108
18. JADE-LEAP: http://sharon.cslet.it/project/jade.
19. Estrin, G., et al: Parallel processing in a Restructurable Computer System. In IEEE Transactions on Computers, Vol. EC-12, (1963)
20. Xilinx Corporation: http://www.xilinx.com
21. Guccione, S., Levi, D., and Sundararajan, P.: JBits: Java Based Interface for Reconfigurable Computing. In Proceedings of 2nd Annual Military and Aerospace Applications of Programmable Devices and Technologies Conference (MAPLD), (1999)

A Programmable Network Enabling Content Adaptation

Bertrand Mathieu, Yannick Carlinet, and Yvon Gourhant

France Telecom R&D, 2 av. Pierre Marzin 22300 Lannion, France
bertrand2.mathieu@francetelecom.com

Abstract. Content adaptation, for delivering personalized information based on terminal capabilities, user preferences and access network topology, is still challenging although many standardization works have been done. These works lead to several formats for specifying user session information. This is based on content adaptation by service providers insofar as they know about terminal and access network capabilities. This paper presents a new solution based on a programmable network that inserts dynamically user session information into client/server exchanges. Different software modules associated to different formats can be deployed dynamically into the network on behalf of the service providers. The programmable node ensures transparency from the client point of view even in the case of TCP exchanges. The performance results show that our solution behaves better than a solution based on a proxy when no insertion is needed. On the other hand, the additional delay of this dynamic insertion is largely less than the average time for transmitting and processing requests.

1 Introduction

In the last few years, a large diversity of heterogeneous terminals has been introduced on the market, especially in the domain of mobile computing. Each kind of terminal has its own features: screen size, number of colours, CPU, memory... Moreover, these terminals have network interfaces with different characteristics. This can be extended to user preferences, user location and to access network topology. Content adaptation and personalization allows the service providers to customize services delivering.

The question we address in the paper is how to inform service providers about user session information (USI): terminal features, user preferences, and possibly access network topology as well as user location.

The first range of solutions enforces mechanisms on the client side (user terminals). The idea is that the client application inserts USI into each request and the server analyses those parameters and builds a customized response.

Three groups have worked in standardisation bodies in this direction: the CC/PP group [1] (Composite Capabilities / Profile Preferences) at the W3C (World Wide Web Consortium) that lead to the RFC3507 and that is now included in the Device Independence Group («CC/PP Exchange protocol based on HTTP Extension Framework» [1]), the Conneg group at IETF (Internet Engineering Task Force) and the MPEG-21 of MPEG (Motion Pictures Expert Group [2]) at ISO/IEC.

Some web servers implement CC/PP: Jigsaw [3] (implemented by the W3C), Dice [4] (from Wales University) running over a "servlet engine" (like Apache Tomcat), a solution built upon the Apache Web server [5].

A. Karmouch, L. Korba, and E. Madeira (Eds.): MATA 2004, LNCS 3284, pp. 108–117, 2004.

There are also some works that take into account the client side, [6] or CSCP [7] as an extension of CC/PP, but their use is limited because of the lack of compliant Web Browsers and therefore the non-availability on many terminals.

Another possibility is to have a USI database and let the Service Providers fetch the USI when they want (periodically for instance; fetching it at each user's request is not realistic since it generates a delay in the response time). This solution is not optimal since the USI may be out-of-date between the time the user modifies his/her information and the time the Service Provider fetches it. Furthermore, it may not be safe to authorize service providers to access the database.

In this paper we are looking at the solutions in the network insofar as the network provides advanced mechanisms for dynamic third-party software module deployment.

The idea is that the service provider deploys its software modules into the network instead of the user terminals. Such modules take the user requests as input and insert USI and/or user location in the user requests as output. Since these modules are deployed in the network, they may append network conditions (available bandwidth, congestion...) to the USI.

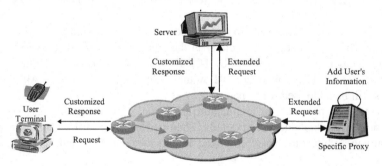

Fig. 1. Use of a Proxy for Inserting User Information

Solutions based on applicative proxies (figure 1), such as http proxy [8] are possible candidates but suffer from some limitations. The user needs to manually configure the browser. Proxies in cascade for the same protocol (for caching or tunnelling) have to be explicitly configured. The proxy is dedicated to a given protocol format: one proxy is needed to insert data in CC/PP format, another one for insertion in the CSCP format.... Thus one proxy per format needs to be deployed in the network. Moreover, the network path between a client and a server is intuitively not optimal, particularly in case of user mobility, since every packet must go through the proxy before going to the destination (one TCP connection established from the user to the proxy and another one from the proxy to the server in the case of http). Solutions like ICAP [9] (Internet Content Adaptation Protocol) or OCP (OPES Callout Protocol) [10], aimed to be the new version of ICAP, more generic and open, currently defined at IETF OPES Working Group, improve proxy-based solutions but are still CPU-consuming and not efficient since all packets are processed at the application-level.

We propose a solution based on a programmable network (see figure 2). It consists of programmable nodes and classical network elements such as routers and B-RAS

(Broadband Access Server). A programmable node is a special network element that is half way between a router and a computer. It intercepts packets of inspected flows and applies application-level processing on the fly: analysis (such as the detection of a signature) or modification (insertion of USI within client requests) and routes at the lower level the others flows. The software module associated to this processing is deployed dynamically on a selected node under the control of a network manager and on behalf of a service provider.

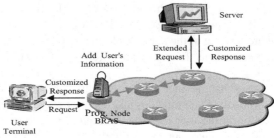

Fig. 2. Use of a Programmable Node for Inserting User Information

This raises several questions. How to introduce such programmable nodes within existing network architectures, especially in the data path? Then, since the programmable node may modify a packet of the TCP flow, is it possible to ensure the consistency of the whole TCP connection? How the whole system performs? All of these questions will be addressed in the paper.

The paper first presents our architecture based on a programmable network. The next section gives implementation details. Then performance of the solution is compared with an architecture based on proxy. Finally, we conclude and give some perspectives.

2   Our Programmable Network Architecture

Our architecture has been designed on programmable network principles [11, 12] that form a prerequisite for deploying third-party code deployment in the network of a network under the control of this last. Our solution is modelled on the P1520 architecture [12] (figure 3).

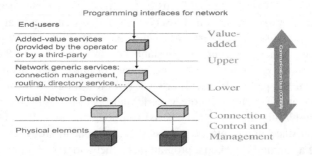

Fig. 3. P1520 Architecture Reference Model

P5120 defines three layers, namely Virtual Network Device, Network generic services and Added-value services. The Virtual Network Device is itself divided in two sub-layers: physical elements and virtual elements. The Lower interface of the Virtual Network Device offers a local abstraction of a programmable node. The Upper interface provided by the Network generic services offers a global transport level abstraction. Then the Upper interface offers a set of added-value services. These open interfaces allow a service provider to manage the programmable nodes of an operator network. The service provider can then have a global view of the network and manage it efficiently while new services are deployed.

Our solution is based on programmable nodes that apply application level processing on some packets. Since this process is CPU consuming, traditional routers reroute selectively only a subset of packets to these programmable nodes. These programmable nodes are themselves divided in two levels. The lower level checks very quickly if an insertion must be included in the packet. The programmable node only intercepts packets fulfilling some conditions (IP Addresses, Protocol). The second level modifies the request for inserting USI. Our network architecture encompasses dynamic deployment mechanisms in order to be able to deal with different formats for delivering this information. The selection of the format is done by the content provider.

2.1 Network Architecture

The architecture we have defined (figure 4) relies on programmable nodes that are between the B-RAS (in the ADSL access network)[1] and the edge router (router NC) in order to be in the path between client and server.

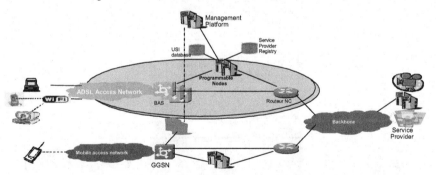

Fig. 4. Integration of Programmable Nodes within a WAN Architecture

Each time a content provider registers a server, the B-RAS is dynamically configured to redirect all the traffic toward this server (IP addresses given as parameters) to pass through the programmable node. Otherwise the traffic directly goes to the edge router. Reciprocally, the edge router is also configured for re-routing the selected traffic going in the other direction (from the server to the client). These two configurations reduce the traffic managed by the programmable router.

---

[1] We expect this may be also extended to mobile access networks although we don't have set up physically for them.

Several B-RAS in the same POP (Point Of Presence – not represented on the figure –) are associated to the same programmable node by now and will be associated to several nodes as soon as the number of servers and/or requests on these servers will overload the capacities of a single node. This schema is replicated on every POP.

2.2 Programmable Node Architecture

Our USI contains terminal capabilities (CPU, memory, screen size, audio format, video format, operating system...), user preferences (wishes video or not, pictures or not, sound or not, preferred language...), network information (like the network access technology: DSL, Wifi), user location and the user IP address. The IP address is used for referencing the user access session.

Two modules are associated to the USI database (figure 5): a *Writing Module* that adds USI at configuration time and a *Reading Module* that is used by the *USIManager* for picking selected information and inserting them in the user requests on the fly. This information is inserted by the selected module in the format of the content provider (*CCPP Module, Proprietary Module*). On the other hand, since the *USIManager* maintains a cache on the USI database, it is informed by the *USIUpdate Manager* when information on the database is modified by the *Writing Module*.

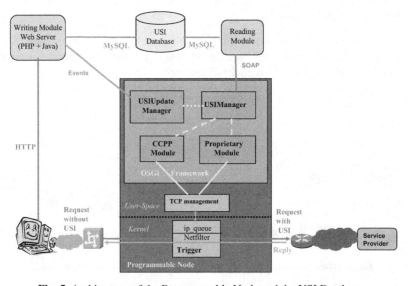

Fig. 5. Architecture of the Programmable Node and the USI Database

These applicative modules are based on a generic programmable node architecture that has two parts (figure 5). The first part is the management of TCP Seq and Acq fields for all the packets of a flow as soon as one packet has been modified for inserting USI. The second part is the triggering function in charge of forwarding incoming packets to their associated module. It is dynamically configured by the first in order to let packets passing quickly through the programmable node or to trigger them to the modules (if insertion is required).

2.3 Management Architecture

The applicative modules are deployed dynamically by the management architecture. The management architecture is in charge of registering software modules that can be dynamically deployed on behalf of the service providers, and deploying them under the control of the network operator. The management architecture is made of a network management platform and of local managers.

The network management platform has a global vision of network resource usage. This includes node resources (CPU load) and not only network resources. It can therefore choose the appropriate node although in our case there is only one node candidate since the selected node must be in the path between client and server.

Each local manager is in charge of the deployment mechanisms on the node. It also instantiates and starts the appropriate code of the deployed software module.

The software modules are registered in and retrieved from a service repository.

3 Implementation Issues

In this section, we first describe the modules specific to the insertion of USI, then the programmable node technology choices, and finally the TCP connection management.

3.1 User Session Information Database

The USI database is filled in by the user through a dedicated web server with PHP pages and Java scripts (*Writing Module*). The USI Database is based on "MySql". The user IP address is used an index for the USI database. Its value is set automatically each time the user authenticates and initiates a PPP/radius connection. To obtain USI information, the programmable node sends request to the *Reading Module* that retrieve selected information from the database.

3.2 Programmable Node

Several programmable network platforms exist. The FAIN project [13] has provided a full active network architecture that could be useful here on the deployment part [14]. Unfortunately, the FAIN programmable node (the *Demultiplexer* component) does not manage TCP streams (only UDP streams are processed) transparently. The ALAN platform [15] allows code deployment but it acts as an application-level proxy and therefore is not transparent to the end user application. Therefore, no programmable network platform, as it is, fulfils the requirements of our use case.

Rather than modifying an existing platform, we decided to build a programmable node based on complementary on-the-shelf technologies then to write a module for TCP management. Our implementation integrates: (1) the Linux *"netfilter"* mechanism, efficient for intercepting packets and passing them to a user-level application via *ip_queue*, (2) an OSGi (Open Services Gateway Initiative) framework, designed at the OSGi Forum, chosen for its ability to dynamically deploy new modules and to resolve dependencies between bundles. The "Jeffree" [16] OSGI framework was chosen for implementing the execution environment of the programmable node. It deploys a CC/PP module or a proprietary module into the same programmable node. The CC/PP module inserts data in the CC/PP format and the proprietary module inserts only the parameters "Device", "ScreenSize" and "Sound" in a specific format.

We have implemented three modules (or bundles, in the OSGi terminology). *USIBundle* handles the interactions with the USI database and the USI management. It retrieves information from the database at the first received packet, stores in a cache, forwards it to the "format" modules and listens events from the *Writing Module* (PHP Web server). The *USIBundle* is notified by the *Writing Module* when the user changes the USI during browsing, so that it can modify the cached information. *CCPPBundle* retrieves USI from the *USIBundle* and inserts this information in a CC/PP format in the user HTTP requests. *ProprietaryBundle* retrieves USI from the *USIBundle* and inserts this information in a proprietary format in the user HTTP requests. There are dependencies between these bundles since the *CCPPBundle* (respectively *ProprietaryBundle*) needs the USI bundle to retrieve USI information before inserting data.

3.3 TCP Connexion Management

Since programmable nodes intercept packets of HTTP requests sent by users and pass them to the OSGi framework that modify http requests for inserting USI, they have to manage the Acknowledgment (ACK) and Sequence (SEQ) TCP fields of the whole HTTP connection [17]. This is achieved by the module we have written, called *nfInterface*.

The *nfInterface* module is connected to the Linux *Netfilter* [15] in order to manage these TCP connections. *nfInterface* receives packets sent by *Netfilter*. If it receives an HTTP request, *nfInterface* forwards the packet to the right module registered for this connection (the CC/PP module or the proprietary module). If it receives a "Seq" or "Ack" then it modifies the fields Seq and Ack to the right values and forwards them. *nfInterface* dynamically configures *Netfilter* in order to let packets passing transparently through the router or to trigger them to the modules (if insertion is required).

4   Performance Tests

In order to compare our programmable node to a proxy, we have extended the open source Apache Proxy to insert user information in the CC/PP format.

4.1 Test Configuration

Figure 6 and the following table show the configuration of the performance tests. The network is an Ethernet 100 Mb LAN. Three machines were used.

The HTTP traffic generator, used for simulating clients, is a java program. The simulation tests have been done with successively 10, 25, 50, 75, 100 and 150 simultaneous clients with an interval of time set to 10 ms. Every client sends a HTTP request.

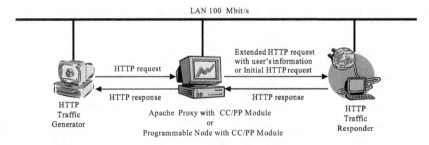

Fig. 6. Test Configuration

Role	Model	Processor	RAM	OS
HTTP Generator	Compaq Armada M700	Pentium III, 700Mhz	392 Mb	Windows 2000 Server
Proxy/Prog. Node	HP Omnibook 6100	Pentium III, 1 Ghz	256 Mb	Linux Debian 2.4.20
HTTP Responder	Compaq Armada M700	Pentium III, 1 Ghz	392 Mb	Linux Debian 2.4.17

The HTTP Responder is made of *servlets* within a web server. It is used for replying to client requests. It analyses the requests, retrieves the requested HTML file from the hard disk and replies to the client. The requested file is always the same.

The last machine is a proxy with CC/PP Module (in the case of tests on proxy) or the programmable node with the CC/PP Module. The same computer plays alternatively the role of the proxy or the role of the programmable node.

4.2 Test Results

We compare results of 5 tests (the first one is not represented on figure 6):

1. Direct: the clients connect directly to the Web Server.
2. Proxy with CC/PP: the clients connect to the Web Server through a proxy that inserts USI.
3. Proxy No Insertion: the clients connect to the Web Server through a proxy that checks in its cache if USI insertion is needed and forwards the request unchanged.
4. Programmable Node with CC/PP: the clients connect to the Web Server via the programmable node that inserts USI by the CC/PP Module.
5. Programmable Node No Insertion: the clients connect to the Web Server via the programmable node that only forwards the request. It is done at the kernel level after the *Netfilter* configuration.

Every test was performed 10 times and the average values are given in milliseconds in figure 7. The values represent the elapsed time between the request sent by the client and the reception of the response. The purpose is not to test how many requests per second the architecture supports but rather the time needed for inserting user session information into the requests at node level, in two different cases: with a programmable node and with a proxy. Likewise, we aim at measuring the overhead of the node architecture when no user information needs to be inserted in the requests.

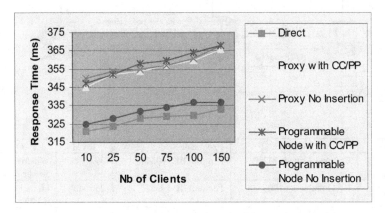

Fig. 7. Performance Comparison between Proxy and Programmable Node

The programmable node yields better performances than the proxy (around 10%) if no insertion is required as the packet is directly forwarded by *Netfilter* running at kernel level, and does not go up to the application. In this case, the response time is very close to the result obtained when using a direct connection.

The implementation of our programmable node (*CC/PP Module* with OSGI built upon Linux *Netfilter*) performs approximately as well as the extended Apache Proxy.

Finally, the delay for inserting USI into requests (around 30ms) is less than the average delay of ADSL networks (around 60ms) and is largely less than processing most of http requests and adapting the content at server side [18]. Moreover, it increases linearly and slowly when the number of simultaneous clients increases.

5   Conclusion

We have defined and implemented a new solution for inserting USI within requests in respect with formats expected by the service providers (CC/PP, proprietary) that can adapt their content and deliver personalized information.

The programmable node integrated within an ADSL access network enables the insertion of network information in requests (hint on user location, access network topology) whereas it is impossible if data was inserted in the user terminal.

Our architecture based on a programmable network performs better than a classical architecture on proxies because no extra routing is necessary for flows that do not need content adaptation. Moreover our programming node consumes less network and computation resources than a proxy. Typically, if only 20% of servers have subscribed to the USI insertion service, then all the programmable nodes will only process the flows on 20% of servers. In addition, the programmable node performs also 10% better locally thanks to the use of the *netfilter* and *ip_queue* mechanisms.

But since data are modified on the data path, one limitation occurs in the case of a secure connection. One solution consists of sharing the keys with the user and the web server as so to be able to decrypt and re-encrypt the data. Another limitation relies on the use of the IP address for finding the USI because it is not relevant in case of Network Address Translation. Our current studies are tackling these limitations.

References

1. «CC/PP Exchange protocol based on HTTP Extension Framework», W3C Recommendation http://www.w3.org/TR/NOTE-CCPPexchange; CC/PP :
   http://www.w3.org/Mobile/CCPP/
2. MPEG : http://mpeg.telecomitalialab.com/
3. Jigsaw : http://www.w3.org/Jigsaw
4. DICE : http://dice.ccpp.info
5. C. Papachristos, E. Markatos, "A CC/PP Aware Apache Web Server", 7th CabertNet Radicals Workshop, Bologna, Italy, 13-16 Oct 2002
6. Kari Pihkala, Mikko Honkala, and Petri Vuorimaa, "A Browser Framework for Hybrid XML Documents," Proc. of the 6th IASTED IMSA 2002, August 12-14, 2002, Kauai, Hawaii, USA. http://www.xsmiles.org
7. A. Held, S. Buchholz, A. Schill, "Modeling of Context Information for Pervasive Computing Applications", SCI 2002, Orlando, USA, 15-18 July 2002
8. J. Magalhaes, A. David, "An End-to-End Framework for Mobile Multimedia Applications", WTC-ISS 2002, Paris, France, 22-27 Sept 2002
9. ICAP : IETF, RFC 3507, April 2003 : http://www.ietf.org/rfc/rfc3507
10. OCP : IETF, Internet-Draft, May 2004 : http://www.ietf.org/internet-drafts/draft-ietf-opes-ocp-core-05.txt
11. Andrew T. Campbell, Herman G. De Meer, Michael E. Kounavis, Kazuho Miki, John B. Vicente, and Daniel Villela, "A Survey of Programmable Networks", ACM Computer Communications Review, April 1999
12. A. Lazar, "Programming Telecommunication Networks", IEEE Network, Septembre/Octobre 1997, pp. 8-18
13. A. Galis and al "A Flexible IP Active Networks Architecture", IWAN 2000, Tokyo, Japan, 16 – 18 Octobre 2000; FAIN: Future Active IP Network http://www.ist-fain.org
14. M. Solarski, M. Bossardt, T. Becker, "Component-Based Deployment and Management of Services in Active Networks", IWAN 2002, Zurich, Switzerland, Dec. 2002
15. ALAN : M. Fry, A. Ghosh, "Application level active networking", Computer Networks, 31 (7) (1999) pp. 655-667; http://dmir.it.uts.edu.au/projects/alan/
16. Jeffree : http://jeffree.objectweb.org/; OSGI : www.osgi.org
17. D.A. Kidston, "Transparent Communication Management in Wireless Networks", thesis presented at University Waterloo, Orlando, Canada, 1998
18. K. Yasuda, T. Asada, T. Hagino, "Effects and Performance of Content Negociation Based on CC/PP", Second conference, MDM 2001, Hong Kong, China, January 2001

Agents Technology Extended with Mobile Devices

Fábio Calhau, Lino Pereira, Paulo Costa, and Luís Botelho

"We, the Body and the Mind" Research Lab", ADETTI / ISCTE,
Avenida das Forças Armadas 1600-082 Lisboa, Portugal
{fabio.calhau,lino.pereira,paulo.costa,luis.botelho}@iscte.pt
http:\\adetti.iscte.pt

Abstract. This paper presents a framework that can be used for improving working conditions. We have extended intelligent agents technology for the Internet with cell phone technology. This extension allows the mobile worker to have access to the full power of server based computation using cheaper, smaller, mobile devices. The most demanding part of the computation is performed by agents running on Internet servers while cell phone computations are concerned only with the interface between end-users and server-based agents. Although we have focused only on Cell Phones, the same technology can be used with, Smart Phones and other mobile devices.

1 Introduction

Mobility has become the principal aspect for enterprises. Becoming mobile means being reachable anywhere, anytime, making the work more profitable. By combining mobility with agent technology the advantages of both technologies to create applications that were never thought to be available in a mobile scenario are achieved. This will bring an enormous advantage since it will contribute to the reduction of the necessary physical work space, the increase of enterprises' geographic coverage [9], and also contribute to the decrease of car traffic and consequently the improvement of environmental quality. With this technology, people can work while they travel, improving their comfort, their overall quality of life, and their productivity.

We have used a combination of mobility and agents technologies in a concrete multi-agent system that allows people to easily find restaurants of their preference and consequently, to book tables for their meals in these. This application has been developed by ADETTI's *We, the Body and the Mind* research lab in a partnership with Vodafone Portugal.

The paper describes the generic multi-agent system architecture and technology(Section 2), and details the mentioned application (Section 3). Section 4 compares our proposals with related work. Finally, Section 5 presents conclusions and future work.

2 Agent Technology Extended with Mobile Devices

This section presents the reference model for multi agent systems using the proposed extensions for mobility and describes adopted technological solutions. In our framework, cell phone programs are not seen as autonomous agents but as interfaces to existing agents running on Internet based servers. Each cell phone is associated to an agent running on an Internet server.

A. Karmouch, L. Korba, and E. Madeira (Eds.): MATA 2004, LNCS 3284, pp. 118–126, 2004.

2.1   The Mobile Solution for Agent Technology

Mobility is a necessity in our days. Many of the things we used to see in non mobile environments are now becoming available in mobile environments. Agent technology is not an exception. This paper presents an approach for the integration of mobility with agent technology. Because agent platforms are heavy and mobile devices do not possess the same computational power as a server, instead of using mobile devices as agent platforms, we have used them only as interfaces associated with agents running on Internet servers. With this, most of the computational effort is done by the server instead of the mobile device. This is the best solution for the integration of the two technologies, given the computational limitations of the current generation of mobile devices.

In our proposal, the only agents aware of the existence of mobile devices are those associated with the mobile interface. The other agents completely ignore their existence. This way, all agents in the application communicate with each other using a single kind of communication technology.

Using the power of agent computation associated with mobility, several new types of application can be developed. The architecture presented in this paper is an example of the power and flexibility of these types of applications since it represents a generic framework for developing several types of applications based on service discovery and execution. Agent technology provides flexibility and value added service composition to the user. Mobility allows the user to access this powerful structure in any place, while traveling or while going to work, improving reach ability and productivity.

Since one of the greatest advantages of agent technology is its modularity. New functionalities can be implemented very easily by just adding new agents that provide the new services. This modularity enables users to extend the functionalities available on their mobile devices just by upgrading or adding new interfaces to existing agents without ever worrying about the complexity of the agent network necessary to fulfill their demands.

2.2   System Architecture

The system backbone in the proposed architecture is a service providing agent network with personal assistance agents and basic service representatives. These are the end points of the agent network. Personal assistance agents provide personalized user access to the networked agent application. Service representative agents provide the agent interface that allows the integration of component services in the networked agent application. Finally the agent network between personal assistance agents and service representative agents creates all sorts of value added services for people from the basic component services. These may range from simple information agents such as yellow pages agents, to service brokers, negotiators, reputation agents, and service composition planning agents.

The fundamental idea is the association of mobile devices such as cell phones with Internet agents. Since cell phones and other mobile equipment are used by the end-user, the Internet agents to whom they are associated are personal assistance agents and service representative agents (Fig. 1).

The tight association of terminal mobile devices with personal assistance and service representative agents allow users (consumers and producers) to have access to

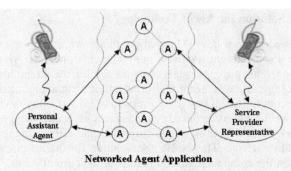

Networked Agent Application

Fig. 1. Reference Architecture

the full computational power of networked agent applications using small less power-ful devices. Most of the computation is provided by the agents to whom they are associated and by the other agents in the network. Equally important, this type of organization allows other agents in the network to forget about the existence of mobile equipment with specific requirements. Mobile equipment programs are hidden by the agents to which they are associated from the other agents in the network. Therefore, agent interaction works exactly as if no mobile equipment were integrated; only a single interface is used. The interaction with the mobile equipment is completely handled by the specific agents associated with that kind of interface device.

2.3 Adopted Technological Solutions

This sub-section presents the technological solutions we have adopted to keep the mobile device programs as simple and as small as possible, to signal mobile device users that they should activate the interface programs on their mobile equipment, and for the communication between mobile devices and associated Internet agents.

Bootstrapping and Configuration. In order to keep the mobile equipment computational requirements to a minimum, the programs running on the mobile equipment are as simple and as small as possible. At bootstrap, they request the necessary information from the Internet agents to whom they are associated in order to proceed. The requested information consists mostly of configuration data. We have used the Java Micro Edition to write the programs in the mobile devices. The communication between mobile devices and associated Internet agents uses serialized Java objects over the HTTP protocol.

Since more than one mobile device associated agent may be running on the same computer, we use a database containing the port of the internet agent to whom the mobile device is associated. All that is required is for the mobile device interface program to use its unique identifier to ask the agent port from the database in the Internet based computer. This is a very flexible process coping with possible changes of the ports of the Internet agents. Even if the Internet agent is temporarily disconnected, when it resumes its operation and its port is settled, it registers the port in the database. This way, mobile devices will always have access to the actual ports of their associated Internet agents.

Once the port is acquired, the mobile device program sets the communication channel with its agent so that it can ask for and send information to the agent.

Short Message Service. Using currently available technology for cell phones, it is impossible to trigger the interface program on the side of the mobile device when information is available for being processed. In order to overcome this difficulty, we use SMS messages to signal mobile device users that they should activate the interface program on their devices so that the available information is processed. For instance, when there is information in the personal assistance agent that should be displayed in the user cell phone, the personal assistance agent sends a SMS message to the cell phone signaling the user that the interface program should be executed.

Cell Phone-Agent Communication Language. We have developed a domain-independent communication language for the interaction between the mobile device interface program and the associated Internet agent. This language includes a set of communicative acts including requests, queries and information messages.

3   Application Description

This section describes the application we have developed in which the proposed framework has been tested. In the implemented application, users find restaurants of their preference using their cell phone interface with the networked agent application running on the Internet. Once the restaurant is found, users may book a table for their meals. Table booking is done through the communication between the restaurant representative agent and the restaurant cell phone.

The implemented system is not a complex and sophisticated system but it is fully implemented and its main goal is to be used as a proof of concept for the propose approach.

3.1   System Architecture and Functionality

In the restaurant table booking application, there are personal assistance agents, an intermediate agent network, and restaurant representative agents. Each user has its own personal assistance agent, and each restaurant has its own restaurant representative agent. The intermediate agent network is formed by a single information agent containing summarized information about all existing restaurants and the identifications of their representatives. The personal assistance agent accepts restaurant preferences and table booking requests from the user, through his or her cell phone interface, and interacts with the intermediate agents' network to discover a restaurant satisfying the user preferences. Once the desired restaurant and its representative agent have been found, the personal assistance agent directly sends the table booking request to the restaurant representative agent. By turn, the responsible person in the restaurant uses the mobile interface to negotiate the table booking, and may accept the required booking or suggest changes such as the hour of the meal, two tables instead of just one, or one table as specified but only in the smoking area. The acceptance or the suggested changes are sent to the restaurant representative agent, which sends them to the personal assistance agent. The acceptance notification or the suggested changes are then presented to the user through the cell phone interface. The user just has to accept or decline the possible changes. If the user does not accept the suggested changes, he or she may initiate another restaurant discovery process to make a new booking request.

If desired, the interaction between users or restaurants and the agent application can be done through a web page instead of the cell phone interface. This possibility is not further explained in this paper since its main focus is the use of mobile device interfaces.

Besides the described restaurant discovery and table booking operations, the implemented application allows other operations. Each time a restaurant is registered data has to be filled by the restaurant representative. A restaurant may modify its representative agent data. Finally, representative agents must update the summarized information regarding its restaurant in the intermediate restaurant information agent. Fig. 2 represents the table booking protocol described above.

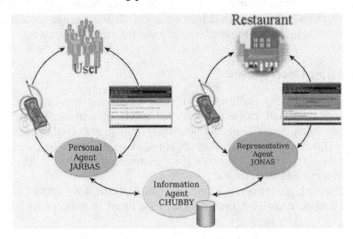

Fig. 2. Table Booking Interaction Protocol

When the personal assistant agent (PAA) sends a table request to the restaurant representative agent (RRA), it may accept the table request specified conditions, it may reject the request altogether, and it may also suggest changes to the specified conditions.

If the RRA accepts the specified table request, the client is automatically bond to the request. If the RRA suggests modifications to the original request the client cannot suggest counter-modifications. The client may only accept or refuses the suggested changes.

Finally, if the table booking request is confirmed, the RRA informs the PAA of the assigned reservation number.

The protocol depicted in Fig. 3 governs the interaction between the RRA (and possibly the associated cell phone) and the PAA (and possibly the associated cell phone).

Since it was not possible to automatically activate the interface program in the restaurant cell phone when a message is received, the restaurant representative agent sends a SMS message to the restaurant cell phone informing the restaurant manager that a reservation request is ready for being processed and thus the cell phone interface application should be launched.

When booking a table, there is mandatory and optional information accompanying the table booking request message. Mandatory information includes preferred meal hour, number of people, and the name of the person responsible for the reservation. Optional Information includes smoking / non-smoking preferences, table location preferences, and special features specifications (e.g., facilities for the disabled such as wheel chair facility).

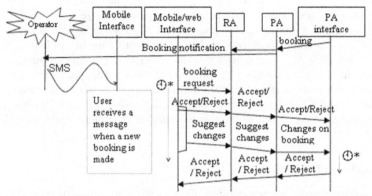

* - The response to the booking request and the response for the suggested changes are time limited. After that time if there is no response the system assumes that it is negative

Fig. 3. UML Interaction Protocol

The booking request sent to the restaurant cell phone has five states, which can be visualized on the cell phone screen.

1. "Not answered", means the booking request is not answered or visualized by the restaurant manager.
2. "Visualized", means that the restaurant manager has visualized the request but has not sent the reply (rejected, accepted, or suggested changes).
3. "Pending", means that the confirmation message of the booking or the Suggested changes are hanging, waiting to be accepted or rejected by the client.
4. "Rejected", means the client has rejected the received booking confirmation or the change suggestion for the original booking.
5. "Accepted", indicates that the client has confirmed the booking or accepted the change suggestions.

3.2 Agent-Mobile Devices Interaction

As referred above, we have developed a domain independent communication language for the communication between mobile devices and associated Internet agents. This communication is based on serialized java objects that are sent through http requests. This is used in all operations that require sending information from the mobile device to the associated agent or the other way around. For this to happen both the mobile device and the associated agent must be aware of the types of objects that can be sent.

The use of serialized java objects is preferred because less information is sent, and although it may seem that the communication will be dependent of using JAVA it is not quite so. Since there is no serialization in JAVA Micro Edition, we had do develop our own serialization classes and, by doing that, we ensured that the serialization process is language independent. Each JAVA object is simplified to its most simple parts, which are serialized and then aggregated to form the final result of the serialization. Since only the simple object parts are transformed into bytes, and since this simple data objects are common in every object oriented language, it is possible to desserialize the object using a different programming language.

When talking about mobile devices the amount of information sent is very important because the communication costs are high, less information means less cost.

Another important factor to consider when referring to mobile devices is bandwidth availability. Since the device has limited bandwidth, our application only sends information to the associated agent when it is necessary (i.e. when changing the restaurant data the application only sends the new data when the user finishes all the changes he wants to make). By doing this the number of connections is significantly reduced.

3.3 Agent-Agent Interaction

Unlike the connection between the mobile devices and the associated agents, the connection between the agents is fixed, allowing a different kind of communication. Inter-agent communication uses ACL and SL communication and content languages. The ACL and SL have been developed by FIPA and are increasingly used in agent communications [6],

When an agent associated with a mobile device receives a request from the device it has two options. It can either solve the problem by itself or it can send an ACL/SL request message to another agent to solve the problem, receive the response from that agent and then send the response to the mobile device. The interaction between agents involves more communication when making a booking request, which requires all the application agents to participate. When making the booking request several ACL/SL messages are sent, asking for the list of restaurants satisfying the user search criteria, or consulting detailed information about the selected restaurant, and booking the table. The booking request is initiated by the personal agent, which sends an ACL/SL message to the representative agent associated with the selected restaurant .

3.4 Implementation Technology

We have used the JADE agent platform [1], which is a FIPA compliant agent platform [6]. We have used FIPA ACL [7] and Extended FIPA SL [8][2] as the agent communication and content languages over the HTTP protocol. We have used serialized JAVA objects over the HTTP protocol for the communication between cell phones and Internet agents. Finally, we have used JAVA for the Internet agents' implementation and JAVA Micro Edition for the cell phone interface program implementation.

4 Related Works

Mobility is a very important factor[5]. Using agents extended with mobile devices, we associate the interesting computational power, flexibility and autonomy of agents with the ubiquity of mobile devices.

In the MAP Agent platform [12], mobile users are supported through the migration of agents from host to host of the network, being possible to sleep and awake agents.

In order to overcome the comparatively little computational power of mobile devices in the Ruse system [11], the mobile device acts only as a keyboard and display, the computation being done in remote applications. This is exactly the same approach we have taken in the described system. On the other hand, the Ruse system does not take advantage of the agents' architecture, because it just does not use it.

In Ruse, popup boxes and scrollbars where used to fit the information in the small screen space. We have used scrollbars, optimized menus, and we have especially tried to reduce the amount of displayed information to the indispensable.

Another reason why it is important to reduce the amount of information is the limited bandwidth available to smart phones and cell phones [15].

In the MOVE project [4] a scenario is presented where a website is accessed by the mobile client to search for a hotel. In this application a self-interface cell phone is used to avoid problems with page presentation and to minimize the user interactions (e.g. scrolling, box selection, etc), since walking through the information in a cell phone is a lot more laborious than in a laptop or in a desktop.

In the MOVE project, as in our system, user requests are sent to the agent through HTTP.

There are some search engines for cell phones as Vodafone Portugal service *"perto de mim* [close to me]*"* [13] where a place (like a bar or restaurant) close to you is searched, or as WithAir Mobile Search Engine [10], where keyword predictive navigation and regional information search is used. With our model, we go further than simple searching. It is possible to make reservations, interact in the process with the restaurant through a defined message protocol, register our own restaurant, and authenticate the restaurant account through the insertion of login/password.

5 Conclusions and Future Work

In this paper we present a proposal to extend traditional agents technology with mobile devices technology. The main contribution of the proposal consists of avoiding overloading mobile devices with heavy computational processes. This goal was achieved by the tight association between personal assistance agents or service representative agents and their mobile device applications. In this framework, mobile devices play the role of mere interfaces to the Internet based agents. Most of the computations are performed by the agents to whom they are associated and by the other agents in the network with which they interact.

The technology concept was proved through the implementation of a concrete application in which the proposed framework was successfully used.

In the near future we intend to use the developed technology for different scenarios such as virtual auctions and virtual enterprises' applications. The exploration of other types of mobile devices such as pocket PCs and PDA's with capability to make phone calls (usually called smartphones) will also be considered.

Maybe more importantly, we will improve the complexity and sophistication of the agent layer between the service representative agents and the user personal assistance agents. This layer will be extended with powerful brokering capabilities [3] developed in our group during the Agentcities project [14] and dynamic context-dependent service composition planning capabilities to be created in the forthcoming European IST project CASCOM.

Finally, we will work on the improvement of the personal assistance agent with the aim of making it more autonomous. One of the obvious directions is the possibility to learn user preferences through user feedback and also through collaborative filtering.

Although the implemented system is a simple testbed, it clearly proves the concept that, using current mobile computing technology and using mobile devices as mere interface Internet agents, is an adequate approach to enable mobile device users to have access to agent technology as a way of using homogeneous communication technology through out the system for agent interaction.

References

1. Bellifemine, F; Poggi, A.; and Rimassa, G. "JADE - A FIPA-compliant agent framework". CSELT internal technical report. Partially published in Proceedings of PAAM'99, 1999; pp.97-108.
2. Botelho, L.M.; Antunes, N.; Ebrahim, M.; and Ramos, P. "Greeks and Trojans Together". Proceedings of the Workshop "Ontologies in Agent Systems" of the Autonomous Agents and Multi Agent Systems Conference (AAMAS 2002), 2002.
3. Botelho, L.M.; Mendes, H.; Figueiredo, P.; and Marinheiro, R. "Send Fredo off to do this, send Fredo off to do that". Proc, of the International Workshop on Cooperative Information Agents (CIA2003), p152-159, 2003
4. Carrega, D.; Fournier, E.; Hope, S.; Muyal, H. "Delivering Integrated Voice and Data Services for Mobile Customers with the MOVE Middleware Architecture", 1999
5. Chlamtac, Imrich; Redi, Jason; "Mobile Computing: Challenges and Potential"; The University of Texas at Dallas and Boston University. Encyclopedia of Computer Science, 4th Edition, International Thomson Publishing, 1998.
6. Foundation for Intelligent Physical Agents. "FIPA Agent Management Specification". Document SC00023J, 2002. http://www.fipa.org/specs/fipa00023/SC00023J.html
7. Foundation for Intelligent Physical Agents. "FIPA Communicative Act Library Specification". Document SC00037J, 2002.
http://www.fipa.org/specs/fipa00037/SC00037J.html
8. Foundation for Intelligent Physical Agents. "FIPA SL Content Language Specification". Document SC00008I, 2002. http://www.fipa.org/specs/fipa00008/SC00008I.html
9. Gateway Group, Offshore Development. 2003.
http://www.gatewaytechnolabs.com/en/offshore/advgateway.asp?lid=222
10. Kawai, H.; Akamine, S.; Kida, K.; Matsuda, K.; Fukushima, T. "Development and Evaluation of the WithAir Mobile Search Engine", 2002.
http://www2002.org/CDROM/poster/102.pdf
11. Landay, James A.; Kaufmann, Todd R.; "User Interface Issues in Mobile Computing"; School of Computer Science - Carnegie Mellon University. Appeared in the Proceedings of the Fourth Workshop on Workstation Operating Systems, Napa, CA, October 1993.
12. Tomarchio, Orazio; Vita, Lorenzo; Puliafito, Antonio; "Normadic users' support in the MAP agent platform" Dipartimento di Ingegneria Informatica e Telecomucazioni, Università di Catania and Dipartimento di matematica, Università di Messina, 2000.
13. Vodafone, "perto de mim". A portuguese mobile phone service, 2003.
http://www.vodafone.pt/main/funandinfo/localizar/Pertodemim/default.htm
14. Willmott, S.; Dale, J.; Burg, B.; Charlton, P; and O'Brien, P. 2001. "Agentcities: a world-wide open agent network". Agentlink News, 8:13-15
15. Wooldridge, Michael; Ciancarini Paolo; "Agent-Oriented Software Engineering"; Dept of Computer Science, University of Liverpool and Dipartimento di Scienze dell'Informazione, University of Bologna. Handbook of Software Engineering and Knowledge Engineering Vol. 0, No. 0 (1999)

Agent Migration as an Optional Service in an Extendable Agent Toolkit Architecture

Peter Braun[1], Ingo Müller[1],
Sven Geisenhainer[3], Volkmar Schau[2], and Wilhelm Rossak[2]

[1] Swinburne University of Technology, School of Information Science
Hawthorn Victoria 3122, Australia
{pbraun,imueller}@it.swin.edu.au
[2] Friedrich Schiller University Jena, Computer Science Department
Ernst-Abbe-Platz 2, 07743 Jena, Germany
{schau,rossak}@informatik.uni-jena.de
[3] University of Applied Sciences, Department of Applied Computer Science
99013 Erfurt, Germany
geisenhainer@fh-erfurt.de

Abstract. In this paper we report on first experiences with a new software architecture for agent toolkits. Agent toolkits mainly consist of a software system that defines an *agency*, which is responsible to host software agents. Most architectures developed so far already define a large set of services, for example for agent migration, communication, and tracking. We propose to employ a kernel-based approach, where the kernel only provides fundamental concepts and functions common in all toolkits and abstracts from any of these services. We were able to show that in particular agent migration can be implemented as an optional service. We believe that this architecture is a useful foundation for research on agent-related topics as it allows research groups to implement their own results as a service which can be used by other groups running an agent system based on the same architecture.

1 Introduction

The interest in mobile agents as a new design paradigm for distributed systems seems to have dwindled over the last years. The number of research groups working on mobile agent related topics is becoming smaller, some conferences and workshops cease to exist or are aligned with more general topics regarding mobility of code.

It is argued that mobile agents were not able to satisfy some of the main expectations, for example regarding their ability to reduce network traffic overhead. Vigna [1] states that mobile agents are very expensive and provide worse performance in the general case than other design paradigms, as for example remote procedure call or remote evaluation. Compare Vigna's early work regarding network load of different design paradigms [2] and a discussion of his approach in [3]. He also points to security problems, which are unlikely to be solved completely and will, therefore, impede the acceptance of mobile agents. Other authors try to get to the bottom of this problem and analyze whether

A. Karmouch, L. Korba, and E. Madeira (Eds.): MATA 2004, LNCS 3284, pp. 127–136, 2004.
© Springer-Verlag Berlin Heidelberg 2004

mistakes of the research community have caused the current disappointing situation. For example, Roth [4] questions Java to be the best programming language to cope with unresolved security problems. Johansen [5] points out that far too many groups have focused on the development of yet another prototype of a mobile agent toolkit with only small contributions to the fundamental research questions. In fact, the current situation is characterized by a few tens toolkits.

We agree with Johansen about the high number of research prototypes. However, some research groups were obliged to develop their own prototype because of the lack of any reference architecture for agent toolkits. We believe that many toolkit prototypes were tailored to specific research topics, for example agent communication, security, tracking, or migration protocols. Only to name two examples, we mention Semoa [6] as a system with a very strong focus on security issues and our first implementation of Tracy [7] which was designed around early ideas regarding high-performance migration protocols. At first, agent communication was not in the focus of neither of these systems – but added later in both of them. Other groups focused on agent tracking and communication problems, e.g. [8] but their algorithms are not adopted in other systems. We see these isolated islands of research as another obstacle for the acceptance of mobile agents as there is no single agent toolkit available that provides at least an almost up-to-date set of features.

Our thesis is that the research community would benefit from the possibility to exchange research results in form of definite software components. Publication of research results in form of algorithms and protocols could be complemented by implementations, allowing other groups to use them immediately. This would also encourage a fair quantitative comparison of different approaches, for example different protocols for agent migration or tracking. We do not propose a new standard yet but we propose a way towards a standard architecture.

As a very first step towards such a framework, we report in this paper on first experiences with our software architecture for agent toolkits that we are developing as a joint project between Swinburne University and the University of Jena[1]. The main goal of this project is to develop an agent toolkit where the migration component is *not* essential part of the whole design but can be plugged into the system later. Hence, we have not designed a *mobile* agent toolkit but a general and extendable multi-agent toolkit.

In this paper, we provide two contributions:

- We define a new architecture for agencies which consists of a three-layered design. This architecture makes intensive use of the concept of a *kernel* and *core service* components (Chapter 2).
- We report on first experiences in developing a core service for agent migration (Chapter 4). This core service adopts an independent software component named Kalong [3] that was developed without regard to any specific Java-based mobile agent toolkit. We report on how Kalong was adapted to work as core service within our software architecture.

---

[1] See **www.mobile-agents.org** for more information.

2   The Tracy Architecture

As motivated in the introduction, we want to address the possibility to exchange research results between research projects in form of software components. Therefore, we propose to split an agency into a single *kernel* and several additional software components, where each component provides a single service. The resulting model for an agency has, therefore, a layered design (compare Fig. 1), where the kernel can be seen as lowest layer. On top of the kernel, all service components form the middle layer. Finally, agents are executed as part of the agency and form the topmost layer.

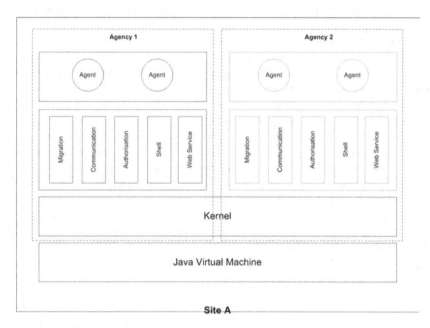

Fig. 1. Block diagram of the Tracy software architecture.

2.1   Kernel

The kernel is responsible to manage service components and agents. It provides a secure environment for running agents, maintains a directory of agents currently residing at this site, defines and monitors an agent's life-cycle and defines a basic interaction model between services and agents. The kernel provides means to group services and agents in logical units, comparable to the concept of *agencies* or places in other toolkits, which are separated from each other using different Java class loaders for each unit. Agents and services can only access those services that are located in the same logical unit. Every agency has a globally unique name [9]. The kernel provides an interface for services that defines methods to start and stop agents and new service components and to retrieve information about them. All these functions are guarded by Java permissions, which makes it possible to prohibit agents or service to access any of these methods.

2.2   Services

On top of the kernel there are several *core service components* that can be plugged into an agency (even dynamically during runtime). Each service component provides a specific service (which is identified by a *service name*) and extends the functionality of the agency. It bears a unique *name*, which is used to unambiguously identify a service component, if necessary, for example when there are two components providing the same service. When a service component is started, it is loaded using a new class loader in order to separate it from other components and agents.

Service components can start and stop agents simply by calling the corresponding kernel methods, request a list of all agents currently residing at this agency and a list of all services. Our agency model also defines the reverse communication direction using the observer pattern. A component can register with the kernel to become notified in case of specific events. A description of the most important events follows in the next section.

Our architecture defines a loose coupling between service components among each other and between agents and components. Direct method calls are prohibited and replaced by so-called *context* objects, comparable to proxies. A service component must assure that each client (agent or another service) holds only a single context object in order to prevent denial of service attacks and to eliminate inconsistencies between different context objects. The main advantage of this concept is that clients do not hold a strong reference to a service, which makes it possible to invalidate a context object, if a client must not use a service any more and to even exchange a service during runtime without giving notice to the agent or other services.

As part of the Tracy project, we have already defined several core service components and correspondent interfaces for context objects. They range from very simple adapter plugins that provide agents access to its name and to the hosting agency, to complex services to manage logical networks of agencies. We refer to [9] for a description of the most important core services.

2.3   Agents

In our model, each agent must have a globally unique name which must be representable as a *String* object. For details concerning agent names, we refer to [9]. Agents are represented as objects of type *Runnable*, i.e. they must provide at least a single public method *run*, which serves as central starting point. The consequence of agents as *Runnables* is of course, that an agent is unaware of itself and its environment. It does know neither its name nor its hosting agency and must use services to obtain these information.

The life-cycle of an agent actually consists only of two states. The first one is *Running* which is characterized by assigning a thread to this agent that executes agent's *run* method. After this method has terminated, the agent might switch to state *Waiting* where no thread is assigned to this agent or the agent's thread is waiting to become activated again. Thus, the agent is now only a passive object that waits to become activated again, for example waiting for a message or another external signal or event. Details about the life-cycle will be presented in the following section, where we introduce the basic functions of an agency.

If an agent wants to communicate to a service, it must request its context object by invoking a static method *getContext* which is provided by class *Context* (which is defined as part of the kernel). Consider the following example:

```
public class Agent implements Runnable
{
  public void run()
  {
    IAgentMessageContext cxt;
    cxt = (IAgentMessageContext)Context.getContext("message");

    cxt.sendMessage( ... );
  }
}
```

The agent requests a context object of a service that has registered under service name *message* and uses it to send a message. We omit to discuss problems that arise from multiple components providing the same service.

Method *getContext* first identifies the agent that has requested a context by determining the current thread (the kernel maintains a directory for this). Second, the kernel selects the component that provides service *message* and requests an agent context object, which is then returned to the agent. If the agent requests a context object from this service component for the first time, it is created. In the other case, the component must return the same object as before. In [9] we describe how we solved the following two problems: (a) if there is no service component providing a service under the given name, then class *IAgentMessageContext* does not exist, which must not result in an error; (b) if the service registered under the given name *message* does not return a context object that is assignable to variable *cxt*, the agent must be able to react on this situation.

3   The Kalong Mobility Model

In the following two sections, we will report on the integration of an already existing software component for agent mobility, named Kalong, into the Tracy architecture. The migration component was developed independently of the Tracy architecture and is specified in [3]. We start with a very short introduction into the basic concepts of Kalong.

The main difference of Kalong as compared to other mobility models is that Kalong provides a flexible and fine-grained migration protocol, which leads to a higher migration performance of mobile agents and to a flexible implementation of security protocols. Current mobility models only offer a single *migration strategy*. For example, in Grasshopper [10] the agent migrates only with its data but without any code, which is dynamically loaded on demand. Other systems always transmit the agent as a package of code and data to the next destination agency. In [11] it was proofed that none of these simple migration strategies leads to an optimized network load and transmission time and proposed in the thesis that mobile agents should be able to adapt their migration strategies according to specific environmental parameters, as for example, the code size of each class, the probability that a class is used at the next destination, network bandwidth and latency, etc.

Therefore, Kalong defines a virtual machine for agent migration with a small set of methods to fully conduct the migration process by the agent resp. by the agent programmer. A program for this virtual machine is called *migration strategy* and about a dozen migration strategies have already been implemented. The simplest ones imitate the migration techniques of Aglets and Grasshopper and the most sophisticated ones take several parameters into account, e.g. code execution probability, which is determined by static program analysis and network quality information. In [3] first results of several experiments are presented, where mobile agents migrate in wide-area networks using Kalong and need about 30% to 50% less execution time for a complete round-trip. Also compare [12] for more results on migration optimization.

The Kalong component defines hot spots within the migration protocol, where each message that is sent or received via network is processed by a set of so-called *protocol extensions*. Every protocol extension can modify network messages, e.g. compress, sign, or encrypt it. In [3] first protocol extensions were presented for agent authentication, code signing, and protecting data items against illicit tampering.

4   Integration of Kalong into the Tracy Architecture

Kalong was designed to work with all Java-based mobile agent toolkits where mobile agents are objects are assignable to type *Serializable*. To integrate Kalong as a service component it was only necessary to develop an adapter class. In this section we will explain how kernel, services, and agents interact with each other. We will describe the basic functions according to the agent's life-cycle with regard to the integration of Kalong into the Tracy architecture.

4.1   Registering an Agent

Registering an agent can be done by services in two ways. In the first case, an agent (as Java object) has not been instantiated yet. To register an agent, a nick name, the name of the agent's main class and a URL where the agent's classes can be found must be specified. The agent object is instantiated and a full agent name is computed. In the second case, the agent has already been instantiated, e.g. by a service component, and must now be registered with the kernel. This function is used to start agents that were received by the migration component. In this case the agent already has a full name as it was transmitted as part of the migration protocol. In both cases, the agent is finally enrolled with the agent directory and then started (explained below).

Before an agent is registered, all services are informed that have been registered a listener for this event. Each service can access all information about the agent and is now able to vote against registering. For example, a service that scans the agent's code for pattern of malicious behavior, is able to prevent registering and starting of this agent. If no service has voted against, the agent is registered with the local agent directory. Finally, a second event is fired, by which registered services are informed about the finalization of the registering process. For example, a graphical user interface can now update its list of agents. Finally, the agent switches to state *Running*, which is described in the next section.

4.2   Running an Agent

When an agent is started, its *run* method is invoked within an own thread of control. In our current implementation we use a thread pool. If an agent switches from state *Waiting* to state *Running*, a sleeping thread from the thread pool is activated to execute the agent. After agent's method *run* has terminated, this thread is responsible to carry out a voting protocol, which is described the next section. As agents must be strongly separated from each other, no two agent threads must be member of the same thread group.

While the agent is running, it can request context objects from services as shown above. If an agent wants to migrate, it must request its own context object from the migration service component and then define the name or a URL of the destination agency by invoking method *setDestination*. Optionally, the agent can also define a migration strategy that should be used for the next migration, for example only to migrate with the agent's main class and load all other classes dynamically on demand. This is done by invoking method *setMigrationStrategy*.

4.3   Termination of Agent's Main Method

After agent's method *run* has terminated, it is decided whether the agent should be killed (i.e. deleted from the agent directory and finally garbage collected) or remain as passive object. It is important to note that this decision is not only up to agents but is decided by the kernel resp. the service components. The *voting protocol* that is proposed for this works as follows: The kernel asks all service components sequentially, about the local status of the agent. A component might announce that it wants the agent to be immediately restarted again, or to continue to live without restart, or raise no objection to kill the agent. The migration component will always answer that it does not object to kill the agent.

If there is at least one service component that wants the agent to be restarted, then agent's method *run* is invoked immediately again. If no service component wants the agent to be restarted, but there is at least a single one that wants the agent to continue to live, then the agent's thread might terminate or wait and the agent continues to live as passive object waiting to become started again. If no component raises an objection to kill the agent, the agent is removed from the agency and is eventually garbage collected.

4.4   Agent Termination

Before an agent is removed from the agent directory, all registered observers are notified about this event and they can perform some final clearance. This notification process is implemented as a transaction using a two-phase commit protocol. In the first phase, each service component is preparing to delete the agent's context object. Only if all service components are ready to delete the agent's context then the transaction is finalized. Otherwise, if any component raises an exception, the transaction is rolled back and the agent is re-started again.

During the first phase of the two-phase commit protocol, the migration component starts the migration process, if the agent has defined a migration destination in its context object. It uses the information stored in the agent's context object in order to open a network connection to the migration destination. After that, the agent's code and data are sent to the destination agency. However, during this first phase of the protocol, the migration process is not finalized and the network connection between sender and receiver agency is not closed. In case of any error during the migration process, this service throws an exception.

When the transaction is committed, the migration component sends a command to the destination which finalizes the migration process. Otherwise, in case of an error during the first phase of the protocol, a different command is sent to roll back the whole migration process at the destination agency.

5   Conclusions and Outlook

The main motivation for the work presented in this paper was the lack of any widely accepted implementation of a mobile agent toolkit that can be used by researchers to implement and test their own research results. Our thesis is that research on mobile agents might benefit from our kernel-based approach, where we only define basic concepts and functions common to all toolkits. Core services, e.g. agent migration, communication, management of logical agency networks, and parts of security issues are implemented as software components. All research groups are appealed for contributing to our idea by implementing their own research results as plugins for Tracy. In this paper we reported on work to integrate an already existing software component for agent mobility, named Kalong, as core service in our Tracy architecture.

We see as major weakness of the current approach a different programming style in case of migration errors. As the migration process is only started when the agent's main thread terminates, the only way to inform an agent about migration error is to re-start it on the same host. In the current approach, the agent must request an error code from its context object in order to determine whether the last migration was not successful. One of our next steps, besides developing more core services to proof our concept, is in particular to integrate another mobility model as a second migration component and to let agents decide dynamically which model to use for the next migration.

In our opinion, our Tracy approach differs from already existing architectures for mobile agent toolkits in the following aspects: Current models for agencies [10, 13] include design decisions for several core services already. We see as major drawback of such an agency model that it creates many dependences between actually independent services. In fact, our model abstracts from these services and in contrast attempts to move as many functional requirements of a mobile agent toolkit into such services. We mention two mobile agent toolkits as examples for kernel-based approaches, namely JavaSeal [14] and MobileSpaces [15]. In both toolkits a kernel is defined comprising of core functionality and additional basic services. In JavaSeal these services are migration, communication, and security - in MobileSpaces it is mainly migration, as services are provided by mobile agents in this toolkit. Our approach goes a step further by defining core services such as migration and communication as exchangeable components that are not part of the kernel, but where services are clearly distinguished from agents.

Finally, we mention Semoa [6] as an example of another extendable toolkit. Agents are also represented as *Runnables* in Semoa and the concept to decouple agents and services using context objects is comparable to our approach. Agents offer application-specific services by registering a service object with the single *environment*. We see as main difference to our approach that Semoa handles application-specific services and the two *core services* for agent migration and communication differently. Whereas the first class of services can be plugged into the system during runtime, core services seem to be strongly coupled into the design of the whole toolkit.

References

1. Vigna, G.: Mobile agents: Ten reasons for failure (panel). [16] 298–299
2. Vigna, G.: Mobile Code Technologies, Paradigms, and Applications. PhD thesis, Politecnico di Milano (1998)
3. Braun, P.: The Migration Process of Mobile Agents – Implementation, Classification, and Optimization. PhD thesis, Friedrich Schiller University Jena (Germany), Computer Science Department (2003)
4. Roth, V.: Obstacles to the adoption of mobile agents (panel). [16] 296–297
5. Johansen, D.: Mobile agents: Right concept, wrong approach (panel). [16] 300–301
6. Roth, V., Jalali, M.: Concepts and architecture of a security-centric mobile agent server. In: Proceedings of the Fifth International Symposium on Autonomous Decentralized Systems (ISADS 2001), Dallas, (USA), March 2001), Los Alamitos, CA, IEEE Computer Society Press (2001) 435–442

7. Braun, P., Eismann, J., Erfurth, C., Rossak, W.: Tracy – A Prototype of an Architected Middleware to Support Mobile Agents. In: Proceedings of the 8th Annual IEEE Conference and Workshop on the Engineering of Computer Based Systems (ECBS), Washington D.C. (USA), April 2001, Los Alamitos, CA, IEEE Computer Society Press (2001) 255–260

8. Moreau, L.: A Fault-Tolerant Directory Service for Mobile Agents based on Forwarding Pointers. In: The 17th ACM Symposium on Applied Computing (SAC '2002) – Track on Agents, Interactions, Mobility and Systems, Madrid, Spain (2002) 93–100

9. Braun, P., Müller, I., Geisenhainer, S., Schau, V., Rossak, W.: A service-oriented software architecture for mobile agent toolkits. In: Proceedings of the 11th Annual Conference and Workshop on the Engineering of Computer-based Systems (ECBS-2004), Workshop on Security, Interoperability, and Applications (SIAMAS), Brno (Czech Republic), May 2004, IEEE Computer Society Press (2004) 550–556

10. Bäumer, C., Breugst, M., Choy, S., Magedanz, T.: Grasshopper – A universal agent platform based on OMG MASIF and FIPA standards. In Karmouch, A., Impey, R., eds.: Mobile Agents for Telecommunication Applications, Proceedings of the First International Workshop (MATA 1999), Ottawa (Canada), October 1999, Teaneck, NJ, World Scientific Pub. (1999) 1–18

11. Braun, P., Erfurth, C., Rossak, W.: Performance Evaluation of Various Migration Strategies for Mobile Agents. In Killat, U., Lamersdorf, W., eds.: Fachtagung Kommunikation in verteilten Systemen (KiVS 2001), Hamburg (Germany), February 2001. Informatik aktuell, Springer-Verlag (2001) 315–324

12. Erfurth, C., Döhler, A., Rossak, W.: A first look at the performance of autonomous mobile agents in dynamic networks. In: Proceedings of the 37th Annual Hawaii International Conference on System Sciences (HICSS'04), Big Island (Hawaii), January 2004. (2004) Available online.

13. Hammer, D.K., Aerts, A.T.M.: Mobile Agent Architectures: What are the Design Issues? In: Proceedings International Conference and Workshop on Engineering of Computer-Based Systems (ECBS'98), Maale Hachamisha (Israel), March/April 1998, Los Alamitos, CA, IEEE Computer Society Press (1998) 272–280

14. Bryce, C., Vitek, J.: The JavaSeal mobile agent kernel. In Milojicic, D.S., ed.: Proceedings of the First International Symposium on Agent Systems and Applications (ASA'99)/Third International Symposium on Mobile Agents (MA'99), Palm Springs (USA), October 1999, Los Alamitos, CA, IEEE Computer Society Press (1999)

15. Satoh, I.: An architecture for next generation mobile agent infrastructure. In: Proceedings of International Symposium on Multi-Agent and Mobile Agents in Virtual Organizations and E-Commerce (MAMA'2000). (2000) 281–287

16. Joshi, A., Lei, H., eds.: IEEE International Conference on Mobile Data Management (MDM'04), Berkeley (USA), January 2004, IEEE Computer Society Press (2004)

Remote Database Administration in Mobile Computational Environments

Fernando Siqueira and Angelo Brayner

University of Fortaleza (UNIFOR), Av. Washington Soares, 1321
60811-341 Fortaleza, Ceara, Brazil
fsiqueira@edu.unifor.br, brayner@unifor.br

Abstract. This paper presents the architecture and functional characteristics of MDBA (Mobile Data Base Administrator), a context-aware tool for remote data base administration that is executed in mobile devices. The MDBA enables database administrators (DBAs) to perform their tasks by automatically identifying databases and the wireless communication structure of a given mobile computational environment. The proposed tool has properties which integrate features of mobile computation pervasive computation paradigms. The MDBA introduces the notion of remote database administration, which is supported by a new computational paradigm, denoted ubiquitous computation. Therefore, the MDBA tool provides database administration services anywhere and anytime. Furthermore, the MDBA enables DBAs to manage databases residing in mobile hosts or fixed hosts. The proposed tool has been developed based on the J2ME technology.

Keywords: database administration, mobile computing, pervasive computing

1 Introduction

The database technology has already been consolidated as efficient data management tool. Modern companies require efficient strategies for administration and management of database systems (DBS). The database administrator (DBA) is responsible for assuring the complete functioning of database systems, keeping them always functioning (to guarantee a great data availability) and with a performance adequate to the company's needs. For an efficient database (DB) administration, it is important to use tools that provide fast, safe and immediate execution of tasks.

Many database management systems' manufacturers make efficient administration tools available, when executed in a computer with fixed address in a network. In other words, such tools have to be previously configured for computer networks, where some nodes in those networks are computers in which databases systems reside. However, these tools become inefficient when any problem happens in the DBS and the DBA is out of the company, but the problem has to be solved immediately. A solution for this problem is to allow remote administration of the DBs through mobile computational technology support.

By means of mobile computation technology, users carrying portable devices are able to access services provided through a wireless communication infrastructure, regardless of their physical location or movement patterns. In this new scenario, a mobile computer can change its physical location constantly and, at the same time, keep functioning as distributed environment component. Therefore, although a mobile computer does not present fixed location in a network, it can access and make resources available in a distributed environment.

A. Karmouch, L. Korba, and E. Madeira (Eds.): MATA 2004, LNCS 3284, pp. 137–146, 2004.

The properties of physical and logical mobility (of the mobile computing paradigm) can be used in the database administration activity in order to enable DBAs to manage database systems anywhere and anytime.

Another paradigm that presents interesting properties to be incorporated into the database administration task is the pervasive computing [12]. The pervasive computing enables a computational device to obtain information from the computational environment (in which it is a component) in order to use this information to build computational models dynamically. Furthermore, the computational environment has the property to recognize the presence of a new computational device. Hence, the concept of pervasive computing can provide the capability of adaptation to the location to a database administration tool.

The main goal of this work is to present a database administration tool that incorporates properties from mobile computation and pervasive computation. It is important to notice that the integration of paradigms from mobile computation and pervasive computation is denominated as ubiquitous computation. The tool, called Mobile Database Administrator (MDBA), allows DBAs, independently of their physical location, to perform a database administration task in a mobile computational environment through a mobile computational device like: handhelds (Palm, iPaq, Personal Digital assistant-PDA), cell phones or notebooks. The tool is also sensible to the location (or context), recognizing, for example, the wireless structure (Bluetooth, Wi-Fi or cell phone network) of the environment where the mobile device is located (where the MDBA tool is being executed). With this information, the tool can be configured to establish a connection through the environment's available structure.

This paper is organized as follows. Section 2 describes the mobile computational environment, characterizing the various components of this environment. In section 2, a discussion about pervasive computation and ubiquitous computation is introduced. In section 3, the remote database administration is defined, highlighting the goals this new approach, as well as the features and functioning of MDBA. Section 4 describes the architecture of the tool and the aspects of the implementation. Finally, Section 5 concludes this work.

2   Ubiquitous Computation Environment Model

In a computational environment with support to mobility, the mobile computers (mobile devices) are grouped in components called cells. As depicted in Figure 1, each cell represents a certain region of space covered by a wireless communication service. These cells can represent a wireless local network (WLAN), an ad hoc network, a covered area (also called cell) of cell phone network or a combination of these communication technologies (like, for example, an ad hoc network located in a covered area of a cell phone service). In Figure 1, the cell C1 represents a WLAN, while the cell C2 represents a covered area of a station of support to mobility in a cell phone network. It is important to note that when a cell represents a WLAN or an ad hoc network, the mobile computers of the cell can communicate with each other. On the other hand, if a cell represents a covered area of a cell phone network, the mobile unities of the cell need an intervention of a device, denoted mobile support station (or base station), to communicate among themselves. A mobile computer can use different communication technologies. Thus, a mobile unit can migrate from one communication technology to another. Such a feature is called vertical handoff. The communication between two mobile support stations is performed through a fixed network. The mobile support stations have the functionality of guaranteeing the communication among mobile devices in distinct cells. In figure 1, the component access point represents the mobile support station connected to the fixed network, responsible for connecting mobile devices from cell C1 with other components either in the fixed network or from other cells that are part of the computational environment. In C2, there is a base station of a cell phone network connected to a fixed network.

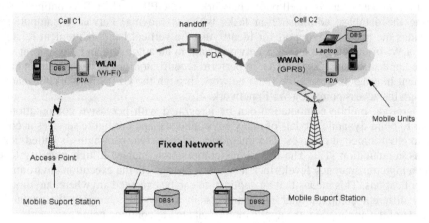

Fig. 1. Mobile Computational Environment

Wireless networks can be divided into 4 main categories according to the covered area: Wireless Personal Area Networks (WPANs); Wireless Local Area Networks (WLANs); Wireless Wide Area Networks (WWANs) and Satellite Networks [13]. In such wireless communication infrastructures, the moment when the vertical handoff happens represents a critical issue, since the mobile device needs to have its parameters reconfigured in order to continue executing its services normally, while moving among cells of different wireless networks.

Pervasive computing provides mobile devices the capability of obtaining information from the computational environment in which it is inserted and using it to build computational models dynamically. The implementation of context-aware applications allows the specification of contexts that can be used in order to guarantee pervasive computing properties, such as wireless communication infrastructure changes (vertical handoff) or its location. The process of developing such class of applications (that include context treatment in their code) is called context-aware programming [10]. Context is any information that can be used to characterize the situation of an entity which can be a person, place or object. The entity should play a key role in the interaction between a user and an application [3]. Hence, context-aware applications contribute for pervasive computing paradigm, since they provide transparently and automatically the necessary support for adaptation and portability. Context-aware applications have the property of executing specific procedures (code fragments) according to a context.

To illustrate the use of the pervasive computing paradigm in remote database administration, suppose a mobile device with support for Bluetooth, Wi-Fi, and GPRS wireless communication infrastructures. Thus, the mobile device can be a node of WPAN, WLAN and WWAN wireless networks. At an instant t1, the device is located in the cell C1 (see Figure 1). Consider that in C1 there is only support for communication through Wi-Fi technology. Thus, mobile devices in C1 can only be nodes of a WLAN. Suppose now that a DBA, located in spatial point inside the geographical area of C1 area, is executing database system administration tasks in database system DBS1 (located in the fixed network). For that, the DBA is using his/her mobile device. Observe that there is an access point for the WLAN in C1 (see Figure 1). For some reason, the DBA moves to the geographical area of cell C2, where the communication infrastructure is a cell phone network (e.g., GPRS). The DBA continues executing the database administration tasks while is moving. Pervasive computation provides the necessary support for identifying the vertical handoff moment (change from a Wi-Fi network to a GPRS network) and, in an automatic and transparent way to the application and user (DBA), to perform reconfigurations in the execution environment in order to access the fixed network through the GPRS network, instead of through the access point of a Wi-Fi network.

Therefore, mobile computation can be integrated with pervasive computation in order to build dynamic models of many environments, and configure services according to environmental changes. The integration of these two paradigms is called ubiquitous computation [12]. The ubiquitous computation enables a high mobility level with a high transparency level, since it supports changes in the execution environment of applications. This means that an application can be executed anywhere, anytime, in many different computational environments, in a way that changing the execution context of the application, the application is adapted to continue being executed.

3   Remote Database Administration

As mentioned before, the DBA is responsible for the control of many functional aspects of the DBMS, like: definition and scheme modification, access authorization, integrity rules specification, security proceedings definition, data access performance monitoring, creation of indexes, control of buffers' size, number of users allowed. These tasks have to be efficiently executed to guarantee that a database system is active. The activity of database administration can be categorized in two different classes according to the host where the database system resides. One can have administration of database systems that are located in computers connected to a fixed network (fixed hosts) or administration of database systems that are located in mobile computational devices (mobile hosts).

We define remote database administration as the functionality that integrates the paradigm of ubiquitous computation with the database administration activity. Therefore, one can use the notion of remote database administration in order to develop tools which provide the necessary support to DBAs to execute their activities through mobile devices. Such mobile devices should behave as nodes in a wireless network.

In the next section, a tool, called MDBA, that implements the remote database administration functionality will be described. The MDBA enables DBAs to manage databases residing in mobile hosts or fixed hosts.

3.1   MDBA Architecture

The MDBA architecture comprises two modules: Client and Coordinator. The client module, installed in a mobile device, provides an interface of the application to the database administrator and performs the connectivity of the mobile device, with the fixed network, through a wireless communication structure available in the equipment. The coordinator module manages the requests from mobile devices, performs the sending of information about modifications of the computational devices for the mobile devices connected to the fixed network and performs the communication with database systems from the computational environment.

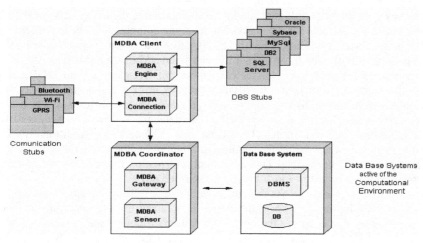

Fig. 2. MDBA Architecture

Figure 2 presents the MDBA architecture. The client module has two layers: the MDBA engine layer and the MDBA connection. The MDBA engine layer consists of a remote application installed in the mobile device and executed on Java Virtual Machine (JVM). The application is a graphic interface containing functionalities of database systems' administration that are made available according to the selection of the DBMS by the DBA. The graphic interface implementation is structured according to the context-oriented programming, which allows, at runtime, to process parts of selected codes. This part of the code is called Stub. With respect to the graphic interface, the MDBA engine presents a list of DBSs provided by the MDBA gateway. Thus, the DBA can choose a specific DBS. By doing this, it is necessary to load of the functionalities of the DBS selected by the user (DBA). In other words, only the stub corresponding to the functionalities of the selected DBS has to be incorporated into the application structure at runtime. Such an approach makes possible to process only the stub of a given DBS, instead of having all codes from all available DBSs. Hence, that feature minimizes the consumption of storage resources of mobile devices. Recall that storage resources have severe limitations in mobile devices.

The MDBA connection layer is responsible for the communication between the client module and the coordinator. This layer also consists of a context-aware application, executed under JVM. The MDBA connection sends requisitions from MDBA engine to MDBA gateway layer, to pass it to the database Server of the computational environment and return the result of these requisitions to MDBA engine. This communication between MDBA connection and MDBA gateway is made through a protocol http (Hypertext Transfer Protocol). The MDBA connection uses a context-aware approach to execute parts of the code when establishing the connectivity with the coordinator. This is because a mobile device can support many wireless communication structures and migrate from one technology to another during the execution of the application. To support vertical handoff without interruptions in the application's execution, a stub of communication (available in the mobile device and specific for a given computational environment), it is inserted in the application structure when the vertical handoff occurs. Thus, the MDBA connection layer guarantees a dynamically reconfiguration of the wireless communication structure's parameters.

The key goal of the coordinator module is to coordinate the requisitions of the client module and pass them for database systems in the computational environment and to obtain necessary information for the MDBA tool execution. This module is executed in another host, which can be a unity with fixed address or a mobile unity.

The coordinator module comprises two layers: MDBA gateway and MDBA sensor, both implemented in Java. The MDBA gateway layer is responsible for sending requisitions from the MDBA engine to a given DBS. This requisition is sent by the MDBA connection layer and it is passed to the database Server. The Access to the DBMS is performed via JDBC (Java Data Base Connection). Additionally, The MDBA gateway is responsible for sending information, gathered by the MDBA sensor layer, to the client module. This additional information is necessary for ensuring pervasive computing features in MDBA, as described next.

The MDBA sensor layer has the functionality of acquiring information from the computational environment. This information is obtained through programs installed in a web Server that searches the computational environment and passes them to a specific layer (MDBA engine or connection layers) through the MDBA gateway. Examples of information which are collected by the sensor layer are: which DBSs are installed in the computational environment and which communication infra-structures are available for the mobile device.

The database system presented in Figure 2 represents the different available DBSs in the computational environment that are managed by the MDBA. The DBS receives the solicitation from the MDBA engine, processes it and return the result for the coordinator. The coordinator sends it back through http protocol, for the MDBA connection layer to pass the final result to MDBA engine.

3.2 System's Requirements

The MDBA is a remote database administration tool which has the following properties: (i) Flexibility to support functionalities from different DBMSs and allow connectivity with different wireless access technologies, like Bluetooth, Wi-Fi, and GPRS; (ii) Adaptability to reduce the frequency of interruptions during the tool's execution when context changes occur (e.g., vertical handoff); (iii) Portability to allow its execution in PDAs and in cell phones as well; and (iv) Modularity, since each developed component is independent and can be reused in other applications.

Those properties provide the necessary support for the execution of administration tasks for several heterogeneous database systems (installed in a fixed network or mobile one) and access to them, avoiding the use of a specific tool for each DBMS and making possible remote database administration possible through any kind of PDA (or mobile phones). Furthermore, MDBA's properties ensure that only the loading to the mobile device of the functionalities of the selected DBMS. Such a feature is critical, since the storing capacity in these devices is still limited. Finally, those properties support dynamically reconfiguration of the connectivity of the wireless communication structure's parameters when vertical handoffs occur.

It is important to observe that the identification of the context (place) of a mobile device makes possible the recognition of where the mobile device is physically located, the type of wireless communication structure which is being used and the DBSs running in the identified context. Based on this information, the application can automatically perform the reconfiguration of the connectivity when the wireless communication structure changes, and to dynamically load the functionalities of the identified DBMSs. Therefore, the MDBA guarantees the properties of pervasive computing.

4 Implementation

For implementing the MDBA tool, we have decided to use the Abstract Factory design pattern [5] and the context-oriented programming paradigm. By using those techniques, the idea was to introduce in the MDA the ability of manipulating several heterogeneous DBMS and of loading the administration functionalities to the MDBA at runtime according to awareness of which DBMS should be manipulated. Figure 3 presents the class diagram which describes the implementation of such properties in the proposed tool. Observe that the diagram comprises an interface class, five concrete classes, a class for instantiating objects of a given concrete class, and the main class of the application. The interface class, denoted Imdba, defines the methods which implement the functionalities of the MDBA tool. The concrete classes have methods specified in the interface class. Those methods are implemented according to the particularity of each DBMS. For example, a functionality that executes a command to list users in Oracle is different from the one in MySql. For that reason, it is codified a method defined in the interface class, called *getUsers*. In each concrete class, it is implemented in this method the functionality to list users according to the DBMSs syntax (late binding and overloading properties). The class mdbaFactory defines a method to instantiate objects of a concrete class indicated by the main class. This method is responsible for loading the functionalities (of a given DBMS) in the mobile device that corresponds to the load of the concrete class and the instantiation of the object of that concrete class. The main class, denoted MDBA, implements the graphic user interface with database administration functionality options. This class is responsible to list the DBMSs installed in the network and to require the indication of one of these DBMSs to be manipulated. After the selection, it is required to a method of the mdbaFactory class, the corresponding object of the concrete class of the DBMS indicated by the DBA during execution.

From the context-oriented programming point of view, the concrete classes presented in Figure 3 are the stubs; pieces of code executed according to the context, in this case the DBMSs available in the network. Another set of stubs is defined for the connectivity establishment of the mobile device in the mobile computational environment, where each concrete class represents a type of connectivity infrastructure available in the environment, such as GPRS, Wi-Fi, and Bluetooth.

A prototype was developed for mobile computational environments that have a wireless interface of the WLAN kind, a fixed unity containing different database systems, and a mobile unity connected to the wireless interface by an access point (base station). The following technologies were used to implement this prototype:

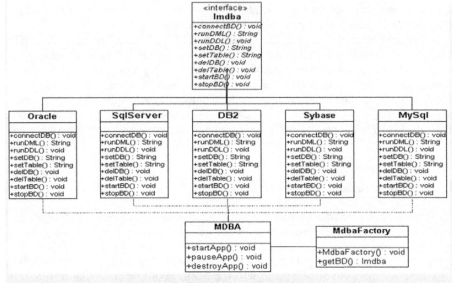

Fig. 3. MDBA Class Diagram

J2ME (Java Micro Edition), Servlets, SQL Server 2000, MySql, J2ME Wireless Toolkit, Apache Tomcat 4.0, and Palm OS Emulator.

The J2ME platform was chosen because it provides a bigger number of mobile devices compatible with the proposed tool. The application and the connectivity on the client side were developed in J2ME, one of the Java technology's specifications that Sun Microsystems developed for mobile devices. The connectivity application on the server side was developed using the concept of Servlet. Likewise the client connectivity and the MDBA, it was developed using the Java. The software Apache Tomcat 4.0 was the web server chosen because it is the server recommended by Sun Microsystems to execute Servlets. Finally, the DBMS SQL Server and MySql were used to simulate the diversity of database systems installed in a fixed network.

The following functionalities were implemented in the MDBA: i) execution of commands DDL (data definition language) and DML (data manipulation language), through QBE (Query By Example) strategy or typing DDL or DML expressions from SQL 99; ii) information about connected users and processes; iii) creation, removal and modification of objects: databases' instances, tables, columns and indexes; iv) creation and execution of stored procedures, triggers, visions; and v) start and Stop of DB server. To illustrate the use of the MDBA tool, consider that a DBA carrying a mobile device (cell phone or handheld) comes to a wireless communication network (Wi-Fi, Bluetooth, GPRS) area. When the execution of the MDBA tool is started, an initial screen with a list of available DBMSs in the mobile computational environment will be presented (in which the DBA is located), as shown in Figure 4. The DBA should select, then, one of the listed DBMSs. After a DBMS is selected, the DBA (user) identification and authentication screen is displayed, as shown in Figure 5.

After filling out data, the administrator can perform any operation on the indicated DB. Figure 6 illustrates the screen of the main menu that has all functionalities implemented in the MDBA, independently of DBMS is being manipulated.

Fig. 4. Initial Screen   **Fig. 5.** Identification Screen   **Fig. 6.** Options Screen

Observe that Figure 4 and 5 present the MDBA being executed in two different mobile devices, in a cell phone and in a PDA.

The solution presented in this work proposes facility and rapidity when executing tasks of a DBA in a computational environment that has several DBSs. Of course, such a feature contributes for the raise of productivity of a DBA and minimizes time for used by a DBA to connect in fixed computers using traditional administration tools. Another advantage of the MDBA is to be implemented in J2ME. Recall that the J2ME platform allows an application to be executed in any mobile device which has a JVM, without the need to rewrite it for each device.

5 Conclusion

This work proposes a database administration tool which integrates properties from mobile computation and pervasive computation. Therefore, the idea was to introduce the paradigm of ubiquitous computation into database technology. For that, this paper has described a context sensitive tool, denoted Mobile Data Base Administration (MDBA), whose key goal is to allow remote database administration through mobile devices (PDAs or cell phones) considering the aspect of the diversity of existing DBMS and wireless communication networks' structures.

Using the implemented prototype, we can observe that the DBA can execute any database administration command. For example, with this tool implemented, it is possible to create and remove tables (and databases), initialize the DBS, deactivate the DBS, activate Backup processes, functions that guarantee the complete functioning in the DBS, keeping them always working with a performance adequate to the needs specified by users anytime and anywhere, and in a safe and immediate form.

References

1. Alonso, Rafael; Korth, Henry F. *Database System Issues in Nomadic Computing*. ACM *SIGMORD Record*, v. 31, n. 2, mai. 1993.
2. Brayner, Angelo, Aguiar, Monteiro F. *Sharing Mobile Databases in Dynamically Configurable Environments*. 15th International Conference on Advanced Information System Engineering (CAiSE 2003).
3. Dey, A.K. *Understanding and Using Context*. Personal and Ubiquituos Computing, Springer-Verlag, v.5, n. 1, p. 4-7. 2001.
4. Dunham, Margaret H.; HELAL, Abdelsalam (Sumi). *Mobile Computing and Databases: Anything new?*. ACM *SIGMORD Record*, v. 24, n. 4, dez. 1995.

5. Gamma, Erich; Helm, Richard; Johnson, Ralph; Vlissides, John. *Design Patterns: Elements of Reusable Object-Oriented Software.* Addison-Wesley, 1994.
6. Imielinski, Tomasz; Badrinath, B. R. *Mobile wireless computing. Communications of the ACM*, 37(10):19-28, oct. 1994.
7. Ioannidis, John; Maguire Jr., Gerhald Q. *The design and implementation of a mobile internetworking architecture. In Proceedings of the 1993 Winter USENIX Conference*, p. 491-502, jan. 1993.
8. Johnson, David. *Ubiquitous mobile host in- ternetworking. In Proceedings of the Fourth Workshop on Workstation Operating Systems. IEEE*, oct. 1993.
9. Kagal, L.; Korolev, V.; Avancha, S.; Joshu, A.; Finin, T.; Yesha, Y. *Highly Adaptable Infrastructure for Service Discovery and Management in Ubiquitous Computing. Technical report, TR CS-01-06, Department of Computer Science and Electrical Engineering, University of Mary-land Baltimore County, Baltimore*, MD (2001).
10. Keays, Roger; Rakotonirainy, Andry. *Context-Oriented Programing. Proceedings of the Third ACM International Workshop on Data Engineering for Wireless and Mobile Access*, p. 9-16, sep., San Diego, USA. 2003.
11. Kuramitsu, Kimio, Sakamura, Ken. *Towards Ubiquitous Database in Mobile Commerce. ACM MobiDE*, p. 84-89. 2001.
12. Lyytinen, Kalle; YOO, Youngjun. *Issues and Challenges in Ubiquitous Computing. Communications of the ACM*, v. 45, n. 12, dec. 2002.
13. Mallick, Martin. *Mobile and Wireless Desing Essential.* New Jersey: John Wiley & Sons, 2003.
14. Raatikainen, Kimmo; Christensen, Henrik B.; Nakajima, Tatsuo. *Aplication Requeriments for Middleware for Mobile and Pervasive System.* ACM SIGMOBILE Review, v. 6, n. 4, oct. 2002.

MobiGrid*

Framework for Mobile Agents
on Computer Grid Environments

Rodrigo M. Barbosa and Alfredo Goldman

Department of Computer Science
Institute of Mathematics and Statistics
University of São Paulo
{rodbar,gold}@ime.usp.br

Abstract. This paper presents a project which focuses on the implementation of a framework for mobile agents support within a grid environment project, namely InteGrade. Our goal is to present a framework where time consuming sequential tasks can be executed on a network of personal workstations. The mobile agents may be used to encapsulate long processing applications (*tasks*). These agents can migrate whenever the local machine is requested by its user, since they are provided with automatic migration capabilities. Our framework also provides to the user a manager that keeps track of the agents submitted by him.

1 Motivation: Mobile Agents on Computational Grids

In the past, high-performance computation was done only on supercomputers. These computers were parallel computers, composed of many processors with shared or distributed RAM, interconnected by a high-speed bus. Nevertheless, this kind of computer has a very expensive price and when it is not being used, there is a huge waste of resources, since plenty of computation time is lost.

Facing this problem, researchers looked for a new paradigm in order to build non-expensive high-performance computers: the *clusters*. A *cluster* is a set of many ordinary computers - usually PCs - interconnected by a high-speed network. Even though the price problem is faced by this solution, the waste problem still remains: when a *cluster* is not being used, plenty of resources are still being wasted.

So, a new paradigm was created: the *grid* [1]. The *computational grid* idea was clearly inspired by *clusters*, in the sense that we have many computers interconnected by a network in order to provide together greater computational power. However, a *grid* does not rely on high speed networks and is more available; they can be composed of computers spread around the world, interconnected by Internet, for example. The idea is to provide computational resources similarly to the way we get power supply: when you want power supply, you may

---

* Project supported by the Research Support Foundation of the State of São Paulo - FAPESP. Process number: 02/11165-6

A. Karmouch, L. Korba, and E. Madeira (Eds.): MATA 2004, LNCS 3284, pp. 147–157, 2004.

connect your device to the power grid; when you want computational resources, you may connect your device to the *computational grid*. The waste problem is addressed in a way that whenever a computer is idle, its computational power can be supplied to the *grid*.

On this context, the idea of mobile agents can be interesting. They can be used to encapsulate opportunistic applications, which can use small slices of the available computational time of personal workstations, migrating to another machine whenever the local user requests his machine, always preserving the processing already done. On this way, mobile agents can be considered as a complementary tool to decrease even more the idle time of a *grid*.

This text proposes our solution to provide a mobile agents environment in a *grid* and is organized in the following way: Section 1 explains the motivations to provide mobile agents support in a *grid*, specifically InteGrade; Section 2 introduces the InteGrade project; Section 3 describes our project objectives; Section 4 introduces some mobile agents environments; Section 5 gives a general overview of the framework; Section 6 shows the class structure of our framework; Section 7 shows some tests we made for measuring the overhead; Section 8 provides ideas for future work and concludes this paper.

2   InteGrade

InteGrade project [2] is building a middleware infrastructure which enables idle time utilization of machines already owned by public or private institutions. One of InteGrade's goals is to use this idle time to solve many kinds of parallelizable problems, including strongly coupled applications.

InteGrade is being built using the most modern technologies of distributed objects systems, industry standards, and high-performance distributed computing protocols.

The main requirements that are considered in the InteGrade development are:

1. the system must know itself: this means the necessity of maintaining a database refreshed dynamically which contains information on the system, on hardware and software platform of each machine, on the links interconnecting the machines, besides the grid dynamic state, which means the use of resources like disk, processor, memory and bandwidth;
2. almost no overhead for the clients: the middleware must be able to use the available idle resources of the client machines with the least possible impact on the overall performance perceived by their users;
3. security guarantee: since it will be possible to dynamically load executable code at the clients machines, it is important to guarantee that this code will not harm the correct functioning of other applications being executed at the client machine. It is also important to guarantee that this code will not modify or gain access to personal information, possibly confidential, stored at the client machines.

2.1   InteGrade Differentials, Compared to Other Grid Projects

1. reutilization of the installed computer base with low overhead to machine users: it is one of the major points on the InteGrade project. Reutilization can be observed in other projects, being not a very important concern in Globus [3] and Legion [4], and a major concern in Condor [5]. The InteGrade differential is in the fact that this concern was considered in the development of its architecture;
2. utilization of modern distributed objects technologies: exclusive feature of InteGrade, that will use mostly CORBA [6] on its implementation. With these characteristics we get two main advantages: we can reuse a lot of services already available in CORBA architecture; the integration of other services and applications on the Grid will be easier and faster. Even though our framework is not directly based on CORBA, it can easily be connected to InteGrade via CORBA.

3   Objectives

This project consists in the implementation of a mobile agents infrastructure for InteGrade. The main idea of our framework is to allow an efficient utilization of computational resources for large sequential or for embarrassing parallelizable applications.

Mobile agents migration ability meets two major InteGrade goals: the system must be transparent to the machine user, in other words, the machine user must have the highest priority compared with InteGrade applications; the idle resources must be used in the best possible way.

In the case where there is the necessity to free the machine resources for the local user, for example, if this is a machine running mobile code, this code can migrate to another machine without losing the partial results already computed. On this process, the InteGrade architecture provides information about the network and the other machines, allowing the mobile agent to choose a machine with more adequate available computational resources. In order to do that, utilization patterns of other machines resources can also be used.

It would also be very interesting to allow the migration of mobile agents to more powerful machines that may become available. But this migration would bring benefits only if this machine utilization pattern shows that it will be on this state for some time, since the migration process is costly.

On this way, mobile agents can be used in a complementary way to InteGrade applications, allowing a even better utilization of computational resources. Among the applications that could be executed using mobile agents, there are loosely coupled parallel applications like SETI@home [7] and BOINC [8], or sequential applications that demand long processing time.

4   Mobile Agents Environments

In an IBM's pioneer report *Mobile Agents: Are They a Good Idea?* [9], Chess et. al analyze the potential of mobile agents and introduce, among other ideas, the possibility of using mobile agents in order to use idle computational resources. That could be done by using mobile agents to encapsulate processes that would migrate through a network always looking for the resources they need. On this process, they take with them their execution state, creating a new paradigm that takes the program to data instead of taking data to the program. Yet in this report, it is stated that the mobile agent support should be done over a interpreted language. This strategy faces the problem of saving the execution state besides the platform heterogeneity. Another report, *e-Gap Analysis* [10], which makes a study about the way scientists do science nowadays with technology support - what is named *e-Science* - points, among other gaps, the absence of mobile agents support in the existent grid infrastructures.

These articles lead us to the idea of creating a Java framework for mobile agents support on grids. The choice for Java was motivated by two reasons: the main reason is due to the fact that Java is a robust, popular and modern language; the second reason is due to the results of a comparison made among many mobile agents environments [11]. In this comparison, where lower grades represent better performance, the environments Grasshopper [12] and Aglets [13], both in Java, are placed among the best, with grades 9.25 and 10.15, respectively.

Grasshopper has excellent documentation and respects the OMG MASIF standard [6]. However, Grasshopper producer, IKV++ Technologies, restricts its utilization inside other projects without royalties payment, as well as to do comparisons with it. These factors were crucial and did not allow us to use this environment, leading us to choose Aglets.

Aglets is a Java environment for mobile agents development and implementation. Aglets Software Development Kit, ASDK, was prototyped and created by IBM. It has become a open source initiative, ruled by IBM license for open source, which allows the code utilization and modification, as well as comparisons. The product documentation, although incomplete, is relatively organized, and the environment provides all the basic resources for the creation of our framework, besides more advanced resources. Resources for mobile agents creation, migration, clonation are provided in addition to advanced resources of security, synchronization and message exchange.

Aglets utilization for grid computing is not a new idea. Aversa et al. [14] have already used this environment in a case study, implementing a dynamically load-balanced distributed version of an algorithm for the (0 - 1) *knapsack problem* - a combinatorial optimization problem. Aglets provides a class structure whose main elements are [15]:

1. `Aglet`: it is the class that represents the mobile agent. It provides methods for migration, clonation, suspension among other features. An object of this class is named *aglet*;
2. `AgletProxy`: represents the *aglet* proxy. It serves as a interface between the *aglet* and the object that references it;
3. `AgletContext`: represents the *aglets* host. There can be many *aglets* in a *context* and many *contexts* in a server;
4. `AgletID`: corresponds to an unique global identifier of the *aglet*.

5   Framework Overview

The main idea of our framework is to provide the programmer with a programming environment for long running applications, which we call *tasks*. We will mention all the components of our framework at a high level:

1. *task*: long running application, encapsulated in a mobile agent. On the implementation of this *task*, the programmer must take care of the *task* state, since the standard Java environments for mobile agents provide weak migration, in other words, only the objects states and variables are preserved, not the state of execution stacks. This comes from the fact that Java Virtual Machine (JVM) forbids threads inspection by the user application, for security reasons. There are a several implementations of mobile agents which allow strong migration [16]. Nevertheless, these environments use modified versions of JVM, what is not desirable, since such JVMs usually become obsolete compared to new versions of Java 2, not following Sun Microsystems standardization;

2. *manager*: it is the component responsible for registering *tasks*. The user who submits *tasks* must have the *manager* active at his machine. The two most important functions of the *manager* are:

   (a) migration: when a *task* is submitted, the *manager* queries the InteGrade infrastructure searching for an idle machine which has a chance of remaining on this state for a given time. With such information, the *manager* dispatches the *task* to such a machine. A similar procedure is used when the *tasks* need to migrate;

   (b) *liveness*: the *manager* also creates a clone of the *task* and dispatches it to another machine. In the context of our work, a *task* that is being executed in more than one machine has *liveness*. When one of the clones dies - which can occur for many reasons, for example, a energy supply interruption at the machine where it is running - the *manager* makes a copy of the clone still alive and dispatches it to another machine. We call *twins* the two clones of a *task*. The choice for two clones is arbitrary, because we could choose a greater number. However, a greater number of clones would imply more waste, since we would be using many resources for running the same *task*;

3. *light server*: this is the server installed on each machine that provides resources to the framework. It provides a execution environment for the *tasks*. When the machine is requested by the local user, the *server* asks the evacuation of the *tasks* that are being hosted by it. These *tasks* query their *managers*, which communicate with InteGrade looking for idle machines. When the *managers* get such information, they take actions in order to evacuate the *tasks* to new machines. At this point, there is another important discussion: how to build *servers* light enough to not interfere with the local user? We choose two solutions: the first is to implement a minimal server that does not use advanced resources of Aglets which are not necessary to our framework; the other solution is to use a small *daemon* written in C;

4. *daemon*: it verifies whether the machine is idle or not. When the machine is idle, it communicates that to InteGrade and turns on the *light server*. When the machine is requested by its local user, the *daemon* informs the *server*, which evacuates the *tasks* and terminates. This *daemon* can be inserted on InteGrade's LRM (Local Resource Manager) [2], which is responsible for monitoring the local resources. LRMs send this information periodically to the GRM, which uses it for scheduling within the grid. So, the *daemon* is responsible for informing InteGrade that the machine is ready to receive *tasks*;
5. *client*: component that provides the user with tools to submit *tasks* to the framework. Also provides a host environment for the *manager*.

In Figure 1, we have an overview of our framework. Each one of the *clients* hosts a *manager*, which communicates with InteGrade. Client 1's *manager* manages Task 1 and its clone. Client 2's *manager* manages Task 2 and its clone. Observe also that the *daemons* communicate with InteGrade in order to inform it when a local machine is idle, turning on the server then.

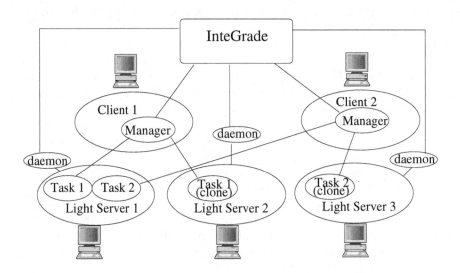

Fig. 1. General architecture of the framework

In the architecture creation, there were two main problems that should be addressed: (1) How to prevent the *tasks* from terminating suddenly? (2) How to use Java on the clients without making the local machine slow for its user?

Two immediate solutions were studied for the first problem: check-pointing and redundance. Check-pointing would demand state saving on disk from time to time and redundance could be considered as having two or more copies of a *task* running on different machines. However, check-pointing cannot be considered a good solution by itself, since a machine could suddenly be turned off and remain on this state for a long time. From this point of view, check-pointing could not work without redundance, since a *task* would need a clone to prevent this undesirable situation. So, we choose to address first this problem by using only redundance. We always have two copies of a *task* running independently, in case of a sudden termination, we could clone the remaining *task*. This solution would fail on the improbable situation of a sudden death of both *tasks* before the *manager* realizes it, but this probability can be reduced by putting them to run on different networks. By using only the redundace solution, we prompt the user for a new submission in case of sudden termination of both *tasks*.

As said before, we addressed the second problem using a *daemon*.

6   Class Structure of the Framework

We will now give a more detailed view of the framework, specifying it by classes:

1. `AgletTask`: this class represents the *tasks* already cited. To define a *task*, the programmer must extend this class and redefine the `defineState()` method, which must return an `AgletState`, that encapsulates the *task* implementation, as well as its state. This class is associated with the `AgletState` class.
2. `AgletState`: class that represents the *task* state, as well as its implementation. The programmer must extend it and implement the following methods:
   (a) `run()`: method that defines literally the *task* implementation, in other words, it defines the long running application that the user wants to submit to the framework. The programmer must have in mind the fact that he is responsible for saving the present state of the application. For this purpose, a feature is being implemented: the method `checkPoint()`. Any Java object implementing `java.io.Serializable` which is referenced inside `AgletState` object will be automatically preserved when the *task* migrates. This `checkPoint()` method will be used to inform the framework that the *thread* has reached a consistent state. The programmer must test the value returned by it: if it returns `true` the *thread* must be stopped in a logical way; if it returns `false`, nothing is done. The reason for that is to prevent the *thread* from entering a inconsistent state. With this feature, the programmer would just take care of calling this method whenever the application reaches a consistent point (a point where the invariants are preserved). The programmer must know also that, at the end of the *task* execution, a call to the `finish()` method must be made.
   (b) `printResults()`: prints the results of the *task* processing. It is called by the framework when the *task* finishes to be executed and returns to the client.
3. `Server`: the class that represents the *light server* already cited. This `Server` hosts the `AgletTasks`. The server is provided with Aglets environment for hosting *aglets*. Also it receives communication of the *daemon* in order to know when it is time to evacuate the `AgletTasks`. We have a simple *light server* already implemented.

4. `AgletManager`: Represents the *manager*. We have implemented the register and evacuation of the `AgletTasks`, as well as the control of their *liveness*. `AgletManager` is nothing more but a special kind of *aglet* which never migrates. We implemented it this way in order to use the Aglets tools for message exchanging among *aglets*. The communication between `AgletManager` and InteGrade is not implemented yet, since it is easier to test it alone.
5. `Client`: Represents the *client*, which means that this class is responsible for `AgletTasks` submission to the framework. It is also used to host the `AgletManager`. For now, we are testing our code by using Tahiti - Aglets visualization tool, which provides an environment for hosting the `AgletManager` and tools to submit *tasks* to our framework.
6. `AgletProxy`: Component of the Aglets environment. It is the class that mediates the communication between two *aglets*.
7. `AgletListener`: Class that executes pre-migration ant post-arriving operations: respectively, `onDispatching()` and `onArriving()`. This class is transparent to the user.

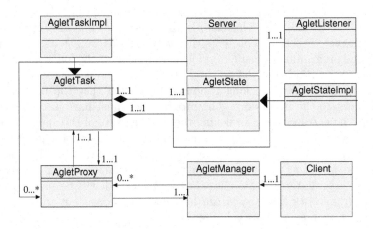

Fig. 2. General UML of the framework

In Figure 2, `AgletStateImpl` and `AgletTaskImpl` are user implementations for, respectively, `AgletState` and `AgletTask`. Notice that each `AgletTask` has one reference to the `AgletState` and `AgletListener`. The `Server` has a list of `AgletProxies` which represents the `AgletTasks` which it hosts. The `AgletTask` has one reference to the `AgletProxy` that represents its `AgletManager`. The `AgletManager` has a list of `AgletProxies` which represents the `AgletTasks` that it manages.

6.1   An Example

Next, we show, as an example, the implementations of a *Hello World task*. This implementation is merely an example of how to use our framework, since it does not have any practical utility. Notice that, whenever the *task* migrates, when it arrives at its new host, the `run()` method is executed. The *task* know how many times it has already said "hello" on other machines, preserving already done processing. When it migrates, all the instance variables of `AgletStateImpl` are preserved: `howMany` and `canSay`.

```
public class AgletTaskImpl extends AgletTask {
   public AgletState defineState () {
      return new AgletStateImpl ();
   }
}
public class AgletStateImpl extends AgletState {
   int howMany = 0;
   public void run () { /* go saying hello until migration_time */
      System.out.println (''I have said hello '' + howMany +
                             ''times'');
      for (;howMany < 1000000; ++howMany} {
         System.out.println (''Hello'');
      }
      if (howMany >= 1000000) finish ();
   }
   public void printResults () { /* processing results */
      System.out.println (''I am back! I have said hello '' +
                             ''1000000 times'');
   }
}
```

7   Tests

We have made some tests in order to determine the migration and state saving overhead. The migration overhead is mostly related to the network speed, while the state saving overhead is related to the serialization of the objects associated with the `AgletTask`, which is a costly process. We submitted *tasks* that solve a *makespan problem*: To determine a distribution of n independent tasks[1] with execution times of $t_1, t_2, ..., t_n \in \mathbb{Z}^+$ in m machines minimizing the time the last task ends. This is a NP-hard problem and we implemented a exponential solution which tests all the possible combinations. Two kinds of implementations were made: a simple implementation that does not take care of state saving nor migration; an `AgletTask` implementation which saves, for each iteration, the last combination analyzed.

In this table, we show tests for applications with parameters n, m in a simple application running on *host 1* and *host 2*, in a `AgletTask` that does not migrate running on *host 1* and in a `AgletTask` migrating 2 and 4 times, between *host 1*

---

[1] Note that here the word *task* has its usual meaning, not denoting the meaning we attributed to it.

Table 1. Tests for a makespan problem

n, m	Simple, *host 1*	Simple, *host 2*	AgletTask	AgletTask, 2	AgletTask, 4
2, 26	22s	13s	50s	30s	25s
2, 28	1min 30s	50s	3min 17s	3min 08s	3min 04s
2, 30	6min 36s	3min 28s	15min 45s	15min 09s	14min 55s

and *host 2*. *host 1* is a Athlon XP 2500, 512 Mb of RAM and *host 2* is a Pentium IV 2.8 GHz HT, 1 Gb of RAM.

We can see that the state saving overhead is significative, what has motivated our study on this area leading to the `checkPoint()` method. Also, we verify that the migrating overhead may not be very significative, being absorbed when the *task* migrates to a faster machine. That happens because when the *task* migrates to a faster machine, its execution speed is increased, compensating the migration time loss. Even though the `AgletTasks` stayed most of the time on *host 1*, it was worth to migrate to *host 2*, which is a faster machine.

8   Future Work and Conclusion

For now, we have implemented a working part of the framework. We have `AgletTask` and `AgletState` classes implemented, so the user can implement *tasks* which will be submitted to the framework. We also have a `AgletManager` that takes care of *tasks* migration and *liveness*, as well as a `Server`, which already implements the evacuation function.

Even though the present code is functional, there are many details to be implemented, as well as features which deserve close attention like: *daemon* implementation; *client* implementation; better support to present state saving (already being implemented); communication between the `AgletManager` and InteGrade.

The idea of mobile agents in InteGrade is very instigating and interesting. Our framework, in the future, can be used to implement many kinds of applications from embarrassing parallel applications, like SETI@home, to applications that need many kind of resources not available in a single InteGrade node. Given the opportunistic characteristic of mobile agents, InteGrade can reach near zero idleness on its nodes, what is impossible nowadays. Another interesting point is our concern on building a framework that is transparent for the machine user, so he will not face a performance loss. A strong feature of our framework is its portability, since it is written almost all in Java.

In the future, our framework can be extended to serve a grid infrastructure that manages different kinds of resources available on several machines. This would be a generalization for resources utilization, since for now our framework is focused only in computational resources.

References

1. Ian Foster and Karl Kesselman. *The Grid: Blueprint for a new Computing Structure*, chapter 2,3,5,11. Morgan Kaufmann Publishers, 1999.
2. Andrei Goldchleger, Fabio Kon, Alfredo Goldman, Marcelo Finger, and Germano Capistrano Bezerra. InteGrade: Object-Oriented Grid Middleware Leveraging Idle Computing Power of Desktop Machines. *Concurrency and Computation: Practice and Experience*, 16:449–459, March 2004.
3. Globus. Site of the Globus project, 2004. http://www.globus.org. Last visit on February, 2004.
4. Legion. Site of the Legion project, 2004. http://www.cs.virginia.edu/~legion/. Last visit on February, 2004.
5. Condor. Site of the Condor project, 2004. http://www.cs.wisc.edu/condor/. Last visit on February, 2004.
6. OMG. Site of the Object Management Group, 2004. http://http://www.omg.org. Last visit on February, 2004.
7. SETI@home. Site of the SETI@home project, 2004. http://setiathome.ssl.berkeley.edu/. Last visit on February, 2004.
8. BOINC. Site of the BOINC project, 2004. http://boinc.berkeley.edu. Last visit on February, 2004.
9. David Chess, Colin Harrison, and Aaron Kershenbaum. Mobile Agents: Are They a Good Idea? Technical report, T.J. Watson Research Center, 1995.
10. Geoffrey Fox and David Walker. e-Science Gap Analysis. Technical report, Indiana Univesity and Cardiff University, june 2003.
11. Josef Altmann, Franz Gruber, Ludwig Klug, Wolfgang Stockner, and Edgar Weppl. Using Mobile Agents in Real World: A Survey and Evaluation of Agents Platforms. 2000. www.umcs.maine.edu/~wagner/workshop/05_altmann_et_al.pdf.
12. Grasshopper. Site of the Grasshopper project, 2004. http://http://www.grasshopper.de. Last visit on February, 2004.
13. Aglets. Site of the Aglets project, 2004. http://aglets.sourceforge.net. Last visit on February, 2004.
14. Rocco Aversa, Beniamino Di Martino, Nicola Mazzocca, and Salvatore Venticinque. Mobile agents for distributed and dynamically balanced optimization applications. In *Proceedings of the 9th International Conference on High-Performance Computing and Networking*, pages 161–172. Springer-Verlag, 2001.
15. Mitsuro Oshima and Guenter Karjoth. Aglets Specification 1.0. Technical report, IBM, may 1997. http://www.research.ibm.com/trl/aglets/spec10.htm.
16. Sara Bouchenak. Making Java Applications Mobile or Persistent. In *Proceedings of the 6th USENIX Conference on Object-Oriented Technologies and Systems*, january 2001. http://citeseer.ist.psu.edu/bouchenak01making.html. Last visit on May, 1994.

Negotiation Process for Resource Allocation in Grid Using a Multi-agent System

Lilian Noronha Nassif[1], Mohamed Ahmed[2],
José Marcos Nogueira[1], and Roger Impey[2]

[1] Federal University of Minas Gerais, Department of Computer Science
Av. Antônio Carlos, 6627, CEP: 30.123-970, Belo Horizonte, Brazil
{lilian,jmarcos}@dcc.ufmg.br
[2] National Research Council Canada, Institute for Information Technology
1200 Montreal Road, K1A 0R6, Ottawa, Ontario, Canada
{Mohamed.Ahmed,Roger.Impey}@nrc-cnrc.gc.ca

Abstract. Grid technology is used for large-scale resource sharing among different institutions or individuals. A recent challenge in this environment is to provide guarantees for the service delivery in a job submission. It is important to know when a job will finish and the performance and costs involved. We present here a multi-agent system that considers such aspects to decide about the best place to run a job in grid. The main component of our solution is the negotiation process, which relies on resource access policies and performance prediction based on past cases of job submissions. The negotiation final goal is to establish Service Level Agreements that register user's expectations and service provision according to price, quality, performance and scheduling.

1 Introduction

Grid technology is used for large-scale resource sharing, for modern applications, among different organizations and individuals. Resource sharing requires mechanisms of security, data management, resource management, and information services that constitute the core of a grid middleware such as Globus [1]. We are particularly interested in the open issues related to resource allocation, scheduling and job submission in this environment.

A job submission in grid can be done using brokers, grid middleware command line or specific portals of a grid community. Although current mechanisms allow users to submit jobs in grid, the new challenge that motivates the grid community is to articulate a workflow in a service-based environment [2]. Actually, there is no consensus about how to guarantee a grid service delivery. It is necessary to know when a job will finish and the performance and costs involved. Indeed, we argue that the current methods used to select a resource to run a job are very naive. Such methods match user's requirements with resource descriptions and select the faster machine or the first machine that meets the requirements. The current solutions also do not consider access policy related to price, quality and time to use a resource.

We present here a multi-agent system for resource allocation in grid. Recently, agent technology has been considered as one of the most promising approaches to

A. Karmouch, L. Korba, and E. Madeira (Eds.): MATA 2004, LNCS 3284, pp. 158–167, 2004.
© Springer-Verlag Berlin Heidelberg 2004

complex scheduling systems because of its autonomous, distributed and dynamic nature [2]. We make use of robust features from agent technology, such as distributed communication, migration and security, to elaborate our solution to the negotiation of distributed resources.

Our framework covers several aspects to succeed in grid resource allocation, mainly the service guarantee and the intelligent choice of resources. The negotiation process of our multi-agent system is able to predict the resource performance in a service delivery by using past cases of job submission. Our negotiation process considers resource access policy according to user profile, price and time to access a resource. The outcome of the negotiation process is a Service Level Agreement (SLA) that registers consumer, providers and conditions about a grid service delivery. Such aspects of performance prediction, policy-based negotiation and use of SLAs are not used or properly explored in other solutions for the problem.

The paper is organized as follows: An overview of related work is presented in section 2. In section 3, we describe the multi-agent system, highlighting the negotiation processes. Section 4 presents a testbed and some considerations arising from the implementation of our work. We present our final comments in section 5.

2   Related Work

The work in [3] presents a protocol called Service Negotiation and Acquisition Protocol (SNAP). SNAP uses three types of SLAs: Task, Resource and Binding Service Level Agreement. This work, like ours, considers SLA in the negotiation process of resource allocation. They establish agreements by using a scheduler community. Our work, on the other hand, treats negotiations in a decentralized fashion using agents. The SLA representation of SNAP is very superficial, they focus on a weaker form of agreement, and no cost model is associated.

Condor [4] is a system for compute-intensive jobs. It uses a framework, called Matchmaking, to associate jobs with resources. Although the matching process is well defined, another Condor method, called Claiming, lacks a more robust way to negotiate. Our work shows how the negotiation process can be improved.

GRMS [5] is a meta-scheduling system for resource management. GRMS does not incorporate SLA guarantees for the service delivery. In our solution we can provide guarantees expressed in SLAs.

In [6], the problem is not related with resource allocation, but with grid interoperability for different platforms. In [7], authors focus on server performance for scientific programs. Our work, on the other hand, considers not only execution time, but also time to transfer data, quality of service and price.

We argue that these related works do not present a suitable negotiation process. We believe that this is a way to give flexibility to the job submission. With negotiation we can associate a job to a faster, cheaper, and higher quality resource. Our solution incorporates features in the negotiation process that are not well explored in these related works such as resource performance prediction, resource access policies and service level agreement.

3 Multi-agent System

An overview of our Multi-Agent System architecture, called MASK, is illustrated in figure 1. It consists of negotiation, migration and interface modules. In the negotiation module we group agents and functions of the negotiation process. The migration module matches SLAs established by agents and decides where to run a job. The interface module integrates agents into the OGSA (Open Grid Service Architecture) [1]. MASK architecture has two different hierarchical levels associated with global and local aspects such as security and scheduling. MASK architecture modules are described in the next sub-sections.

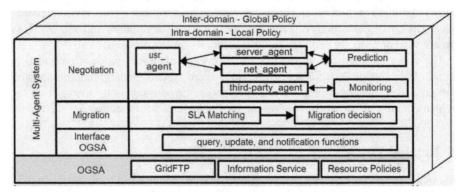

Fig. 1. Mask Architecture

We are working with Jade[11], a robust environment for agent deployment. We are integrating our solution into Globus, *de facto* standard for grid. Figure 2 illustrates the system flow. Initially, the user configures the user_agent providing information about price, quality, time schedule, and job arguments. The user also creates a proxy that will permit the user_agent to submit the job for him. The user_agent uses the

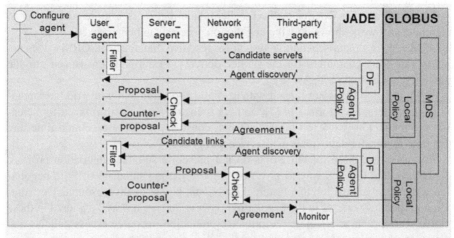

Fig. 2. System Flow with Jade and Globus

information service component of Globus, the Monitoring and Discovery Service (MDS) to find out resources that match the job description. The user_agent selects a group of servers to negotiate with. The server_agent negotiates according to restrictions defined in the local resource policies. The objective of the negotiation is to establish a SLA. A third-party agent will manage all SLAs. The user_agent also negotiate with a group of network_agents associated to network links that connect sites where data are available to sites where servers selected by the user_agent are located. A group of SLAs is chosen to provide the service (details about SLA choice in section 3.2). This choice must meet the user's preferences concerning price, quality and schedule time. Agents transfer data to the selected server and monitor SLAs.

3.1 Negotiation Module

In the negotiation module it is described who is negotiating, what is being negotiated, the types of negotiations, and how negotiations take place. The negotiations are between user_agent and server_agent or between user_agent and network_agent. The negotiation elements are represented in a tuple $<Id,P,Q,Ts,Tf,G,JD>$ where Id is the proposal identification, P is the price negotiated; Q is a set of quality of service; Ts is the time to start the job; Tf is the time to finish the job; G is a set of guarantees, and JD is the job description in Extensible Markup Language (XML) format. The negotiations can be bilateral, multi-issue and chaining. A bilateral negotiation occurs when there are only two parts involved. In a multi-issue negotiation, different aspects are negotiated. The negotiation between user_agent and network_agent is also called chaining negotiation. It occurs after finishing the negotiation between user_agent and server_agent.

A user_agent elaborates proposals and negotiates with a set of server_agents, which, in turn, elaborate counter-proposals considering resource access policies and resource performance prediction. The procedures concerning negotiation filter, policy-based negotiation and performance prediction are described as follows:

Negotiation Filter. The negotiation filter is a procedure used by user_agents to select some servers to negotiate with. It is defined as RS= (L, Perf, NS, PS, **CS**) where RS are resources selected to negotiate with; L is the server location related to data location, where L = {LN,RN} for Local Network (LN) or Remote Network (RN), in such a way that, if the server is in the same local network where the data is available, then L=LN; Perf is the machine's performance; NS is the number of SLAs established for the same time interval requested; PS is the percentage of servers to be selected to negotiate with; and CS is the set of candidate servers. The server selection is done using a utility function. First we associate weights (p1,p2,p3) to characteristics; after we calculate the utility function U=(L*p1 + Perf*p2 + NS*p3), and sort the set; finally we select PS*CS servers (with higher utility function from the set) to negotiate with.

Policy-Based Negotiation. This procedure is used by server_agents or network_ agents for elaboration of a counter-proposal based on resource access policies. In our policy model each constraint can assume two values. This allows the server_agent to evaluate each argument of the proposal and to elaborate a counter-proposal with a value opposite to the value received, in case such argument cannot be accepted.

Table 1. Sample of values for negotiable objects

Policy constraints	User	Time	Price	Quality		Guarantee		
				Function	Schedule	Validate	Predicate	Actions
Example of values	NRC domain	business hours	>20	minimum	hourly	business hours	greater than	10% price off
	out NRC domain	off hours	<20	average	every minute	weekend	less than	send e-mail

Table 1 presents an example of values that can be used to build policies associated with arguments that are being negotiated in our negotiation process. For each negotiated metric it is necessary to define qualities and guarantees. The metrics we are considering for a server are: number of processors and application run time. The metrics we are considering for a network link are: bandwidth and packet loss. There is a function that computes the defined metric. "Schedule" defines intervals during which the function is executed. The guarantee has a validity period called "validate". Operators defined in "predicate" compare the metric measurement with a threshold. "Actions" are trigged in the case of guarantee violation. We are using quality and guarantee definitions according to WSLA specification [9]. We implemented resource access policies using XACML[10]. In addition to defining a standard format for policy, XACML defines a standard way of expressing requests. Server_agents build request files in execution time according to the values included in the user_agent proposals. Requests are evaluated against policies.

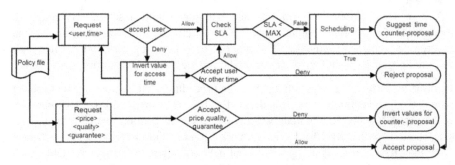

Fig. 3. Policy analysis functional model

Figure 3 presents our policy analysis functional model. It shows the possibilities of acceptance, rejection, and inversion of values for the elaboration of counter-proposals. First, it is necessary to check if the user has permission to run a job in the resource at the time suggested. If the answer is positive, it is necessary to verify if the number of jobs already submitted for that resource do not exceed the maximum allowed at the same time (Max SLA). In the case of exceeding such limit, the server_agent schedules the job to another time. Price, quality and guarantee are checked and accepted if the proposed values are allowed by the policy file, otherwise the server_agent inverts the argument value according to table 1 and includes this value in the counter-proposal. If the user cannot execute a job in any given time in that resource, the proposal is rejected.

We defined the schedule problem using the notation used in [8]. The schedule problem has three parameters that represent, respectively, the number of machines involved, the number of jobs and the optimization function. We model the schedule problem as [1 machine| 1 job |SLA load balance]. Our scheduler optimization function balances job execution by choosing the interval with less SLAs associated. We are considering that the machine negotiated can be a cluster head.

Negotiation Based on Performance Prediction. This procedure uses a prediction technique in order to know when a job will finish. We incorporate Case-Based Reasoning (CBR) technique in our negotiation process in order to give confidence to SLAs. CBR predicts resource performance based in past cases. If a job with similar characteristics has already been run in the same or similar machine, it is possible to predict the job run time. With prediction, we can estimate how many SLAs are associated to each resource at the same time and improve scheduling process [12].

Table 2. Job submission experiences expressed in cases

	Case attribute	Case 1	Case 2	Case 3
Problem	File name	Simulator 1	Simulator 1	Simulator 1
	Arguments(no.exec, tempo exec)	1, 2h	1, 2h	1, 2h
	Operating System, Version	Suzie, 9.0	Suzie, 9.0	Red Hat 8.0
	Local resource management	Pbs	Pbs	Pbs
	Minimum RAM required	512 MB	512 MB	512 MB
	Minimum no. processors	2	2	2
	Minimum CPU performance	2GHz	2GHz	2GHz
Solution	Host where job was executed	HPCBC129219	HPCBC129219	Ontario
	CPU	2 GHz	2 GHz	2 GHz
	RAM	1 GB	1 GB	1 GB
	No. processors	2	2	4
	Job submission time	08:10:54	11:00:05	15:20:19
Result	Job finish execution time	09:11:25	12:11:25	16:11:25
	Max SLA	20	20	30
	Estimated execution	1:00:00	1:00:00	-
	Estimation method	Identical case	Relative case	CPU speed
	SLAs during execution	12	6	18
	No. users during execution	63	48	54

Performance prediction in grid is rare [7]. But, it becomes essential in a solution that intends to solve problems associated with guarantees to the grid service delivery.

Table 2 shows part of our CBR information structure where experiences are expressed in some case examples. The attributes are grouped according to the problem, the solution and the result associated to a case. A server_agent uses the parameter *JD* with the job description to check if there are similar cases into problem group. Solutions used, that is, servers selected to run similar jobs and conditions provided in past cases, are described in the solution group. Result group registers data monitored during the job execution. We infer from result group the success or fail of past cases.

The similarity between a new case and past cases can be acquired using similarity measures like Euclidean distance, where smaller distances indicate increasing similarity [14]. In the Euclidean measures, for each pair of values (here interpreted as arguments of past case (x) and arguments of new case (y)) we can calculate the distance using the formula $Ed(x,y)=((x0-x1)^2 + (y0-y1)^2)^{1/2}$. In our project, the estimations for a job run time can be of three types: identical case, analogous case or no past case. With no acceptable past case in the case library, the server selection must be based, mainly, in the server CPU speed.

3.2 Migration Module

Migration module is responsible for making the decision of "where" to run the job. It is formed by the SLA Matching and Migration sub-modules.

SLA Matching Sub-module. It matches SLAs that are interconnected and are providing the same service. For example, a service can include a SLA established between user_agent and server_agent (SSLA) and a SLA established between user_agent and network_agent (NSLA). The combination of both will show when the job will start and finish, the total price, and the quality of service for both services.

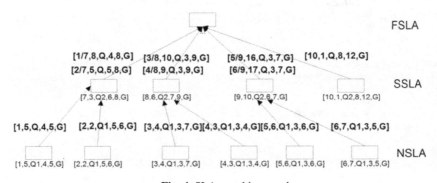

Fig. 4. SLA matching graph

We are using a graph G, directed and acyclic, to model the SLA matching procedure. G=(V,E), where V={s} and each vertex in V represents a SLA. Each edge denotes the precedence between SLAs in time schedule and accumulates SLA parameters. A node is represented as a tuple <Id,P,Q,Ts,Tf,G> where Id is the SLA identification; P is the price negotiated; Q is a set of quality of service; Ts is the job start time; Tf is the job finish time; and G is a set of guarantees.

The time to start a Final SLA (FSLA) is the time to start the NSLA and the time to finish the FSLA is the time to finish the SSLA, so fsla.start = nsla.start and fsla.finish = ssla.finish. The price of FSLA is the price accumulation for all SLAs interconnected, defined as A(s) = nsla.price + ssla.price. The QoS and guarantee of the FSLA is a set of different QoS and guarantees established in the NSLA and SSLA respectively, where fsla.qos= {(nsla,ssla).qos} and fsla.guarantee= {(nsla,ssla).guarantee}.

Figure 4 shows an example of a graph that matches all SLAs established in negotiations of a job submission. Layers represent FSLA, NSLA and SSLA. The root of the graph is a node where all SLA combinations converge and it represents the Final SLA (FSLA) that will be selected by the migration decision sub-module.

Migration Decision Sub-module. This sub-module is responsible for making the decision of "where" to run a job. It takes into account the user preference among price, quality of service or performance. It chooses the best combination of SLAs involved in a service delivery and discards alternative SLAs. The migration is done using agents and GridFTP [1]. This sub-module also submits job to the selected resources using Globus commands. The SLAs selected are activated in the MDS.

3.3   Interface OGSA Module

This module provides the interface between the multi-agent system and the OGSA. It groups functions associated with query, notification and grid commands. We are integrating our multi-agent system into the grid environment by the following implementations: 1) Extension of the grid directory service schema by adding SLA attributes. A complete SLA is formed by SLA tuple, presented in 3.2 section, and is complemented by other agreement information. A partial example of some SLA attributes generated by our information provider can be viewed in figure 5; 2) Definition of a proxy for agents in grid; 3) Inclusion of negotiation objects into grid resource access policies. We defined such policies using XACML [10].

```
nassifl@hpc129219:/opt/globus-2.4/etc> /home/nassifl/informationprovider/grid-info-SLA-core -
devclassobj -devobjs -dn Mds-Host-hn=hpc129219.iit.nrc.ca,Mds-Vo-name=local,o=grid -validto-s
ecs 21600 -keepto-secs 240800
dn: Service-Level-Agreement=agent, Mds-Host-hn=hpc129219.iit.nrc.ca,Mds-Vo-name=local,o=grid
objectclass: UoOAgentSLA
objectclass: UoOAgentSLAPartiesServiceProvider
objectclass: UoOAgentSLAPartiesServiceConsumer
objectclass: UoOAgentSLAPartiesSupportingParty
objectclass: UoOAgentSLAServiceObjectSLAParameter-Metric
objectclass: UoOAgentSLAServiceGuaranteesServiceLevelObjective
UoO-Agent-SLA-ID:15012204103598
UoO-Agent-SLA-Parties-ServiceProvider-Contact: hpc129219://nrc/agent/agentnetwork2
UoO-Agent-SLA-Parties-ServiceConsumer-Contact: ontario://nrc/agent/agentlilian
UoO-Agent-SLA-Parties-SupportingParty-Contact: cobra://nrc/agent/third-party-agent
UoO-Agent-SLA-Parties-SupportingParty-Role: Manager
UoO-Agent-SLA-Service-Object-Schedule-Period:Mon Jun 28 08:50:00 EDT 2004
UoO-Agent-SLA-Service-Object-SLAParameter-Metric-Name:bandwidth
UoO-Agent-SLA-Guarantees-ActionGuarantee-Expression: if transfer_time > transfer_prediction
Mds-Service-hn: hpc129219.iit.nrc.ca
Mds-Service-port: 2135
Mds-Service-Ldap-timeout: 30
Mds-Service-admin-contact: Mohamed.Ahmed@nrc.cnrc-gc.ca
Mds-Service-Executable-PID: 9616
Mds-Service-Path: /opt/globus-2.4
Mds-Service-admin-comment: This is an MDS 2.2 deployment.
Mds-Service-Ldap-suffix: Mds-Vo-name=local,o=Grid
Mds-Service-Ldap-suffix: Mds-Vo-name=site,o=Grid
Mds-validfrom: 200406281407172
Mds-validto: 200406282007172
Mds-keepto: 200407010900372
```

Fig. 5. Information provider with SLA parameters

4 Testbed

In order to test our system, we will make use of a controlled testbed in a grid infrastructure. Such environment should allow replications of scenarios with identical characteristics. The testbed is the most viable way to analyze the system, since current grid simulators and emulators do not implement middleware we would like to test, such as Condor, GRMS and Mask. The scenario for this testbed involves the use of datagrid applications, which, in general, demand a great amount of data to be processed by an application. The time to transfer data and the quality of service provided by network links are significant in this context. Although the scalability in this testbed is reduced, the proof of concept is possible and we can compare different functionalities and results for each middleware. The test will be executed with the same workload and will be performed in an isolated way for each middleware. Some parameters can be changed during the tests, such as: workload, resource policies, user's preferences, addition or removal of machines, and the location of application and data. The test must be repeated for each middleware, for each set of changes.

The testbed was created at National Research Council Canada, with two sites interconnected. The total amount of CPUs is fifteen. The environment was configured properly for each middleware. Condor demands the installation of clients and central manager and GRMS requests service and broker software. Mask demands a definition of Jade platform and containers. The tests analyze the choice of the server, the service delivery guarantee, and the SLA establishment by considering user's preference and resource policies. We have conducted preliminary tests with policies in XACML format for some machines of our testbed. We also developed an information provider that reads SLAs created by agents and upgrades this information in MDS structure.

5 Conclusions

In this paper we consider that guarantees for grid service delivery and resource intelligent allocation are still challenges in the Grid middleware which needs more robust and adaptable alternatives to solve this problem.

We presented here a multi-agent system that decides the best place to run a job. In our solution, the negotiation process is the main aspect developed to achieve this goal. The negotiation is based on resource access policy and resource performance prediction using the CBR technique. The negotiation is established as a Service Level Agreement. The migration process complements the negotiation process. It matches SLAs established between agents and considers the set of SLAs that best fits the user preferences to make a migration decision. The SLA matching process is described in a graph notation.

We are currently integrating our multi-agent system into Globus middleware. We expect to compare our system with other middleware mainly concerning benefits obtained with the use of SLA, resource performance prediction and policy-based negotiation. Our future work concerns explore the monitoring module, where the mobility of agents can help to find out the real conditions of job executions. We also intend to address our multi-agent system to the meta-schedule problem in grid by including such feature in the second level of our hierarchical architecture.

Acknowledgment

The first author thanks CAPES and Prodabel for financial and institutional support.

References

1. Globus. http://www.globus.org
2. Andrieux, A., Berry, D., Garibaldi, J., Jarvis, S., MacLaren, J., Ouelhadj, D., Sneling, D.: Open issues in Grid Scheduling. Report of workshop at e-Science Institute, 2003.
3. Czajkowski, K., Foster, I., Kesselman, C., Sander, V., Tuecke, S.: SNAP: A Protocol for Negotiation of Service Level Agreements and Coordinated Resource Management. Workshop on Job Scheduling Strategies for Parallel Processing (JSSPP'02), Edinburgh, 2002.
4. Raman, R., Livny, M., Solomon, M.: Matchmaking: Distributed Resource Management for High Throughput Computing. Proceedings of The Seventh IEEE International Symposium on High Performance Distributed Computing, p.140, Chicago, 1998.
5. GRMS. http://www.gridlab.org/WorkPackages/wp-9.
6. Overeinder, B. Wijngaards, N., Steen, M.van, Brazier, F.: Multi-agent Support for Internet-Scale Grid Management. AISB Symposium on AI and Grid Computing, London, 2002.
7. Cao, J., Jarvis, S., Saini, S., kerbyson, D., Nudd, G.: ARMS: An Agent-based Resource Management System for Grid Computing. Scientific Programming, Special issue on Grid Computing, IOS Press, 2002.
8. Pinedo, M.: Scheduling: Theory, Algorithms, and Systems. Prentice-Hall, 2nd Ed., 2002.
9. Dan, A., Franck, R., Keller, A., King, R., Ludwig, H.: Web Service Level Agreement. (WSLA) Language Specification WSLA, 2002.
10. Godik, S., Moses, T.: eXtensible Access Control Markup Language (XACML) Version 1.0, OASIS Standard, 2003.
11. Jade. http://sharon.cselt.it/projects/jade/
12. Smith, W., Foster, I., Taylor, V.: Predicting Application Run Times Using Historical Information. 4th Workshop on Job Scheduling Strategies for Parallel Processing, USA, 1998.
13. Kolodner, J.: Case-Based Reasoning. Morgan Kaufmann Publishers, 1993.
14. Lewis, L.: Managing Computer Networks A Case-Based Reasoning Approach. Artech House Publishers, 1995.

Mobile Agent Oriented Software Engineering (MAOSE)

Li Wang and Qiao Guo

Network Information Center, Beijing Institute of Technology, Beijing 100081, China
{victorwang,guoqiao}@bit.edu.cn

Abstract. Mobile agent (MA) has gained a lot of researchers' interests for its outstanding superiorities. For a long time, it is regarded as a subsidiary subject of agent technique. Accordingly, people tend to develop MA-based system relying on the methodologies of Agent Oriented Software Engineering (AOSE). In fact, they are not well suitable for mobile agent. Most agent methodologies have not sufficiently considered the migration characteristic of mobile agent, and the spatial coordinate is unconsciously ignored. Migration is in the network, so the network's island property should be taken into account. Mobile agent should be manageable, and their population must be controlled in proportion to environment resource. In this paper, a novel subject – Mobile Agent Oriented Software Engineering (MAOSE) is represented, which is based on the improvement of MAS-CommonKADS and MESSAGE, with spatiotemporal concept and the idea of ecology introduced. The new methodology consists of agent model, organization model, clan model, task model, interaction model, migration model and knowledge model, which can describe mobile agent system and contribute to the design of MA-based software system.

1 Introduction

These years, mobile agent (MA), as the combination of distributed computing and agent technique, has drawn a lot of attention for it can migrate in the network autonomously and carry out the specified task given by users [1]. If used appropriately, it can efficiently save bandwidth, distribute the computing burden, increase the service intelligence and flexibility, and enhance the system scalability and robustness. It has been tentatively applied to many fields, such as electronic commerce, personal assistance, information retrieval, network management and parallel processing etc.

For a long time, mobile agent is regarded as a subsidiary subject of agent technique, so people are inclined to develop application system in the method of Agent Oriented Software Engineering (AOSE). We have seen that AOSE has a lot of superiorities to traditional Object Oriented Software Engineering (OOSE). The former can deal more complicated problem if given enough intelligence and ability. The methodology of AOSE has made great progress especially in recent years. Kinny [2] defines a methodology for MAS extending OMT in two main levels: agent, and interactions. Burmeister [3] describes an agent-oriented methodology in three models, agent model, organizational model and a cooperation model. MASB [4] proposes an agent-oriented methodology that covers analysis and design. CoMoMAS [5] proposes also an extension to CommonKADS for MAS. DESIRE [6] is a formal framework for multiagent modeling, which covers task, agent and expertise models. CoLa [7] is a

A. Karmouch, L. Korba, and E. Madeira (Eds.): MATA 2004, LNCS 3284, pp. 168–177, 2004.

specification language for task decomposition, transactions and contracts. MAS-CommonKADS [8] extends the knowledge engineering methodology Common-KADS with techniques from object oriented and protocol engineering methodologies, which consists of seven models, agent model, task model, expertise model, organization model, coordination model, communication model and design model. MESSAGE [9] presents a set of five analysis models, which can be used by analysts to capture different aspects of an agent system. They are organization model, goal/task model, agent model, domain (information) model and interaction model.

All these methodologies can effectively solve some problems in different fields. However, they are not well suitable for mobile agent. Most agent methodologies have not sufficiently considered the migration characteristic of mobile agent. Accordingly, the spatial coordinate is unconsciously ignored, which is the most important for mobile agent. Migration in the network should correspond to the properties of real network. The network's *island* characteristic should be taken into account. Mobile agent should also be manageable, though it can autonomously move. Their population must be controlled in proportion to environment resource. Agent is firstly natural, secondly social. In this aspect, the idea of ecology can be introduced into the management of mobile agent.

Based on the improvement of MAS-CommonKADS and MESSAGE, with spatio-temporal concept and the idea of ecology introduced, a novel engineering model Mobile Agent Oriented Software Engineering (MAOSE) is established, which can lively describe mobile agent system and contribute to the design of software system based on mobile agent.

2 Model Descriptions

2.1 Model Framework Overview

The MAOSE model framework is composed of seven models, agent model, organization model, clan model, task model, interaction model, migration model and knowledge model. These seven models, related and overlapped with each other, together build up our defined framework. Among these models, we call agent model, organization model and clan model as autonomous entities for they have initiatives, while the left are called non-autonomous entities.

2.2 Agent Model (AM)

Agent is a simple individual, which can autonomously sense, reason, decide and act. AM is used to describe MA's identifier, attributes, characters and its environment. The value of MA exists in its function. In order to explain MA's function, we still inherit the *role* concept. A MA can take on different roles according to its capabilities. In addition, the spatiotemporal concepts, time and location are also added, i.e. a MA must know current time and location and let it be controlled by some other model elements. This is helpful for the management of MAs, for MA often migrates from here to there. AM's structure is depicted as bellow in Fig. 1. Several concepts about Fig. 1 are also given out.

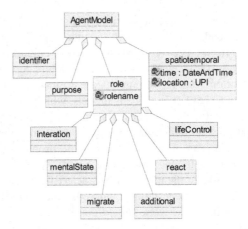

Fig. 1. Agent model structure

- $AM_{identifier}$: $AM_{identifier}$ is MA's identifier to differentiate from each other. The same naming mechanism can refer to FIPA org.
- $AM_{purpose}$: $AM_{purpose}$ expresses what to guide MA's decision and actions.
- AM_{role}: AM_{role} generally describes what task the agent can undertake in the process. In many applications, it can easily represent the MA's capability in some aspect.
- $AM_{spatiotemporal}$: $AM_{spatiotemporal}$ is to describe the information of time and location where the MA exists. Time can adopt an absolute timestamp DateAndTime in network management, while UPI [10] is suggested to name location that consists of a physicalAddressID and a placeID. From these spatiotemporal and environment information, MA can determine what to do next.
- $AM_{ability}$: $AM_{ability}$ is corresponding to AM_{role}. The abilities include iteration, mental state, reaction, migration, life control and some additions. Iteration includes communicating, understanding and resource control and access. Mental state includes desire, belief, intention, knowledge storage, guide and decision. Reaction includes sensing and performing actions to the environment. Migration includes movement and stay. Life control includes generation, suspension and termination. The ability can be separated into two layers, the basic ability and the special ability. Basic ability is loosely coupled with knowledge model of specific domain, while special ability is strictly coupled with the knowledge model of specific domain. Both of them are related to interaction model and migration model.

2.3 Organization Model (OM)

Organization is a community established by a group of MAs for a same goal or task. OM describes this community's purpose, right, responsibility, owned resources, complied guide, workflow, structure, MA's role and their mutual relations. Note that OM can be described iteratively, i.e. an organization can be divided into several subsidiary organizations if needed. Fig. 2 depicts OM's structure.

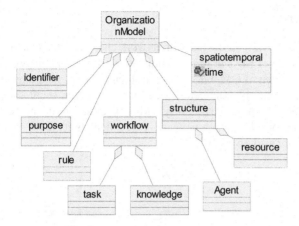

Fig. 2. Organization model structure

- $OM_{identifier}$: $OM_{identifier}$ is the organization's identifier to differentiate from each other. Since the needs are diverse, we can refer to maintenance of MIB tree in network management. An international institute, such as IANA, can be authorized to divide organizations by numbering. Some common MAs sharing the same function should be in the same organizations. And, some other number should be preserved for extension of enterprises' private applications. For example, {1,3,6,1, 2,1,1} refers to common flux monitoring organization, while {1,3,6,1,4,1,X,1,1,1} refers to X enterprise's private fault processing organization.
- $OM_{purpose}$: $OM_{purpose}$ is a comprehensive concept to guide organization's decisions and actions.
- $OM_{resource}$: $OM_{resource}$ describes the physical or logical resource an organization requires to operate. The resource can be memory, CPU processing time or database etc.
- OM_{rule}: OM_{rule} explains the norm how the organization operates and controls itself, or the resolving mechanism when a conflict occurs.
- $OM_{workflow}$: $OM_{workflow}$ describes the schedule and arrangement on how to deal with a task [9]. It is generally expressed with the power relations between MA's roles. Power relations can be separated into two types, isInfluencedBy and isSubordinateTo. For instance, companion relation can be seen as isInfluencedBy no matter they are in competition or cooperation, while the relation between stuff and head is isSubordinateTo.
- $OM_{spatiotemporal}$: An organization should know its time, while location is not necessary. A MA can only join in a currently existing organization, so here we focus on the time concept. However, an organization's office could be virtual and unlimited to one place, so location concept is not emphasized. Since interaction in OM cannot be ignored, which is often concerned with location, no matter mailbox, blackboard or direct communication, location is also important to OM.

2.4 Clan Model (CM)

Clan model is put forward on the basis of network characteristic. Clan is a community composed of a group of MAs or organizations located in a specific area. The function of CM is similar to that of OM, but the former focuses on its natural ecology concept. MAs in one area cannot be innumerable, and the population should be in proportion to resource and environment. That is why CM is specifically advanced. A clan can be a host, a computer or a local area network. Fig. 3 depicts its main structure, and the related concepts are also given out.

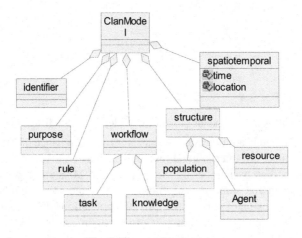

Fig. 3. Clan model structure

- $CM_{identifier}$: Clan's identifier should be bound with IP address or a number assigned by some international organizations like $OM_{identifier}$. It is sometimes analogous to *domain* concept in network management.
- $CM_{purpose}$: $CM_{purpose}$ is the whole guide for clan to decide or act.
- $CM_{resource}$: $CM_{resource}$ includes the physical or logical resource the clan needs to operate.
- $CM_{population}$: $CM_{population}$ refers to the population of all agents stayed in the specific area.
- CM_{rule}: CM_{rule} explains how the clan operates and controls it.
- $CM_{workflow}$: Different from $OM_{workflow}$, $CM_{workflow}$ does not care how to cooperate and solve the task. $CM_{workflow}$ just explains that the task or problem is detected and assigned to some MA, and the assigned MA is in responsibility of cooperation with other MAs or doing more. In fact, as far as task is concerned, the relation between role and task in $CM_{workflow}$ is loosely coupled. The settlement of task still resorts to OM. For example, the relation in $CM_{workflow}$ can be isAssignedBy.
- $CM_{spatiotemporal}$: Since clan is located in one area, time and location concepts are both important to CM.

2.5 Task Model (TM)

Task model describes the goal, which the autonomous entity aims to reach at a certain time and a certain location. Task can be decomposed into subtask to reduce its complexity. Actually, it is often simplified into a series of activities in purpose. Here, it is necessary to mention the principle of task decomposition. The task in MA-based system often needs to be done in many different locations, so decomposition according to locations is often the first principle. At the same time, some other common principles should also be conformed to. The first child task's pre-condition must be implied in its parent task's pre-condition, and the last child task's post-condition must be included in its parent task's post-condition [9]. If a single agent can complete the task independently, it is really unnecessary to decompose any more. TM's structure is depicted in Fig. 4, and several concepts are shown as followed.

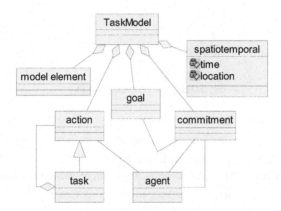

Fig. 4. Task model structure

- TM$_{goal}$: Goal is a series of environment situations, which a MA, an organization or a clan want to attain. It generally comprises an informal name, a formal aliases and a .description [9]. Goal can be decomposed according to the principle that child goal must satisfy parent goal.
- TM$_{action}$: Action is an element behavior which can influence or change system environment. The difference between the pre-condition and the post-condition indicates whether the action has taken place or not. Note that the action mentioned here does not include migration.
- TM$_{commitment}$: Commitment refers to a ternary relationship between two agents and a task. One sender agent commits the task to the receiver agent. The latter is obligated to fulfill the task.
- TM$_{spatiotemporal}$: TM$_{spatiotemporal}$ means that a task has its limitation of time and space. Time concept implies that a task has its start time and lifecycle. Space concept implies where the task has been executed.

2.6 Interaction Model (IM)

Interaction model describes how the autonomous entities communicate with each other, in which a communicating method is defined. Interaction model consists of communicating relations, agent roles, communicating protocols and communicating tools. Its structure is shown in Fig. 5.

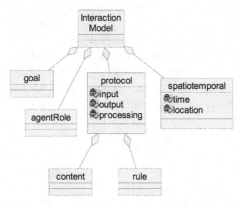

Fig. 5. Interaction model structure

- IM_{goal}: IM_{goal} explains the aim to interact.
- $IM_{agentRole}$: $IM_{agentRole}$ constitutes the main members in the interaction, which may include interaction sponsor, interaction responder, etc.
- $IM_{protocol}$: Protocol comprises two parts, the content, which both sides can understand, and the rule, which both sides can observe. Content consists of input and output, which correspond to the content of sponsor and that of responder.
- $IM_{spatiotemporal}$: IM concerns both time concept and space concept. An interaction must be completed in a period of time. An interaction without time limit is meaningless. Because of migration in the network, it is hard for MA to know exactly where its partner is. Blackboard and mailbox as the communicating tool have been widely accepted. Space concept is the location of blackboard or the server for e-mail, generally represented in UPI.

2.7 Migration Model (MM)

Migration Model is specifically put forward for mobile agent system. It describes the migration style and itinerary pattern. Fig. 6 depicts its structure.

- $MM_{stayedPlace}$: $MM_{stayedPlace}$ describes where MA currently stays.
- $MM_{destination}$: $MM_{destination}$ describes the next station of MA.
- $MM_{migrationStyle}$: $MM_{migrationStyle}$ defines MA migration level is strong migration or weak migration. In strong migration, program state, data state and execution state must be captured and transferred to the destination machine. Whereas, in weak migration only program state and data state are transferred.

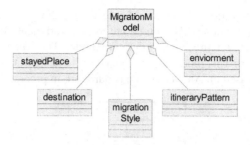

Fig. 6. Migration model structure

- $MM_{itineraryPattern}$: MA's itinerary pattern includes two kinds, pre-planned and conditional. In the former, MA's itinerary is determined according to needs before it start migration. In the latter, MA does not know which one is the next station, which will depend on the environment situation at that time.
- $MM_{environment}$: $MM_{environment}$ refers to all the factors, which can influence migration itinerary.

2.8 Knowledge Model (KM)

Knowledge model is the domain information database, which a MA requires to deal with a task. It consists of terms, rules and some other additional attributes. Fig. 7 depicts its structure.

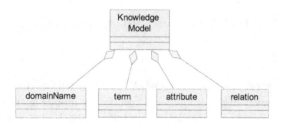

Fig. 7. Knowledge model structure

- $KM_{domainName}$: $KM_{domainName}$ identifies different domain knowledge.
- KM_{term}: KM_{term} refers to the basic concepts in the domain knowledge.
- $KM_{attribute}$: $KM_{attribute}$ consists of some other additional attributes.
- $KM_{relation}$: $KM_{relation}$ provides the rules of concept connection and knowledge reasoning.

3 Modeling Process

The main modeling process is shown in Fig. 8. Task description in detail according to customer requirement is the first step. Then the task model is in conception. When the relevant domain knowledge is collected, the knowledge model framework is setup. At the same time, organization model for MA to cooperation to solve task and clan model to balance population and resource are also in rudiment. The next step is to define and specify iteration model and migration model. The process is recursive until all the details are clear. This modeling has been used to design QoS-guaranteed adaptive routing system based on AntNet, which is our work in processing.

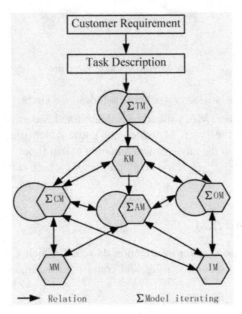

Fig. 8. Development workflow for MAOSE

4 Conclusions

Based on the absorption of MAS-CommonKADS and MESSAGE, inspired by the idea of ecology, a novel engineering model specific for mobile agent system is established, which consists of agent model, organization model, clan model, task model, interaction model, migration model and knowledge model. This methodology has been attempted to apply to the development of MA-based network management system specific for QoS-guaranteed adaptive routing based on AntNet.

The motive of study on agent is to adopt the thoughts of different fields (such as ecology, sociology, economics, philosophy and logic etc.), and abstract more natural and reasonable model for developing complicated system. MA is an agent that can move. From this aspect, the system based on MAs is much more like human society. Undoubtedly, sometimes stationery agent is more efficient than a mobile one, while sometimes it is on the contrary. Just like in life, it is convenient to collect some information by fax if both sides have been equipped with it, but if not, it is a better way to send a person to do the job on the spot and return it back, for it is too expensive and impractical to install a fax temporarily. Mobile agent is such a flexible way to enrich service logic dynamically at running time. We believe stationary agent and mobile agent, complementary with each other, will build up next generation software system. Frankly speaking, it is hard to perfectly simulate a human society in programming. Though a lot mentioned above are still worth discussing in detail, we are sure MAOSE, as a new subject for mobile agent, will play an important role in the future software development.

References

1. A. Puliafito, O. Tomrchio, and L. Vita: MAP: Design and implementation of a mobile agents' platform, Journal of Systems Architecture, 46 (2000) 145–162
2. D. Kinny, M. Georgeff, and A. Rao: A methodology and modelling technique for systems of BDI agents, Agents Breaking Away: Proceedings of the Seventh European Workshop on Modelling Autonomous Agents in a Multi-Agent World MAAMAW'96, Springer-Verlag, Germany, Vol. 1038 (1996) 56–71
3. B. Burmeister: Models and methodology for agent-oriented analysis and design, Working Notes of the KI'96 Workshop on Agent-Oriented Programming and Distributed Systems, Saarbrücken, Germany (1996)
4. B. Moulin, and L. Cloutier: Collaborative work based on multiagent architectures: A methodological perspective, Soft Computing: Fuzzy Logic, Neural Networks and Distributed Artificial Intelligence, Prentice-Hall, USA, (1994) 261–296
5. N. Glaser: Contribution to Knowledge Modelling in a Multi-Agent Framework (the Co-MoMAS Approach), PhD thesis, L'Universtit´e Henri Poincar´e, Nancy I, France, November 1996.
6. F. M. T. Brazier, B. M. Dunin-Keplicz, N. R. Jennings, and J. Treur: DESIRE: Modelling multi-agent systems in a compositional formal framework, International Journal of Cooperative Information Systems, January (1997) 67–94
7. E. Verharen, F. Dignum, and S. Bos: Implementation of a cooperative agent architecture based on the language-action perspective, Intelligent Agents IV, Springer-Verlag, Germany, (1998) 31–44
8. C.A. Iglesias, M. Garijo, J.C. González, and J.R. Velasco: Analysis and Design of Multi-agent Systems using MAS-CommonKADS, Proceedings International Workshop on Agent Theories, Architectures, and Languages (ATAL'97), USA, (1997) 313–327
9. EURESCOM: MESSAGE: Methodology for Engineering Systems of Software Agents, http://www.eurescom.de
10. D. Rossier: Towards Active Network Management with Ecomobile, an Ecosystem-inspired Mobile Agent Middleware, PhD thesis, Imprimerie Uni-Print, Universit´e de Fribourg, (2002)

A Probabilistic Transmission Control Scheme
for Low Power Consumption in Sensor Networks*

Jungpil Ryu, Minsu Kim, Sungho Hwang, Byeongjik Lee, and Kijun Han**

Department of Computer Engineering,
Kyungpook National University, Korea
{goldmunt,kiunsen,sungho,leric}@netopia.knu.ac.kr,
kjhan@bh.knu.ac.kr

Abstract. In this paper, we propose a probabilistic transmission control scheme to reduce the redundant consumption of computation power, storage, energy resources, and radio technology in sensor networks. Our scheme dynamically determines the transmission probability at application layer of each node based on the neighbor information within two-hop span. Simulation results are presented, which show our scheme may offer a better performance over the deterministic transmission control approach.

1 Introduction

Sensor network is an important emerging area of mobile computing that presents novel wireless networking issues because of their unusual application requirements, highly constrained resources and functionality, small packet size, and deep multi-hop dynamic topologies. Although many high level architectural and programming aspects of this area are still being resolved, the underlying media access control (MAC) and transmission control protocols are critical enabling technology for many sensor network applications. These problems are well-studied for traditional computer networks, however, the different wireless technologies, application characteristics, and usage scenarios create a complex mix of issues that have led to the existence of many distinct solutions. [1-5].

Application behavior in sensor networks leads to very different traffic characteristics from that found in conventional computer networks. The primary function of a sensor network application is to sample the environment for sensory information, such as temperature, and propagate this data back to the infrastructure, while perhaps performing some in-network processing, such as aggregation or compression. The network tends to operate as a collective structure, rather than supporting many independent point-to-point flows. Traffic tends to be variable and highly correlated. Over lengthy periods there may be little activity or traffic, but for short periods the traffic may be very intense. For example, when an abnormal event, such as a fire, is detected, many devices will initiate communication at once. [6]

In recent years, a number of studies for reducing the power consumption of sensor network have been carried out. These studies mainly focused on data-aggregated routing algorithm and energy efficient MAC protocols. For more inherent solution to

---

* University Fundamental Research Program supported by Ministry of Information & Communication in Republic of Korea.
** Correspondent author.

A. Karmouch, L. Korba, and E. Madeira (Eds.): MATA 2004, LNCS 3284, pp. 178–185, 2004.

reduce energy consumption problem, however, application level should be also considered. In this paper, we suggest a probabilistic approach to reduce the redundant packet transmission while maintaining reliability above some acceptable level. In our scheme, each node probabilistically decides whether to transmit a packet to its neighbors or not, based on the geographical distribution of nodes. In other words, each node adaptively determines the transmission probability using local density information at each node. The local density information means the number of neighbors. Our paper is organized as follows. Section 2 introduces our scheme and simulation results are presented in section 3. Finally, section 4 contains the conclusions.

2   Probabilistic Transmission Control Scheme

The sensor nodes are usually scattered in a *sensor field* as shown in Fig. 1. Each of these scattered sensor nodes has the capabilities to collect data and route data back to the *sink*. Data are routed back to the sink by a multihop infrastructureless architecture through the sink. The sink may communicate with the *task manager node* via Internet or satellite. [10]

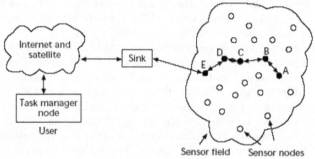

Fig. 1. Sensor nodes scattered in a sensor field

Due to the tight restricts of sensor node, power consumption has been considered as one of the most important issues. In addition, fairness is also a highly desirable requirement for construction of efficient sensor networks. For example, we may want to collect roughly the same amount of temperature data from each deployed sensor in a field to infer the temperature gradient during a fire. Therefore, a fair allocation of bandwidth delivered to the base station from each node over multiple hops is desired. It is not sufficient to share the channel fairly in an individual cell, we would like to achieve a crude level of end-to-end fairness even in a deep and self-organized multihop networks, which may change dynamically and originate data at each intermediate node. To satisfy requirements of the low power consumption and fairness, we should control the transmission of sensing information by considering the local density which means the geographical density of nodes.

For implementation of an efficient sensor network, energy efficient routing algorithm and MAC protocols have mainly been studied. However, application level has not been considered although it might make more inherent solution to reduce energy consumption. In this paper, we propose a traffic control scheme to reduce transmission redundancy at application level as shown in Fig. 2.

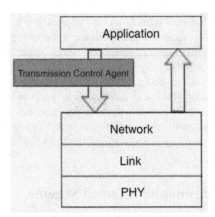

Fig. 2. Transmission control agent

The redundant sensing traffic is apt to be generated when a number of nodes are located in a relatively small area. Under the highly dense distribution of nodes, the solutions for reducing transmission attempts at network layer or at link layer can not guarantee the satisfactory results. Control of the transmission rate at application layer is absolutely needed to make sensor networks more effective.

Here, we propose a dynamic probabilistic scheme to reduce the redundant packet transmission while maintaining acceptable reliability. In our scheme, each node probabilistically decides whether to transmit a packet to its neighbors or not, based on geographical distribution of nodes. In other words, each node adaptively determines the transmission probability using local information at each node. In our scheme, each node determines its own transmission probability depending on its local information within two-hops to minimize the redundancy overhead while obtaining acceptable reachability. We assume that the local information can be simply achieved through periodical packets and from other protocols such as the routing protocols. To explain our scheme, some parameters are defined as follows.

- S_W = set of one-hop neighbors of node W

- S^2_W = set of two-hop neighbors of node W

- U_{W,X_k} = set of two-hop neighbors that can be reached only through one-hop neighbor X_k from W (for $k=1,2,3,...,n$)

- $N(.)$ = size of a set.

It was shown in [8], [9] that the probabilistic scheme offers poor reachability. This is because every node tries to transmit its packet with the same probability, regardless of its local information.

When the node W senses and makes a packet to transmit, it computes the transmission probability using one of the following four versions.

- Version 1
$$P_W = \text{Constant} \tag{1}$$

- Version 2
$$P_W = \frac{1}{N(S_W)} \cdot \sum_{k=1}^{N(S_W)} N(U_{W,X_k}) \tag{2}$$

- Version 3

$$P_W = \frac{N(S_W)}{N(S_W) + N(S^2{}_W)}$$

(3)

- Version 4

$$P_W = \frac{N(S^2{}_W)}{N(S_W) + N(S^2{}_W)}$$

(4)

The first version gives the same probability of transmission to every node. The second version is based on the density of two-hop neighbors that can be reached only through one-hop neighbor. The third version determines the transmission probability by the fraction of one-hop neighbors within two-hop coverage. On the other hand, the forth version chooses the transmission probability by computing the fraction of two-hop neighbors within two-hop coverage.

Our scheme can be figured out using an example shown in Fig. 3.

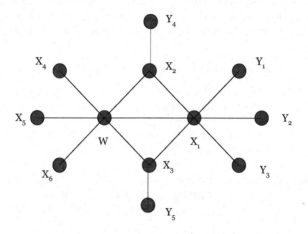

Fig. 3. Example for one-hop and two-hop neighbors

$$S_W = \{X_1, X_2, X_3, X_4, X_5, X_6\}; N(S_W) = 6$$
$$S_W^2 = \{Y_1, Y_2, Y_3, Y_4, Y_5\}; N(S^2{}_W) = 5$$
$$U_{W,X_1} = \{Y_1, Y_2, Y_3\}; N(U_{W,X_1}) = 3$$
$$U_{W,X_2} = \{Y_4\}; N(U_{W,X_2}) = 1$$
$$U_{W,X_3} = \{Y_5\}; N(U_{W,X_3}) = 1$$

Version 2: $P_W = \dfrac{1}{6} \cdot (3+1+1) = 0.833$

Version 3: $P_W = \dfrac{1}{6} \cdot (3+1+1) = 0.833$

Version 4: $P_W = \dfrac{5}{6+5} = 0.4545$

3 Simulations

We have carried out a discrete event simulation to evaluate performance of our scheme. We first define the square grid model which consists of $m \times m$ grid with nodes placed at each intersection [9]. A geometric area called a map and the size of overall area is 20×20. A radio range radius is given 500m, a unit on map is 100m and all the nodes which are inside this radius (500m) are considered as the direct, one-hop neighbors. In our simulation, we consider a map of 20, 40, 60, 80, 100, 150 and 200 nodes randomly distributed. We have performed simulation runs with various topologies of networks. In each case, 1,000 packets are generated.

In our simulations, some assumptions are made as follows [8-9]:

- There are no unidirectional links. Each link between a pair of nodes is a perfect bidirectional link;
- The only traffic carried within the network is that of the diffusion of packet;
- Each node always maintains the set of one-hop and the two-hop neighbors. For this, each node attaches the list of its own neighbors, while sending its HELLO packets.

The performance metrics to be observed are as follows:

- *Average RE (Reachability)* : it measures how many packets are successfully arriving at the destination and is calculated by

$$RE = \frac{\sum N_{RCV}}{\sum N_{SNT}} \tag{5}$$

where N_{RCV} means the number of packets which successfully reach the sink node and N_{SNT} indicates the total number of packets sent by all source nodes.

- *Average OH (Overhead)*: it means the redundancy, and is given by

$$OH = \frac{(Area \ of \ \text{Sensor})W_A}{(Area \ of \ \text{Sensor Field})} \tag{6}$$

where W_A is the number of active nodes which try to transmit packets.

First, we investigate the average reachability as the number of nodes varies. Fig. 4 shows the reachability obtained when the constant transmission probability is used (Version 1). We can see that a small probability P is sufficient to achieve satisfactory reachability in high dense situation while a larger P is needed if the host distribution becomes sparse. This result can be utilized for finding the optimal number of nodes which can cover the given sensor field. In this figure, we can find out the optimal number of nodes maintaining the RE close to 1 in the given sensor field is 40 when $P = 1$.

Fig. 5 shows the transmission probability averaged over all nodes when three versions of schemes are applied. As shown in this figure, the average transmission probability of Version 2 and Version 3 decreases as the number of nodes grows up. This is because the number of nodes is directly related with the local density. We can see that Version 4 offers the largest OH.

Fig. 6 and Fig. 7 depict RE, OH, respectively. As shown in these figures, there is a tradeoff between the RE and the OH. In other words, the RE should be sacrificed to

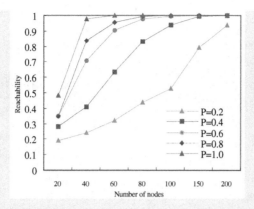

Fig. 4. Reachability with Version 1: constant transmission probability

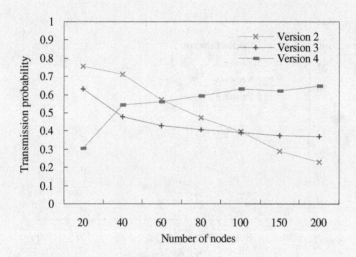

Fig. 5. Average transmission probability with Version 1, 2, and 3

reduce the OH. Version 2 represents this contradiction most obviously. It is clear that if we increase the transmission probability in Version 2, the RE performance can be apparently improved.

4   Conclusions

This paper presented a probabilistic transmission control scheme to reduce the transmission redundancy while maintaining reachability and accuracy within acceptable levels in sensor networks. Our scheme uses the local density information, namely, the one-hop and the two-hop neighbor information, to dynamically determine the transmission probability. Simulation experiments have demonstrated the efficiency of theses improvements with a significant reduction of the number of redundant packets.

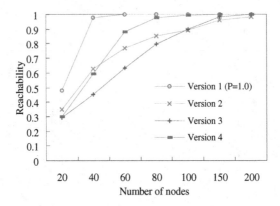

Fig. 6. Reachability with Version 1, 2, 3, and 4

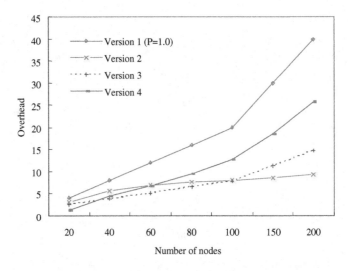

Fig. 7. Overhead with Version 1, 2, 3, and 4

Reference

1. B. Albrightson, J. Garcia-Luna-Aceves, and J. Boyle, "EIGRP - a fast routing protocol based on distance vectors," *Proceedings of Networld/Interop*, May 1994
2. B. Chen, K. Jamieson, H. Balakrishnan, and R. Morris. "Span: An energy-efficient coordination algorithm for topology maintenance in ad hoc wireless networks," *International Conference on Mobile Computing and Networking (MobiCom 2001)*, pages 85–96, Rome, Italy, July 2001
3. D. Ganesan, B. Krishnamachari, A. Woo, D. Culler, D. Estrin, and S. Wicker. "Complex behavior at scale: An experimental study of low-power wireless sensor networks," Technical Report UCLA/CSD-TR 02-0013, Feb. 2002
4. D. Johnson and D. Maltz, "Dynamic source routing in ad hoc wireless networks," *Mobile Computing*, pages 153–181. Kluwer Academic Publishers, 1996

5. E. Shih, P. Bahl, and M. J. Sinclair, "Wake on wireless: an event driven energy saving strategy for battery operated devices," *Proceedings of the 8th annual international conference on Mobile computing and networking*, pages 160–171. ACM Press, 2002
6. A. Woo and D. Culler. "Evaluation of efficient link reliability estimators for low-power wireless networks," Technical Report UCB//CSD-03-1270, U.C. Berkeley Computer Science Division, September 2003
7. M. D. Yarvis, W. S. Conner, L. Krishnamurthy, A. Mainwaring, J. Chhabra, and B. Elliott. "Real-world experiences with an interactive ad hoc sensor network," *International Conference on Parallel Processing Workshops*, Aug. 2002
8. Y.C. Tseng, S.Y. Ni, Y.S. Chen, and J.P. Sheu, "The broadcast storm problem in a mobile ad hoc network," *Wireless Networks*, vol. 8, pages 153–167, Mar. 2002
9. Y. Sasson, D. Cavin, A. Schiper, "Probabilistic broadcast for flooding in wireless mobile ad hoc networks," *IEEE WCNC'03*, vol. 2, pages 1124–1130, Mar. 2003
10. I. F. Akyildiz, W. Su, Y. Sankarasubramaniam, and E. Cayirci, "A Survey on Sensor Networks," *IEEE Communications Magazine*, vol. 40, issue8, pages 102–114, Aug. 2002

Designing a Self-organizing
Wireless Sensor Network

Fabrício A. Silva[1], Linnyer Beatrys Ruiz[1,2], Thais Regina M. Braga[1],
José Marcos Nogueira[1], and Antonio A.F. Loureiro[1]

[1] Department of Computer Science
Federal University of Minas Gerais
Belo Horizonte, MG, Brazil
{fasilva,linnyer,thaisrb,jmarcos,loureiro}@dcc.ufmg.br
[2] Department of Electrical Engineering
Federal University of Minas Gerais
Belo Horizonte, MG, Brazil
linnyer@cpdee.ufmg.br

Abstract. Wireless Sensors Network are generally designed with hundreds or thousands of autonomic devices called sensor nodes. These sensor nodes organize themselves in a wireless ad hoc network that performs data sensing, processing and dissemination services. A wireless sensor network should perform, besides services related to the applications, self-management services with the goal to promote productivity and quality of service. In this work we have developed and evaluated management services related to the formation of groups and sensing area coverage maintenance, defined by the MANNA architecture, using a set of policies. The results show that this set of policies can lead to more productive sensor networks.

1 Introduction

Wireless Sensor Networks (WSNs) can be seen as a special kind of mobile ad hoc network and as one of the sources of the ubiquitous computing [1]. A WSN can be used to monitor and, sometimes, control an environment. This kind of network is typically comprised of hundreds or thousands of autonomic devices called sensor nodes. The main components of a sensor node are: transceiver to perform wireless communication, energy source, sensing devices, memory and processor. Sensor nodes tend to be designed with small dimensions and this size limitation imposes restrictions to nodes resources, such as energy source, transceptor and processor capacities. The logical component of a sensor node is the software that runs in its processor. Despite the fact that nodes individually possess small computational and energy capacities, a cooperation among them allows the performing of a larger task [1].

Sensor nodes can be dropped over remote areas (oceans, volcanos, rivers, forests, etc.) and have to operate without human intervention, to form an ad hoc wireless network that collects data of interest, performs local processing and

A. Karmouch, L. Korba, and E. Madeira (Eds.): MATA 2004, LNCS 3284, pp. 186–195, 2004.
© Springer-Verlag Berlin Heidelberg 2004

disseminates information to an Access Point (AP) in a multi-hop communication scheme. A WSN can organize itself into groups of nodes with the goal of to reduce energy consumption and communication problems such as collision and congestion. Each group should have a leader that will be responsible for receiving data collected by common nodes, to perform some processing and send those information to the AP. When it comes to heterogeneous WSNs (networks containing nodes that present different hardware capacities), nodes with greater processing and energy capacities may be the cluster heads.

Considering certain applications, sensor nodes can be launched from aircrafts, helicopters and other means that do not guarantee an uniform coverage. During the deposition, some nodes can be lost and do not enter in service. To minimize this problem and to reduce uncovered areas (areas without monitoring), a larger amount of nodes is dropped over the area of interest. Besides fault-tolerance, the high density of nodes can increase the information precision provided by the network, since many nodes will be collecting information of the same phenomenon and disseminating these data through different paths in the network. However, this strategy can lead to more nodes disputing the media access and increasing the congestion, collision and interference probabilities [2].

It is not a trivial task to manage a network with such characteristics. In [3], we proposed an architecture to the management of WSNs called MANNA. This architecture defines a set of management functions and services that when performed in an automatic way, gives to WSNs characteristics of an autonomic system [4], i.e., systems that can manage themselves without human intervention [3]. In the scope of this work, there is a focus on two of these self-management services: formation of groups (self-organization) and sensing area coverage maintenance (self-configuration). There exists some ways through which these functions and services can be specified. One of them is to use policies [5], which are described through a set of rules. The conditions to execute the rules can be obtained through models, also called maps by the MANNA architecture. A map represents the network state using a certain abstraction level. The management policies define how the network behavior should be, using the available information of its current state.

This text is organized as follows. Section 2 presents an introduction to autonomic WSNs, showing the self-organization and coverage area maintenance services proposed by the MANNA architecture. Section 3 describes the set of policies proposed as an autonomic solution to the formation of groups considering the network density maintenance. Section 4 describes the results obtained from the simulations performed. Finally, the conclusion and future work can be found in Section 5.

2   Autonomic Wireless Sensor Networks

In this section, we present an overview of autonomic wireless sensor networks, and discuss both the self-organization and coverage area maintenance services.

2.1   Overview

Given the discussion presented in Section 1, it is clear that there exists important differences between traditional management and WSN management. Probably, the fundamental question is how the management can promote the network productivity and how it can integrate, in an organized way, the configuration, operation, administration and maintenance functions of all network elements and their services. Energy is a critical resource to WSNs and, therefore, all the operations performed by the network should be energy efficient, including the management tasks. One of the most important computer management goals is to promote resource productivity and to keep the quality of the provided services. An architecture to WSN management called MANNA is proposed in [3]. The MANNA architecture vision is that WSNs will became autonomic systems, i.e., systems that manage themselves without direct human interference [4].

A self-managed WSN performs services and functions without direct interference of a network administrator. According to the necessity, a WSN should organize itself into groups (self-organization) and adapt itself to environmental, topological and connectivity changes (self-configuration). A WSN should negotiate the accomplishment of a service from three quality levels: sensing quality, processing quality and dissemination quality. Other automatic services that a WSN should perform are described in [3].

The WSN management entities (managers and agents) can act according to policies established to achieve the management services and functions. The management strategies define where and how services and functions must be performed into the network. The MANNA architecture allows the centralized and decentralized management strategies.

This work proposes an integration between the formation of groups and sensing coverage area maintenance services, in a hierarchical heterogeneous WSN, implementing a distributed management strategy. The managers are localized at cluster head nodes and they cooperate among themselves to form groups and to make the network balanced, i.e., with a number of nodes per monitored area next to the ideal one. In this way, policies were defined to allow nodes to perform this task, in an automatic fashion and without any human interference. A Voronoi Diagram [6] algorithm is used to perform the sensing area coverage maintenance service. The services and policies defined to perform the above tasks are described below.

2.2   WSN Self-organization Service

The self-organization of a wireless sensor network is the ability to perform structural changes in its organization without human interference, in order to make it scalable and robust to changes in the network operational state. The WSN self-organization problem can be solved using a global vision of the entire network [2, 7]. However, this solution may not be efficient for some applications if we consider some metrics such as packet loss and delay.

In this work, we evaluated an automatic and localized formation of group service, which also considers the coverage area service of a hierarchical hetero-geneous WSN using a distributed management approach. This type of man-agement has the advantage to be scalable. The goal is to develop a decentral-ized self-organization service based on policies, where the cluster heads interact among themselves, in a cooperative fashion, to achieve a desired overall goal: to form groups of nodes, control the network density and keep the coverage of the WSN area. There are some challenges to be overcome to achieve this goal that are restrictions related to the sensor node, such as energy, processing capacity, available bandwidth and the large number of nodes.

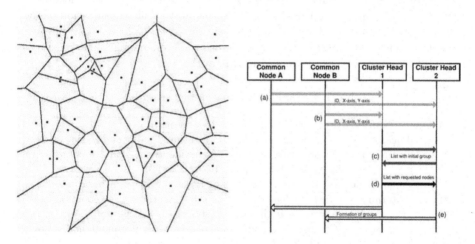

Fig. 1. A Voronoi Diagram.   **Fig. 2.** Flow Messages.

2.3   Coverage Area Maintenance Service

The sensing coverage area maintenance service is one of the services defined by the MANNA architecture. This service identifies backup nodes on a dense net-work, i.e., nodes that have sensing coverage areas similar to the others in the network. These backup nodes generate redundant data, traffic congestion and collision. In this case, the management takes them out of service temporarily making the network more balanced. After a while, the backup node turn itself on and asks the manager if it is allowed to return to service. Therefore, the manager answers yes (the node should turn it on) or no (the node should con-tinue as a backup). Given that sensor nodes can fail, run out of energy or even being destroyed, there may appear sparse areas, which will not be completely monitored. When a sparse area is identified, the service tries to activate one or more backup nodes that can lead to a balanced network again.

In [7], it is proposed the use of Voronoi Diagram to identify backup nodes, considering a centralized management approach. Given a set comprised of N nodes, the Voronoi Diagram algorithm [6] builds, for each node, a corresponding region, called *Voronoi area*, such that inside of which area any point is closer to this node rather than to any other node present in the network, as depicted in Figure 1. It can be seen that a node that has a small Voronoi area can be considered a WSN backup node and, therefore, taken out of service if there exists other nodes on its neighborhood with a similar sensing range.

3 Policy Definition

In the following, we present the policies and rules defined in this work. The implementation of the self-organization and self-configuration services is based on a set of policies that describe the desired behavior of each sensor node according to local information. These rules are applied during the self-organization of the network when groups are formed and the sensing coverage area is established. Table 1 presents identifiers, names and descriptions of management messages that implement the policies proposed in this work.

Table 1. Definition of management messages.

Identifier	Name	Description
M_L	Localization	Common node sends its identifier, and x and y coordinates
M_G	Initial Group	Cluster Head node sends its identifier, x and y coordinates and lists of active and backup nodes
M_N	Negotiation	Cluster Head node sends its list of active or backup nodes
M_P	Paternity	Cluster Head node sends its identifier to a common node informing it that the cluster head is its parent
M_D	Density	Cluster Head node sends a message to a common node taking it out of service temporarily

In the following, we describe the management policies proposed in this work.

Cluster Head Election Policy (P1): The network used in this work is heterogeneous, and, thus, the functions performed by a cluster head need a hardware with a larger capacity.

Topology Discovery Policy (P2): Network common nodes send a M_L message to all cluster heads that are inside their communication range, as illustrated in Figure 2(a) and (b). We are assuming that the nodes are able to discovery their position (X-axis and Y-axis). This is still a WSNs problem that other researchers are trying to solve.

Group Formation and Initial Density Control Policy (P3): Each cluster head receives a set of messages M_L, and, after a period of time, accepts this set as its initial group, running the Voronoi Diagram algorithm over it. These cluster heads keep a list of nodes considered *active* and another one with nodes considered *backup*. After that, cluster heads exchange among themselves M_G messages, as shown in Figure 2(c).

In this case, some common nodes may be present in the lists of two or more cluster heads, causing a conflict among them, that needs to be negotiated resulting in the cluster head that will keep such a node. In the following, we present a set of negotiation rules that are fair and efficient, that treat all possible types of conflicts.

- **Rule R1 – Backup × Backup Conflict:** if two leaders have the same node in their lists of backup nodes, a conflict of this kind will occur. In this case, the cluster head that has the smallest number of backup nodes in its list holds this node. In case the cluster heads have the same number of backup nodes in their lists, then the cluster head that is closer to the node is going to keep it. Another option is to keep the common node in both cluster heads list. In this way, both will be able to turn it on when desired. We have decided to use the first approach.
- **Rule R2 – Active × Active Conflict:** this conflict must be treated similarly to Rule R1 observing however that cluster heads must consider their lists of active nodes.
- **Rule R3 – Active × Backup Conflict:** if a cluster head has a given node in its active list, whereas another cluster head has the same node in its backup list, a conflict of this type will occur. In this case, it is considered that the cluster head that labeled it as a backup node, has a more precise vision of that particular area, given by the common nodes radio range, since it perceived that there exists one or more nodes that can cover that region. Thus, this cluster head keeps this node and manages it.
- **Rule R4:** consider Figure 2. If cluster head node 1 receives message M_G from cluster head 2, and they have already negotiated when cluster head 2 received message M_G from cluster head 1, they are not going to negotiate again. As the negotiation has already been performed, this rule eliminates the redundance and inconsistence of previous negotiations, reducing the energy consumption with processing, transmission and reception of unnecessary messages.
- **Rule R5:** when a cluster head decides that should keep some common nodes in conflict, it sends to the other cluster heads a message M_N requesting them (Figure 2(d)). The cluster head that receives this M_N message takes these common nodes out of its list of active or backup nodes.
- **Rule R6:** when a cluster head decides that should not keep some common nodes in conflict, it takes them out of its lists of backup or active nodes immediately.
- **Rule R7:** when there exists more than two cluster heads disputing the same common node, the negotiations take into account the order in which the messages arrived.
- **Rule R8:** after a period of negotiations, the cluster head nodes send M_P messages to the common nodes, communicating them of their paternity (Figure 2(e)).

Coverage Area Maintenance Policy (P4): Each cluster head node must send to the common nodes of its group that are identified as backup nodes, a M_D message taking them out of service temporarily.

4   Simulations and Experimental Results

The evaluation of the proposed solution of policies and rules described in this work was performed through simulations using the Network Simulator 2 (NS-2) tool. In the following, we present the main results.

4.1   Scenarios

Scenarios containing a hierarchical heterogeneous WSN with common sensor nodes and cluster heads with a larger hardware capacity were built. The characteristics of these two types of nodes were configured according to Mica Motes [8] (common nodes) and WINS [9] sensor nodes (cluster heads). Three different nodes positioning were evaluated, each of them corresponding to a simulated scenario. **Scenario 1** has all nodes positioned in a grid, **Scenario 2** has all nodes distributed randomly, and **Scenario 3** has the cluster head nodes positioned in a grid and the common nodes distributed randomly.

Table 2. Characterization of performed simulations.

Network Configuration	Simulation Configuration
Cluster Head Nodes Number: 16;	*Simulation Time:* 50 seconds;
Common Nodes Number: 196;	*Number of Simulations:* 33;
Transport Protocol: UDP;	*Scenario Size:* 145m × 112m;
MAC Protocol: IEEE 802.11;	
Management Protocol: MannaNMP;	
Cluster Head Nodes Configuration	**Common Nodes Configuration**
Range: 250 meters;	*Range:* 40 meters;
Processing Consumption: 0.360W;	*Processing Consumption:* 0.024W;
Transmission Consumption: 0.6W;	*Transmission Consumption:* 0.036W;
Reception Consumption: 0.3W;	*Reception Consumption:* 0.024W;
Sensing Consumption: –	*Sensing Consumption:* 0.015W;
Delivery Type: Continuous;	*Delivery Type:* Continuous;
Collection Type: –	*Collection Type:* Continuous;
Battery Capacity: 100J;	*Battery Capacity:* 10J;
Bandwidth: 100kbps;	*Bandwidth:* 28.8kbps;

Table 2 presents a summary of the characteristics of simulations performed in this work. The protocols used in both MAC and transport layers are not specific to WSNs. In the network layer, it was used a broadcast mechanism offered by the NS-2 simulation tool, in which all nodes perform only a single-hop transmission. In this case, a message reaches its destiny or it is lost. The metrics used to evaluate the functioning of the proposed solution are consumption of energy with processing, number of orphan nodes and number of exchanged messages.

4.2   Evaluation of the Number of Orphan Nodes

To determine the efficiency of the formation of groups proposed in this work, the number of common nodes that could not be associated with any cluster head was determined. Figure 3 shows the results obtained for each scenario.

As it was expected, the scenario with random distribution (Scenario 2) has in average more orphan nodes than the other scenarios. This occurs because of the irregularity of node localization, when some common nodes do not directly reach any of the cluster heads.

When comparing Scenario 1 with scenario 3, we verify that the former has, in average, more orphan nodes than the latter. In Scenario 1, there always exists a fixed number of nodes that will not reach any cluster head because of the deterministic distribution. However, in Scenario 3 common nodes have random localization and the cluster heads are distributed in a deterministic way. Therefore, there are more chances to have a higher number of nodes that can reach at least one of the cluster heads.

In all scenarios, the total number of orphans is also influenced by the loss of M_L messages that occur because of packet collision int the network. In average, 4% of the network sensor nodes became orphans.

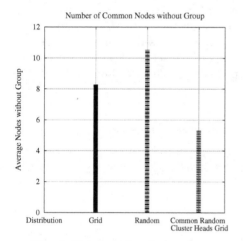
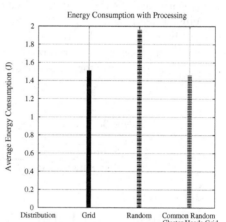

Fig. 3. Number of orphan nodes.   **Fig. 4.** Processing Energy consumption.

4.3   Evaluation of Energy Consumption

Energy is a critical resource in wireless sensor networks and any solution to this kind of network must verify its consumption. In particular, it is interesting to evaluate the amount of energy spent by the cluster heads with processing, since they must run the Voronoi algorithm, which has a $O(n \log n)$ complexity, and there is also a need for searches in lists, when policy P3 rules are evaluated. Figure 4 shows the average energy amount consumed with processing by the cluster heads of Scenarios 1, 2 and 3.

The scenario with random distribution (Scenario 2) is the one that has cluster heads presenting the highest energy consumption for processing. The irregular distribution of nodes makes possible for several common nodes to reach more than one cluster head, forming initial groups larger than the groups of the other scenarios, according to policies P2 and P3. Larger groups lead to higher energy consumption with processing. The amount of energy spent to calculate the Voronoi Diagram is directly proportional to the number of nodes involved.

Moreover, the backup and/or active nodes lists are larger, which leads to a higher energy spent with the searches that are performed over those lists at the moment of the negotiations defined in P3. It was spent, in average, 1.6J of energy with processing considering the entire process proposed.

4.4   Evaluation of the Number of Exchanged Messages

The messages considered by this metric are those necessary to perform the management services, and not those messages containing data collected from sensor nodes. Table 3 presents the results obtained to the simulated scenarios. Messages M_L are not computed into these results.

All scenarios presented a similarity regarding this metric. When an average is performed among the 16 cluster head nodes of all scenarios, we can see that each cluster head should send 16 messages, including messages M_G, M_N and M_P, foreseen by P2, P3, and P4, respectively. The impact caused by those messages is relatively small when compared to the benefits of the achieved results, since it is provided an autonomic formation of groups that considers the network coverage area.

Table 3. Number of necessary management messages.

Scenario	1	2	3
Messages Number	261	262	266

5   Conclusion and Future Work

Wireless sensor networks present a great variety of new problems that were not studied yet or that are still incipient. In the future, remote sensing will become part of our lives and will be used on a variety of applications in different areas, such as security, medicine, traffic control, environment monitoring and education.

Comparing the simulation results, we can see that the solution proposed in this work provides better results to networks with more uniform distributions. However, is it worth to mention that the results of all simulated scenarios are relatively close. The results show that, to all simulated scenarios, the goals were achieved: groups were formed and the backup nodes were identified, making the network hierarchical and balanced. The impact related to the energy consumption with processing and communication has almost no relevance, given the advantages and benefits offered by the solution. In applications where human maintenance is impracticable, this solution can increase the productivity and network lifetime by configuring the network in the best way that is possible, given the initial conditions.

The focus of this work is not on the simulation results, but it is on the definition of policies for self-management of wireless sensor networks. In particular, the work defines policies to self-organize and self-configure WSNs, forming groups of nodes and controlling the density from the identification of redundancy, using a distributed management strategy.

A possible extension of this work is to introduce fault-tolerance in the messages sent to their cluster heads. There is also the possibility of evaluating, in terms of computational cost, the sorting of lists used during the negotiations, so the searches are more efficient. Another interesting aspect is to perform simulations with broadcast algorithms that allows nodes to send their messages through the use of multi-hop communication.

References

1. Akyildiz, I., Su, W., Sanakarasubramaniam, Y., Cayirci., E.: Wireless Sensor Networks: A Survey. Computer Networks Journal **38** (2002) 393–422
2. Ruiz, L.B., Silva, F.A., Braga, T.R.M., Nogueira, J.M.S., Loureiro, A.A.F.: On impact of management on wireless sensors networks. In: NOMS – Network Operation and Management Symposium, IEEE/IFIP (2004) 657–670
3. Ruiz, L.B.: MANNA: A Management Architecture for Wireless Sensor Network. PhD thesis, Computer Science Department - Federal University of Minas Gerais. Available in http://www.sensornet.dcc.ufmg.br/ (2003)
4. Kephart, J.O., Chess, D.M.: The Vision of Autonomic Computing. IEEE Computer (2003) 41–50
5. Damianou, N., Dulay, N., Lupu, E., Sloman, M., Ponder: A Language for Specifying Security and Management Policies for Distributed Systems. Technical report, Imperial College Research Report DoC (2001)
6. Voronoi: Voronoi Website. Available in http://www.voronoi.com (2004)
7. Vieira, M.A., Ruiz, L.B., Vieira, L.F., Loureiro, A.A., Fernandes, A.O.: Scheduling nodes in wireless sensor network: A voronoi approach. In: IEEE LCN – Local Computer Network. (2003) 423–429
8. Mica Motes: The Commercialization of Microsensor Motes. Available in http://www.sensorsmag.com. (2003)
9. WINS: WINS Wireless Integrated Network Sensors. Available in http://www.janet.ucla.edu/WINS . (2003)

Ambient Networks Management Challenges and Approaches

Marcus Brunner[1], Alex Galis[2], Lawrence Cheng[2], Jorge Andrés Colás[3],
Bengt Ahlgren[4], Anders Gunnar[4], Henrik Abrahamsson[4], Robert Szabo[5],
Simon Csaba[5], Johan Nielsen[6], Alberto Gonzalez Prieto[7],
Rolf Stadler[7], and Gergely Molnar[8]

[1] NEC Network Laboratories, Kurfürstenanlage 36, 69115 Heidelberg, Germany
brunner@netlab.nec.de
[2] University College London, Department of Electronic and Electrical Engineering,
Torrington Place, London WC1E 7JE, United Kingdom
{a.galis,l.cheng}@ee.ucl.ac.uk
[3] Telefónica Investigación y Desarrollo, Emilio Vargas, 6, 28043 Madrid, Spain
jorgeac@tid.es
[4] 4SICS, Box 1263, SE-164 29 Kista, Sweden
{bengta,aeg,henrik}@sics.se
[5] Budapest University of Technology and Economics,
Department of Telecommunications and Media Informatics,
H-1117, Budapest, Magyar Tudosok krt. 2
robert.szabo@tmit.bme.hu, simon@david.tmit.bme.hu
[6] Ericsson Research, Ericsson AB, SE-164 80 Stockholm, Sweden
johan.nielsen@ericsson.com
[7] KTH – Royal Institute of Technology, Laboratory of Communication Networks- IMIT
{gonzalez,rolf}@imit.kth.se
[8] Ericsson Hungary Ltd., H-1037 Budapest, Laborc u. 1., Hungary
gergely.molnar@ericsson.com

Abstract. System management addresses the provision of functions required for controlling, planning, allocating, monitoring, and deploying the resources of a network and of its services in order to optimize its efficiency and productivity and to safeguard its operation. It is also an enabler for the creation and sustenance of new business models and value chains, reflecting the different roles the service providers and users of a network can assume. Ambient Network represents a new networking approach and it aims to enable the cooperation of heterogeneous networks, on demand and transparently, to the potential users, without the need for pre-configuration or offline negotiation between network operators. To achieve these goals, ambient network management systems have to become dynamic, adaptive, autonomic and responsive to the network and its ambience. This paper discusses relationships between the concepts of autonomous and self-manageability and those of ambient networking, and the challenges and benefits that arise from their employment.

1 Introduction

In the recent years, we have witnessed a liberalization of the telecommunications market. This liberalization has triggered the appearance of new operators, which has multiplied the offered access connectivity. However, end-users cannot take full advantage

A. Karmouch, L. Korba, and E. Madeira (Eds.): MATA 2004, LNCS 3284, pp. 196–216, 2004.
© Springer-Verlag Berlin Heidelberg 2004

of this extensive access connectivity today. Operators only grant connectivity access to those users with whom they previously have signed an agreement. This gives rise to a situation where end-users cannot obtain the service quality they require despite the fact that operators have the resources to offer such a service. Similarly, the cooperation among operators is based on off-line negotiations and therefore quite limited and static.

The goal of Ambient Networks is to allow the establishment of inter-network agreements on-demand without the need for pre-configuration and offline negotiation between network operators [1]. The key concept of Ambient Networks is network composition. Networks compose and gain connectivity through instant establishment of inter-network agreements. This will provide access to any network instantly. From the point of view of the end user, Ambient Networks will provide ubiquitous connectivity. Users are able to obtain connectivity instantly at any place at any time. Moreover, the user obtains ubiquity through network compositions that do not require manual interaction.

During recent years, we have also seen the proliferation of wireless link layer technologies like WLAN, GSM, 3G, etc, for access networks. This heterogeneity of technologies hinders cooperation among networks, and complicates dynamic composition. Heterogeneity requires the provision of innovative link layer solutions for easy adaptation of existing radio interfaces and incorporation of new ones. In this sense, the vision of Ambient Networks is to create a new, robust, and technology independent platform for mobile and wireless communication networks beyond 3G.

Network composition brings new challenges to network management. For instance, during composition, the networks' management must agree to provide a consistent common control space for the newly created composed network. Similarly, when networks decompose, the associated management systems decompose. Nodes in an Ambient Network must be able to act autonomously without direct interaction with a central management station. Additionally, since whole networks come and go, the traffic patterns and topology change significantly, making monitoring and traffic engineering a challenging task.

In this paper, we present and analyse the challenges Ambient Networks pose on network management. At this point, we do not aim to provide an integrated solution, but rather to identify research issues and discuss how we intend to address them. From a management point of view we focus on management technologies dealing with the composition of networks as well as with self-managing technologies for automation and reduction of costs. More specifically we propose four different approaches in this area: 1) peer-to-peer management for dealing with composition networks for exchanging management information, 2) pattern-based management for a fully distributed management of dynamic networks, 3) plug and play for easy configuration, and 4) control-loop based management for self-optimisation of networks. Other aspects of AN i.e. multi-radio access, network connectivity and mobility, smart routing, context awareness and security are presented in [1, 2]. The rest of the paper is organized as follows: firstly the characteristics of ANs are presented, through which the idea of an integrated control space for composed ANs known as the Ambient Control Space (ACS) is presented. Next, an AN scenario is described to highlight the characteristics of ANs and the respective AN management requirements. The management challenges raised by the need of network composability and self-manageability in AN management systems are then presented.

Then, four approaches that have been identified in the AN project to tackle AN management challenges are presented and discussed. Lastly, an implementation plan for these approaches is outlined.

2   Ambient Networking

Since its beginning, the Internet's development has been founded on a basic architectural premise: a simple network service is used as a universal means to interconnect intelligent end-systems. The end-to-end argument has served to maintain this simplicity by pushing complexity into the endpoints, allowing the Internet to reach an impressive scale in terms of inter-connected devices. However, while the scale has not yet reached its limits, the growth in functionality - the ability of the Internet to adapt to new functional requirements - has slowed with time. In addition, the ever-increasing demands of mobile applications and network services currently face the relative inflexibility of the IP infrastructures. In this sense, the pervasive use of the Internet in mobile networks to support such applications has revealed important deficiencies. One such structural deficiency is the lack of ambient control [1, 2].

2.1   Main Characteristics of Ambient Networks

The main characteristics of an Ambient Network (see Fig. 1) are:

- All-IP Network: Ambient Networks are based on all-IP based mobile networks and can be regarded as the outcome of a continued adoption of Internet design principles.
- Heterogeneity: Ambient Networks are based on a federation of multiple networks of different operators and technologies.
- Mobility: In dynamically composed network architectures, mobility of user group clusters would support effective local communication. An Ambient Network mobility solution will have to work well across business and administrative boundaries, which requires solutions for ensuring the security of inter-domain operation.
- Composability: An Ambient Network can be dynamically composed of several other networks. Cooperating Ambient Networks could potentially belong to separate administrative or economic entities. Hence, Ambient Networks provide network services in a cooperative as well as competitive way. Cooperation across different Ambient Networks is facilitated by the Ambient Network Interface (ANI). Note that the ANI is the interface through which management systems and network elements of different AN domains may communicate with each other.
- Provisioning of well-defined control interfaces to other Ambient Networks and to service platforms or applications.
- Explicit Control Space: Provisioning (at least a subset of) the Ambient Control Space functions. When Ambient Networks and their control functions are composed, care must be taken that each individual function controls the same resources as before: by composing two Ambient Networks, resources shall not become a common asset but rather an asset that can be traded.

- Accessing the services of an Ambient Network is via the Ambient Service Interfaces (ASI).
- Autonomic and self-management: system management in the ambient network environments.

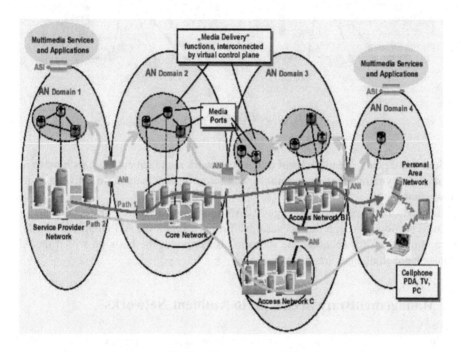

Fig. 1. ASI and ANI in AN

The notion of the Ambient Control Space (ACS) is introduced (i.e. Fig. 2) to encompass all control functions in a certain network domain. The Ambient Control Space together with a (possibly legacy) connectivity network is called an Ambient Network (AN). The Ambient Control Space hosts a set of control functions. In addition to the basic functions required for management, security, and connectivity, the ACS hosts additional control functions. For instance, control functions for supporting mobility, connectivity, multi-radio access, smart media routing, security and management in ANs, as well as more abstract functions like the provisioning of context information. Each of these control functions is accommodated in different aspects of the AN project.

The challenges in developing AN management systems are complicated by the increased complexity of composed heterogeneous ANs. Management for such composed networks must handle network composition in a simple and low cost approach (specifically for user networks), it has to be scalable and robust and it ultimately makes these networks themselves scalable and robust. Note that advanced network management is also an enabler for the creation of new business models and value chains, reflecting the different roles the "operators" and users of Ambient Networks can assume. To

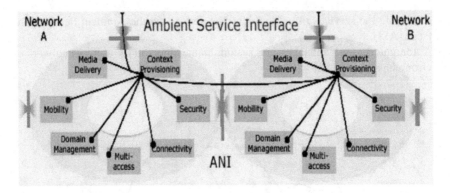

Fig. 2. Ambient Control Space (ACS)

achieve these goals, components of ambient network management systems have to become more dynamic, more autonomous, and have to participate more active in (inter) networking.

In order to explain the challenges of AN management, a scenario is described in the next section. Through this scenario we further explain the AN characteristics that were outlined in this section. The scenario also provides the basis on which the AN management challenges are presented.

3   Managementware Scenarios in Ambient Networks

In order to create use cases for ambient networks several scenarios have been developed. In this paper we present a train scenario, which illustrates the management issues and challenges raised by ambient networks.

This scenario is built around the entertainment industry's possible future use of ambient technology for the production, marketing, distribution and consumption of live and recorded content. This scenario is based on the AN Rock Express scenario presented in [1] but the main focus in this paper is the management aspects of the scenario.

This scenario takes place somewhere in Europe during summer of 2015. We follow a rock band, Rusty Zigglers Travelling Hearts Club Band, while they tour Europe in a special rock train which they use for travel between gigs, as a concert stage and also to host exclusive interviews and present material to special guests and fans who pay to travel with the band.

This scenario also focuses on Buffy Vamp and Dianh Dolittle as fans of the rock band, Pearl Parlay as a radio/TV reporter who is painting a portrait the life of a rock band on the road, and Nurdtendo Opus as the network technician responsible for planning and maintaining enough network capacity to allow all other players to fulfil their roles.

Other players are the rock band promoter who is responsible for content production (i.e. the rock band) and content owner, the train operator as owner of infrastructure and network provider (i.e. the train itself as well as physical network access on board the trains and between the train and its surroundings) and public network operators providing network access and extra features to its subscribers on board the train.

Multiple ANs will be set up between different actors on board the trains as well as between actors on and off the train. Temporary ANs will also be set up at the concerts to facilitate information sharing and content distribution between the band and the audience and friends not able to attend the concert. Potentially, all these ANs will be using different access technologies, and end users will be minimally affected when their connection is transferred from one access technology to another, or when new traffic is added to already restricted resources. At the same time ANs will allow for ad hoc changes in network capacity configuration with minimum human interaction.

3.1   The Scenario Story

This scenario, originally developed as an overall AN scenario presented in [20] network management aspects in mind, exhibits the dynamic environment that AN represents and nicely highlights the management challenges of Ambient Networks. The scenario has two main parts, "At the Concert" and "the Exclusive Rock Train Travel" and a short prequel in which the train is prepared for the tour.

3.1.1 Prequel. As preparations for the Rusty Zigglers Hearts Club Band tour through Europe a train and several carriages are rented from a train operator. Almost all of the carriages in this train will be occupied by fans and specially invited guests while the train moves between the different venues, but one will be the "private Rock band" carriage.

The AN in the carriages used by the fans and guests is operated by the train company, and composed into one AN domain using the absorption model. However, the AN in the private rock band carriage is operated by the rock band technician, and the composition of this AN (carriage) and the AN in the other carriages is done using the gatewaying model. The terms absorption and gatewaying refer to different modes of network composition. Absorption takes place when the administrative tasks of one network are completely taken over by another, resulting in a single administrative domain. Gatewaying refers to the situation where administrative tasks for a composed network are carried out between administrative domains, resulting in a composed network but with separate administrative domains. Management information sharing between administrative peers in a gatewaying model is done through the ANI.

3.1.2 At the Concert. As the train rolls into the concert area it is hard to believe this was "the middle of nowhere" just a few hours before. What used to be empty fields far out on the countryside is now crowded by at least 50,000 people waiting for their rock band to perform. The train stops near several access points of a local ground network, connected to the Internet.

What is even more amazing is that these fields, which previously had barely enough network coverage and capacity to support the few tourists crossing the landscape now has the capacity to serve all the fans' communication, plus several TV companies covering the event "live". In addition to this, the network supports content distribution and file downloads (audio, video, text) from the rock band infrastructure to the fans being at the concert. All this with almost no human interaction.

During the concert, fans form, modify and break AN domains with each other. They also digitally record parts of the concert, which they stream to absent friends by using the "see what I see" application.

Suddenly a base station is tipped over by some fans climbing the mast to get a better view. Luckily, no one gets hurt, and the AN domains closest to the base station automatically reconfigure themselves to reroute the traffic through other AN domains.

As the concert draws to a close, the band solicits feedback on their performance. The fans have been asked to rate the concert using their PDAs, and at the end the network technician instructs his AN to issue a pattern-based information collection pattern. 30 seconds later 50,000 votes are displayed confirming that this was a very good concert.

3.1.3 The Exclusive Rock Train Travel.

After the concert, the invited guests and fans that have bought special e-tickets via their PDAs enter the train. They start mingle with each other as the train departs, exchanging their personal experiences of the concert, and all kinds of information about the rock band. Fans are also able to "browse the train" to find other fans on board the train, and based on this information form new ANs and/or recompose existing ones to include the newly found people. Temporary AN domains form and break rapidly as "everybody talks to everybody", using multiple radio accesses, but the Ambient Networks are cope with the situation.

Imagine the roar of happiness from the fans when they realise there is some very special material available on the train to be accessed only by the people onboard the train. Some material is free and some material is sold at a good discount. Fortunate fans with subscriptions with an operator can securely buy the content and obtain an extra discount, and they will be billed directly by the operator.

Meanwhile the band decides to relax in the bar of the private carriage for a few minutes before going out to meet the fans. All the band members go to the bar, except the drummer who checks his gear one more time. However, the band members continue to discuss and evaluate the concert by forming an AN domain by themselves, using the train network to keep the connection between the drummer and the rest of the band. This overlay is completely private and no one will be able to listen in to what the band members discuss, even though the traffic goes through other physical equipment.

The TV crew starts interviewing the band members, and this interview is broadcast live to the people on the train. The interview is simultaneously streamed to the TV station office, and these video clips are automatically uploaded to a website where customers with special subscriptions can access the material. The videostream is also saved for future by the TV station.

Fans on the train are able to send questions to the band members, and these are "instantly" answered by the band. The band also randomly distributes special electronic content to selected members of the audience, much like they did with physical gadgets 20 years or so previously.

Finally the band emerges out and mingles with the fans and guests. They are wearing advanced head-mounted micro-camera-PCs and microphones that allow the fans to see what their idols see. These streams are also uploaded to the rock band's homepage to allow fans all over the world to access and enjoy the clips for a small fee. The band starts to play some of their songs on acoustic instruments, and this content is distributed to those fans on the train that cannot see the band, as well as to fans accessing the band's homepage.

3.2 Scenario Analysis

The above scenario has highlighted the key requirement and the capabilities of AN management systems to interact to provide services in a ubiquitous manner. When this scenario is analysed from a network management point of view, it can easily be broken down to 3 parts: static configuration, dynamic configuration, and movement of the train (or even trains). We explore the different parts below.

3.2.1 Static Configuration. In the prequel to the scenario, several carriages are connected to each other, with some of the carriages belonging to the same domain, while one carriage is reserved for the rock band. This implies different models of composing the carriages' networks, as presented in Fig. 3. Initially, as the carriages of the same operator are attached (the two carriages at the right hand side), their AN can be fully composed. The result is a new AN forming one administrative domain, this composition model being referred to as the *absorption model*. The rock band's carriage (the leftmost carriage in Fig. 3) is under the control of the bands' tour management, therefore on attaching their carriage to the rest of the train a different model is followed, the *gatewaying model*. In this model the ANs communicate through well-defined interfaces but they remain two distinct administrative domains.

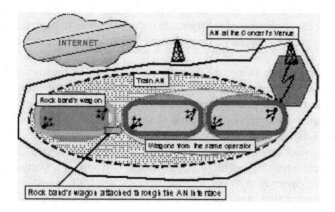

Fig. 3. Different Network Composition Cases

The type of network composition we see in the prequel is quite static, once a network composition is completed the new AN will not likely change soon. The same applies to setting up the extra network capacity at concert place prior to the concert; these ANs will also remain rather static.

3.2.2 Dynamic Configuration. As the train arrives at the concert venue, one carriage is linked to the ground network, resulting in a new gatewayed AN. From this point the fans can use the network resources on the train. They form several new PAN-like ANs between themselves while being part of the larger AN. Based on the policies of each new AN and of the ANs already merged in the larger AN (fully composed AN of the carriages, gatewayed AN of the train, gatewayed AN of the train and ground AN, the ground AN), the composition process differs. For example, the AN of a group of fans that is allowed to enter the carriages of train might have the right to fully merge with the carriage's AN (absorption model). Other fans just remain outside the train, and their AN connects to the train's gatewayed AN (gatewaying model). Although all these new ANs will eventually compose the larger AN, we may say that they join it at different *hierarchy levels*. By introducing hierarchical composition we believe it will ease the management of the different AN compositions.

At the same time, all the PAN-like ANs communicate and negotiate their level of composition on a peer-to-peer basis in order to avoid going through a third, central node. Instead, the PANs negotiate directly with each other and agree which resources and information, and their management, to share.

The TV crews also utilise peer-to-peer network management to connect to their home TV stations. When they reserve network resources and capacity, they use peer-to-peer technology to program the base stations and routers to provide them with sufficient quality. When the train moves, and the connection between the TV crew and the home TV station has to be updated, peer-to-peer technology is used for reprogramming the new nodes in the new path between the crew end their home office.

Pattern-based information gathering tools are used to collect feedback during the concert. During the concert, members of the audience express their opinion of the show, and in the end these votes are collected and processed using patterns.

Patterns are also used to collect connectivity statistics. These statistics are highly dynamic due to the movement of the trains. In order to be able to track this dynamicity, real-time monitoring is necessary. A pattern-based monitoring system provides it.

3.2.3 Moving the Train. Due to the high network volatility on the train and at the concert, near real-time information about connectivity status and distribution is required to distribute the traffic load over the networks. These statistics are provided to the appropriate management node(s) as the basis of their decisions. Patterns can be used to distribute the decisions of the management node(s).

With the network mobility introduced by the moving train, several new traffic engineering aspects have to be dealt with. At station hotspots of a station the network operator must engineer its network to cope with sudden traffic bursts when the train moves into a hotspot area. Another aspect is if and how to reroute traffic from one access type to another when possible, how to do this in an optimal way, and how to make the applications aware of the new conditions.

Also, while the train moves, it will travel through several networks. The reservation of resources to support traffic with QoS requirements between operators has to be investigated, in particular how TE information can be passed between different operators.

In this scenario, we have presented the major characteristics of AN, namely the heterogeneity of each of the to-be-composed ANs and the mobility of AN. These characteristics highlight the dynamic network composability of AN. This paper suggests that a self-managed management system is needed to handle dynamic AN network composition. These two management criteria of AN management systems are discussed in the next section.

4   Managementware in the Ambient Networks

4.1   Management Features of Ambient Networks

In the previous section we introduced a reference scenario that showcases all the possible features of the candidate Ambient Management System (AMS). We analysed these scenarios to pinpoint the specific management mechanisms required to deploy a working management system. This section takes a detailed look on the features and concepts to be supported by the AMS. We propose novel approaches to achieve these goals.

Fig. 4 shows the contrasts between traditional management systems and AMSs. The key features of AN management are dynamic network composability between heterogeneous ANs, and self-manageability.

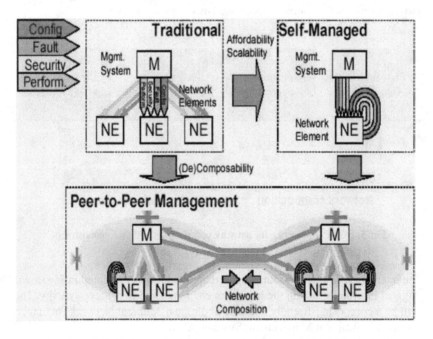

Fig. 4. Going beyond existing network management paradigms

In general, network management includes the set of functions required for controlling, planning, allocating, deploying, coordinating, and monitoring the resources of a network. The appearance of novel wireless technologies, and the concept of network composition, where networks agree to share a common control space, represents a challenging scenario from a network management perspective. In order to respond to these challenges, novel protocols and approaches are required to go beyond existing network management paradigms. Management for such composed networks has to be simple and low cost (especially for personal networks), while scalable and robust, which will make the networks themselves scalable and robust.

To achieve these goals, management systems have to become sensitive, adaptive and responsive to their ambience. That is, they have to interwork with other management systems in an autonomous and dynamic way.

When composing two separate networks, one crucial challenge is to join the management systems of both networks into a consistent management system for the composed network. Similarly, when a network separates in two parts, its management system has to be separated as well. In order to deal with the complexity of composition and decomposition, two novel approaches will be analysed: usage of peer-to-peer technologies and pattern-based management.

In addition, innovative self-management technologies will be explored in order to reduce the cost of network deployment and operation and to increase scalability and affordability of Ambient Networks. Two approaches have been selected to enable AN self-management, plug-and-play configuration at individual networking element level and closed-loop-based optimisation mechanisms at network level.

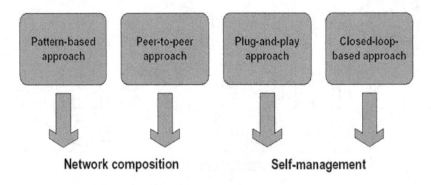

Fig. 5. Novel approaches for network composition and self-management

The interaction among the four proposed approaches, as presented in Fig. 5 will be investigated in order to obtain the best from each one, and to achieve synergy. The result will be a composing-friendly, scalable and robust Ambient Networks management framework, the Ambient Management System (AMS).

4.2   Main Concepts and Research Challenges

Network composition refers to the situation where multiple heterogeneous networks - each of which is an Ambient Network (AN) owning an Ambient Management System (AMS) controlling an Ambient Control Space (ACS) accordingly to a set of predefined policies - join together in a new AN in order to transparently provide new services to end users. From a management perspective, the result of this composition will be a common ACS being controlled by a common AMS based on a set of policies agreed during the composition process. The composition of different management systems faces several challenges:

- A simple, efficient and scalable mechanism is needed to pool and share management information across heterogeneous networks, i.e. to control the common ACS.
- Composable AMSs should be service-oriented: they should be capable of supporting new services on demand through dynamic reconfiguration of network elements.
- Composed networks are autonomous, i.e. AMSs may leave or join arbitrarily.

It is in the interest of AN to evaluate four different network management approaches in order to deal with such challenges. These approaches will be integrated through the concept of AMS, which will provide a set of useful features (a network management toolbox) for the implementation of the global AN solution. The AMS of a composed AN will consist of various distributed and co-ordinated AMSs that will facilitate different ways of managing of the common ACS. By combining these AMSs – co-ordinated through the ANI – an AN will adapt itself to its context based on network conditions or administrative policies.

The features provided by an AMS should include: access to the totality of context policies for an AN; pro-active action triggering due to context changes in the AN based on the composition agreement; conflict resolution in AN based on the composition agreement; co-ordination of composition-aware AN entities; inter-AN path optimisation; policy negotiation between ANs during composition processes.

From a business point of view, a network composition can be seen as a temporary agreement among independent networks collaborating towards a common business goal. This agreement would match the diversity and complexity of the market offerings and products structure, and would increase the ability to react to the rapidly shifting demands of today's markets. In this way, composition should be as transparent as possible for member networks and end users to enable effective business activities. For instance, in the previous proposed scenario, carriages of different rail companies join their network infrastructures in order to offer passengers a full-coverage connectivity service inside the train, with seamless handover between the network infrastructures of both companies. Another problem hindering the formation of compositions is the lack of applications that support the automated creation and administration of the composed network. The creation process includes the finding of adequate ANs, negotiation among them, the definition of business relations, the collection of configuration information and requirements and the reservation of appropriate resources of the network infrastructure. In this way, a highly dynamic and flexible information infrastructure is needed in order to successfully run services over a composed AN. This information infrastructure must be able to provide connectivity with guaranteed quality on demand. Conventional solutions like the currently available Virtual Private Networks (VPNs) provide mostly few and fixed QoS guarantees or no guarantees at all. The major drawback of the today's VPNs is their low flexibility to quickly adapt to the changing requirements. Therefore, a new kind of programmable information infrastructure is needed to supply advanced communication and connectivity services, with guaranteed QoS, to the composed AN. This infrastructure will be called Virtual Private AN (VPAN), which can be seen as a programmable, dynamic, QoS guaranteed VPN that can be directly configured according to the demand of the ACS.

These challenges highlight the problem space of AN management. This paper proposes that these challenges should be tackled through different approaches. The AN project has identified four different approaches to handle the network composition and self-management challenges of AN management. These approaches are discussed in the next section.

4.3   Management Approaches in Ambient Network Project

As explained in earlier chapters, dynamic network composition and self-management present major challenges that must be met if Ambient Networks are to be realised. The Peer-to-Peer (P2P) approach and the Pattern-based approach are discussed in this section as a means of solving the network composition challenge, whereas the Plug- and-Play (PnP) and the Traffic Engineering (TE) approaches are also discussed, targeting the self-management challenges.

4.3.1   Peer-to-Peer Approach. The distributed approach of P2P [19] realises interaction between individual management systems (or AMS following the AN terminology) to establish a consistent management system for the entire composed network. P2P management defines interaction between managers as well as between (self-managed) network elements. P2P also carries high potential of realising a management system with higher scalability. A further key design goal is to minimise management costs; and so simple protocols for transportation should be used.

Based on the above we consider relevant to *network composition* the following main areas.

- *Network architecture for control and data plane:* where focus is on novel architectural concepts that allow easy combination (grouping/partitioning) of several networks.
- *Address allocation* must ensure a consistent addressing structure regardless of the frequent reorganisation of network structures. Issues here are plug and play configuration of network components, duplicate address detection etc. Since neighbour discovery is usually done at MAC or IP layer, we also address the network discovery within this topic, as well.
- *Routing* enables the basic connectivity service. Issues here are how to support this basic service in a dynamically changing environment; results available for ad-hoc networks may be reused because of the similar conditions that apply.
- *Policies* are upper level, generalised descriptions of management rules. Since different merging networks contain different rule sets, merging them into a consistent new rule set is not a trivial task.

Additionally, flexibility is needed in composable P2P AN management stations in terms of service placement, as well as in terms of variable functionality that might be required over time. Consider an AN environment in which two networks offering different levels of QoS connection are composed. Nodes in the network with lower QoS connection service should be re-configured in order to support a higher QoS connection. Dynamic re-configuration of network elements can be achieved through programmable techniques. Incremental, composable and self-organising software modules should be launched on demand to adapt to variable operational conditions.

Experience in P2P service networks shows P2P techniques to be capable of providing distributed services in a scalable and efficient manner. The distributed nature and the use of simple protocols, make P2P an ideal candidate for supporting inter-working between large-scale, autonomous composable management systems. Although the major focus of existing P2P techniques is on resource handling on the edges of the network, P2P techniques could be developed further to manage management information between heterogeneous ANs to support network composition.

In fact, AN could be modelled and realised as P2P networks. A main feature of P2P is the immediate interaction among equal partners that are called 'peers'. In P2P architectures, the networked nodes are highly autonomous: peers may leave or join a P2P network arbitrarily. Similarly in an AN environment, end users move across different ANs, resulting in dynamic network de/composition. As a consequence, from the user's point of view, AMSs of different ANs are also autonomous: they come and go as he changes location traverses, which is very much the same in the case of P2P. Thus AMSs in AN have a highly variable topology. Both P2P networks and AN networks are expected to be large-scale. As a consequence, any management approach that suits P2P networks is highly adaptable to AN networks. The selforganising aspect of P2P management provides sensitive contributions towards a selfmanagement system in AN.

Architectures of P2P networks vary between two extremes: pure P2P and pure client/server distributed architectures. A pure P2P architecture is completely decentralised. Peers operate in a highly autonomous mode and are de jure equal entities. De facto, however, if left to themselves, most P2P architectures evolve into a hybrid structure, where some peers are 'more equal than others'. Hybrid structures may form themselves due to preferential attachment of peers to distinct peers. One key concept is the Active Virtual Peer (AVP). As its name suggests, an AVP is a virtual entity, which interacts with other peers inside a P2P network. An AVP is a representative of a community of peers. Its purpose is to enhance, control, and make the P2P relation more efficient inside that community.

Despite of all these advantages, owing to its distributed nature, P2P requires enhancement in four areas of control, in order to deploy P2P techniques on information sharing between AMSs [3, 20]:

- *Access control* is needed since management information is valuable; so AMSs must enforce strong access control and authentication among peers.
- *Adaptive Topology control:* due to the autonomous nature of AN, P2P overlay connections between composable AMSs may be established or broken arbitrarily. Service reliability may be enforced through topology control over redundant connections. Thus a highly flexible infrastructure that allows new software modules to be launched on demand to control dynamically overlay creation and management over the AN management station topology is needed.

- *Overload traffic control* copes with traffic flows inside the P2P overlay. Its goal is to balance the traffic and load in order to maintain sufficient throughput inside the overlay, while also protecting other network services by mapping this load in an optimum way onto the underlying network infrastructure.
- *Resource Management:* AN domains are composed/de-composed dynamically, thus there is a need to utilize the shared resources among different domains. The resources of individual peers must be treated with care. For example, low-bandwidth connected peers should not be overloaded with traffic flows.

This composable network management system approach is also considered as a top-level reflection of the concept of re-configurability within the network layer i.e. to enable the dynamic configuration of network elements as well as to support new services on demand. Such an advanced service management system should be selfmanaging and apply context at the network level. Flexibility in ANs' network infrastructure in deploying new services to meet these requirements is therefore needed in composable P2P AN management stations in terms of service placement, as well as in terms of variable functionality that might be required over time. Dynamic re-configuration of network elements can be achieved through programmable techniques [18]. With a flexible network infrastructure, incremental, composable and self-organising software modules should be launched on demand to adapt to variable operational conditions. For instance, a QoS assured management service overlay can be created dynamically between P2P administrative peers through the use of programmable techniques.

4.3.2 Pattern-Based Approach. Centralised network management has well-known drawbacks [11–13]. It presents poor scalability regarding: a) management traffic; b) processing load on the management station, and c) execution times. A centralised network management approach does not fit into an AN environment, where domains are composed dynamically.

The pattern-based management paradigm [14, 17] aims to address these limitations through investigating a distributed management approach based on the use of graph traversal algorithms to control and coordinate the processing and aggregation of management information inside the network From the perspective of a network manager, the algorithm provides the means to 'diffuse' or spread the computational process over a large set of nodes. A key feature of the approach is its ability to separate this mechanism of diffusion and aggregation from the semantics of the management operation. The paradigm achieves this through the development of two important concepts: the navigation pattern and the aggregator. The former represents the generic graph traversal algorithms that implement distributed control, while the latter implements the computations required to realise the task. A navigation pattern controls the flow of execution of a (distributed) management operation. It is described by an asynchronous network algorithm, which can be analysed for its complexity and scalability properties.

The main benefits of pattern-based management, all of them useful for AN network management purposes, are that it (i) separates the semantics of the task from its flow control, (ii) enables building scalable management systems, and (iii) facilitates management in dynamic environments.

Previous work on pattern-based management has identified the *echo* pattern, which has proved useful for distributed monitoring [14, 16]. The defining characteristic of the echo pattern is its two-phase operation:

- *Expansion phase*, where the flow of control messages (explorers) emanates from a management node. Nodes, upon receiving an explorer for the first time, send copies along all direct links, except for the link where the explorer came from, and then perform the local management operation specified in the explorer. An explorer that arrives at an already visited node triggers the second phase of the pattern, by generating a control message called an *echo*, which is sent out on the link where that explorer came from.
- *Contraction phase*, where a node waits until it has received an *echo* for each explorer it has sent out. It then aggregates the results from its own operation and those contained in the *echo* messages and, finally, it propagates an *echo* with the result of that aggregation back.

The echo time complexity increases linearly with the network diameter, which results in fast execution times in networks with a connectivity distribution that follows the power law (such as the Internet). Its traffic complexity grows linearly with the number of network links and the management traffic produced by executing this pattern is distributed evenly cross all links, without causing hot spots, where congestion can occur.

Other identified patterns are the progressive wave pattern and the stationary wave pattern. They can be used to update Internet routing protocols and interactions between peer nodes in peer-to-peer networks, respectively. In [17], the authors describe how the stationary wave pattern can be used for self-stabilization in peer-topeer networks. The pattern provides a medium for disseminating state updates. Instrumenting the pattern permits us to monitor the dynamic behavior of the peer-topeer system.

Pattern-based management has a strong potential for providing real-time connectivity information (e.g.: flow performance, traffic statistics) in the context of dynamic network composition of AN. However, in order to apply its concepts in such a scenario, it is necessary to investigate (among others) the following issues: a) how a decentralised management system can dynamically reconfigure to accommodate changes in the connectivity among network domains (network composition) [15]; b) how robust patterns can execute during topology changes (network compositions) and failures (potentially); c) how to apply concepts beyond fixed IP networks (WLAN, etc.); d) how to extend current monitoring model towards push functions (event triggered); e) how to reconfigure services dynamically; f) how effective inter-domain management can be realised in the context of decentralised management, involving domains with different administrative domains.

4.3.3 Plug-and-Play Approach.

The plug-and-play approach aims to minimise configuration (ideally selfconfiguration) of base stations, mobile terminals and mobile routers extending, complementing, and/or replacing already existing technologies, such as DHCP, IPv6 address auto-configuration, and policy-based management.

The plug-and-play paradigm for networked devices/routers is very appealing from a business point of view, however it is very difficult to apply in practice in view of its unwanted consequences in some environments. In fact, there are still many networks whose administrator wants to strongly control configuration in order to maintain an advantage over competitors and, on the other hand, IP-based networks and devices distributed into various environments, where no knowledgeable staff are available to manage the network and devices. We assume most medium to small companies, as well as most home users, are not capable of configuring networks correctly. Since the Internet is becoming more and more widely used, user-friendlier configuration, or even better no user configuration at all, is the goal.

For plug-and-play of a network infrastructure device (mostly routers) in an AN context we would need some method to obtain or generate necessary configuration information that makes the device fully functional in an AN domain. Developing this method, the AN device has to have functions to establish connectivity to the working and configured part of the network. It must communicate with the rest of the network and a new device to get and provide configuration information respectively. Some configuration information can be inherited from the working part of the network and would be obtained from management entities of the working network.

Nowadays routers are manually configured when installed. Automatic configuration is needed for ANs. Thus, methods for detecting and establishing IP connections to the rest of the network (practically, to the neighbouring routers, where the new router(s) is (are) connected) are needed. The 'packages' of functions to be configured should be defined. The necessary configuration parameters for these functions and where the values for these parameters can be read (i.e. which can be read from the working routers, which can be read from a central management entity, and which can be guessed/generated by the new device itself, etc.) must also be defined. For the values that can be read from routers, a 'service' has to be defined in AN routers that can serve these values for a new device. For values can be read from a centrally management entity, this entity has to be defined and the method by which the new routers find/reach it and read the values also has to be defined. For values that can be generated by the new router itself (using information obtained from other routers or from a central management entity), a new method has to be defined.

A *flexible* and *self organising management* system needs to be developed and integrated, incorporating the following properties: support for optimisation of resource usage of P2P overlays, and its adaptation on demand to changing patterns of request profiles and traffic loads, and to new application type requirements. Adaptation should be possible both in time and space, and the adaptation pattern should reflect the granularity of significant structural overlay changes and the timescale of such events. The use of mobile code with an appropriate programming environment [18] seems an attractive solution to some of the important questions.

We consider two types of plug-and-play scenario. First, the plug-and-play of a single device. Second, the plug-and-play as a starting point for network composition in the case where two or more AN domain interact. A full plug-and-play proposal for AN would cover both scenarios.

4.3.4 Closed-Loop-Based Approach. The closed-loop-based approach explores the use of traffic engineering mechanisms [4] as a way to optimise the network resources usage, i.e. link bandwidth. A promising approach that has recently been investigated is to use optimisation to tune the link weights of a link-state routing protocol in order to minimise the risk of congestion.

For a network operator, it is important to analyse and tune the performance of the network in order to make the best use of it. The process of performance evaluation and optimisation of operational IP-networks is often referred to as traffic engineering. One of the major objectives is to avoid congestion by controlling and optimising the routing function, or in short, to put the traffic where the capacity is. However, current routing protocols are designed to be simple and robust rather than to optimise the resource usage.

Several attempts have been made to make the routing more adaptive to the current traffic situation. With large and complex networks and with constantly changing and often unpredictable traffic demands this can be a challenging task, and much research is going on in this area. Different traffic engineering methods are categorised depending on whether there is centralised or distributed control, whether the method requires global or only local network state information, whether the calculations are performed on-line or off-line, to mention a few.

Different timescales apply within traffic engineering. From capacity planning that works on a timescale of months or years, through adaptation to weekly and daily variation in traffic patterns, down to reaction to sudden changes in traffic on the timescale of seconds. Different traffic engineering approaches are suitable for different time scales.

Existing intra-domain routing protocols such as OSPF (Open Shortest Path First) and IS-IS (Intermediate System to Intermediate System) are simple, highly distributed, and scalable. But these protocols do not consider network utilization and do not always make good use of network resources. More specifically, in these protocols, traffic is always routed though the shortest path, even when the path is overloaded, and alternative paths are not considered.

Network administrators can coarsely control how traffic is distributed over the network by manually adjusting the link costs. But this approach is often imprecise and difficult because changing the weight of a link can affect traffic in other parts of the network. With an extension to routing protocols such as ECMP (Equal-Cost Multiple Path), the problem remains, because an under-utilized longer path cannot be used and every equal cost path will have an equal share of load. Thus one of the paths may end up carrying much more traffic than other paths because it also carries traffic from other sources.

The general problem of finding the best way to route traffic through a network can be mathematically formulated as a multi-commodity flow (MCF) optimisation problem. This has recently been used by several research groups to address traffic engineering problems [5–9]. In the simplest case, the optimisation result can be used as a benchmark when evaluating the performance of the network to see how far from optimal the current routing is. The optimisation can also be used as a basis for setting the optimal weights in OSPF or IS-IS [6, 9] or for traffic engineering using MPLS [8, 10].

A long-term research goal would be to construct a new multi-path routing protocol based on flow optimisation [5]. With a multi-commodity flow optimisation the network capacity constraints and overall traffic characteristics are taken into account.

An extra dimension is added to the complexity of traffic engineering when mobility is taken into account. The fluctuations in the traffic matrix of a network infrastructure in a scenario with a moving network (e.g. a train with an internal access network) pose a challenging problem, which TE has to cope with, providing the most optimal usage of the available network resources. In addition, the situation where there are several available access networks will provide opportunities to dynamically adapt to the total capacity available, as well as bringing into being the role of virtual access operator over the same access network.

4.3.5 Initial Management Integration. At this stage of the research it is beneficial to gather together the major concepts and functionalities of each of the approaches, and to create an initial management node concept, which provides a basis for future integration, work discussion.

In this integration approach the pattern-based approach is used for providing real-time traffic information to the traffic engineering approach and the P2P approach. Base on the real-time traffic information, the P2P approach will create a management service overlay with desired QoS with programmable techniques. An attempt for an integrated solution is currently undergoing in a reference model for the AN Management plane as an enhancement and control of the AN. The purpose of this reference model is to enable flexibility and adaptively by the use of self-organization. The information included in this model should ease also the definition of ASI and ANI. It should accommodate the management functional areas of the four approaches as well as the series of service layers on which these functionalities may be deployed. For instance, the monitoring function of network elements is deployed on the selfware layer i.e. a control loop is formed based on the monitoring function of network elements for continuously monitoring network activities and to autonomously react (self-ware) accordingly based on a set of pre-defined policies upon an event. A full integration of different management approaches are envisage in the 2nd phase of the AN project [2].

5   Implementation Plan

In the following we outline some implementation aspects of the four approaches in order to give a better understanding of the approaches and their challenges.

5.1 Peer-to-Peer Approach

The development platform envisaged for use in one peer-to-peer prototype is DINA (www.cs.technion.ac.il/Labs/Lccn/DINA/). DINA is a Java-based platform, which inherits the concepts and ideas from ABLE (www.bell-labs.com/topic/swdist/). DINA is a modular and scalable software architecture that enables deployment, control, and management of active services (sometimes called sessions or active sessions) over network entities such as routers, WLAN access point, media gateways, and servers that support such services in IP-based networks.

5.2 Pattern-Based Approach

The concepts of pattern-based management have been implemented in Weaver [16], a decentralized management platform to execute patterns. Weaver is a scalable platform that facilitates the collection, correlation, and processing of information from very large networks. Weaver will be used to investigate pattern-based management in AN scenarios.

5.3 Plug-and-Play Approach

Existing methods (described in [3]) have to be examined with respect to their applicability and usability in AN scenarios. It is expected that, for some functionality, new methods and protocols will be needed. In fact, plug-and-play is needed in two different situations: a new device joining an AN (i.e. a network composition following an absorption model); and the AN discovery phase prior to the network composition processes. Both cases should be satisfied with the results obtained with this approach in AN.

5.4 Closed-Loop-Based Approach

Performance of proposed traffic engineering mechanisms will be analyzed through Maryland Routing Simulator (MaRS) and Network Simulator 2 (www.isi.edu/nsnam/ns/). The former is more focused on routing mechanisms research, while the latter supports a wider range of network technologies: MPLS, UMTS, WLAN, etc.

6 Conclusions

In this paper we presented the characteristics of a new networking approach, called Ambient Network, in terms its dynamic composability, mobility, and heterogeneity. AN aims to enable the co-operation of heterogeneous networks, on demand and transparently, to the potential users, without the need of pre-configuration or offline negotiation between network operators. An integrated control space known as the Ambient Control Space (ACS) is needed in AN for control purposes. An ACS contains different control elements for different aspects of AN such as connectivity, mobility, media routing, context-awareness support, security and management. To achieve these goals, Ambient Network management systems have to become dynamic, adaptive, autonomic and responsive to the network and its ambience. A scenario was described to highlight specific AN management characteristics. The management challenges i.e. dynamic network composability and self-manageability in ACS were outlined. Four approaches to these AN management challenges i.e. peerto- peer, pattern-based, plug-and-play, and closed-loop-based were analyzed. These four approaches will be investigated individually during the first stage of the AN project. Whereas an integrated management approach built based on the four approaches will be developed in the next stage of the project.

Acknowledgements. This paper describes work undertaken in the context of the Ambient Networks - Information Society Technologies project, which is partially funded by the Commission of the European Union. The views and conclusions contained herein are those of the authors and should not be interpreted as necessarily representing the Ambient Networks Project.

References

1. Niebert, N., Flinck, H. Hancock, R. Karl, H. Prehofer, C. "Ambient Networks – Research for Communication Networks Beyond 3G"- 13th IST Mobile and Wireless Communications-Summit 2004, 27-30 June 2004, Lyon, www.mobilesummit2004.org
2. WWI-AN Ambient Networks Project WWW Server - www.ambient-networks.org
3. R8-1 Report, "State of the Art of dynamic network composition and self-management ", Ambient Networks project internal report, IST-2002-507134-AN/WP1/R8-1, March 04.
4. D. Awduche, A. Chiu, A. Elwalid, I. Widjaja and X. Xiao, "Overview and principles of Internet Traffic Engineering", Internet RFC 3272, May, 2002.
5. H. Abrahamsson, J. Alonso, B. Ahlgren, A. Andersson and P. Kreuger, "A Multi Path Routing Algorithm for IP Networks Based on Flow Optimisation", In Third COST 263 International Workshop on Quality of Future Internet Services, QoFIS, 2002.
6. B. Fortz and M. Thorup, "Internet Traffic Engineering by Optimizing OSPF Weights", In Proceedings of IEEE INFOCOM, 2000.
7. B. Fortz and M. Thorup, "Optimizing OSPF/IS-IS Weights in a Changing World", IEEE Journal on Selected Areas in Communications, 20(4): 756-767, May2002.
8. D. Mitra and K. G. Ramakrishnan, "A Case Study of Multiservice, Multipriority Traffic Engineering Design for Data Networks", In Proceedings of Globecom'99, Brazil, 1999.
9. A. Sridharan, R. Guerin and C. Diot, "Achieving Near-Optimal Traffic Engineering Solutions for Current OSPF/IS-IS Networks", In Proceedings of IEEE Infocom, San Francisco, March, 2003.
10. D. Awduche, J. Malcolm, J. Agogbua, M. O'Dell and J. McManus, "Requirements for Traffic Engineering Over MPLS", Internet RFC 2702, September 1999.
11. M. Baldi, S. Gai and G. Picco, "Exploiting Code Mobility in Decentralized and Flexible Network Management", First International Workshop on Mobile Agents (MA'97), Berlin, Germany, April 97, pp. 13-26.
12. M. Baldi, G. Picco, "Evaluating the Tradeoffs of Mobile Code Design Paradigms in Network Management Applications", First International Working Conference on Active Networks (IWAN'99), June/July 1999, Berlin, Germany.
13. Liotta, G. Knight, G. Pavlou, "On the Performance and Scalability of Decentralized Monitoring Using Mobile Agents", DSOM '99, Zurich, Switzerland, October 1999.
14. K.S. Lim and R. Stadler: "Developing pattern-based management programs", 4th IFIP/IEEE International Conference on Management of Multimedia and Network Services (MMNS'01), Chicago, Illinois, October/November 2001, pp. 345-358.
15. K.S. Lim, C. Adam and R. Stadler; "Decentralizing Network Management", submitted to IEEE electronic Transactions on Network and Service Management
16. K.S. Lim and R. Stadler; "Weaver: realizing a scalable management paradigm on commodity routers", 8th IFIP/IEEE International Symposium on Integrated Network Management, 24-28 March 2003, Colorado Springs, Colorado, March 2003, pp: 409 – 424
17. C. Adam, R. Stadler, "Patterns for Routing and Self-Stabilization", in Proc. of Network Operations & Management Symposium (NOMS 2004), Seoul, Korea, April 19.23, 200
18. Galis, A., Denazis, S., Brou, C., Klein, C. (ed) – " Programmable Networks for IP Service Deployment" ISBN 1-58053-745-6; March 2004 - Artech House Books, 46 Gillingham Street, London SW1V 1AH, UK; www.artechhouse.com
19. Cohen, E., and Shenker, S., "Replication Structures in Unstructured Peer-to-Peer Networks," *ACM SIGCOMM*, 2002.
20. R8-2 Report, "Description of concept and scenarios for network composition management and self-management", Ambient Networks project internal report, IST-2002-507134-AN/WP8/R8-2, May 04.

Scalability, Security Technologies
and Mobile Applications

Larry Korba and Ronggong Song

Institute for Information Technology
National Research Council of Canada
Ottawa, Ontario K1A 0R6, Canada
{Larry.Korba,Ronggong.Song}@nrc.ca

Abstract. Multi-agent applications are expected to take an important role in the future of e-business applications. However, security for multi-agent applications has become a critical issue. Unfortunately, effective security technologies often tend to require considerable computational and network resources, leading to scalability issues. Thus, scalability of the security technologies is a vital issue when developing practical agent-based applications. In this paper, we present the results of measurements of implementation of various security technologies operating in the JADE multi-agent platform.

1 Introduction

Multi-agent applications have been more and more applied in a wide range of information technology applications. However, security protection for multi-agent applications has become critical issue, especially for agent-based e-commerce applications. On the other hand, in order to make multi-agent-based applications practical and efficient, careful attention must be placed on the scalability of the security technologies embedded within those applications.

In this paper, we first propose a testing model for assessing the scalability of several important security technologies. These include: authentication, IPSec [1]-[4], RSA [5], 3-DES, MD5, etc. Using the testing model, we measure the scalability of the security technologies as applied to the JADE multi-agent platform [6], and present an analysis of its scalability.

The rest of the paper is organized as follows. Several security technologies are briefly introduced in the next section. In Section 3, a simulation model is designed for testing purposes. In Section 4, the simulation and testing metrics are briefly discussed. In Section 5, we show the testing results and analyze the scalability problems. In Section 6, we present some concluding remarks.

2 Security Technologies

There are many security technologies that could be deployed in support of security protection for agent-based applications. We only test a few of them. However, they are important, basic security technologies that may be part of many different multi-agent applications. They are described as follows.

- **Entity Authentication:** Entity authentication is the testing process whereby one agent is assured of the identity of a second agent. This ensures that the agent is what it claims it is. There are two kinds of entity authentication methods: one is

A. Karmouch, L. Korba, and E. Madeira (Eds.): MATA 2004, LNCS 3284, pp. 217–223, 2004.

based on the shared secrets such as password or shared key; another is based on the certificates. The former usually uses the cryptographic algorithms such as hash function (e.g., MD5) or symmetric-key cryptography (e.g., 3-DES). It suits more "lightweight" applications. The latter usually uses public-key or signature algorithms such as RSA. It has strong protection for the authentication.

- **Data Confidentiality:** Confidentiality is a security service used to keep the content of the application data from all but those authorized to have it. Two kinds of cryptographic mechanisms could be used for the confidentiality: one is symmetric-key cryptography such as 3-DES and AES; another is asymmetric-key cryptography such as RSA.
- **Non-repudiation:** Non-repudiation is a security service to prevent an agent from denying its previous actions. Signature algorithms are often used for this purpose (e.g., RSA, DSS).
- **Integrity:** Integrity is a security service to address the unauthorized alteration of data. Usually, we use a hash function or Message Authentication Code (MAC) for this (e.g., MD5).

3   Simulation Model

The objective of this work is to test the scalability of several security technologies: entity authentication, IPSec, RSA, 3-DES, and MD5 as applied in a multi-agent environment. These technologies are vital and foundational security measures for information systems. The network and computational overhead required for implementing these technologies can have a major impact on multi-agent system scalability. Our approach was to test sample implementations of these security technologies operating in the model client-server environment.

4   Simulation Platforms and Metrics

The testing platform includes the hardware and software. The hardware used for the testing includes two computers and local Ethernet. Testing was performed on an Intel Pentium 4 computer. The CPU clock speed and memory size were 1.50GHz and 256 MB respectively, and the operation system was Windows 2000. The network used during the tests was 100Mbps Ethernet.

The software environment used for the tests included the operating system and testing software platform. The operating system was Windows 2000. The testing software platform was the JADE multi-agent platform (version 3.0). All software implementing the testing model was built in the JAVA programming language (Standard Edition (J2SETM) version 1.4.2). The crypto package IAIK JCE (3.0) [8] was used for the testing cryptographic package.

Throughout the simulation, the main simulation parameters that were measured included message size, user size, and total processing time for all messages. The total processing time includes the computing complexity cost for security processing in the testing model above.

- Message size: the number of the messages sent by the user agents, where each message contains 1Kbits content;
- User agent size: the number of the user agents;

- T_Time: the total processing time for the user agents to send all messages to the server agent, and for the server agent then to processes all messages and send a reply message to each user agent.

5 Testing Results

5.1 Entity Authentication Mechanisms

Using the testing model, we first tested the authentication mechanisms under the JADE multi-agent platform. The server agent is run in the main container, and the user agents are run in another container, all running on the same computer. The simulation test is described as follows.

The testing was performed with the user agents using different entity authentication mechanisms. These mechanisms included: password-based authentication (using MD5) and certificate-based authentication (using IAIK JCE 1024bit RSA and 2048bit RSA). We also tested the effect of the number of the user agents on the T_Time. During testing, the number of user agents ranged from 1 to 2048, where all user agents simultaneously send one request-message to the sever agent. Table 1 and Figure 2 depict the total processing time for the request and reply messages for the different numbers of user agents and authentication approaches.

Note: For these authentication systems, the workload usually is on the server side. Normally, we use the short key as the verification key for certificate-based authentication in order to make the server agent more efficient for testing as would be the case for real applications.

Table 1. T_Time for the Different Authentication Mechanisms

No. of User agents	1	2	4	8	16	32
MD5 (ms)	80	110	170	320	501	831
RSA 1024 bit (ms)	110	140	200	280	531	901
RSA 2048 bit (ms)	120	150	220	341	551	952
No. of User agents	64	128	256	512	1024	2048
MD5 (ms)	1281	1833	2954	4696	7811	13489
RSA 1024 bit (ms)	1352	2103	3425	5648	9724	17325
RSA 2048 bit (ms)	1772	2804	4646	8062	14220	26479

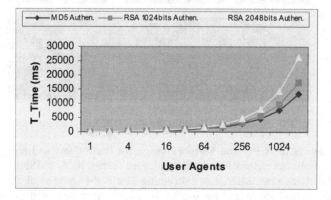

Fig. 1. Comparison of T_Time for the Different Authentication Mechanisms

Figure 2 depicts the CPU and Memory usage for the request and reply messages with password-based authentication. Considering first the CPU usage history, the first pulses are the results for one user agent sending 1 request and reply message, the second flurry of pulses are for two user agents and each agent sends 1 request and reply message, ..., the last pulses are for 2048 user agents. Note that in Figure 2, each pulse group has two peaks, and the first peak is the CPU usage for JADE platform start-up and application system setup. The second peak is the CPU usage for the processing of the authentication messages.

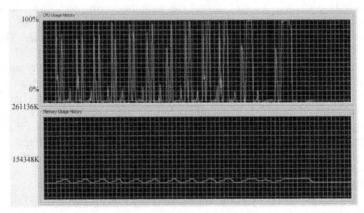

Fig. 2. CPU and Memory Usage for the Password-based Authentication

Figure 3 depicts the CPU and Memory usage for the request and reply messages under the certificate-based authentication technologies (RSA 1024bit). Other things are same as the above description.

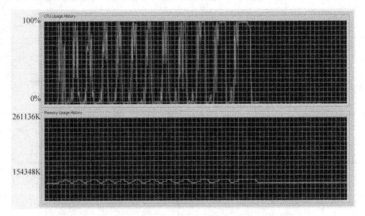

Fig. 3. CPU and Memory Usage for the RSA (1024bit) Authentication

Figure 4 depicts the CPU and Memory usage for the request and reply messages under certificate-based authentication technologies (using RSA 2048bit certificates). Other than the change in certificates, everything else is the same as above. However, in this situation, the CPU usage for the JADE platform start-up and the application system setup is much more than that of the above two situations.

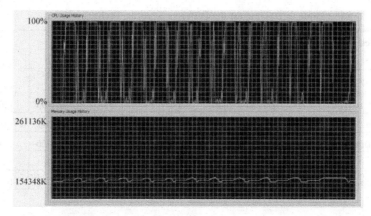

Fig. 4. CPU and Memory Usage for the RSA (2048bit) Authentication

From the testing results, we know that the password-based authentication has the best scalability, and the certificate-based authentication (using 1024bit RSA algorithm) also scales reasonably well, but the 2048bit certificate-based authentication scales less well. On the other hand, as we mentioned, since the verification key (public key) usually is very short (about 14bit) for certificate-based authentication, its scalability is reasonable for the real applications. With this approach, according to the testing, we also would get a balance between the scalability and the security level for the real applications.

5.2 Other Security Technologies

In this part, we test and compare different security technologies that may be used in the multi-agent applications. During testing, the user agents and server agent are run in the different computers. The simulation test is described as follows.

During simulation tests, the user agents are equipped with different security technologies such as IPSec (AH+ESP), RSA, 3-DES, etc. We assess the scalability using different numbers of user agents (ranging from 1 to 128), with each user agent sending 100 request-messages. Table 2, Figure 5, and Figure 6 depict the total processing time for the request and reply messages employing the different security technologies.

Note: In the simulation with RSA algorithm, each message is signed using RSA signature algorithm with a 2048 bit modulus by the user agent and verified by the server agent, but during testing we only collect and calculate the processing time in the server agent side (i.e., the verification time) since this is most germane to our measurement model. In this testing, we also measure the situation wherein the request messages are encrypted by the user agents and decrypted by the server agent. Similar to the signature scenario, we collect and calculate the decryption processing time with the server's private key at the server agent side.

From the testing, notice that most basic security technologies such as RSA authentication, IPSec, SSL, 3-DES, MD5, only have a small impact on the multi-agent system scalability. But some public-key cryptography operations like digital signature and decryption would have a huge impact on multi-agent system scalability if the operations are running on the server side since the key pairs would be large (e,g, 2048bit RSA algorithm).

Table 2. T_Time for the Different Security Technologies

User agents	1	2	4	8	16	32	64	128
Messages	100	200	400	800	1600	3200	6400	12800
RSA Decrypt. (ms)	20960	39296	78823	156325	312049	621223	1242907	2481669
RSA Authen. (ms)	2694	3254	5147	9264	18226	33578	64493	126311
IPSec (ms)	2524	3535	6079	10615	19898	37204	70642	136046
3-DES (ms)	2224	3345	5578	9544	18316	35441	66856	124459
MD5 (ms)	1993	3134	4686	7841	15322	29462	56331	109348
None (ms)	1902	2814	4196	7571	14260	27420	52245	102217

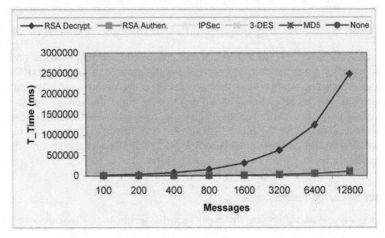

Fig. 5. T_Time for the Different Security Technologies

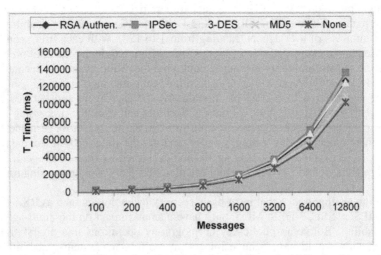

Fig. 6. T_Time for the Different Security Technologies. Note the different time scale from Figure 6

6   Discussion and Conclusions

In this paper we have presented results of testing a variety of core security approaches in operation within a Java agent development environment (JADE). The test results show the impact of using technologies such as: RSA (decryption and authentication), IPSec, 3-DES shared key encryption, MD5 (MAC) on processor overhead and execution times. The security mechanism that has the most profound impact upon performance is RSA decryption. While this aspect may have been predicted based upon an understanding the RSA encryption/decryption process as compared to the other security functions tested, the test results indicate the relative costs of the different processes. The results of this work provide figures for calculating the effect of adding any of a variety of security primitive to a multi agent system. Developers using the JADE environment may in fact use these results to assess how well security functionality will scale for their multi-agent applications. Through the methodology presented, one can develop performance fitting curves for scalability related to many more security technologies in JADE or any other agent environment.

Multi-agent systems will play important roles in the future information society, especially for e-business applications, in which security is considered to be the gating factor for their success. Security, privacy and trust mechanisms have become important aspects for practical multi-agent applications. This paper presents a methodology for assessing scalability of different technologies used to implement security, privacy and trust functions. Overall, the measurements show that most security technologies only have a small impact on the multi-agent systems. However, some public-key algorithms such as signature and decryption would have a large impact on the systems when they are used in the server side.

Acknowledgements

We would like to thank the Communications Security Establishment of Canada for their support towards our Security and Privacy R&D program, and our IST-EU Fifth Framework Project, Privacy Incorporated Software Agent (PISA), partners [7].

References

1. S. Kent and R. Atkinson. Security Architecture for the Internet Protocol. IETF RFC 2401, November 1998.
2. S. Kent and R. Atkinson. IP Authentication Header. IETF RFC 2402, November 1998.
3. S. Kent, R. Atkinson. IP Encapsulating Security Payload. IETF RFC 2406 November 1998
4. D. Harkins and D. Carrel. The Internet Key Exchange. IETF RFC 2409. November 1998.
5. R. L. Rivest, A. Shamir and L. Adleman, "A method for obtaining digital signatures and public-key cryptosystems" Communications of ACM, Vol.21, No.2, pp.120-126 Feb 1978
6. JADE – Java Agent Development Framework. http://sharon.cselt.it/projects/jade/
7. PISA web site: http://www.pet-pisa.nl/.
8. Institute for Applied Information Processing and Communications Home Page. http://jcewww.iaik.tu-graz.ac.at/.

Detecting and Proving Manipulation Attacks in Mobile Agent Systems

Oscar Esparza, Miguel Soriano, Jose L. Muñoz, and Jordi Forné

Technical University of Catalonia
Jordi Girona 1 i 3
08034 Barcelona, Spain
{oscar.esparza,soriano,jose.munoz,jforne}@entel.upc.es

Abstract. Mobile agents are software entities consisting of code, data and state that can migrate autonomously from host to host executing their code. Unfortunately, security issues restrict the use of mobile agents despite its benefits. The protection of mobile agents against the attacks of malicious hosts is considered the most difficult security problem to solve in mobile agent systems. In a previous work, the Mobile Agent Watermarking approach (MAW) was presented as a new attack detection technique based on embedding a fixed watermark into the agent's code. In this paper, some improvements are introduced in MAW. Instead of a fixed watermark, the origin host embeds a watermark that can change dynamically during execution. In each host, the marked code creates a data container where the watermark will be transferred and the results will be hidden. When the agent returns home, the origin host applies a set of integrity rules that the containers must fulfill. These rules can be inferred from the modifications performed in the agent's code during the watermark embedding. If a container does not fulfill the rules, this means that the corresponding host is malicious. This paper also presents how these containers can be used as a proof to demonstrate that a manipulation attack has been performed.

1 Introduction

Mobile agents are software entities consisting of code, data and state and that can migrate from host to host performing actions autonomously on behalf of a user. Mobile agents are especially useful to perform functions automatically in almost all electronic services, like e-commerce or network management. Despite their benefits, massive use of mobile agents is restricted by security issues.

This paper introduces some improvements on the Mobile Agent Watermarking approach (MAW) [3]. Instead of a fixed watermark that is located into the results in some positions previously known by the origin host, the watermark can change dynamically during execution. In each host, the agent creates a data container that will be used later to assure the execution integrity and to hide the results. During the execution, the agent puts information inside the container in an ordered way, for example some dummy data, input data or even intermediate variable values. When the execution finishes, the results are also fitted

A. Karmouch, L. Korba, and E. Madeira (Eds.): MATA 2004, LNCS 3284, pp. 224–233, 2004.

into the container. When the agent returns to the origin host, it applies a set of integrity rules to all the data containers. These rules can be inferred from the modifications performed in the agent's code during the watermark embedding. If a container does not fulfill the rules, this means that the corresponding host is malicious. The proposal not only detects manipulation attacks performed during the agent's execution, but it also proves the malicious behavior of the host. Consequently, a Trusted Third Party (TTP) [4] can punish a malicious host by using its tampered container.

The rest of the paper is organized as follows: Section 2 describes the existing approaches to protect mobile agents; Section 3 details how to detect and prove manipulation attacks using the MAW approach. Finally, some conclusions can be found in Section 4.

2   Malicious Hosts

The attacks performed by a malicious host that is executing the mobile agent are considered, by far, the most difficult problem to solve regarding mobile agent security. Notice that while it is possible to assure the integrity and authentication of the code, the data or the results that come from other hosts by using digital signature or encryption techniques, it is difficult to detect or prevent the attacks performed by a malicious host during the agent's execution. Malicious hosts could try to get some profit of the agent reading or modifying the code, the data, the itinerary, the communications or even the results due to their complete control on the execution. The agent cannot hold a decryption key because the hosts could read it. Furthermore, it is not sure that the host runs the complete code in a correct manner, or it simply does not allow the migration.

An example of search agent is included in Figure 1 to illustrate how the executing hosts can attack a mobile agent. The example agent visits several airline sites to find the cheapest flight from Barcelona to Paris. When the last host of the itinerary finishes its execution, the agent returns to the origin host with the cheapest prize in the variable *bestprize* and the airline that provides this prize in the variable *bestairline*. For simplicity, cryptographic protection to any part of the mobile agent is not provided.

Now consider what would happen if the last of the servers acts dishonestly and changes the prize in its database to a value that is lower than the prize contained in the variable *bestprize*. As a result, the variable *bestairline* is set to this dishonest server and the product is finally bought to it. In this case the host carries out an eavesdropping attack reading the variable *bestprize*, and with this privileged information the host changes its database in order to sell the product. Eavesdropping attacks cannot be detected nor avoided because the host can always save a copy of the agent to analyze it. The problem gets worse when a malicious server carries out a manipulation attack. For example, the first server can set directly both variables to the values that it wants and can make the agent returning home. While there are techniques to protect the mobile agent's route [8], the proposals that have been published until now do not protect the

```
DATA BLOCK
Address home=myPC;
City origin= Barcelona;
City destination=Paris;
Address itinerary[]=[Airfrance,Iberia,Spanair];
Integer index_itinerary=0;
Integer bestprize=300;
Address bestairline=void;
```

```
CODE BLOCK
1 public void cheapestFlightAgent () {
2  if (itinerary[index_itinerary].flightprice(origin,destination) <
bestprize) {
3    bestprize=itinerary[index_itinerary].flightprice(origin,destination);
4    bestairline=itinerary[index_itinerary];
5  }
6  if (index_itinerary >= (itinerary.length - 1) go(home);
7  go(itinerary[++index_itinerary]);
8 }
```

Fig. 1. Example of a Search Agent

rest of the parts of the agent properly against manipulation attacks performed during the execution.

There are two main types of approaches: attack avoidance approaches, that try to avoid the attacks before they happen, and attack detection approaches, whose aim is detection after the attack has been performed. Detection techniques are less effective for services where benefits for tampering a mobile agent could be greater than the possible punishment. In those cases, attack avoidance approaches are recommended. The rest of the paragraph summarizes some of them. Yee introduces the idea of a closed tamper-proof hardware subsystem [12] where agents can be executed in a secure way, but this forces each host to buy a hardware equipment and to consider the hardware provider as trusted. Roth presents the idea of cooperative agents [9] that share secrets and decisions and have a disjunct itinerary. This fact makes collusion attacks difficult, but not impossible. Hohl presents obfuscation [6] as a mechanism to assure the execution integrity during a period of time, but this time depends on the capacity of analyzing the code of the malicious host. The use of encrypted programs [10] is proposed as the only way to give privacy and integrity to mobile code. The difficulty here is to find functions that can be executed in an encrypted way.

Existing attack avoidance approaches are difficult to implement, computationally unfeasibles or do not avoid the attacks completely. On the contrary, attack detection approaches are more promising or, at least, possible to use in some scenarios. In [7], the authors introduce the idea of replication and voting. In each stage, a set of hosts execute the agent in a parallel way and send several replicas of the agent to the next stage. This offers a fault-tolerant mechanism to execute agents, but only can be used as an attack detection approach in those scenarios in which the hosts in the same stage are independent, i.e. they must have different interests to attack an agent. In [11], Vigna introduces the idea of cryptographic traces. The running agent takes traces of instructions that alter the agent's state due to external variables. If the agent owner suspects that a host acted maliciously and wants to verify the execution, it asks for the traces and executes the agent again. Despite being the most widely known attack detection approach, it still has some major drawbacks that deter its implementation. At first, the executing hosts must store the traces for an indefinite period of time because the origin host can ask for them. Furthermore, verification is performed only in case of suspicion, but how a host becomes suspicious is not explained. In [5] a Suspicious Detection Protocol (SDP) was introduced to solve the drawbacks of the cryptographic traces approach. Using both the traces and SDP jointly it is possible to offer a complete attack detection mechanism. However, we consider that the proposal is still too expensive.

3   Mobile Agent Watermarking

In [3], the authors introduced the Mobile Agent Watermarking approach, a lightweight attack detection approach that permits to verify the execution integrity of all the hosts without thinking in terms of suspicion. In the proposal, the origin host embeds a fixed watermark into the code. As a result, the running of the agent creates marked results. When the agent returns to the origin host, these results are examined in order to find the watermark. If the watermark has changed or disappeared, this means that the executing host is malicious.

In this paper, some improvements are introduced in MAW to make the proposal more secure and resistant to collusion attacks. To do so, the running of the agent creates a data container where the watermark will be transferred. During the execution, the agent puts some data inside the container in an ordered way, for example some dummy data, input data or even intermediate variable values. When the execution finishes, the results are also fitted into the container. Consequently, the transferred watermark changes dynamically during the execution. When the agent returns to the origin host, it applies a set of integrity rules to all the data containers. If a container does not fulfill the rules, this means that the corresponding host is malicious. These rules can be inferred from the modifications performed in the agent's code during the watermark embedding.

3.1   Watermark Embedding and Transference

Just like any other attack detection approach, the MAW must provide proofs to the origin host to verify that the execution has not been tampered. For this reason, the origin host embeds a watermark into the agent's code by using software watermarking techniques [1]. In each host, the execution of the marked code creates a logically-structured data container where the watermark will be transferred. During execution, the agent puts some information into the container, for example dummy data, input data, intermediate variable values, data that come from communications, and finally the results. In fact, the data of the container can be made up of:

- Fixed values located in some positions previously known by the origin host, like it was in [3].
- Values that can change dynamically during the execution and fulfill a set of logical rules.

The way this information is put into the container and the information itself constitute the transferred watermark. In short, the container is the digital cover where the agent's code must transfer the embedded watermark, and hence it can be used as a proof to verify the execution integrity. Furthermore, the container is hiding the results from malicious hosts, that is to say, a malicious host should not tell the difference between the results and the transferred watermark.

3.2   Detecting Manipulation Attacks

When the agent returns home, the origin host tries to detect the attacks performed during execution. To do so, the origin host verifies that all the containers fulfill a set of integrity rules. These rules can be inferred from the modifications performed over the original agent's code to embed the watermark. If a container does not fulfill the rules, this means that the corresponding host modified the mobile agent, so it is malicious. Notice that the way the origin host uses to verify the execution integrity is the same for all the hosts, but this does not mean that all the containers have the same watermark. In fact, the transferred watermark is different because it depends on the execution.

3.3   Proving Manipulation Attacks

Attack detection approaches are not enough to protect the agent on their own. This kind of mechanisms must be attached with some punishment policies. Usually, a host will turn into malicious behavior only in case that the benefits for tampering the agent would be greater than the punishment. Thus, the harder the punishment, the less attacks will be performed by the hosts. Obviously, the TTP in charge of the punishment will only penalize a host if there are proofs that it behaved maliciously [4].

The way to verify that the execution has not been altered is by applying the integrity rules to the containers. The problem arises because these rules are not public, only the origin host knows them. So then, the TTP needs proofs that these rules matches the agent's code. This can be done by executing the agent (once or several times) with random input data. If the new container created during this random execution fulfills the rules, then the integrity rules can be considered as valid. Once the rules have been validated, the TTP can verify if a host is malicious by applying the integrity rules to its container.

3.4 Example

Figure 2 shows some easy modifications that can be applied to the agent of Section 2 to detect manipulation attacks. Just remark that the modifications performed in a real agent should be much more complicated than these of the example. Again for simplicity, cryptographic protection to any part of the mobile agent has not been provided.

The agent's code must transfer the watermark and hide the results into the container. The techniques used in the example are based on diffusing[1] and confusing[2] the information into the container:

- The agent's code can introduce any kind of available data into the container, like input data, constants or intermediate variable values, and finally the results. However, these data should be changed before putting them into the container.
- The agent can ask for information in which the user is not interested in. For instance, the agent of Figure 2 asks for the price of a flight from Madrid to Paris, but the user is only interested in the flight from Barcelona to Paris.
- The container must be dependent on the execution flow in order to detect any change in it.
- None of the parts of the mobile agent must give information about its intentions to make the code harder to analyze. The more difficult to understand is the code, the more secure is the approach. In this sense, the use of techniques like obfuscation [2, 6] can be additionally useful.

Figure 3 shows the containers that would be obtained if all the three airline servers act honestly and give the real prices of their databases to the agent. The containers of the example are located inside the array of integers $f[\,][\,]$. Figure 4 shows some of the integrity rules that can be inferred from the marked code. Applying these rules to the containers it is possible to verify that all the hosts were honest.

3.5 Advantages

MAW is a lightweight attack detection approach if it is compared to the most widely known, the cryptographic traces approach [11]. These are some of the advantages of MAW regarding the use of traces:

- The size of the containers is determined by the programmer and can be little enough to be carried in the agent. On the contrary, the size of the traces depends on the amount of input data, that can be huge.
- The origin host can verify the execution integrity of all the hosts because the containers return with the agent. On the other hand, in the cryptographic traces approach the verification is performed in case of suspicion.

---

[1] Diffusing values means repeating these values into several different places.
[2] Confusing values means modifying these values to different ones, for example by adding constant values.

```
DATA BLOCK
City c1= Barcelona;
City c2=Madrid;
City c3=Paris;
Address d=myPC;
Address i[]=[Airfrance,Iberia,Spanair];
Integer b=0;
Address a1;
Address a2;
Integer p1=753;
Integer p2=1154;
Integer f[][];

CODE BLOCK
1   public void example_agent () {
2   Integer h,j,m,n,k=0,z=3;
3   h=i[b].flightprice(c1,c3)*2+107;
4   f[b][k+z]=h+234;
5   j=i[b].flightprice(c2,c3)*3+125;
6   m=p1-h+132+z*3;
7   k++;
8   f[b][k+z]=j-120;
9   z--;
10  n=p2-j+73+k*5;
11  if (m>87) p1=h-54;
12  if (m<=87) p1=m+h-141;
13  f[b][z-k]=p1+132;
14  z--;
15  f[b][z-k]=b*4+5;
16  if (n>57) p2=j-21;
17  if (n<=57) p2=n+j-78;
18  z--;
19  f[b][2*k-z]=p2+56;
20  z++;
21  f[b][3*(z+k)]=h+j;
22  k++;
23  f[b][3*k-z]=p1+p2;
24  if (b >=(i.length -1) go(d);
25  go(i[++b]);
26  }
```

Fig. 2. Search Agent Using MAW

- In MAW, the hosts do not need to store any kind of proof. On the contrary, the hosts must store the traces for an indefinite period of time because the origin host can ask for them.
- To verify the execution of a host, the origin host has to apply the rules to the container. In the cryptographic traces approach, it is necessary to execute the agent again.

f[][]

5	725	1000	881	845	1537	1612	→ Container Airfrance
9	685	1000	841	875	1497	1482	→ Container Iberia
13	685	910	961	755	1407	1602	→ Container Spanair

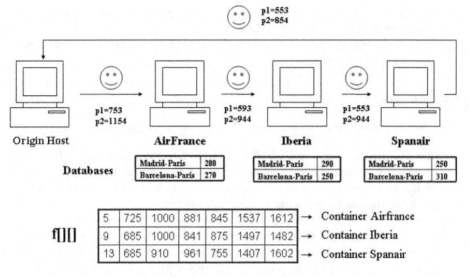

Fig. 3. Honest Execution of the Example Agent

RULES IN A CONTAINER
f[i][0]=i*4+5
f[i][3]>=f[i][1]+156
f[i][4]+155>=f[i][2]
f[i][1]+f[i][2]=f[i][5]+188
f[i][3]+f[i][4]=f[i][6]+144

RULES BETWEEN CONTAINERS
f[0][1]>=f[1][1]>=f[2][1]>=...>=f[N-1][1]
f[0][2]>=f[1][2]>=f[2][2]>=...>=f[N-1][2]
f[0][5]>=f[1][5]>=f[2][5]>=...>=f[N-1][5]

RESULTS
Result=(p1-53)/2
Result=(f[N-1][1]-185)/2
Result=(f[N-1][6]-f[N][2]+3)/2

where N is the length of the agent's itinerary

Fig. 4. Rules that Must Fulfill the Containers of the Example

3.6 Drawbacks

These are the main drawbacks that can be found in the mobile agent watermarking approach:

- The origin host must embed the watermark into the agent's code and must infer the rules from these modifications.

- There is an increase in the code size. Embedding a mark always means that some overhead is added to the code.
- The mobile agent must carry a data container for each host, instead of just the results of execution.

3.7 Attacks

These are the main attacks that the malicious hosts can perform to MAW:

- Eavesdropping: all non-encrypted data in the agent can be read by the hosts. Although it is possible to modify the agent to make it harder to analyze, for instance by using obfuscation [2], a malicious host with enough time can guess the intentions of the agent.
- Manipulation: a malicious host can manipulate any part of the agent to achieve an execution on its own profit. The aim of the malicious hosts is modifying the agent without altering the watermark, because any change in it can be used as a proof to punish them. In this sense, the strength of MAW is making the watermark imperceptible enough to an observer, because a malicious host will be easily detected if it tries to modify the agent with no knowledge about where the watermark is.
- Collusion: it is difficult that a group of colluding hosts locate the transferred watermark by comparing their containers, because the watermark is different (dynamically generated) for each host.

4 Conclusions

In this paper, some improvements have been added to the MAW approach. Instead of a fixed watermark like it was in [3], the origin host embeds a watermark that changes dynamically during execution. This makes the proposal more secure and resilient to collusion attacks. In each host, the agent's code creates a container to transfer the watermark of the code and to hide the results. These containers are the proof of the good or bad behavior of the hosts. When the agent returns home, the origin host applies a set of integrity rules that the containers must fulfill. These integrity rules can be inferred from the modifications performed in the agent's code during the watermark embedding. If a container does not fulfill the rules, this means that the executing host has modified the agent. Consequently, these containers are the proof that assures the agent's execution integrity.

Acknowledgments

This work is supported by the Spanish Research Council under the project DIS-QET CICYT TIC2002-00818.

References

1. C. Collberg and C. Thomborson. Software watermarking: Models and dynamic embeddings. In *Principles of Programming Languages 1999, POPL'99*, 1999.
2. C. Collberg, C. Thomborson, and D. Low. A taxonomy of obfuscating transformations. Technical Report 148, The University of Auckland, 1997.
3. O. Esparza, M. Fernandez, M. Soriano, J.L. Muñoz, and J. Forné. Mobile agent watermarking and fingerprinting: tracing malicious hosts. In *Database and Expert Systems Applications (DEXA 2003)*, volume 2736 of *LNCS*. Springer-Verlag, 2003.
4. O. Esparza, M. Soriano, J.L. Muñoz, and J. Forné. Host Revocation Authority: a Way of Protecting Mobile Agents from Malicious Hosts. In *International Conference on Web Engineering (ICWE 2003)*, volume 2722 of *LNCS*. Springer-Verlag, 2003.
5. O. Esparza, M. Soriano, J.L. Muñoz, and J. Forné. Implementation and Performance Evaluation of a Protocol for Detecting Suspicious Hosts. In *Mobile Agents for Telecommunication Applications (MATA'03)*, volume 2881 of *LNCS*. Springer-Verlag, 2003.
6. F. Hohl. Time Limited Blackbox Security: Protecting Mobile Agents From Malicious Hosts. In *Mobile Agents and Security*, volume 1419 of *LNCS*. Springer-Verlag, 1998.
7. Y. Minsky, R. van Renesse, F. Schneider, and S.D. Stoller. Cryptographic Support for Fault-Tolerant Distributed Computing. In *Seventh ACM SIGOPS European Workshop*, 1996.
8. J. Mir and J. Borrell. Protecting Mobile Agent Itineraries. In *Mobile Agents for Telecommunication Applications (MATA 2003)*, volume 2881 of *LNCS*. Springer-Verlag, 2003.
9. V. Roth. Mutual protection of cooperating agents. In *Secure Internet Programming: Security Issues for Mobile and Distributed Objects*, volume 1906 of *LNCS*. Springer-Verlag, 1999.
10. T. Sander and C.F. Tschudin. Protecting mobile agents against malicious hosts. In *Mobile Agents and Security*, volume 1419 of *LNCS*. Springer-Verlag, 1998.
11. G. Vigna. Cryptographic traces for mobile agents. In *Mobile Agents and Security*, volume 1419 of *LNCS*. Springer-Verlag, 1998.
12. B.S. Yee. A sanctuary for mobile agents. In *DARPA workshop on foundations for secure mobile code*, 1997.

MASS: A Mobile Agent Security Scheme for the Creation of Virtual Enterprises

Michelle S. Wangham, Joni Fraga, Ricardo Schmidt, and Ricardo J. Rabelo

Department of Automation and Systems
Federal University of Santa Catarina
C. P. 476 – 88040-900 – Florianópolis – SC – Brazil
{wangham,fraga,rschmidt,rabelo}@das.ufsc.br

Abstract. This article describes a security scheme, based on crypto-graphic protocols and SPKI/SDSI chains of trust, for protecting agent platforms and mobile agents in large-scale distributed systems. In addition, it proposes an approach on how trust building in mobile agent-based architectures can be reinforced by using security mechanisms in the process of searching and selecting partners to create a Virtual Enterprise.

1   Introduction

A mobile agent in a large-scale network can be defined as a software agent that is able to autonomously migrate from one host to another in a heterogeneous network to perform tasks on behalf of its creator [1]. In order for these agents to exist within a system or to form a system themselves, they require a computing environment – an agent platform – for deployment and execution.

The ability to move agents allows deployment of services and applications in a more flexible and dynamic way with respect to the client-server paradigm [2]. Despite its many benefits, the mobile agent paradigm introduces new security threats from malicious agents and platforms. Mechanisms currently available for reducing the risks of this technology do not efficiently cover all the existing threats. Moreover, they introduce performance restrictions that frequently out-weigh the benefits from the use of this paradigm. This paper focuses on security scheme applied to a mobile agent-based application for searching and selecting partners in the formation of Virtual Enterprises (VEs) – *MobiC-II* system [3].

Cooperation in the form of Virtual Enterprises represents a modern strategy which has been applied by many companies over the world to expand their par-ticipation in the market without drastically changing their structures. Actually, a VE corresponds to a set of companies that are selected to meet the require-ments of a given business opportunity (BO) as none of them is able to attend to it alone. The selection of the VE members has been often supported by partner's search and selection systems (PSS), and this search in turn is usually made over a pre- defined group of companies – a cluster. The decision process is performed in an interactive way, in which the company that receives the BO, called broker, negotiates it with the cluster companies. This negotiation lasts until the selec-

A. Karmouch, L. Korba, and E. Madeira (Eds.): MATA 2004, LNCS 3284, pp. 234–243, 2004.

tion of the most suitable subset of members is finished. These members comprise the VE, which is finally created.

Aiming at greater efficiency and flexibility, this paper brings an approach to aid the creation phase of VEs which is based on an agents hybrid architecture - mobile and stationary agents. This work comprises security aspects for the use of mobile agents. These aspects strengthen the trust building process in the VEs' formation. The security threats in the *MobiC-II* scenario are also analyzed and a security policy that aims at mitigating most of these threats is defined.

One of the main concerns about an agent platform implementation is ensuring that agents are not able to interfere with an underlying agent platform [4]. A common approach for accomplishing it is to establish isolated protection domains for each incoming mobile agent and platform, and to control all inter-domain access. Protection against malicious agents is not restricted to confining their execution to their own execution domains in agent platforms; other issues need to be considered when large-scale distributed applications are the focus.

Malicious platforms' attacks against agents are the most difficult security problems to overcome and have still been left without an appropriate solution. While mechanisms directed towards the platform security are a direct evolution from traditional mechanisms that emphasize techniques of prevention, mechanisms directed towards agent security usually correspond to detection measures. This occurs due to the fact that an agent is totally susceptible to a platform and that it is difficult to prevent the occurrence of malicious behaviors [5].

Based on cryptographic protocols and on decentralized authentication and authorization controls that use SPKI/SDSI certificates [6], we defined the **MASS** – *Mobile Agent Security Scheme* for large-scale systems. In the present study, we proposed security mechanisms to protect the communications infrastructure, agent platforms and agents themselves. In our scheme, the flexibility needed for the implementation of a security policy to the *MobiC-II* system is given by the ability to select only the subset of mechanisms desired by this application.

2 *MobiC-II*: The Partners Search and Selection System

The PSS System proposed in this work is based on an agent hybrid architecture. This system exploits the benefits of the mobile agents' paradigm to improve agility in the presentation of business opportunities to the cluster of companies and to achieve higher efficiency in the formation and analysis of the possible virtual enterprises to be constituted. Stationary agents, which represent every real company of a virtual organization, are responsible for interactions with the companies' legacy systems.

A prototype which implements the PSS system – *MobiC-II* – was developed for the TechMoldes cluster, a group of mold makers in southern Brazil whose members have been collaborating to enhance their global competitiveness. The main idea of Techmoldes is to act as a *single*/larger productive entity in the market, combining the individual skills and resources of each member; *transparent* to the final customer, however. When collaborating within Techmoldes, each member remains independent and autonomous, even to the extent of making business out of the cluster. Three classes of agents compose *MobiC-II* system:

- **Broker Agent:** it is a stationary agent responsible for receiving BO, distributing it to the potential enterprises, sending a mobile agent to them, and collecting/electing the final VE composition.
- **Mobile Agent:** it is a mobile agent responsible for delivering a BO to the enterprises, negotiating locally with them, and travelling through the net to the other enterprises and finally back to the broker. This agent may have to perform different roles (missions) - from acting as a simple information messenger agent, as a data researcher, to acting as a negotiator capable of making decisions and negotiations independently - without counting on the orders sent by the broker agent during the accomplishment of a task. Thereby, roles are created to the agents according to their desired function.
- **Enterprise Agent:** it is a stationary agent that represents an enterprise and is responsible for receiving a BO, evaluating it, accessing the local database to get the required information, and answering the BO to the mobile agent.

The PSS System is shown in Fig. 1. Mobile agents are used as a means to travel through the selected enterprises in order to interact with the stationary agents for receiving the required information (e.g., delivery time and capacity) or for negotiating lower costs or shorter delivery time.

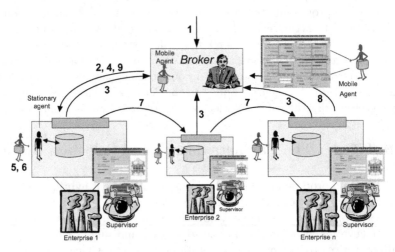

Fig. 1. Scenario for PSS System

When a business opportunity appears, it is received by the broker, which identifies (only) the potential enterprises that can supply each mold (**step 1**, 1). A summary of the mold specification is immediately sent out to the enterprises (**step 2**). Each enterprise receives it, evaluates its preliminary interest and capacity, and sends back an answer to the broker, either *yes* (expressing its interest) or *no* (**step 3**). The broker receives the answers and sends a mobile agent to the enterprises that answered *yes*, provided with the full BO specification and the list of candidate enterprises to visit (**step 4**). The mobile agent arrives at the first enterprise and interacts with the local stationary agent, asking for its delivery time and capacity (**step 5**). The local agent, acting as the enterprise's representative, retrieves this information from its legacy system or local database. After that, the mobile agent asks the local supervisor about the price, as it is a very important piece of information in the molding sector. A negotiation process may be carried out locally (**step 6**). Then, the mobile agent moves to the next enterprise of the list with these information (**step 7**). This process is repeated until all the candidate enterprises in the list are visited, when the mobile agent then returns to the broker agent with their proposals (**step 8**). The agent broker generates a set of possible VEs, assesses every VE composition and a human broker elects the most suitable one. Afterwards, the human broker sends a *win* or *lose* message to the enterprises (**step 9**). The election criteria applied on this case are global lowest cost and shortest delivery time.

The trust building process is indeed one of the most difficult issues to be overcome by the developers of VE solutions. *MobiC-II* considers the need of having more than one broker acting within a VE. This characteristic brings advantages to the *MobiC-II* due to the fact that (1) there is a reduction of a number of activities into a sole element and that (2) having many brokers makes a decentralized system's hierarchy possible, which aids trust building process among participant enterprises. However, even though the members know one another and are aware of what they are supposed to do in order to be a candidate for a BO, they get reluctant to share some kinds of information, such as prices, delivery dates and capacities. Cultural, ethical, managerial, besides other "pure" IT-related problems, have been pointed out as obstacles for a wider adoption of the VE paradigm by the companies [7]. Therefore, security mechanisms that ensure the confidentiality, integrity and availability of information, according to the cluster security policy, should be introduced aiming at trust building. This paper presents an approach on how trust building in mobile agent-based architectures can be reinforced by using some security mechanisms in the process of searching and selecting partners to create a Virtual Enterprise.

3   Security in Mobile Agent Systems

Mobile agent platforms face several threats, such as [4]: (1) *masquerading*, when an agent poses as an authorized agent in an effort to gain access to services and resources to which it is not entitled; (2) *denial of service*, when an agent launch attacks to consume an excessive amount of the agent platform's computing resources; and (3) *unauthorized access-* for example, when an agent obtains read or write access to data for which it has no authorization.

The establishment of isolated protection domains for each incoming mobile agent and control of system domains entrances is an approach that has been commonly adopted with the purpose of offering protection to agent platforms. In addition to this approach, other techniques were proposed based on conventional security techniques. Some of these techniques are safe code interpretation, digital signatures, path histories, State Appraisal, and Proof-Carrying Code (PCC).

The dangerous attacks of agents platforms against mobile agents are critical security problems to solve. The set of threats includes [4]: (1) *masquerading*, when a platform poses as another platform in an effort to deceive a mobile agent misleading it from its true destination; (2)*denial of service*, when a malicious platform ignores agent service requests, introduces unacceptable delays for critical tasks, or simply does not execute the agent's code; (3)*eavesdropping*, when a platform monitors every instruction executed by the agent, and all the subsequent data generated on the platform; and (4) *unauthorized access*, when a platform modifies a mobile agent by changing its code, its state, or both.

The security of mobile agents mainly involves (1) the agent's **integrity**, in order to prevent the platforms from altering the code or the data which are collected during the visits, and (2) the **confidentiality** of the code and of the agent's state, in order to avoid violating the intellectual property. Some mechanisms for agent protection include Secure Hardware, Partial Result Encapsulation, Computing with Encrypted Functions, and Time Limited Blackbox. However, these techniques cannot be considered suitable and flexible when a mobile agent needs to travel through several sites in a large-scale system. This occurs because mobile agents run under the control of a platform and it is very difficult to prevent attacks against them.

3.1   *MASS*: A Mobile Agent Security Scheme

The security scheme proposed – **MASS**[1] – is based on an agents' model that assumes free itineraries and multi-hops. The Mobile Agent Facility (MAF) specification [9] is used as a guideline to achieve interoperability between mobile agent systems. *MASS* is composed of security mechanisms to protect the communications infrastructure, agent platforms and agents themselves. Figure 2 shows the procedures defined in the security scheme, which are composed by prevention and detection techniques. we analyze some aspects of the mechanisms in the following proposed scheme.

Techniques for Creating a Protected Mobile Agent

During a mobile agent creation process, the owner, who is the authority that an agent represents, provides a set of SPKI/SDSI authorization certificates defining the agent's privilege attributes (its credentials). The owner of the agent has to put in an object that will contain the list of previously visited platforms (called the *path register*) a signature indicating its identity and the identity of the first platform to be visited. This object is attached to the agent. Also, agents can have attached platform lists that indicate which platforms are authorized to execute the agent. Visited platforms must be associated with the agent's authority. The agent programmer can protect items in the agent's state so they are only accessible to certain platforms. To accomplish this, the programmer can

---

[1] Further details on the security mechanism of *MASS* can be found in [1], [8].

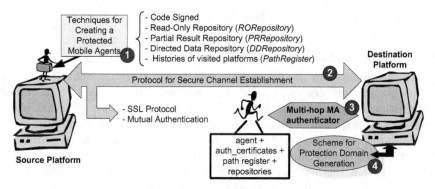

Fig. 2. *MASS*:Security Scheme to Mobile Agent Systems

use a directed data vector – *DDRepository*. This allows for selective disclosure of the agent's state [10]. Moreover, we propose that platform-generated sensitive data should be stored in a repository to be carried by the agents. These sensitive data should be signed by the generating platform so that possible modifications can be detected. So, the programmer can create the partial result repository – *PRrepository* – to protect visited platform-generated data. Finally, the agent's owner must first sign the agent's code and the data defined by the programmer as read-only (in *RORepository*), and then create the agent in its home platform.

Protocol for Secure Channel Establishment

In the proposed scheme, mutual authentication between the involved platforms must be established before agents can be transferred, which creates a secure channel in the communications infrastructure. This is performed via a Challenge/Response protocol based on SPKI/SDSI certificates of the owners of the platforms. The basis for authentication in SPKI/SDSI are chains of authorization certificates [6]. The establishment of a secure channel will remain valid in the subsequent interactions. For secure channel establishment, an underlying security technology (Secure Sockets Layer - SSL) is used for ensuring confidentiality and integrity of the communications between agent platforms.

Mobile Agents Authentication

Before instantiating a thread to an agent, the destination platform must authenticate the received agent. We define a multi-hop authenticator that establishes trust on an agent, based on the authenticity of the owner of the agent, and on the authenticity of the platforms visited by the agent. As a platform receives a mobile agent, it must first check, through verification of the code's signature and of the RORepository's signature, that this agent has not been corrupted and confirm its association to a principal, that is, to its owner. Thus, modifications introduced by malicious platforms can be detected by any platform visited by the agent. In addition, for detecting other possible modifications and checking the multi-hop agent's traveling history (*path_register*), the destination agent platform must analyze the record of the agent's path. If defined by the agent owner, the authenticator should verify the *PRRepository*'s and the *DDRepository*'s integrity.

Procedure for Generation of Protection Domains

Protection domains and the permissions assigned to them are defined after the trust in an agent has been established. They are based on the agent's SPKI/SDSI authorization certificates. The authorization chains carried by an agent, which represent its credentials, need to be verified by the platform guardian for the set of permissions to be defined and for the protection domains to be generated. This scheme decouples the privilege attributes granted to principals (agent's credentials) from the attributes required to access resources protected by the platform (control attributes or policies), offering a more flexible and dynamic access control for large-scale systems with respect to the Java access control.

3.2   The *MASS* for *MobiC-II*

The selection of the security mechanisms that were applied to the partners search and the selection system was carefully evaluated in the design phase of the proposed hybrid agent system. This enhances the quality of the system in the sense that the most suitable mechanisms can be conceived without losing their potentialities, which usually happens when they are implemented afterwards. Security policies and mechanisms determine which agents will be mobile and which will stay stationary, the scope of the agents' functionalities, and others.

All the security threats (identified in section 3.1) against the agents and the mobile agent platforms are also found in the *MobiC-II* system's steps – steps 2, 4, 5, 6, 7, and 8 (see Figure 1). The threats against the communications channel that can compromise the dispatch of agents as well as the sending of messages among mobile agents platforms, such as unauthorized modification, and eavesdropping, are found in steps 1, 2, 3, 7, and 8 of the *MobiC-II* system.

Security Policy to the TechMoldes Scenario. An organization security policy is a set of rules and practices imposed by an organization to establish the operating limits of the users of a system, aiming at protecting the organization's sensitive data. During the project period of the *MobiC-II* system, a security policy was defined to the TechMoldes scenario and an answer was planned against systems threats – the *MASS*' security objectives for the *MobiC-II* system. A summary of the security policy's rules is listed as follows:

- **P1:** The integrity of read-only data carried by mobile agents (e.g.: summary of the mold specification) should be provided by the *MASS*;
- **P2:** Only the cluster's enterprises may have access to the summary of the mold specification and the full BO specification;
- **P3:** Only the cluster's enterprises may take the broker's role and thus only these enterprises will be able to send (1) mobile agents with the BOs' specifications as well as (2) researcher agents and (3) negotiator agents;
- **P4:** The *MASS* may control the access of mobile agents to the platforms' sensitive data;

- **P5:** The authenticity origin of a mobile agent (its creator) must be verifiable;
- **P6:** Only the participant enterprises may reply to a given BO (through the negotiator or researcher mobile agents). These collected proposals must be revealed only to the broker and their integrity must be assured;
- **P7:** The integrity and authenticity of the origin of all messages exchanged between the mobile agents' platforms, while being sent by the communications channel, must be assured by the *MASS*;
- **P8:** The integrity and authenticity of mobile agents, while being sent through the communications channel, must be assured by the *MASS*;
- **P9:** Only a mobile agent's owner may change its code;
- **P10:** An enterprise may not deny that it has received a given BO;
- **P11:** An enterprise may not repudiate a proposal, that it has presented, in reply to a given BO.

Analysis of Security Mechanisms. After identifying the threats and defining the organizational security policy, we analyzed the security mechanisms supported by the *MASS* and the mechanisms needed to minimize or eliminate the exploitation of one or more vulnerabilities that would hinder trust building in the *MobiC-II* System. These mechanisms are listed in the Table 1.

Table 1. Security Mechanisms to the *MobiC-II* System

Security Mechanisms	Rules satisfied
Repository of read-only data (*RORepository*)	P1
Repository of Partial Results (*PRRepository*)	P6 and P11
A list containing the platforms authorized to receive mobile agents	P2 and P6
A signature of the mobile agent's code	P9
Multi-hop authenticator – use of the *PathRegister* object	P2 and P10
Multi-hop authenticator – verification of *RORepository*' and *PRRepository* integrity	P1 and P6
Multi-hop authenticator – verification of the mobile agent signature	P3, P5, and P9
Procedures for Protection Domain Generation	P4
Secure channel establishment – mutual authentication	P3
Secure channel establishment – use of SSL Protocol	P7 and P8

4   Implementation

A prototype of the *MASS* was implemented and integrated to *MobiC-II* in order to demonstrate its suitability for distributed applications with mobile agents.

For the mobile agents support layer we have chosen IBM Aglets[2], an open-source platform that uses Java as its mobile code language. The Aglets software development kit (ASDK) provides mechanisms for code and state information mobility, and a computational environment.

---

[2] http://aglets.sourceforge.net/

In order to aid the agent creation process and the use of secure data repositories, a GUI was implemented. This interface enables an owner to define which data repositories are going to be used and attached to the agent. The algorithm of the *multihop* authenticator was implemented to a stationary agent called `SecurityInterceptor`. This agent must be initiated in all platforms that are to receive the mobile agent and has as a role to intercept the mobile agent receiving process. This interception enables the verification of the incoming mobile agent's integrity prior to its initiation in the platform.

The protocol for the secure channel establishment and the multi-hop authenticator (see section 3.1) were implemented with the SDSI 2.0 library [11] and with Java 2 cryptographic tools. The SSL support is provided by the iSaSiLk toolkit[3] and was integrated to the Aglets platform.

As the agent platform chosen for the prototype is based on Java, the secure interpretation of the agents' code and the definition of the protections domains to mobile agents are provided, in part, by the Java 2 security model. The process for generating the set of permissions was defined to overcome the limitations related to the Java 2 access control model. Some extensions to the Java 2 security model were needed for generating the protection domain.

As described in [3], in *MobiC-II*, agents were placed in two platforms. The mobile agents were coded in Java and the Aglets platform was used. The stationary agents were coded in C++ and the MASSYVE-KIT platform[4] was used. CORBA is the technology applied to support the multi-platform interoperation.

5   Concluding Remarks

Security issues still hamper the development of applications with mobile systems. Current security mechanisms do not present satisfactory results for protecting mobile agent platforms. There are even more limitations when we consider large-scale systems, which impose stronger requirements with regard to flexibility and scalability. *MASS* was motivated by the perception of these limitations and a concern about aspects of security specific to large-scale applications. This article proposes an approach to improve trust building in Virtual Enterprises, especially in their creation phase (searching and selecting partners). To accomplish this, *MASS*'s security mechanisms were used for the conception of the *MobiC-II*.

Comparing secure data repositories presented in section 3.1[5] to related works described in [10],[12], one can ascertain that the proposed repositories overcome some of the limitations and vulnerabilities described in this works. In comparison to the static model in Java 2 and to the platforms that extend the Java Security Manager [10], our scheme has the advantage of decoupling privilege attributes (credentials) from control attributes (policies), its use of some Java security features notwithstanding. This means that, although a policy configuration file still needs to be statically defined, the proposed mechanisms add the

---

[3] http://jce.iaik.tugraz.at/products/02_isasilk/

[4] http://www.gsigma-grucon.ufsc.br/massyve/mkit.htm

[5] These repositories were described in detail in [8].

flexibility offered by SPKI certificates to domain generation. That is, domains are dynamically defined when an agent aggregates the delegated certificates received during its itinerary to its credentials. Besides, in the agent authentication process described in section 3.1, the information used to determine an agent's set of access rights is based not only on the identity of the agent's owner, but also on the public keys of the owner of the visited platforms, which avoids global name resolutions in large-scale systems. The work described in this paper was fully implemented. Integration and adaptation of the *MASS* to the *MobiC-II* system was done in order to demonstrate its usefulness. At present, its performance is being properly measured and evaluated.

Acknowledgments

The authors thank the "IFM (Instituto Fábrica do Milênio)" and "Chains of Trust" project (CNPq 552175/01-3) members for their contributions. The first and the second authors are supported by CNPq (Brazil).

References

1. Wangham, M.S., da Silva Fraga, J., Obelheiro, R.R., Jung, G., Fernandes, E.: Security mechanisms for mobile agent platforms based on spki/sdsi chains of trust. In: Software Engineering for Multi-Agent System II. Volume 2940 of LNCS. Springer (2004) 207–224
2. Vigna, G., ed.: Mobile Agents and Security. Volume 1419 of LNCS. Springer (1998)
3. Rabelo, R., Wangham, M., Schmidt, R., Fraga, J.: Trust building in the creation of virtual enterprises in mobile agent-based architectures. In: 4Th IFIP Working Conference on Virtual Enterprise. (2003)
4. Jansen, W., Karygiannis, T.: Mobile agent security. Technical Report NIST Special Publication 800-19, National Institute os Standards and Technology (1999)
5. Chess, D.M.: Security issues in mobile code systems. In Vigna, G., ed.: Mobile Agents and Security. Volume 1419 of LNCS. Springer (1998)
6. Elisson, C.: SPKI Requirements (RFC 2692). The Internet Engineering Task Force. (1999) http://www.ietf.org/rfc/rfc2692.txt.
7. Camarinha-Matos, L., Afsarmanesh, H.: Dynamic virtual organizations, or not so dynamic ? In: Third IFIP Working Conference on Virtual Enterprise (PRO-VE'2002). (2002) 111–124
8. Wangham, M.S., da Silva Fraga, J., Deitos, R., Fernandes, E.: Repositórios seguros de dados para protecão de agentes móveis contra plataformas maliciosas. In: IV Workshop em Seguranca de Sistemas Computacionais. (2004) (in portuguese).
9. OMG: Mobile agent facility specification. OMG Document 2000-01-02 (2000)
10. Karnik, N.: Security in Mobile Agent System. PhD thesis, University of Minnesota (1998) http://www.cs.umn.edu/Ajanta.
11. Morcos, A.: A java implementation of simple distributed security infrastructure. Master's thesis, Massachusetts Institute of Technology (1998)
12. Karjoth, G., Asokan, N., C.Gulcu: Protecting the computing results of free-roaming agents. In: Proc. of the Second International Workshop on Mobile Agents. (1998)

APHIDS: A Mobile Agent-Based Programmable Hybrid Intrusion Detection System

Ken Deeter[1], Kapil Singh[1], Steve Wilson[1], Luca Filipozzi[2], and Son Vuong[1]

[1] Department of Computer Science, University of British Columbia
Vancouver, Canada
[2] Department of Electrical Engineering
University of British Columbia
Vancouver, Canada

Abstract. Intrusion detection systems are quickly becoming a standard requirement in building a network security infrastructure. Although many established techniques and commercial products exist, their effectiveness leaves room for improvement. We propose an intrusion detection system architecture which takes advantage of the mobile agent paradigm to implement a system capable of efficient and flexible distribution of analysis and monitoring tasks, as well as integration of existing detection techniques. Our architecture defines a high-level application specific scripting language to specify the interaction between monitoring agents and analysis agents.

1 Introduction

Intrusion detection systems (IDS) are quickly becoming a standard component of network security architectures, complementing conventional techniques such as firewalls, encryption, and authentication. The purpose of an IDS is to detect and report unusual and malicious behavior in a network – often caused by the intentional circumvention of an existing security measure by a malicious user.

This task requires a system to be able to characterize patterns in the context of a complex network environment. As networks gain in size, complexity, and variation, the task of analyzing different parts of the network and maintaining a cohesive view of the entire system becomes increasingly difficult. While the initial problems of performance have been overcome, the effectiveness of current intrusion detection systems remains limited. The primary difficulties include the management and correlation large amounts of data and the frequent occurrences of *false positives* – when a system identifies harmless behavior as malicious.

This paper pressents a novel IDS architecture, which we call APHIDS, that employs mobile agents to perform monitoring and analysis in a distributed and timely manner. This architecture delegates data capture and detection tasks to existing monitoring systems. Distributed search and analysis tasks are implemented with mobile agents, and the system provides a high level scripting facility to define how analysis results from these agents should be combined and reported. Our approach is complementary to existing IDS techniques – it aims

A. Karmouch, L. Korba, and E. Madeira (Eds.): MATA 2004, LNCS 3284, pp. 244–253, 2004.

to effectively combine the strengths of existing technologies to provide more effective results.

This paper is structured as follows: the following section provides a background for readers not familiar with intrusion detection and the mobile agent paradigm. Section 3 summarizes our motivations and design goals for the system. Section 4 details our system architecture and Sect. 4.2 introduces our automation system known as *distributed correlation scripts*. Finally, several conclusions and ideas for future work are offered.

2   IDS Background and Related Work

Intrusion detection techniques are largely classified into two areas: *misuse* detection and *anomaly* detection. In the *misuse* approach, malicious behavior is characterized and expressed in machine readable form, and the IDS checks for the existence of this behavior using a deterministic method. The work of specifying the malicious behavior is left entirely to the developers and users of the system. An example of such a system is the Snort network IDS [1]. Snort is configured using a database of *signatures* which characterize network packets that are potentially malicious. Using this database, Snort monitors a network connection and logs all occurrences of network packets that match any of the configured signatures. As is the case with any *misuse* based system, however, Snort cannot detect events for which no signatures have been developed.

Anomaly detection refers to an approach where a system is trained to learn the "normal behavior" of a network. An alarm is raised when the network is observed to deviate from this learned definition of normality. This type of system is theoretically capable of detecting unknown attacks, overcoming a clear limitation of the *misuse* approach. However, because an alarm is based on a detected change in an abstract representation of the network behavior, information about the root cause of the deviation may be difficult to infer.

Intrusion detection systems are also traditionally classified as either *network-based* or *host-based*. *Network-based* systems monitor network traffic and inspect packet transmissions for suspicious behavior. A network-based system can be used to provide detection for multiple hosts by locating the monitoring component appropriately (at a network ingress point, for example). *Host-based* systems operate on single hosts, and operate on low-level system data, such as patterns of system calls, file access, or process usage. They can monitor for suspicious behavior, or they can scan configurations to detect potential vulnerabilities.

Log correlation refers to the process by which an IDS combines captured data that is distributed both spatially and temporally, and tries to extract significant and broad patterns. For example, a similar type of attack detected at different points in time may indicate an automated, coordinated attack. Likewise, an event detected at different monitoring locations may be indicative of a distributed attack. In general, the more data that can be collected related to a specific event, the easier it is for a security administrator to respond in an effective manner. The automatic correlation process reduces the need for an administrator to search through large log files manually, saving valuable time.

The established approach to the log correlation process involves the collection of distributed sensor data into a central location, and the application of searching and data aggregation techniques to discover patterns.

2.1 Agent-Based IDS Research

The applicability of mobile agents and software agents to intrusion detection has been explored in several other projects. The AAFID [2] [3] system from Purdue University's COAST Laboratory (now CERIAS) introduced an autonomous agent-based IDS, which formed a reference for comparison for many of the mobile agent-based systems introduced since. Related work on this system has been reported recently as well [4].

The key differentiating factor between the AAFID approach and the mobile agent-based approach is the mobility of the agents participating in the IDS. Many independent projects have explored the advantages of the mobility aspect of mobile agents in the context of intrusion detection. The IDA system [5] employs mobility to identify the source of attacks. Systems which use mobile agents to model biological immune systems have been proposed [6] and elaborated on[7]. The Micael system [8] and the MA-IDS system [9] both use mobile agents to aggregate distributed information related to attacks. The Sparta system [10] uses mobile agents to provide a query like functionality to reconstruct patterns of related events distributed across multiple hosts. The MAIDS project at Iowa State University explored the usage of dynamic agent composition techniques to create an array of lightweight agents to perform a full range of IDS-related tasks.

The APHIDS architecture presented in this paper represents a variation of the existing mobile agent-based approaches (with some similarities to the SPARTA and MAIDS systems). Our system shares a common goal of exploiting the mobility of the agents to perform distributed correlation. It differs, however, in the mechanism by which these mobile agents are coordinated and combined. APHIDS provides a scripting capability that aims to automate evidence gathering tasks that system administrators would otherwise perform manually. Our system also attempts to utilize and integrate existing IDS technologies and implementations instead of replacing their functionality.

3 Motivation

The initial motivation for our work is to address limitations of current IDS systems by taking advantage of the mobile agent paradigm. Specifically, we address the following limitations of conventional centralized approaches to the log correlation task:

- *Bandwidth Scalability:* The bandwidth required to collect large, distributed data sets from distributed sensors can pose a significant overhead cost, affecting network performance.

- *Processing Scalability:* The processing capability of the centralized approach is limited by the computational power of a single analysis center, even though other resources may be available.
- *Analysis Delay:* In the centralized approach, logs are collected only periodically, delaying results by at most one collection and analysis cycle. Long delays can hamper a timely and effective response.
- *Integration:* Existing commercial IDS's are sold and developed as standalone products, and they do not support aggregation of data between various systems[1].

4   APHIDS Framework

4.1   Network-Level Architecture

From a deployment perspective, the structure of our system is trivial. It requires the placement of an agent engine at every relevant location, including network monitoring devices, web servers and other service-providing hosts, as well as hosts running other IDS systems[2]. APHIDS is realized as a distributed layer which operates on top of a set of distributed agent engines. This design allows us to access network components in a uniform and efficient manner, and allows all of our system components to take advantage of the benefits provided by the agent platform. Mobile agents are used for monitoring the output from other IDS systems, for querying the log files and system state, and for reporting results. These various agents are coordinated using a *distributed correlation script*, which is described in Sect. 4.2.

4.2   Distributed Correlation Scripts

A key feature of our system is that it allows the specification of coordinated analysis tasks using a high-level specification language. This language is used to define a *Distributed Correlation Script* (DCS), which associates a *trigger event* with a series of *analysis tasks* to be performed when the event is detected. A collection of these scripts is provided as input to the system.

4.3   Detection and Analysis

Our system's detection and analysis procedure for a particular attack can be broken down into the three following steps:

1. Detection of a *trigger event*[3]
2. Collection and Analysis of data related to this event
3. Reporting the event

---

[1] Competing commercial IDS's have no incentive to cooperate with each other, even though the data they each collect may yield better results when combined.

[2] Our architecture also requires the existence of one a system console, used for system configuration and display of analysis results

[3] A *trigger event* is an abstract concept that simply refers to any suspicious event occurring on the network. The exact definition of a *trigger event* is left up to a *trigger agent* that is programmed to detect it.

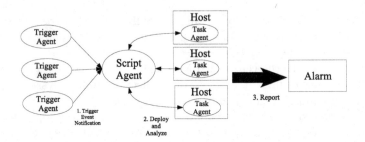

Fig. 1. This diagram shows the interactions between agents in our system. After deployment, trigger agents notify the script agent of occurrences of trigger events. The script agent then launches task agents which migrate to appropriate locations to perform analysis, the results of which are returned to the script agent. The script agent finally conditionally raises an alarm and generates a report

Each DCS specifies exactly one *trigger agent* (along with some initialization parameters) and the types of analysis that should be performed based on a trigger notification from that agent. The tasks are specified by referring to mobile agents called *task agents* that implement each type of analysis task.

When a particular script is enabled, an agent is created to manage it. This *script agent* is responsible for instantiating the *trigger agent*, launching the task agents, and storing the data returned by these various agents. When a trigger agent detects that a trigger event has occurred, it sends a set of values describing the event back to the script agent to which it is associated. The script agent in turn launches task agents according to the script specification. The values received from the trigger agent are made available to these analysis agents. Data returned from each task agent is stored by the script agent and is made available to subsequently launched task agents. The manner in which these values are passed to task agents is determined in each script, allowing for different forms of collaboration to be specified by writing different scripts.

After all the task agents have completed, the script agent can make a decision to report an alarm. This decision process is also specified in the script (the details are described in the following subsection). This entire process is illustrated in Fig. 1.

These scripts allow users and developers to freely mix and match existing monitoring and analysis agents. The correlation task represented by each script is capable of considering data and conditions from distributed sources.

4.4   Script Syntax

The syntax of a distributed correlation script is shown and described below:

```
Trigger <TriggerAgent>(<Parameters>...) : <RetValueName> {
    Task <DataTaskAgent>(<Parameters> ...) : <RetValueName>
      :
}
```

```
alarm {
  <ConditionTaskAgent>(<Parameters> ...) : <ConditionValueName>
    :
  condition((<ConditionValueName> AND <ConditionValueName>)
      OR (NOT <ConditionValueName>))
}
```

A script is composed of a combination of a `Trigger` block and `alarm` block. The `Trigger` block specifies a trigger agent name, along with initialization parameters. The trigger block contains a list of task agents that are to be launched when a trigger event notification is recieved. Each task is specified with the `Task` keyword, the name of the agent which performs the task, and configuration parameters for that agent. We refer to the agents within this block as *data collection agents*.

To facilitate the sharing of results between agents (including information related to the trigger event returned by the trigger agent), each agent is allowed to return an associative array of values, which is referenced by the identifier provided after the colon following the agent's invocation (notated by `<RetValue Name>`).

In the `alarm` block, a second set of task agents are specified. These agents however, can only return a boolean value, and are used only to check for the existence of certain conditions in the network. These agents are referred to as *condition checking agents*. The return value of these condition checking agents are also named and referenced by a variable name provided at the end of the each agent's invocation.

Finally, the alarm block concludes with a `condition` statement. The statement is composed of an arbitrary boolean combination of condition values defined in the same alarm block. This condition determines whether an alarm is generated for this event.

A design decision was made to ensure that none of the analysis or monitoring implementations are directly specified in a DCS. Instead, a script can only refer to an agent that implements the required functionality. This choice allows complex monitoring and analysis tasks to be implemented in a more suitable language (e.g. Java). We wished to avoid replicating an entire programming language to allow complex computational operations to be specified in the scripts themselves. This design also allows the system to be extended in a straightforward manner. For example, new trigger and task agents can be defined after the APHIDS is initially deployed, and new scripts referring to those agents can be incorporated on the fly, without requiring any changes to the existing set of scripts and agents.

4.5   Analysis Scenarios

To illustrate the practical usage of a DCS we present two analysis scenarios that can be handled by a DCS.

In the first example we consider the following scenario: an attacker from host A has gained access to a SSH account on one of several protected servers.

In an attempt to infiltrate other hosts, the attacker performs a portscan (also from host A) of the network. This scenario would be detected by APHIDS by deploying the following script:

```
Trigger SnortPortScan() : PS {
    Task ArgusFindConnections(PS.source, PS.timeRange) : FC
}
alarm {
    LoginCheck(PS.source, FC.targets, PS.timeRange) : C1
    condition(C1)
}
```

This script would first deploy a trigger agent written to capture notifications of a port scan from a Snort system. Once the port scan is detected the trigger agent would notify the script agent. The script agent would then deploy a data collection agent to perform the `ArgusFindConnections()` task. The `PS.source` argument is passed in from the trigger agent to tell the data collector where the port scan originated, as well as the `PS.timeRange` argument to tell the agent what time range to look for connections (we would be interested in a time before the port scan occurred). The data collection agent would then migrate to a host running the Argus network monitor, and discover that a number of SSH connections have been made from the host A to a local host (or possibly several hosts). Based on this information, a condition checking agent implementing the `LoginCheck()` task is deployed. This agent uses the parameter FC.targets, to sequentially move to the hosts that host A has connected to, and checks for login attempts from PS.source. In our example the login from the attacker would be found which would raise our alarm. As a result, the system administrator would be alerted to the fact that a certain user launched a port scan and accessed the network successfully, indicated a potential security breach. The administrator could then investigate further and may discover a compromised user account.

For our second example we consider the following scenario: an attacker makes an unusually high number of connections to a server on the monitored network, possibly with the intent to perform a denial of service attack against a host, or inidicating that the attacking host has been infected with a virus or worm. The following script would respond to this attack:

```
Trigger ConnectionOverLoad(): CL {
    Task CheckUserNames(CL.target, CL.source) : CN
}
alarm {
    UserCount(CN.nameList) : C1
    condition(C1)
}
```

This script would deploy a trigger agent that implements an anomaly-type detection method or interfaces with an external detection system. Once the rate of connections from a certain host reached a defined threshold the trigger agent would report back to the script agent. In response, the `CheckUserNames()` data collection agent would be invoked to collect the list of user names that have logged into `CL.target` from `CL.source`. Finally, the `UserCount()` agent would be deployed to confirm whether a particular user has performed an extraordinarily large number of logins. If a suspect is found, an alarm will be raised. The system administrator could respond by enabling process accounting and auditing for the user in question.

As can be seen from our examples, the actual analysis tasks in our system are always performed by mobile agents that have access to system libraries and that can be written in an expressive programming language. The DCS mechanism only provides a mechanism to coordinate these agents, and combine their results in a simple manner useful for intrusion detection.

5   Discussion

First, we address the specific limitations described by the central approach.

- *Bandwidth Scalability:* APHIDS uses a remote evaluation technique based on mobile agents to remove the need to transfer log data from sensors to an analysis center. If analysis agents are sufficiently small (typically less than 20 kilobytes) when compared to the log data size (often several gigabytes), then bandwidth savings can be realized.
- *Performance Scalability:* Because mobile agents perform distributed search and analysis, the processing work related to each incident is inherently distributed, reducing the amount of work done per host and removing a single host bottleneck.
- *Analysis Delay:* Because each incident is analyzed immediately, the upper bound on the delay between an incident occurence and its corresponding report depends only on the processing time needed for analysis of one incident, as well as the time needed to transfer and collect related data. Delay can be further reduced by launching data collection agents in parallel where possible.
- *Integration:* Our architecture's use of an agent engine guarantees that new components (new IDS's, monitoring systems, etc.) can be integrated without requiring global changes. Our system provides a uniform layer to analysis agents allowing them to effectively combine data from different sensors.

Next we identify other benefits that are realized by our framework:

- Because of the distributed and integrative nature of our framework, it can be adapted to an existing security infrastructure.
- Distributed correlation scripts are able to capture the expert knowledge of security administrator by automating the standard investigative procedures that are performed in response to an incident.
- APHIDS is able to discover and utilize greater amounts contextual information when processing an incident, allowing it to potentially make more informed decisions.

– Our framework is extensible. For example, a user can introduce new types
  of trigger, script, and data collection agents, as well as provide new scripts
  to combine existing agents in novel manners.

The mobile agent approach has several disadvantages which must also be
kept in mind:

– Virtualization and serialization routines required for agent mobility cause
  performance overhead that may be significant without proper design consideration.
– Security of the agent system must be considered, including the potential to
  perform a denial-of-service attack by intentionally triggering analysis agents.

6   Conclusions and Future Work

We have presented a mobile agent-based architecture for a programmable IDS
which incorporates existing IDS technologies. Our next direct step will be to
complete our prototype implementation of the DCS system.

To our knowledge, our IDS architecture is the first mobile agent-based architecture with a explicit primary goal to use mobile agents to form a middle-ware
which ties together separate network and host-based intrusion detection systems.
By using a mobile agent platform that allows us to incorporate object-oriented
design techniques, we are able to treat the agent engines as an uniform interface
for agents to access data generated by each type of monitoring system.

Our system architecture realizes the scalability of mobile agent-based approaches, and addresses flexibility, extensibility, and delay limitations of existing
approaches. Our two examples presented in Sect. 4.5 illustrate how APHIDS can
incorporate both *misuse* and *anomaly* approaches by implementing agents that
employ each technique.

As our current work focuses on the distributed correlation implementation,
in the future we would like to investigate enhancement of the detection portion
of the framework. Detection mechanisms are modularized by the trigger agent,
allowing for the investigation of new detection techniques. This abstraction also
allows the framework to incorporate advanced finite state machine-based detection systems such as the Bro system [11] and STAT-based systems [12]. We
intend for APHIDS to become a useful framework for experimenting with new
intrusion detection techniques, while making the advantages of the mobile agent
paradigm available to new implementations.

Acknowledgments

This research is supported in part by the Directorate of Telecom Engineering and
Certification of the Department of Industry Canada. We would like to thank Peter Chau, Os Monkewich and Sergio Gonzalez Valenzuela for fruitful discussions
and for reviewing the drafts of the paper.

References

1. Roesch, M.: Snort – lightweight intrusion detection system for networks. In: Proceedings of USENIX LISA'99. (1999)
2. Crosbie, M., Spafford, G.: Defending a computer system using autonomous agents. In: 8th National Information Systems Security Conference. (1996)
3. J S Balasubramaniyan, J.O.G.F., Isacoff, D., Spafford, E., Zamboni, D.: An architecture for intrusion detection using autonomous agents. Technical Report 98/05, COAST Laboratory, Purdue University (1998)
4. Wu, Y.S., Foo, B., Mei, Y., Bagchi, S.: Collaborative intrusion detection system (cids): A framework for accurate and efficient ids. In: Proceedings of the 19th Annual Computer Security Applications Conference (ACSAC'03). (2003)
5. Asaka, M., Taguchi, A., Goto, S.: The implementation of ida: An intrusion detection agent system. In: Proceedings of the 11th FIRST Conference. (1999)
6. Faukia, N., Billard, D., Harms, J.: Computer system immunity using mobile agents. In: HP Openview University Association 8th Annual Workshop. (2001)
7. Faukia, N., Hassas, S., Fenet, S., Albequerque, P.: Combining immune system and social insect metaphors: A paradimg for intrusion detection and response system. In: Proceedings of the 5th International Workshop for Mobile Agents for Telecommunication Applications. (2003)
8. Duarte de Queiroz, J., Fernando Rust da Costa Carmo, L., Pirmez, L.: Micael: An autonomous mobile agent system to protect new generation networked applications. In: 2nd Annual Workshop on Recent Advances in Intrusion Detection. (1999)
9. Li, C., Song, Q., Zhang, C.: Ma-ids architecture for distributed intrusion detection using mobile agents. In: Proceedings of the 2nd International Conference on Information Technology for Application (ICITA 2004). (2004)
10. Kruegel, C., Toth, T.: Sparta – a mobile agent based intrusion detection system. In: Proceedings of the IFIP Conference on Network Security (I-NetSec). (2001)
11. Paxson, V.: Bro: A system for detecting network intruders in real-time. Computer Networks **31** (1999) 2435–2463
12. Vigna, G., Kemmerer, R.A.: Netstat: A network-based intrusion detection system. Journal of Computer Security **7** (1999)

Optimistic Blinded-Key Signatures
for ElGamal and Related Schemes

Lucas C. Ferreira and Ricardo Dahab

Intituto de Computação
Universidade Estadual de Campinas (Unicamp)
Caixa Postal 6176
13083-970 Campinas SP
Brazil
Phone: +55-19-3788-5839, Fax: +55-19-3788-5847
{lucasf,rdahab}@ic.unicamp.br

Abstract. If autonomous mobile agents are to be used in electronic commerce environments, they must be able to sign contracts and payment orders without the need to contact their owners. As agents execute in untrusted environments, it is assumed that any information they carry can be read by a malicious host; thus, it is unwise to include secrets, such as private keys, in such agents. Sander and Tchudin proposed the concept of *undetachable signatures* to solve this problem, but gave no practical manifestation for it. Ferreira and Dahab's *blinded-key signatures* were proposed as a practical implementation of Sander and Tchudin's idea, but require the intervention of an online TTP (trusted third party). Later, they proposed an optimistic version of their blinded-key signatures based on the RSA signature scheme. Here we propose a new version of *Optimistic blinded-key signatures* which is based on ElGamal signatures and its variants: DSA and Schnorr.

1 Introduction

Ferreira and Dahab [1] proposed a novel signature scheme that allows mobile agents to carry private keys and sign agreements on behalf of their owners. They call their scheme *Blinded-key Signature*, which is a method for building *undetachable signatures* [2].

In the original version, blinded-key signatures required the use of a Trusted Third Party (TTP), or a Notary, which must be online to validate each transaction. Also, the Notary has access to information that allows the impersonation of agents, raising the level of trust required from all parties in the system.

In another paper [3], they proposed an extension to the basic blinded-key signature scheme, called *Optimistic Blinded-key Signature*, which requires a TTP only for the agent setup and in case any dispute arises. Here, we show that optimistic blinded-key signatures can be built for blinded-key signatures based on ElGamal and its variants (DSA, Schnorr).

This paper is organized as follows: Section 2 presents the mobile agent system model we use throughout this paper; the basic blinded-key signature scheme is presented in Section 3; next, in Section 4, the Optimistic Blinded-key Signature

A. Karmouch, L. Korba, and E. Madeira (Eds.): MATA 2004, LNCS 3284, pp. 254–263, 2004.

scheme is presented and discussed; Section 5 presents some issues unsolved regarding blinded-key signatures and some related work; Section 6 concludes this paper.

1.1 ElGamal Basics and Notation

The ElGamal public key encryption and signature scheme [4] is one of the most commonly used public key cryptosystems. Its security is based on the intractability of the discrete logarithm problem. We present here only the basic operations needed to generate ElGamal keys and signatures. For more details, proofs of correctness and discussion of security, readers are referred to the original paper or the books [5,6].

Before one can use the ElGamal signature scheme, a key pair, consisting of public and private keys, must be generated. The public key is the triple (p, α, y) and the private key is the integer a.

2   Mobile Agent Systems

In this section, we present the model of mobile agent systems on which we based our work. We begin by describing each of its elements and then show how they are related. This description fits most models for mobile agents, in that someone builds agents and releases them on a network in order to achieve some specified goal. Those agents are autonomous in the sense that they do not need to contact their owners after they are released.

We deal with four different players:

Owner: is the entity that will build/configure the agents and specify their mission, releasing them on the network to accomplish their job. They have pairs of public/private keys.

Agents: are mobile pieces of code that will execute some action on behalf of their owners. An agent has a unique ID and the corresponding blinded key for signing agreements.

Foreign Agency: an agency is a place where agents can bind to and execute their code. The foreign agency may be an agent-based marketplace, some entry point to a distributed database and so on. The foreign agency is not trusted by the owner and may try to disrupt an agent behavior or to have access to the agent's internal state.

Notary: is a Trusted Third Party (TTP) that will be responsible for verifying blinded-key signatures and to enforce any agreement signed by the agents.

Now, we show how those architectural elements interact by means of an example. Suppose Alice (owner) wants to send an agent to the Virtual Store, an agent marketplace (agency). The agent's mission is to contract the acquisition of a copy of the original ElGamal paper. The following steps must be executed in the original scheme:

1. Alice blinds (Section 3) it before including it in the agent's state. Alice also sets the agent mission and specifies the maximum price of $10.
2. Alice sends the notary a signed message containing the agent's ID and the blinding factor to the notary, together with a signed policy describing which kind of negotiation and contract this agent is authorized to sign. The policy must include both the agent ID and the blinding factor.
3. Alice releases her agent which will interact with the foreign agency to locate the item it is looking for and to negotiate the price for that item.
4. The agent signs an agreement to buy the original ElGamal paper (or a payment order) using the blinded key it carries (Section 3).
5. The store's agency will contact the notary and ask it to verify the signature (Algorithm 1) and the agreement or payment order with respect to the policy specified by Alice for this agent. The agency accepts the signature if the notary can verify it and the deal conforms to the owner's policy.
6. The agency notifies the agent and releases it to its next stop.

3   Blinded-Key Signatures

In this Section, we present briefly the ElGamal-based version of the general blinded-key signature scheme. The reader is referred to [7], where the general scheme and the specifics for ElGamal variants (DSA and Schnorr) are described in detail.

To prevent agencies from having access to their private keys, owners will blind them before insertion in their agents. All operations needed for the blinded-key signature scheme are described below.

Blinding the key. An ElGamal private key, denoted a, must be blinded by computing

$$a_b = a \times b \bmod (p-1),$$

where $b \in [0, p-2]$ is the randomly chosen blinding factor and a_b is the blinded private key.

Signing with the blinded key. Signature generation with blinded keys uses exactly the same algorithm as signing with standard ElGamal keys, but substituting a_b for a.

Verifying a blinded-key signature. After it receives a signed agreement from the agent, the agency sends the agent's ID and its signature to be verified by the notary. To verify a blinded-key signature S, the notary will use Algorithm 1.

Algorithm 1 ElGamal-based blinded-key signature verification.

Given a signature $S = (r, s)$, a message m and a public key (p, α, y), the notary computes:

$$v_1 = y^{br} r^s \bmod p$$
$$v_2 = \alpha^{h(m)} \bmod p$$

where $h(.)$ is the hash function chosen for the signature scheme.

Output $v_1 \stackrel{?}{=} v_2$.

---

4   Optimistic Blinded-Key Signatures

As shown in Section 3, the original blinded-key signature scheme requires the use of a trusted third party, known as *Notary*. Being aimed to be used by autonomous mobile agents, this is undesirable, and set the main goal for improving the scheme to be the reduction of the need to interact with this TTP. Ferreira and Dahab [3] present an improved version of Blinded-key Signatures in which the TTP can act offline and only be summoned in case the outcome of a transaction is disputed. In the optimistic scheme, the notary has no access to the blinding factor used to hide the private key. The only information sent to the notary is the blinded key itself, which is also assumed to be seen by the agencies and whose knowledge does not empowers any entity to break the signature scheme. In this Section, we extend this previous work for ElGamal-based signature schemes, such as ElGamal itself, DSA and Schnorr.

The main difference of this version with the basic blinded-key signature protocol is that the agent will carry some data which can be used by the foreign agency to verify the signature without interacting with the notary. The agency only needs to contact the notary if it believes the transaction is in error. In this case, the notary will verify the signature and determine the validity or not of this specific transaction.

The blinding operation is not changed from the basic scheme, which means it is executed according to Section 3. After the blinding factor has been chosen, the agent owner executes the protocol described in Algorithm 2 to get a proof of validity for the blinded key. This proof of validity must be included in the agent before it is released in the system. It is important to note that *agent* in Algorithm 2 represents the agent code, not including its state, which will change when the agent is executed.

When the agent arrives at the foreign agency, the agency verifies the proof of validity for the blinded key carried by the agent by executing Algorithm 3 (this can also be done lazily by checking only when a signature is required). The agency must also check the policy attached to the blinded key to verify the class of agreements the agent is allowed to sign. If the blinded key can be correctly verified and the agreement abides to the policy, the signature output by the agent is valid and the agent owner will be bound to its terms.

Algorithm 2 Blinded key proof of validity generation

Given the blinding factor y, the blinded key a_b and a hash function $h(.)$ execute the following steps:

1. Owner sends the Notary: Agent ID, a_b, $h(agent)$;
2. The Notary chooses a random x and computes $z = y^x \times \alpha^{-a_b} \equiv \alpha^{ax-ba} \equiv \alpha^{a(x-b)} \equiv y^{(x-b)}$ (mod p) and sends $s = signed_{Notary}\,[h(agent), h(y^x), z]$ to the agent owner;
3. Upon receipt of s, the owner computes $w = z \times y^b \equiv y^{(x-b)}y^b \equiv y^x \bmod p$ and builds the proof of validity $v = signed_{owner}\,[agent\,ID||s||w]$;

where *agent* is the agent's code.

Algorithm 3 Proof of validity verification

Given a proof of validity $v = signed_{owner}\,[agent\,ID||s||w]$ and the agent owner's public key (p, α, y), execute:

1. Verify the notary's signature on s;
2. Check that the value $hash(agent)$ included in s is equal to the hash of the agent it received for execution;
3. Extract $h(y^x)$ from s and verify that $h(y^x) = h(w)$.

If the three checks above are successful, the proof of validity has been verified.

4.1   Dispute Resolution

As stated before, this optimistic scheme requires the involvement of the notary when errors or unexpected results occur. The notary is usually invoked by the agency when it is unable to verify the signature received from the agent. To start the dispute resolution protocol, the agency sends the notary the signature it wants verified and the agent ID. The notary runs algorithm 4 and sends the agency a signed message stating the validity or not of the signature.

Upon receipt of the validity verification response from the notary, the agency must accept the notary's decision on the agent signature's validity. If the agency refuses to accept a signature that has been verified by the notary, the dispute would have to be settled by some court of law, which should recognize the notary's answer as authoritative. The dispute resolution protocol could also be invoked by the agent, in case the agency refuses to accept a signature it considers valid.

4.2   Example

Now, we show how an Optimistic Blinded-key Signature based system works by adapting the example of Section 2. Suppose Alice (owner) wants to send an agent to the Virtual Store, an agent marketplace (agency). The agent's mission is to contract the acquisition of a copy of the original RSA paper. The following steps must be executed in the optimistic scheme:

Algorithm 4 Dispute resolution

Given and agent ID, a signature S and the message m that was signed, execute:

1. use the agent ID to fetch its owner public key and the value a_b from its database.
2. compute

$$t_1 = r.\alpha^s \equiv \alpha^{k.k^{-1}(h(m)-a_b r)} \equiv \alpha^{h(m)-a_b r}$$
$$t_2 = \alpha^{h(m)-a_b r}$$

3. output $t_1 \overset{?}{=} t_2$.

The notary should sign the output of this algorithm and send the signed message to the entity that requested the signature validity check.

---

1. In order to prevent the agency from having access to its private key, Alice blinds it before including in the agent's state by computing the formula from Section 3. Alice also sets the agent mission and specifies the maximum price of $10.
2. Alice sends the notary a signed message containing the agent's ID, the blinded key and a hash of the agent's code, together with a signed policy describing which kind of negotiation and contract this agent is authorized to sign. These data are required as inputs for Algorithm 2.
3. The notary uses Algorithm 2 to generate s and sends it to Alice, which will generate the proof of validity v and include it in the agent.
4. Alice releases her agent which will interact with the foreign agency to locate the item it is looking for and to negotiate the price for that item.
5. The agent signs an agreement to buy the original ElGamal paper (or a payment order) using the blinded key it carries.
6. The store's agency will then verify the proof of validity carried by the agent using Algorithm 3 and, if the proof is valid verify the agent's policy to make sure the agent was entitled to sign the agreement. If the agency is unable to validate the signature, it invokes the notary's dispute resolution protocol.
7. The agency notifies the agent and releases it to its next stop.

4.3   Security Discussion

The main concerns that may be raised against the Optimistic Blinded-key Signature technique are:

1. Is there any way to build a fake proof of validity?
2. Does the knowledge of several a_b makes it easier to discover a?

To be able to build a fake proof of validity, one would need to build a fake x', which could be done by:

1. inverting the hash function $h(.)$;

2. finding x;
3. or finding a collision for the hash function $h(.)$.

We assume the hash function used is cryptographically secure, which means it is very hard to invert and to find collisions for a given $h(x)$, where x is unknown. This counters the first and last attacks. Finding x is equivalent to finding the discrete log of y^x. Any adversary able to find this discrete log is also able to break the ElGamal signature scheme by computing the secret key a. So, our scheme is at least as secure as the original ElGamal signature scheme.

As shown in [7], knowing several values for a_b is equivalent to knowing a random permutation of several values for b and this gives an adversary no knowledge about a or any value of b.

5   Problems and Related Techniques

In this section, we present some problems that arise from the use of digital signatures by mobile agents and that no technique based on blinded-key signatures deals with. Then we present relevant related work.

5.1   Problems Not Addressed by Variants of Blinded-Key Signatures

None of the techniques presented here can make sure the agency does not generate several signatures by extracting signature-related code and data from the agent. This problem was addressed in the original context of blinded-key signatures by requiring the notary to check each signature against an owner-defined policy. Multiple signatures may be avoided by the use of data hiding and code obfuscation techniques, as discussed in [8].

The agency could use data and code extracted from the agent and sign arbitrary agreements, which the agent owner does not agree with. Including an owner-signed policy with each signature could avoid this problem. This policy could be included in the blinded key's proof of validity since it is required for signature verification. The agency may be able to look at the agent's code and data and discover its negotiation strategy, using this information to its advantage. This is discussed in [1] and can be thwarted by the use of data hiding and code obfuscation techniques, such as black-boxing [9].

5.2   Related Work

We classify related work in two classes: variations of digital signature systems and improvements to the security of mobile agents. We discuss the most relevant of these works below.

Variants of cryptographic signature schemes This area of cryptographic research includes works as different as Chaum's *blind signatures* [10] or distributed key generation and signing of documents (see [11] for an example of distributed signing and [12] for distributed key generation).

Our blinded-key signatures are in some ways similar to Chaum's blind signatures as both use blinding factors to guarantee the secrecy of information. But whereas blind signatures are meant to conceal the contents of the message being signed , blinded-key signatures conceal the signing key. Works on distributed key and signature generation brought many insights used in defining the blinding operation described in Section 3.

Mobile agent security Chess [13] surveys the main security issues in systems with mobile code, including mobile agents. Several aspects of host protection against malicious agents are presented, including authentication, trust and secure languages. Results in protecting the agents against malicious hosts, which is the problem we consider here are also presented.

The main tools for protecting agents against malicious hosts use the concept of black boxes [9], which guarantees that: agent code and data cannot be read (in a meaningful way); agent code and data cannot be modified (in a meaningful way).

Two approaches have been proposed to construct black boxes: *time limited black-boxes* [9] and *mobile cryptography* [2], which includes computing with encrypted functions and computing with encrypted data. Hohl [9] proposes time limited black-boxes, which are based on code and data obfuscation techniques. In Hohl's approach, black boxes are valid only during a time interval, in which the black box properties remain valid. After the time validity expires, it must be guaranteed that future access to its contents has no unwanted effects. This precludes the inclusion of private keys in agents based on this technique.

Two approaches have been proposed for implementing mobile cryptography. Sander and Tchudin [2] propose a scheme for encrypting mobile agents based on homomorphic cryptosystems, which would allow a remote host to execute agents without being able to infer their contents. Cachin et al. [14] construct a black box system combining oblivious transfer and secure function evaluation. Both methods are difficult to understand and to implement and can hardly be considered practical.

Sander and Tchudin [2] propose a simplified mobile cryptography operation that would allow mobile code to execute digital signatures: *undetachable signatures*. Blinded-key signatures and related schemes are specific implementations of the undetachable signature concept. Kotzanikolaou et al. [15] also propose a scheme that implements undetachable signatures based on RSA signatures. Their scheme does not require a TTP and is also vulnerable to multiple signature generation and agent negotiation strategy extraction, as our blinded-key signature schemes. Their use of a policy would require the use of a TTP for resolving disputes, as we use for our optimistic version of blinded-key signatures.

6   Final Remarks

Using trusted third parties is an undesirable feature in protocols aimed at being used by mobile agents since they restrict agent autonomy and their ability to work disconnected or in poorly connected environments. Yet, practical protocols for allowing mobile agents to generate digital signatures, such as blinded-key signature schemes, still rely on the presence of TTPs to validate agent transactions.

Previous work on designing *optimistic blinded-key signatures* aimed at reducing the need for the TTP to interact with the mobile agent during each signature generation operation. This was achieved by allowing the TTP to work offline and to get actively involved in the transaction only if a dispute arises, as in most legal systems. Previous optimistic blinded-key signature schemes were designed for RSA-based signatures. Here, we have shown that ElGamal-based signature schemes may also be extended optimistically and also described a protocol that can be used to make those blinded-key signatures optimistic.

Still, some problems from the basic scheme remain. As shown in [8], a combination of schemes should be used to achieve better agent protection than can be provided by a single technique, each one addressing a specific need from agent security.

References

1. Ferreira, L.C., Dahab, R.: Blinded-key signatures: securing private keys in mobile agents. In: Proceedings of SAC'2002 - ACM Symposium on Applied Computing, Madrid, Spain (2002)
2. Sander, T., Tschudin, C.F.: Protecting mobile agents against malicious hosts. In Vigna, G., ed.: Mobile Agent Security. Number 1419 in Lecture Notes in Computer Science. Springer-Verlag (1998)
3. Ferreira, L.C., Dahab, R.: Optimistic blinded-key signatures. Submited for publication. (2004)
4. ElGamal, T.: A public key cryptosystem and a signature scheme based on discrete logarithms. In: Proceedings of Crypto '84, LNCS 196, California, USA, Springer-Verlag (1984)
5. Menezes, A.J., Oorschot, P.C., Vanstone, S.A.: Handbook of Applied Cryptography. CRC Press (1997) Available online at http://www.cacr.uwaterloo.ca/hac.
6. Stinson, D.: Cryptography: Theory and Practice,Second Edition. CRC/C&H (2002)
7. Ferreira, L.C., Dahab, R.: Blinded-key signatures. Technical Report IC-01-015, Instituto de Computação - Unicamp, Campinas, SP, Brazil (2001)
8. Ferreira, L.C., Uto, N., Dahab, R.: Combining techniques for protecting mobile agents. In: Actas del Segundo Congreso Iberoamericano de Seguridad Informática CIBSI '03, Ciudad de Mexico, Mexico, Servicio de Publicaciones del Instituto Politécnico Nacional (2003)
9. Hohl, F.: Time limited blackbox security: Protecting mobile agents from malicious hosts. In Vigna, G., ed.: Mobile Agent Security. Number 1419 in Lecture Notes in Computer Science. Springer-Verlag (1998)

10. Chaum, D.: Blind signatures for untraceable payments. In Chaum, D., Rivest, R.L., Sherman, A.T., eds.: Advances in Cryptology: Proceedings of Crypto'82, Springer-Verlag (1982)

11. Wu, T., Malkin, M., Boneh, D.: Building intrusion tolerant applications. In: Proceedings of the 8th USENIX Security Symposium. (1999) 79–91

12. Boneh, D., Franklin, M.: Efficient generation of shared RSA keys. In Kaliski, B., ed.: Advances in Cryptology - Proceedings of Crypto'97, Springer-Verlag (1997) 425–439

13. Chess, D.M.: Security issues in mobile code systems. In Vigna, G., ed.: Mobile Agents and Security. Number 1419 in Lecture Notes in Computer Science. Springer-Verlag (1998) 1–14

14. Cachin, C., Camenisch, J., Kilian, J., Müller, J.: One-round secure computation and secure autonomous mobile agents. In: Proceedings of ICALP'2000. (2000)

15. Kotzanikolaou, P., Burmester, M., Chrissikopoulos, V.: Secure transactions with mobile agents in hostile environments. In: Australasian Conference on Information Security and Privacy. (2000) 289–297

A Secure Framework for User Privacy in Heterogeneous Location Networks

Harikrishna Vasanta, Yiu Shing Terry Tin, Colin Boyd,
Mark Looi, and Juan Manuel González Nieto

Information Security Research Centre,
Queensland University of Technology
GPO Box 2434, Brisbane, Australia
{h.vasanta,t.tin,c.boyd,m.looi,j.gonzaleznieto}@qut.edu.au

Abstract. A heterogeneous location network is one that derives location information from multiple sources and provides various location based services to users irrespective of the device used. User privacy is an important issue that needs to be addressed for the growth of heterogeneous location networks. We propose a secure framework for assuring user privacy in heterogeneous location networks. We also present lightweight cryptographic protocols along with an analysis of the computation reqirements and security capabilities of the proposed framework.

1 Introduction

Location information can currently be derived using Global System for Mobile Communications (GSM), Global Positioning System (GPS), Wireless LAN and other proprietary technologies like Active Badges [19] and Radar [3]. The location information derived from each source is of a different level of granularity and can vary from pinpointing the exact location of the user to confining the user to a known perimeter. The location information is used to provide services like guiding systems, location based advertising, and context based authentication and authorisation. The services are provided to users via different devices such as PDA, laptops, and mobile phones.

Currently there is a general move towards heterogeneous data access with the network operator being able to consolidate the billing, transparency of data access and authentication over a technologies such as GSM, 3G and wireless LAN networks. This move can be beneficial to users, network operators and service providers. It helps the user manage and configure desired privacy policies easily and provides the flexibility to choose the granularity of location information being disclosed to a service provider. The service providers can provide a wide range of location based services to the users. The network operator benefits from consolidation of billing and managing user accounts across multiple networks.

The main purpose of this paper is to present a secure heterogeneous location privacy framework that can help users to manage and configure their privacy policies across multiple vendors. This paper also presents secure lightweight cryptographic protocols and analyses the security and computational capabilities of

A. Karmouch, L. Korba, and E. Madeira (Eds.): MATA 2004, LNCS 3284, pp. 264–274, 2004.
© Springer-Verlag Berlin Heidelberg 2004

the framework. The framework forms an essential component in the design of a complete heterogeneous architecture.

2   Background Information

Context-aware computing is a mobile computing paradigm where applications use contextual information, such as user location, to provide services to users. For effective use of context information, issues such as user privacy, communication medium security, collection of the location information and creation of a centralised location dataset must be addressed [7, 16]. Currently, there are different mechanisms to determine the location of a user and efforts are underway to merge this information into a single dataset [6, 15]

In most of the existing technologies (e.g. GSM, wireless LAN) the network operator has the responsibility of safeguarding the user information. When a service provider requests location information, the network operator provides the information by asking if the user wants to provide the information to the service provider. The user has no control over the granularity of information being passed to the service provider and how the information is used [10]. Since the location information provides a track record of user behavior the current authorisation process are inadequate to provide the required level of privacy.

Recently various governments, standardisation organisations and researchers have stated the need for users to have a greater transparency and control over location information [5]. The Fair Information Practices Act of USA [18] states the need for transparency in the collection and use of personal information. The "Location Privacy Protection Act of 2001" emphasises the need for location privacy [5]. Similar legislations also exist in the European Union and Japan [14].

Standardisation organisations like the World Wide Web Consortium and WAP forum have emphasised the need to assure location privacy [20]. Preferential Privacy Practices (P3P) has been standardised to assure privacy on the Internet and meets the requirements of the fair information policies. Thus the forum has endorsed the need for architectures similar to P3P to assure user location privacy [8]. Due to computational constraints on wireless and mobile devices the existing P3P architecture cannot be used.

Server centric P3P was proposed by Agrawal as an enhancement to the existing P3P architecture for mobile environments [2]. However the proposal does not address the issue of location privacy. The ISTF charter for Geographic Location privacy [9], has listed some of the requirements for assuring location privacy and emphasises the need for a heterogeneous approach for location privacy. 3GPP group [1] and GSM LCS [11] standards also provided requirements for location privacy in 3G and cellular environments.

3   Requirement Analysis

This section presents the requirements that need to be addressed for assuring user privacy in a heterogeneous location framework. The various participating entities and the requirements for assuring location privacy are as follows:

- User: The entity that requests a location based service and whose location information needs to be protected;
- Application Service Provider (ASP): Provides the requested service to user;
- Network operator: Provides the required infrastructure to the user;
- Location server: Derives the location information from various location sources, stores the information and provides the user with the location information.

User requirements: The user should have the ability to: (1) choose an ASP; (2) have the flexibility and ability to choose the granularity of location information; (3) have control over the location information; (4) update and refine policies easily; and (5) protect their identities if required.

ASP requirements: The ASP should adhere to the stated privacy policy and the ASP should restrict any collection, use, disclosure of, retention of, and access to customer location information to the specific purpose that is the subject of the express authorization of the customer concerned.

Network Operator requirements: The network operator acts impartially and should act according to the fair information practices while selecting an ASP, thus providing fair competition among similar services.

Location server requirements: The location server must reconcile the user location information derived from various sources like GSM, GPS and should provide the information according to the requested granularity.

General requirements: Only privacy policies relevant to an application should be disclosed to the ASP. The communication should be efficient and accommodate the requirements of thin clients. The privacy policies should be easy to export and import across networks and the privacy policies.

Security requirements: The security properties required are (1) Mutual endpoint authentication between all the participating entities. (2) Data Integrity to stop modification by unauthorized entities. Connectionless integrity during storage of location information and user privacy policy. (3) Data confidentiality to protect from eavesdropping (during transmission and storage)and replay by an adversary.

Additional requirements: The ASP polices should be application specific instead of a generalised privacy policy. Non-repudiation with proof of origin is required to ensure that the ASP abides to the stated policy.

4   The Proposed Privacy Framework

A new framework is illustrated in Figure 1. The framework assuring location privacy in heterogeneous environments and accommodates small devices with limited computational power. The computations takes place at a proxy location with enough resources. Because the network operator can perform complex computation and has access to user personal information, such as addresses and billing information the network operator is suitable to act as a proxy server. The

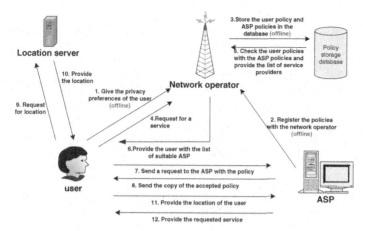

Fig. 1. The proposed privacy framework

ASPs register the preferred privacy policies with the network operator. When the user requests a service to the network operator, the network operator compares the user policies to the policies of ASPs. The network operator provides the user with the list of ASPs that match the users preferred privacy policy along with the minimum and maximum granularity of location information required for the application. The user then selects an ASP for providing the service.

The ASP sends a copy of the accepted privacy policy to the user along with a request for the location information. The user requests the location server for the location information of the chosen granularity. The user then sends the location information to the ASP and the ASP provides the requested service to the user.

5 Protocols for the Proposed Framework

This section focuses on secure protocols for the framework. Public key cryptography is often preferred for key establishment process due to the simplicity in key management. Also the security property of non-repudiation is only possible with the use of public key cryptography. However the use of public key cryptography in small devices is currently not feasible due to the computation limitations.

Our protocols are designed with the assumption that there exists considerable trust between the user and network operator. There is a long term secret key shared between the user-network operator and the user-location server. The network operator and the ASP have enough resources to perform public key cryptography. The core of the proposed protocol is a three party key distribution protocol for communication between the user, network operator and the ASP. The protocol varies from the 3PKD protocol proposed by Bellare and Rogaway [4] in the use of both symmetric and asymmetric key cryptography for establishment of a session key. The proof of security for the core protocol were carried out as part of this work and was presented at ACISP04 [17]. The notations used are shown in Table 1.

Table 1. Protocol notations

Entities	
U	Client reqesting the service (User)
A	Application service provider
S	Network operator who is acting as a proxy for the user
LS	Location server
Keys	
E_{i-j}	Symmetric encryption with secret key between i and j
E_i	Asymmetric encryption with public key of entity i
Elements	
Sig_i	Signature generated by entity i
r_i	Random number generated by entity i
σ	Session key generated for communication between the user and ASP
H	Hash function
$MAC_{k_{i-j}}$	Message Authentication code generated by using symmetric key of i and j
$PriASP_{(i)}$	Privacy policy of the ASP for application i
$PriUser$	Privacy policy of the user
$AppName$	Name of the application along with minimum and maximum granularity
Υ_i	Time stamp generated by i
$GranReq$	Granularity of location information reqired by user
$LocInfo$	Location information of reqested granularity
$ReqService$	Service reqested by the user
S_{ID}	Session identifier

5.1 Configuration and Registration of User Policy

The user configures the preferred privacy policy and sends the policy to the network operator. The policies are written to the current W3C standards for P3P using XML. The network operator stores the user policy in the database. The protocol for the registration of policy is shown in Figure 2. The configuration

$$User(U) \qquad\qquad NetworkOperator(U)$$
$$\xrightarrow{\quad PriUser \quad}$$

Fig. 2. Registration of Privacy Policy by the User

of policies can take place in any device the user is currently operating. The device sends the policy to the network operator who stores the user policy. Alternatively services like 'Over-The-Air-Service-Provisioning' (OTASP) can be used to configure the user policy on the web and then update these to the user and the network operator[12].

5.2 Registration of the Privacy Policy by the ASP

The ASP registers the preferred privacy policies with the network operator. Each application requires varied granularity of information and thus a single privacy policy will not be sufficient for all services the ASP wishes to provide. Thus the policies are designed to be application specific. When there is a change in the policy for a specific application or if the ASP terminates service to a specific application then the privacy policy can be easily updated. This approach gives more flexibility in managing the user information. The protocol for the registration of the policy by the ASP is shown in Figure 3. Non-repudiation

---

$NetworkOperator(s)$ $ASP(A)$

$$\xleftarrow{Sig_{ASP}(PriASP(AppName_j))}$$

Fig. 3. Registration of Privacy Policy by the ASP

between the ASP and the network operator assures that the ASP adheres to the stated privacy policy. If the ASP deviates from the stated privacy policy, the user can then hold the ASP accountable. To achieve this property the privacy policy of the ASP is signed by the ASP's secret key. The higher computation capability between the ASP and the network operator allows the use of public key encryption. For every application that the ASP provides service, the privacy policy will adhere to the requirement of W3C standard for P3P. The privacy policy of the application will also include the name of the application, validity of the policy, minimum and maximum granularity of location information required for the application and date of creation of privacy policy. $PriASP(AppName_j)$ is the privacy policy of the application where $j = 1$ to n, represents the number of the applications the ASP intends to provide service.

The network operator stores the policy of the ASP in a database. If the ASP changes a policy for a specific application then the ASP is required to report the change. The network operator updates the privacy policy of the ASP for the specific application after receiving the new policy from the ASP.

5.3 Providing the Requested Service

A list of service providers suitable for the requested application is provided to the user by the network operator. The network operator also generates session keys for communication between the user and the ASP for a secure session. Figure 4 describes the process. The various steps in the protocol are as follows:

1. User requests the network operator for a suitable ASP matching the users preferred policy for an application.
2. The network operator compares the user policy to the privacy policy of various registered ASPs for the requested application and computes the list of ASPs matching the users preferred policy.
3. The network operator generates the session keys for the communication between the ASP and user. For each ASP that matches the user policy a separate session key is generated. The session ID S_{ID} is the concatenation of the time stamp Υ_S and random number r_U. A MAC of the session key, session identifier, a random number sent. The ASP and the network operator identities are generated by the network operator. The network operator also signs the session keys generated for the ASP with the network operator

secret key. The signature is encrypted with the public key of the corresponding ASP. This assures that an adversary cannot find the identity of the user and the accepted policy by eavesdropping and looking into the information contained in the signature.

4. The network operator then sends the user the list of ASPs and the privacy policy of the ASP containing the minimum and maximum granularity required to provide the requested service. The network operator also sends the session keys generated for the ASPs. The message is encrypted with a long term secret key agreed between the user and network operator. This key is different from the secret key used for generation of MAC and encryption of the session key. $A_i, ..A_l$ is the list of all the ASPs sent by the network operator to the user.

5. The user then chooses a suitable ASP and sends the encrypted package generated by the network operator as a request to provide the service.

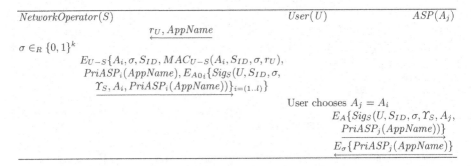

Fig. 4. Protocol for selection of ASP by user and establishment of secure communication between the user and ASP

This stage provides the ability for the user to choose the service provider the user feels is safe and trustworthy. Also the user can decide the granularity of information that needs to be provided. The generation of session keys by the network operator for communication between the ASP and user helps in saving a large amount of computation resources at the user device. Once the ASP gets the encrypted package, it decrypts, checks the privacy policy. The ASP then sends an acceptance to the user which contains the privacy policy of user encrypted with the session key generated by the network operator. The user decrypts the acceptance, verifies the privacy policy sent by the ASP and sends a request to the location server to provide the requested location information.

5.4   Request for Location from Location Server

The user and the location server share two long term symmetric keys which are used for secure communication between them. The user sends a request for location information and the location server responds by sending the location information of the requested granularity. A time stamp is used to assure freshness. The location server also generates a MAC of the random number, the location information and the granularity requested. The key for the generation of the MAC is different from the key used for the message encryption between the user and location server. The user then decrypts the information with the shared secret key. The user checks for the freshness of the information from the time stamp and generating the MAC. The protocol is described in Figure 5.

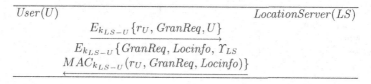

$$User(U) \qquad\qquad\qquad\qquad\qquad LocationServer(LS)$$
$$E_{k_{LS-U}}\{r_U, GranReq, U\}$$
$$\xrightarrow{}$$
$$E_{k_{LS-U}}\{GranReq, Locinfo, \Upsilon_{LS}$$
$$MAC_{k_{LS-U}}(r_U, GranReq, Locinfo)\}$$
$$\xleftarrow{}$$

Fig. 5. Reqest for location by user

5.5   Providing the Requested Service

The user decrypts the information sent by the location server and, after validating the location information, sends it to the ASP. The ASP uses the information to provide the requested service. A fresh key is generated if the user needs to request another application from the ASP. The protocol is described in Figure 6.

$$User(U) \qquad\qquad\qquad ASP(A)$$
$$E_{\sigma}\{Locinfo, A, U, \Upsilon_{LS}\}$$
$$\xrightarrow{}$$
$$E_{\sigma}\{ReqService\}$$
$$\xleftarrow{}$$

Fig. 6. Providing the reqested service

6   Comparing the Framework to the Requirements

User requirements: In the proposed framework the network operator provides the user a choice of ASPs matching the user preferences providing the user the ability to choose a suitable ASP. Legislative requirements require the network operator to provide equal preferences to all ASPs. The privacy policies contain the minimum and maximum preferences and these are within the user preferences. Thus the user can choose the granularity of location information and the service provider. The privacy policies of the user and the network operator need to be similar to P3P thus allowing the easy update of policies.

ASP requirements: The property of non-repudiation provides a mechanism to hold the ASP accountable when the ASP deviates from the stated policy. The non-repudiation is provided by the signing of the privacy policies by the ASP

Table 2. Number of cryptographic operations reqired for the proposed protocols

Cryptographic operations	Registration of user		Registration of ASP		Providing requested service			Request for location		Providing requested service	
	U	S	S	A	U	S	A	U	LS	U	A
Public key encryption	-	-	-	-	-	n*	-	-	-	-	-
Public key decryption	-	-	-	-	-	-	1	-	-	-	-
Digital signature	-	-	-	1	-	n*	-	-	-	-	-
Signature verification	-	-	1	-	-	-	1	-	-	-	-
Symmetric key encryption/decryption	-	-	-	-	2	1	1	2	1	1	1
Hash Function	-	-	-	-	n*	n*	-	1	1	-	-
Key generation	-	-	-	-	-	n*	-	-	-	-	-

where n is the number of ASP the server sends for the user to choose from

as shown in Figure 3. Though existing government legislations require the ASP to seek explicit authorisation before providing the information to a third part there is no mechanism to assure this in the proposed framework.

Network operator requirements: In the current architecture the network operator needs to provide the user with a choice of suitable service providers. The mechanism provides a means for the user to choose the service provider and the granularity of information thus giving the flexibility to the user to get a satisfactory service. The framework provides a means to assure fair competition among service providers whose privacy preferences match the user preferences.

Location server requirements: The information is derived from multiple sources and the location data set is created based on the location derived from various sources. The time stamp enables the user to check the freshness of the information. The MAC further assures the location information is not replayed from an adversary. Since the information is sent to the user and the user then forwards the information to the service provider, the user can verify that the information is of the requested granularity.

General requirements: The user does not disclose his preferred privacy policy to the ASP. The ASP can only know that the user's preferences match the ASP preferences. Since the privacy policy is application specific, the ASP providing the service will only be able to know the privacy policy matches the preferences of application requested by the user.

The processing of the policies takes place at the location of the network operator. The protocols are lightweight and from Table 2 it can be observed that the user is not required to perform complex operations. The user is limited to generating two symmetric encryption/decryption operations and a MAC.

These operations require limited amount of resources and can be performed easily on a smart card. Symmetric key encryption and decryption using DES algorithm can be performed on a Gemplus GPK8000 smart card at 507 kbps. The amount of time taken for the generation of the MAC using SHA is just 0.35

ms. This is quite reasonable compared to the time taken for the generation and verification of a digital signature which usually takes 94ms signature generation and 125ms for a signature verification using a DSS algorithm [13]. The policies designed are in XML and similar to P3P policy to meet the WAP-W3C requirements. Thus they can be easily imported and exported across networks. These are policy requirements that are currently not addressed by the framework but part of work in progress.

Security requirements:

1 Mutual end-point authentication: The authentication between the user-network operator and user-location server is provided by the existing infrastructure. The communication between the user and the service provider takes place after the establishment of the session key.

2 Data integrity: The use of MAC assures that the integrity of communications taking place between the user-network operator and user-location server. The use of signature based authentication for transmitting the session key between the user and ASP along with the time stamp assures the integrity of the session key and in turn the integrity of information between the user and ASP.

3 Data confidentiality: There are three types of important information that need to be secure: (1) user location information between location server and user; (2) session key to be used for communication between the user and ASP generated by network operator; and (3) communication between user and ASP. The long term key shared between the user-network operator and user-location server assure the confidentiality of communication.The time stamp assures the freshness of the session key.

Additional requirements: The framework specifically states that the privacy policy of the ASP needs to be application specific and contains the minimum and maximum granularity required for each application to function. Also the service provided to user is based on the privacy requirements of the user for a specific application. From Figure 3 it can be observed that the ASP signs the preferred privacy policy and sends this to the network operator. This signed privacy policy provides the non-repudiation with proof of origin from the ASP.

7   Conclusion

The proposed framework and protocols help to ensure security and privacy of heterogeneous location networks. Ongoing work in progress involves the representation and formulation of privacy policies focusing on the use of XML. Implementation and performance analysis of the framework will also be conducted.

References

1. 3GPP. LCS service description, Stage1, 2003.
2. R. Agrawal, J. Kiernan, R. Srikant, and YX. Server centric P3P. In   *W3C Workshop on the Future of P3P*, Nov. 2002.

3. P. Bahl and V.N. Padmanabhan. RADAR: An in-building RF-based user location and tracking system. In *INFOCOM (2)*, pages 775–784, 2000.

4. M. Bellare and P. Rogaway. Provably secure session key distribution: The three party case. In *27th Symposium on Theory of Computing*, pages 57–66. ACM, 1995.

5. D. Carney. Location privacy protection act of 2001. *Tech Law Journal.*, 2001.

6. G. Chen and D. Kotz. A survey of context-aware mobile computing research. Technical report, Dept. of Computer Science, Dartmouth College, Nov 2000.

7. D.A. Cooper and K.P. Birman. The design and implementation of a private message service for mobile computers. *Wireless Networks*, 1(3):297–309, 1995.

8. L. Cranor, M. Langheinrich, M. Marchiori, M. Presler-Marshall, and J. Reagle. The platform for privacy preferences 1.0 (P3P1.0) specification. Technical Report REC-P3P-20020416/, April 2002.

9. J. Cuellar, Jr J.B. Morris, D. Mulligan, J. Peterson, and J. Polk. Internet-Drafts: Geographic Location/Privacy (GeoPriv) reqirements. Technical report, March 2003.

10. A.J. Demers. Research issues in ubiqitous computing. In *Proceedings of the thirteenth annual ACM symposium on Principles of distributed computing*, pages 2–8. ACM Press, 1994.

11. ETSI. GSM 02.60 - LCS Stage-1 Service Description. *GSM Technical Specificaton*, April 1999.

12. R. Gellens. Wireless device configaration(OTASP/OTAPA) via ACAP, 1999.

13. Gemplus. GPK Reference Manual, 1999.

14. J. Kempf, L. Ackerman, and T. Miki. Wireless location privacy: A report on law and policy in the USA, the European Union, and Japan. Technical report, Nov,2003.

15. J. Lin, R. Laddaga, and H. Naito. Personal location agent for communicating entities (PLACE). Lecture Notes in Computer Science. Springer, 2002.

16. E. Snekkenes. Concepts for personal location privacy policies. In *Proceedings of the 3rd ACM conference on Electronic Commerce*, pages 48–57. ACM Press, 2001.

17. T. Tin, H. Vasanta, C. Boyd, and J. Nieto. Protocols with security proofs for mobile applications. In *Lecture Notes in Computer Science, ACISP2004*. Springer, 2004.

18. Justice Department USA. The privacy act of 1974.

19. R. Want, A. Hopper, V. Falcão, and J. Gibbons. The active badge location system. *ACM Transactions on Information Systems (TOIS)*, 10(1):91–102, 1992.

20. WAP and W3C. Report from WAP-W3C joint workshop on mobile web privacy. Technical report, WAP and W3C, 2000.

PEARL: A PErformance evaluAtor
of cRyptographic aLgorithms for Mobile Devices*

Bringel Filho[1], Windson Viana[1,**], Rossana Andrade[1], and André Jalles Monteiro[2]

[1] Mestrado em Ciência da Computação (MCC) – Universidade Federal do Ceará (UFC)
{bringel,windson,rossana}@lia.ufc.br
http://great.lia.ufc.br
[2] Departamento de Estatística – Universidade Federal do Ceará (UFC)
Fortaleza – CE – Brasil
jalles@ufc.br

Abstract. Limited computational power imposes new challenges during the implementation of security and privacy solutions for mobile devices. The choice for the most appropriate cryptographic algorithm for each mobile device has become a critical factor. In this paper, we present an approach for performance evaluation of cryptographic algorithms for mobile devices. A tool called PEARL (PErformance evaluAtor of cryptogRaphic aLgorithms for mobile devices) is also introduced in this work to validate the approach. This tool collects and analyzes information related to executions of the cryptographic algorithms in the mobile devices. Moreover, PEARL allows evaluating the performance of symmetrical and asymmetrical cryptographic algorithms, and hash functions for the J2ME platform.

1 Introduction

With the fast evolution of mobile computing, an enormous diversity of mobile devices, such as cellular phones, Palms and Pocket PCs can be found in the market. These devices offer Internet connectivity using wireless communication technologies (e.g., IEEE 802.11, GSM, GPRS) allowing users to get access to information any time and any place. Moreover, mobile devices provide not only applications that are available by manufacturers (e.g., agenda, calculator), but also the possibility of creating new applications to their users. These new applications are implemented using the development platforms supported by the device, for example, J2ME (Java 2 Edition Micron), Superwaba, .Net and Brew.

On the other hand, mobile device developers face new challenges. For example, the increasing availability of information using mobile data networks causes serious risks to the security. Cryptography can be used to assure security in both data transmission and data storage. However, certain cryptographic algorithms, which are simple and efficient when executed in high performance processors available in desktops, can be inefficient or unsuitable to be implemented in low performance processors available in most of the mobile devices mentioned previously. Thus, the limited computational power in these devices imposes new challenges during the implementation

---

* This work is supported by Instituto Atlântico, Fortaleza, Ceará, Brazil.
** Windson Viana is supported by CAPES, Brasília, DF, Brazil.

A. Karmouch, L. Korba, and E. Madeira (Eds.): MATA 2004, LNCS 3284, pp. 275–284, 2004.
© Springer-Verlag Berlin Heidelberg 2004

of cryptosystems. In this context, the choice of the most appropriate algorithm for a certain mobile device has become a critical factor and brought the need for evaluating the efficiency of cryptographic algorithms for these devices.

Different from the works that appear in the literature [6][7], this paper presents an approach and its respective tool that allow performance evaluation of cryptographic algorithms in a large range of mobile device types (e.g., Palms [13], Pockets PC [9]). The tool is implemented in J2ME, which is a largely used platform for developer mobile applications and the great majority of the current mobile devices support J2ME.

The main contributions of this work can be summarized as follows: (1) the tool allows the performance evaluation of cryptographic algorithms in mobile devices; (2) the evaluation results brings the possibility of verifying the viability of the algorithm application in certain device; (3) the tool allows to identify the algorithm that has the best performance for a certain input size; (4) the tool allows to evaluate the algorithm performance in different virtual machines in the same device; and (5) the evaluation results allow the construction of optimized cryptosystems for the analyzed device or an application that can adapt the security layer for each analyzed device.

The remaining sections are organized as follows. Section 2 shows related works. Section 3 introduces our approach for the performance evaluation of cryptographic algorithms for mobile devices. In Section 4, we show our tool, called PEARL, which implements the proposed approach, and, in Section 5, a case study. Finally, Section 6 ends up with final considerations and future works.

2   Related Work

According to the research done in the literature for this work, we consider [6] the closest work related to our approach and its respective tool. The authors had implemented and evaluated libraries of cryptographic systems for the Palm platform. These libraries include implementations in C language of stream ciphers (SSC2, ARC4 and SEAL 3.0), block ciphers (Rijndael, DES, DESX and TripleDES), hash functions (MD2, MD4, MD5 and SHA-1) and integer arithmetical operations of multiple precisions.

In [6], the algorithms had been evaluated in Palm V (16 Mhz processor, 2Mb) and Palm IIIc (20 Mhz processor, 8Mb) devices. The evaluations had consisted of the algorithm executions in these devices by ciphering plaintext of various sizes (2 Kb, 50 Kb, and 4Mb). The amount of ciphered bytes (or digested, in case of hash functions) was calculated in each second (bytes/s). With the evaluation result, the authors had identified that the SSC2 has better performance than ARC4 and SEAL 3.0 for small plaintext (1Kb). For big plaintext (4Mb), SEAL 3.0 performs twice faster than SSC2. From the block ciphers analysis, the authors had observed that Rijndael is four times faster than DES.

The performance evaluation in [6] has also demonstrated the viability of using integer arithmetical operations of multiple precision, which are operations used in asymmetrical cryptographic algorithms. It was also observed that implementations of embedded cryptographic algorithms in applications have better performance than implementations based on system libraries.

It is also worth to mention the work developed in [7], where the authors show a performance analysis of cryptographic protocols in mobile devices. The analysis is applied to SSL, S/MIME and IP/Sec protocols, which are widely used in network applications. The analysis results show that the time necessary to execute cryptographic functions is small, not causing significant impact in the performance of real time mobile transactions. The analysis was done only in the iPAC H3630 device (206 Mhz StrongARM processor, RAM 32 Mb with operational system Windows CE Pocket PC 2002). However, the analyzed device has a performance similar to a desktop and it is still necessary to investigate mobile devices with low computational power.

Our approach, on the other hand, allows evaluating the algorithm performance in any mobile device, if the device presents support for J2ME/MIDP 1.0 platform or higher version. The performance of each algorithm is evaluated according to the time necessary to execute cryptographic operations over an input text of pre-defined size. As a result of the evaluation, we present the amount of bytes that can be ciphered per second (bytes/s), in case of symmetrical and asymmetrical cryptographic algorithms, and the amount of bytes that can be digested per second for hash functions.

3 An Approach for Performance Evaluation of Cryptographic Algorithms in Mobile Devices

This section describes an approach to evaluate the performance of cryptographic algorithms in mobile devices. The approach is divided in two phases, as follows. The first phase consists in collecting information related to the executions of the algorithms in the mobile devices (called samples). This information is used to evaluate the performance of the algorithms in the device. The second phase is responsible for evaluating this information to identify which are the algorithms with the best performance in the analyzed device.

The following sub-sections present the description of the collected sample format for each execution and more details about the approach phases.

3.1 Sample Format Description

The samples contain information related to the executions of the cryptographic algorithms in the analyzed device. The sample format allows identifying the analyzed devices, the virtual machine, the algorithm, the message size, and the initialization and execution times. This information is enough to evaluate the cryptographic algorithm performance in each device. A sample is created and stored for further analysis in each execution of an algorithm with pre-defined input size. Each sample refers to a single execution and contains the following fields:

- *idDevice:* identifies the analyzed device. Each device receives an identification before initiating the information collection;
- *idVM:* identifies the virtual machine;
- *idAlg:* identifies the evaluated algorithm;
- *sizeText:* is the size of the input text;

- *timeInit:* is the algorithm inicialization time. Each algorithm has an specific inicialization time that can change according to the input size;
- *timeExec:* is the algorithm execution time. For each input size and evaluated algorithm, we have a different execution time.

3.2 Sample Collection

As already mentioned in the previous sub-section, a sample contains information related to an execution in the analyzed device of an algorithm with an input text defined previously. The algorithms get input texts from different sizes. For each input size, it is collected the initialization algorithm time and the time necessary for ciphering or calculating the digest. The sample that contains this information is stored in a local repository in the mobile device called SLB – Samples Local Bank (see Fig. 1).

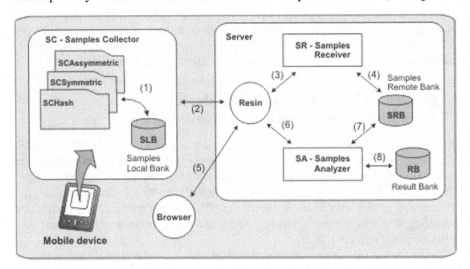

Fig. 1. PEARL Architecture: Components and their relationships

The size of the initial input text is 1Kb that is duplicated until reaching the maximum size multiple of two, which is specified for the evaluation (e.g., 256Kb), or the maximum size supported by the device (e.g. 64KB for palm devices with Sun J2ME VM). The algorithm performance evaluation becomes more precise with this variation in the input size that allows the analysis of the variation on the execution time and the initialization time, according to the increase of the input text size.

A test case corresponds to an execution of an algorithm with a defined input text size. For each input size and algorithm, test cases are executed and they generate a sample for posterior analysis.

After the collection phase, the samples that are stored in the LBS are transmitted to a computer desktop, which has more processing power, to be analyzed. In the desktop, a database, called SRB - Samples Remote Bank (see Fig. 1), stores the received samples. The sample analysis is then executed on the SRB data instead of in the mobile device. The analysis technique is presented in the next sub-section.

3.3 Sample Analysis

In our approach, the test cases (i.e., executions of the algorithms with a specific input size) generate the samples to be analyzed. The sample analysis of an algorithm presents as a result the amount of ciphered or digested bytes per second, for each input size.

For calculating the speed (i.e., bytes/s) of the cryptographic operations, we use the input text size (e.g., 1024, 2048, and 4096 Bytes) and the modal value of the execution time for that size. We use the modal value, which is the value repeated more often in a distribution, since we need to obtain a fast and close measurement that represents the most typical value of the distribution. So, at the end, we have as a result the speed that more frequently occurs for each text size and evaluated algorithm.

4 The PEARL Tool

A tool called PEARL (Performance EvaluAtor of cryptogRaphic aLgorithms for mobile devices) is developed in this work to validate the approach presented in the previous section. Next sub-sections describe the architecture and the main functionalities of the tool.

4.1 Architecture

Fig. 1 illustrates the architecture of the PEARL tool, including its components and the interaction among them.

The SC – Samples Collector module executes the test cases of the cryptographic algorithms in the analyzed device. The SCAsymmetric, SCSymmetric and SCHash submodules store the samples related to the algorithm test cases (1) in the SLB. After the collection phase, it is necessary the user interaction for executing the synchronization (i.e., the sending process) of the collected samples with the server (2, 3). The user invokes the SR servlet to receive and to store the samples sent in the SRB (4). After the sample reception, the user interacts with the system core using any Web browser (5) and invokes the SA servlet to execute the analysis of the received samples (6). This servlet, in turn, recovers the samples stored in the SRB (7) to do the analysis. As a result, we get the amount of ciphered or digested bytes per second (i.e., the algorithm throughput) for each text size and evaluated algorithm. The analysis results are stored in the RB (8).

The tool is developed in Windows environment, using the Java language (J2ME/MIDP 1.0 platform and J2SE), Resin server and MySQL database. PEARL also executes in Linux environment by changing Java servlets (SR – Samples Receiver and SA – Samples Analyzer) to the Apache Tomcat server.

4.2 Samples Collector

As mentioned before, the Samples Collector (SC) module is responsible for the test cases of the cryptographic algorithms in the mobile devices. This module is divided in 3 (three) submodules: SCSymmetric, SCHash and SCAsymmetric.

These submodules are developed in J2ME platform, specifically, we use J2ME Wireless Toolkit 1.0.4_01 [7] and SonyEricsson J2ME SDK [14] tools. The evaluated cryptographic algorithms are implemented and distributed by the Legion of the Bouncy Castle, which is a research group that develops open source Java APIs in the security area.

Each submodule allows to choose minimum and maximum text input sizes, the algorithm to be evaluated, and the amount of test cases that are necessary for the analysis. It is also possible to execute all algorithms with the same minimum and maximum text input sizes and amount of test cases.

For calculating timeExec and timeInit, we apply the java.util.Date class, more specifically, the getTime() method, which returns in milliseconds the amount of time since 00:00 h of January 1st, 1970.

SCSymmetric is responsible for the test cases of the symmetrical cryptography algorithms. They are divided in 2 (two) categories of algorithms: block ciphers and stream ciphers. This submodule allows to evaluate any of the following 18 (eighteen) cryptographic algorithms: AES, AES Fast, AES Light, Blowfish, CAST5, CAST6, 3DES, DES, IDEA, RC2, RC5 32 bits, RC5 64 bits, RC6, Rijndael, Serpent, Skipjack, and Towfish block ciphers as well as RC4 stream cipher. Some of these algorithms are variations of existing block ciphers, for example, the AES Fast and the AES Light are variations of the AES. Other algorithms are different implementations for the same algorithm, such as Rijndael and AES. For each block cipher algorithm and input text size, it is evaluated four ciphering types: Electronic Codebook (ECB), Cipher Block Cleaning (CBC), Cipher Feedback (CFB), and Output Feedback (OFB). Then, four test cases are generated and each of them applies one of the blocks ciphering type mentioned before. In the test cases that use CFB or OFB ciphering types, the block size used is 64 bits and the ciphering key size is 128 bits.

SCHash is responsible for the test cases of the hash functions. We apply 10 (ten) algorithms (functions and variations): MD2, MD4, MD5, RIPEMD128, RIPEMD 160, SHA 256, SHA 384, SHA 512, SHA-1 and Tiger. As mentioned in Section 2, SCHash does not collect the timeInit information, just the timeExec.

Finally, *SCAsymmetric* is responsible for the test cases of the asymetrical cryptography algorithms. It is possible to evaluate the following two public key algorithms: RSA and ElGamal. TimeInit in this case is the amount of time for the key generation. The created key is 1024 bits, with public exponent e = 65537.

4.3 Samples Analyzer and Result Bank

The Samples Analyzer (SA) module is responsible for calculate the throughput (i.e. byte/s) of the cryptographic operations using the approach mentioned in Section 3.3.

The results of SA are stored at the Result Bank (RB). So, at the end of the PEARL tool execution, RB has a result speed for each algorithm at each device. This allows a mobile application developer to know the time that a specific device spends to execute an algorithm of cryptographic.

5 Case Study

As a case study, PEARL tool was executed at Palm M130, Palm M515 and Sony Ericsson P800 smart phone. Table 1 presents more technical details about them.

Table 1. Mobile Devices Investigated

Device	RAM	Processor	SO	VM
Palm M130	8Mb	Motorola Dragonball VZ 33 Mhz	Palm OS 4.1	IBM
Palm M515	16Mb	Motorola DragonBall VZ 33 Mhz	Palm OS 4.1	IBM
Sony Ericsson P800	12Mb	32-bit RISC ARM9 @ 156 MHz	Symbian OS 7.0	Sony Ericsson

For each device, symmetrical and asymmetrical algorithms, as well as hash functions are executed. The initial size of the evaluated text is 1Kb (see section 4), being duplicated until reaching 256Kb. This maximum size is chosen for being the maximum multiple of two that a vector of bytes can be allocated to the memory of the Palm devices listed above using the IBM virtual machine. On the other hand, P800 smart phone does not have such limit, allowing evaluations with a vector of bytes greater than that (e.g., 2048 Kb).

In each device we execute 50 test cases for each input size and algorithm, as follows: 3400 executions of block cipher symmetrical algorithms, 50 executions of the RC4 stream cipher algorithm, 500 executions of hash functions and 100 executions of asymmetrical cryptographic algorithms. The execution results of the asymmetrical algorithms are not able to finish before the end of this paper submission.

Beyond the throughput for each algorithm execution of the device, the analysis of RB generated by AS (see Fig. 1) shows that RC4 stream cipher presents the best performance among the symmetrical cryptographic algorithms for all three devices. On the other hand, the Rijndael algorithm presents the worst performance, it does not matter the operation type (i.e., ECB, CBC, CFB and OFB) and evaluated text size. Table 2 presents a summary of the evaluation results of the symmetrical cryptographic algorithms, considering the ECB operation type in each analyzed device.

Minor throughput shows the worst algorithm throughput (i.e., 61,02 Bytes/s) is the Rijndael algorithm throughput in the Palm M130 device. Similarly, the major throughput column presents the best performance algorithm throughput in the analyzed device. The throughput increasing order is established considering the plaintext size equal to the final size of the evaluated text (i.e., 256 Kb).

We observe with hash function evaluations that the MD4 algorithm presents the best performance. On the contrary, the MD2 presents the worst performance. Table 3 demonstrates a summary of these evaluation results in each analyzed device. The hash function throughput increasing order is established considering the plaintext size equal to 256 Kb.

The analysis results of the Palm devices demonstrates that, despite Palm M515 has twice the amount of memory than Palm M130, the throughput of cryptographic algorithms is very close in these devices (see Table 2 and Table 3). We can also observe

Table 2. Summary of the algorithm evaluations of symmetrical cryptography

Device	Minor throughput (Bytes/s)	Major throughput (Bytes/s)	Throughput increasing order
Palm M130	61,02	1587,6	Rijndael < 3DES < Serpent < Skipjack < RC2 < AES Light < DES < IDEA < CAST6 < RC6 < AES < CAST5 < Twofish < AES Fast < RC5 32 Bits < Blow-Fish < RC5 64 Bits < RC4
Palm M515	60,97	1575,4	Rijndael < 3DES < Serpent < Skipjack < RC2 < AES Light < DES < IDEA < CAST6 <RC6 < AES < CAST5 < Twofish < AES Fast < RC5 32 Bits <Blow-Fish < RC5 64 Bits < RC4
Sony Ericsson P800	5953,49	2048000	Rijndael < 3DES < Serpent < CAST6 < AES < AES Light < Skipjack < RC2 < IDEA < CAST5 < RC6 < DES < Twofish < RC5 32 Bits < BlowFish < AES Fast < RC5 64 Bits < RC4

Table 3. Summary of algorithm evaluations of hash functions

Device	Minor throughput (Bytes/s)	Major throughput (Bytes/s)	Throughput increasing order
Palm M130	88,12	2546,07	MD2 < SHA256 < SHA512 <= SHA384 < SHA1 < RIPEMD160 < RIPEMD128 < Tiger < MD5 < MD4
Palm M515	87,9	2546,57	MD2 < SHA256 < SHA512 <= SHA384 < SHA1 < RIPEMD160 < RIPEMD128 < Tiger < MD5 < MD4
Sony Ericsson P800	9309,1	2048000	MD2 < RIPEMD160 < SHA256 < SHA512 <= SHA384 < SHA1 < RIPEMD128 < MD5 < Tiger < MD4

that the growth order of the algorithm throughput in these devices is equal, differing from the growth order presented in the SonyEricsson P800.

These results show that PEARL tool can be used by a mobile application developer to verify the viability of an algorithm application in J2ME at a specific device, to identify the algorithm that has the best performance for a certain input size, and to know the throughput of a specific algorithm. PEARL results can be also used to construct optimized cryptosystems for the analyzed device or a security layer that can adapt the cryptography algorithms for each analyzed device.

6   Conclusion and Future Work

The performance evaluation of cryptographic algorithms is a requirement for safe and efficient development of cryptosystem in devices of low computational power.

The approach presented in this paper and its respective tool allows evaluating the efficiency of the algorithms in a large variety of mobile devices (e.g., Palm, cellular, Pocket PC). The approach phases allow managing both qualitative and quantitative information. The PEARL tool implements the approach, which identifies the most efficient algorithms in J2ME environments for a certain analyzed device.

The case study validates the approach and its tool, presenting the evaluation results of the cryptographic algorithms in Palm M130, Palm M515, and smart phone Sony-Ericsson P800. The results can interfere directly in the developer's choice of the algorithm that will be composing the cryptosystem developed to provide security during the data transmission and storage. Thus, the analysis results allow either the development of optimized cryptosystems or a security layer with adaptation capability.

However, it is worth mentioning that just the performance factor does not guarantee the development of safe cryptosystems. For each algorithm is necessary to study the security offered for the algorithm and its vulnerabilities to attacks mentioned in the literature.

We consider as future work the development of a framework that will allow the development of safe applications for mobile devices in J2ME platform. From the evaluation results, the developer will be able to choose the algorithms to be added to the framework to guarantee the security in the data transmission and storage of data in the mobile device. Aiming at organizing a repository of the analysis results, we also consider new evaluations in other devices.

More investigation about the plaintext type (e.g., ASCII text, binary text) and its effects on the performance of cryptographic algorithms should also be done as future work. During the evaluations of this work, we have already identified variations on the execution time according to input type changes.

References

1. Winkle W. V.; Palm Business Applications. The Ultimate guide to mobile computing: 2002 mobile Technology. p. 82-89, 2002.
2. Stallings, William. Network security essentials: applications and standards / William Stallings. ISBN: 0-13-016093-8.
3. The Legion of Bouncy Castle. Cryptography API for Java.
   Available at www.bouncycastle.org. Last access in: Feb. 2003.
4. Menezes, A. J.; Oorschot, P. C. V.; Vanstone S. A.; Handbook of Applied Cryptography. Oct, 1996.
5. Susilo, W. Securing Handheld devices. 10th IEEE International Conference, Wollongong, p. 349-354, 2002.
6. Wong, D. S.; Fuentes, H. H.; Chan, A. H.; The Performance Measurement of Cryptographic Primitives on Palm Devices. Boston, p. 1-10, 2002.
7. Java 2 Platform, Micro Edition (J2ME). Available at <http://java.sun.com/j2me>. Last access in: Mar. 10th, 2003.

8. Argyroudis, P. G.;Verma, R.;Tewari, H.;O'Mayony, D. Performance Analysis of Cryptographic Protocols on Handheld Devices, 2003.
9. Windows CE, Disponível em <http://www.microsoft.com/windowsce/>. Last access in: Jan. 10th, 2004.
10. Superwaba: The Java VM for PDAs. Available at <http://www.superwaba.com.br>. Last access in: Mar. 10th, 2003.
11. Microsoft. Mobile ASP.NET Web Applications. Available at <http://www.asp.net/default.aspx?tabIndex=6&tabId=44>. Last access in: Mar. 10th, 2003.
12. Qualcomm. Qualcomm Brew. Available at <http://www.qualcomm.com/brew/>. Last access in: Mar. 15th, 2003.
13. PalmOne. Available at <http://www.palm.com/>. Last access in: Mar. 15th, 2003.
14. SonyEricsson. Available at: <http://developer.sonyericsson.com/site/global/home/p_home.jsp>. Last access in: Mar. 10th, 2003.

On the Performance of Distributed Search
by Mobile Agents

A. Mawlood-Yunis[1], Amiya Nayak[2], Doron Nussbaum[1], and Nicola Santoro[1]

[1] School of Computer Science, Carleton University, Ottawa, ON K1S 5B6, Canada
{armyunis,nussbaum,santoro}@scs.carleton.ca
[2] School of Information Technology & Engineering, University of Ottawa
Ottawa, ON K1N 6N5, Canada
anayak@site.uottawa.ca

Abstract. When using mobile agents in distributed search, the overall performance is influenced by several factors. In this paper, we study some of them and their impact. Several experiments were carried out to study the impact of network size, network topology, and the number of agents. These experiments were performed on two well-known mobile agent platforms: AGLET (a commercial environment), and TACOMA (an academic research environment). The results shed some light on the nature of the functional dependency of performance on these factors. Moreover, the experiments show that, except for the scale, the results are platform independent.

1 Introduction

The performance aspects of the mobile agents have been a subject of several studies. In [2] the scalability of the server, the performance factor that are fundamental to the mobile agent idea, and separately, the performance factor due to design differences of different mobile agent platforms have been addressed. The authors compared a traditional client/server approach with a mobile agent approach on four mobile agent's platforms in the context of a simple informational retrieval application. In [7], analysis of mobile agent performance in a network management and, its comparison with the client/server model used by the SNMP (Simple Network Management Protocol) have been performed. Performance evaluation of mobile agents for e-commerce application have been studied in [4]. In [3], an analytical model that examines the claimed performance benefits of mobile agents over client/server computing for a mobile information retrieval scenario was developed.

In this paper, we study performance behavior of mobile agents in a distributed search using single and multiple agents. In the case of multiple agent search, we suggest three different algorithms. The search has been conducted under variable network size, network topology and number of agents. Several experiments are carried out to measure the performance of mobile agents solution to distributed search problem. The results on two different mobile agent platforms, namely AGLET (a commercial one) [6] and TACOMA (an academic one) [5], have been compared.

A. Karmouch, L. Korba, and E. Madeira (Eds.): MATA 2004, LNCS 3284, pp. 285–294, 2004.

2   Distributed Search with Single and Multiple Mobile Agents

2.1   Structure and Components

Since our objective is to compare the results using AGLET mobile agent with the results obtained by [8] using TACOMA mobile agent, we use similar algorithm to the one implemented in [8]. We start with the construction of a logical spanning tree on top of the physical network. Once a spanning tree constructed, the search problem is reduced to a tree traversal problem. The search time of mobile agent does not include the time to construct the spanning tree, as we assume that the spanning tree was constructed in pre-processing steps. To traverse the spanning tree, agent may start at any node in the network. It obtains its neighboring information and travels to the first host in the list. Once the agent obtains the neighboring information, it changes its internal queue or stack (itinerary). The process of adding neighboring information into the internal data storage in *Single agent* search leads to different spanning tree traversal such as *Breadth_First_Search* (BFS) once the the internal data structure is queue or *Depth_First_Search* (DFS) once internal data structure is stack. The search can be carried out with multiple agents; this we call *flooding*. Agent interacts with the local resources at each node; it opens a file at each site it visits, and carries along the contents of the file. Once all nodes in the network were visited, the agent returns to the initiator node with the search result (file contents).

In our study, we have used a framework that consists of the following components: *Blackboard, Whiteboard, Router,* and *Log.* The purpose of the *Blackboard* is to help terminate the flooding algorithm. The purpose of the *Whiteboard* is to avoid multiple visit to the same node by different agents. The purpose of the *Log* component is to terminate the flooding algorithm without using the *Blackboard* component. A *Log* component is associated with each node in the network. The *Router* is used with both single and multiple agent search. It acts as a global and local *Router* to enable agents to move around the network.

2.2   Search Using Single Agent

At each host, the agent gets the list of the next hosts to visit which becomes the agent's *Itinerary.* The agent checks to see if a parent of the current host or initiator host are in the list. If the list contains the parent or initiator node, the agent removes it to avoid returning to the host it just came from or returning to the the initiator node before completing the search. It adds the remaining hosts (if not null) to the internal container. For the BFS traversal, every time we get a set of new neighbors from the   *Router* we add it to the end of the internal container, this results in BFS traversal. In case of DFS, we add a new set of neighbors to the beginning of the internal list resulting in DFS traversal.

2.3   Search Using Multiple Agents (Flooding)

Flooding is another way to traverse spanning tree and solve the problem of distributed search. The agent starts from a node and duplicates itself as many identical agents as the number of children specified in the local number list; all these copies travel simultaneously to every child in the neighboring list. For the purpose of flooding the network with agents we use three different approaches: *Local flooding*, *Remote flooding*, and *Regular flooding*

In *Remote flooding*, the agent and the *Blackboard* communicate remotely. Here the agent contacts *Blackboard* for removing its ID once it is at the end of the search path and just before moving back to the initiator node. In this way, the agent removes its ID while being host on remote node, and only after its ID has been removed from the *Blackboard* it returns back to the initiator node.

In *Local flooding* the agent and *Blackboard* communicate locally on the initiator node. This contact happens just before agent reports its partial result and after it returns back to the initiator node. The agent contacts the *Blackboard* to remove its ID. Once its ID is removed, it reports the partial result to the initiator node.

In *Regular flooding*, agents start moving from the initiator node all the way down to the end of their search path. Once they reach the end of the search path, each agent reports its partial result to its immediate parent. This continues until the final result reaches the initiator. Once the last agent returns back to initiator, the algorithm terminates. In this approach, we do not have any *Blackboard* component to facilitate termination, as it is the case with two previous algorithms. Instead, we use a *Log* (i.e. local *Blackboard*) at each node which holds information about that node.

3   Experimental Results

In the experiments, agents are injected from any node of the network. The launching application or initiator measures the time in milliseconds before injecting the first agent and after the last agent has arrived. The difference between these two time measurements is the total execution time for the entire search. The strategy followed for testing different schemes consists of a set of test cases aimed at evaluating the impact of certain variables on the overall performance. The objective was to obtain sufficient information to compare the performance between the AGLET mobile agent and the TACOMA mobile agent.

All the experiments were carried out in the absence of failure. The computers were used simultaneously by other users, and no special care was taken to guarantee exclusive access to computer resources or network during these experiments. All the experiments presented herein were developed in the Graduate Lab of the School of Computer Science on 1000 MHz Pentium with 500 MB RAM machines. The agent platform used was AGLET-2.0.1 compiled and run on the Sigma Network (Linux Mandrake 7.1 machines) and the Ultra Network (SunOs 5.7 Generic_106541-06 sun4u sparc SUNW, Ultra5-10). The *Blackboard* associated to each node was implemented as a multi-threaded application using the Java JDK1.2.2. *Router* and *Whiteboard* were implemented in Java JDK1.2.2 and used a RMI server. The size of information carried by the agent was same for all algorithms. Agent(s) performed a dummy search at each site consisting basically of opening a file and reading the content.

3.1   Impact of Network Size

We compared the search time of running single and multiple agents on binary trees of different sizes from 3 to 28 nodes. Each test was run thirty times to get the average search time. The following results were obtained:

1. The AGLET agent performed better than the TACOMA Agent. Searching with a single AGLET agent is almost ten times faster than searching with a single TACOMA agent. In multiple agent search, the AGLET agent performed almost seven times better than the TACOMA agent. This is due to the difference in their respective platforms.
2. For both the AGLET and TACOMA platforms, single agent performed better than multiple agents for small networks whereas multiple agents performed better than single agent in large networks. The only difference here is in the size of the network in which multiple agents outperformed the single agent. In the TACOMA platform, the single agent performed better than multiple agents for a network size up to eighteen nodes, while in the AGLET platform network size of only eight nodes were sufficient for multiple agents to outperform a single agent. This result suggests that we can run multiple AGLET agents on binary tree (i.e. take advantage of parallelism) on network with size as little as eight nodes, whereas we cannot do that with TACOMA agents. In order to take advantage of parallelism with TACOMA agents, we should have a network (i.e. binary tree) size of at least eighteen nodes.
3. The single agent search performance is better than the multiple agents search performance for networks of small size.

The above explanations lead us to conclude that for small networks, the advantages we gain from parallelism by using multiple agents is not enough to overcome the overhead associated with it. In large networks, the advantages of parallelism will overcome the above mentioned overhead, and as a result we get a better search performance with multiple agents than with single agent. Another aspect of the third point of the result is that in multiple agents search, the AGLET system performs better than TACOMA system in small networks. The execution time for a single and multiple travelling agent for both AGLET and TACOMA system are shown in Figure 1 and Figure 2 respectively.

3.2   Impact of Number of Neighbors

In this test, we compared the results of running single and multiple agents of both TACOMA and AGLET systems on various trees with constant size. The trees are differ from each other in the number of children of each node. We started with a binary tree and then increased the number of neighbors for each node at each step by two until we ended up with a star structure.

The result shows that in the case of a single agent search, the number of neighbors did not have significant impact on search time in both systems. This result is predicted, since by increasing the number of neighbors in single agent

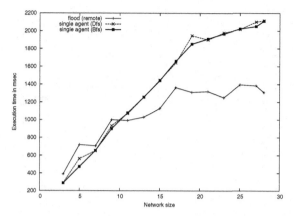

Fig. 1. Average Execution Time for Single and Multiple Agent Search (AGLET)

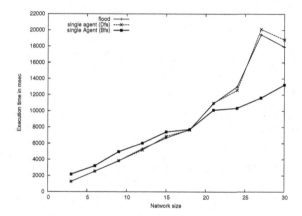

Fig. 2. Average Execution Time for Single and Multiple Agent Search (TACOMA)

search the change occurs only in the visiting sequence of hosts, and this does not have any effect on the search since we working on LAN. For both systems, multiple agents search performed better than single agent search when the number of neighbors was low. As the number of neighbors increased and the search became closer and closer to the sequential search, single agent performed better than multiple agent. This was due to the overhead associated with multiple agents search.

The only difference between AGLET and TACOMA agents here is at the turning point when single agent search starts to become more efficient than the multiple agents search. In the TACOMA system, multiple agents search performed better than single agent search only in the case of binary tree, whereas in AGLET system, multiple agents search performed better than the single agent search in a tree with each node having eight neighbors (k =8) and the best performance came in a tree with each node having four neighbors (k= 4).

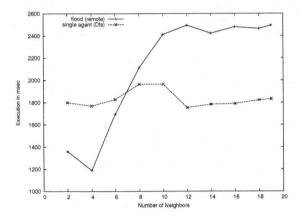

Fig. 3. Single and Multiple Mobile Agents with Various Number of Neighbors (AGLET)

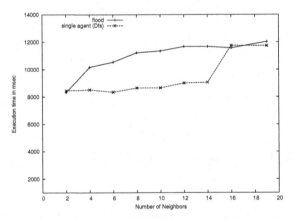

Fig. 4. Single and Multiple Mobile Agents with Various Number of Neighbors (TACOMA)

Figures 3 and 4 show the average execution time for a single and a multiple agent for both the AGLET and the TACOMA system when the network size is constant (N = 20) and the topology changes from a binary tree to a star (k =2, 4, 6, ..., 19).

3.3   Impact of Network Topology

In this test, we compared the search times of running single and multiple AGLET and TACOMA agents in different network topologies of a fixed size. The network for this test consists of sixteen nodes. The topologies which been used for this test are: unidirectional ring, bidirectional ring, hypercube, and binary tree. Beside comparing the search times of AGLET and TACOMA, we also compared the search time of single and multiple agents for the AGLET system as well. We have the following observations:

Single Agent Traversal:

a. The best performance is seen in the bidirectional ring and the worst performance in the hypercube for both the AGLET and the TACOMA systems. Hence, the behavior of both systems is very much similar in different topologies when a single agent is used.
b. Even though we see the best and worst scenario, the performance in all topologies considered is almost the same for both systems.

Multiple Agent Traversal:

a. For deploying multiple agents, the best performance of the TACOMA agent is seen in the bidirectional ring, and the performance is similar in the case of a binary tree. On the other hand, the best performance of the AGLET agent is seen in the hypercube. From the first test, it is evident that the AGLET agents are more efficient than the TACOMA agents; hence, the AGLET agents are more capable of taking advantage of parallelism. The second test shows that the best performance of AGLET agents comes from a tree with four neighbors for each node or a hypercube.
b. The worst performance for the AGLET agent is seen in the unidirectional ring whereas the worst performance for the TACOMA agent is seen in the hypercube.

Single and Multiple AGLET Agent Performance:

The result shows that the AGLET performance is better in the flooding case than in the a single agent case for both binary tree and hypercube, but it is almost the same for bidirectional ring. In the case of bidirectional ring, the single agent performs slightly better than flooding. This is due to the overhead associated with flooding. If we ignore the extra overhead associated with flooding, the single agent search is better in the case of a bidirectional ring.

Figure 5 shows the performance comparison of AGLET and TACOMA mobile agent in single agent search for different network topologies. Similarly, Figure 6 compares the result in the case of multiple agents.

3.4 Three Flooding Algorithms

In this test, we compared the performance of *local flooding*, *remote flooding*, and *regular flooding* in binary trees of different sizes from 3 to 28 nodes. The following observations were made:

1. The difference between all three approaches is very little if the network size is small.
2. Once the network size exceeds nineteen nodes, *remote flooding* performs better the other two algorithms.

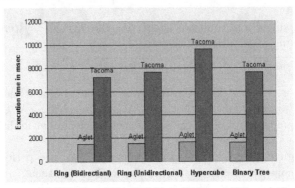

Fig. 5. Performance of AGLET and TACOMA in Different Network Topologies (Single Agent Case)

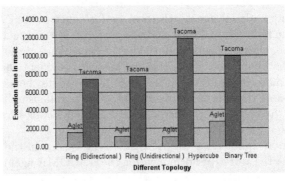

Fig. 6. Performance of AGLET and TACOMA in Different Network Topologies (Flooding Case)

3. The *remote flooding* performs better than *regular flooding*, even though we do not contact the *Blackboard* remotely nor do we have multiple agents running at the same place at one time.

Figure 7 shows the execution time for all three algorithms.

3.5   Cost of Moving AGLET and TACOMA Agents Between Nodes

In this test, we compared the time required for moving a single AGLET and TACOMA agent between any two nodes. The objective was to compare the time required in each case to deploy an agent to a node and to pull back this agent to the source. The result shows that even though the difference in the implementation language is in favor of TACOMA, the AGLET mobile agent is almost ten times faster than the TACOMA agent (162.32 msec in the case of AGLET compared to 1551.57 msec in the case of TACOMA). The difference in performance is due to the difference in their respective architectures. In the AGLET mobile agent case, we compile the agent code to byte code, and when we deploy the agent we serialize the byte code and send it over the socket to

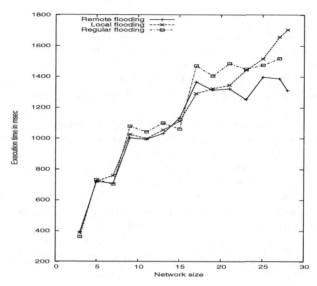

Fig. 7. Execution of remote, local and regular flooding for various network size

be executed at the remote host. In the TACOMA case, on the other hand, once we deploy the agent we send the code which should be compiled and linked for execution at the remote host. This requires more time than having byte code.

4   Conclusions

In all the tests we conducted, single agent performed better than multiple agents in networks of small size, whereas in large networks, multiple agents outperformed single agent. The same result was seen in the TACOMA platform; the only difference between the AGLET and the TACOMA is in the size of the network in which multiple agents outperformed single agent. We identified the crossover points for all our tests which could be used to make decision on the choice of mobile agent platform, search criteria, topology, etc. Comparing the results from both AGLET and TACOMA platforms, it appears that the overall behavior of a mobile agent is platform independent whereas its performance is platform dependent; this is the same conclusion that was found in [1].

References

1. J. Baek, J. Yeo, G. Kim, and H. Yeom. Cost Effective Mobile Agent Planning for Distributed Information Retrieval. *Proc. 21st Conference on Distributed Systems*, pp. 65-72, 2001.
2. R. S. Gray, D. Kotz, R. A. Peterson, J. Barton, D. Chacón, P. Gerken, M. Hofmann, J. Bradshaw, M. Breedy, R. Jeffers, and N. Suri. Mobile-Agent versus Client/Server Performance: Scalability in an Information-Retrieval Task. *Proc. 5th International Conference on Mobile Agents*, pp. 229-243 , 2002.

3. R. Jain, F. Anjum and A. Umar. A Comparison of mobile agent and client-server paradigms for information retrieval tasks in virtual enterprises. *IEEE Academia/Industry Working Conference on Research Challenges*, pp. 209-215, 2000.

4. R. Jha, and S. Iyer. Performance Evaluation of Mobile Agents for E-Commerce Application. *Proc. International Conference on High Performance Computing*, pp. 331-341, 2001.

5. D. Johansen, R. V. Renesse and F. Schneider. An Introduction to the TACOMA Distributed System Version 1.0. Technical Report 95-23, Department of Computer Science, University of Tromso, Norway, 1995.

6. D. B. Lange and M. Oshima. Programming and Deploying Java Mobile Agents with Aglets. Addison Wesley, Massachusetts, USA, 1998.

7. M.G. Rubinstein, O. Carlos, M. B. Duarte and G. Pujolle. Scalability of a Network Management Application Based on Mobile Agents *Proc. 2nd International IFIP-TC6 Networking Conference*, pp. 515-526, 2002.

8. E. Velazquez, N. Santoro, A. Nayak. A Mobile Agent Prototype for Distributed Search. *Proc. 3rd Int. Workshop on Mobile Agents for Telecommunications Applications*, pp. 245-254. 2001.

On the Feasibility of Mobile Video Services for IEEE 802.11b Multicast Networks

Rafael Asorey-Cacheda[1], Francisco J. González-Castaño[1],
José C. Pérez-Gómez[2], Ignacio López-Cabido[2], and Andrés Gómez-Tato[2]

[1] Departamento de Ingeniería Telemática, Universidad de Vigo,
ETSI Telecomunicación, Campus, 36310 Vigo, Spain
{rasorey,javier}@det.uvigo.es
[2] Centro de Supercomputación de Galicia (CESGA), Campus Sur,
Avda. de Vigo s/n, 15705 Santiago de Compostela, Spain
{jcarlos,nlopez,agomez}@cesga.es

Abstract. In this paper, we evaluate the feasibility of mobile video services for IEEE 802.11b multicast networks. We show that progressive encoding (which increases content bandwidth) is not strictly necessary. Depending on the maximum number of multicast content channels in the service, it is possible to achieve negligible demand blocking and expulsion probabilities by increasing the density of access point locations (higher minimum IEEE 802.11b rate available) and/or the number of single-band access points per location (more multicast content channels per location), in a cost-effective way.

1 Introduction

In [1, 2], we proposed a real-time DVB-S-to-IEEE 802.11b transcoding system to generate video contents and an indoor video service to deliver transcoded contents to wireless mobile terminals using IEEE 802.11b multicast. We have focused on IEEE 802.11b because it was the first legal substandard in the European Union with commercial success. Due to EU regulations, IEEE 802.11a was not immediately adopted, which influenced the development of the new substandard IEEE 802.11h (a variant of IEEE 802.11a) [3]. However, the extension of this work to other substandards is straightforward. In [4], we extended the system in [1] to support QoS and inter-LAN roaming.

In this paper, we analyze the feasibility of cost-effective mobile video services for IEEE 802.11b multicast networks. We show that progressive encoding (which increases content bandwidth) is not strictly necessary. Depending on network parameters (number of content channels[1], user arrivals and service times) it is possible to achieve negligible blocking and expulsion probabilities of user requests by increasing the density of access point (AP) locations (higher minimum IEEE

---

[1] A *content channel* is a content transmission, whereas an *IEEE 802.11b channel* is an access point band.

A. Karmouch, L. Korba, and E. Madeira (Eds.): MATA 2004, LNCS 3284, pp. 295–303, 2004.

802.11b rate available) and/or the number of bands per AP[2] (more multicast video channels per location), in a cost-effective way.

The rest of this paper is organized as follows: section 2 reviews the background of this research. Section 3 describes the model of the mobile video service. Section 4 presents simulation results to evaluate mobile video feasibility. Finally, section 5 concludes.

2   Background

Multicast channel scheduling has been studied in the past [5, 6]. However, previous results are not directly applicable to IEEE 802.11. For a given packet slot length, IEEE 802.11 bitrate depends on user position. This has interesting implications from the point of view of content channel scheduling. For example, if we transmit a 1-Mbps stream at 1-Mbps bitrate, 100% of AP bandwidth will be used. However, a 1-Mbps stream at 11-Mbps bitrate will approximately require 10% of available bandwidth, leaving room for more streams. In other words, transmitting a 11-Mbps stream at 11-Mbps requires the same bandwidth as transmitting a 1-Mbps stream at 1 Mbps. Thus, content servers must set the fastest rate possible for a given content channel as far as user location admits it. The strategy in this paper is a novel scheduling approach to support IEEE 802.11 mobile video (to meet blocking and expulsion probability goals and to minimize content channel bandwidth).

Some authors have focused on coding schemes that guarantee QoS regardless of terminal SNR (which depends on user location) [5, 7]. Other authors have investigated the problems that arise when mobile users roam between LANs with different degrees of resource availability, while keeping ongoing connections with remote sources under QoS constraints [8, 9]. In general, they assumed a fixed modulation regardless of user position. In scenarios where modulation varies with user position, it has been argued that progressive encoding such as MPEG-4 FGS is not strictly necessary, since fixed-rate encoding is enough for most wireless applications [10]. Our point is that, *as far as feasibility goals are met*, progressive encoding should be replaced by fixed-rate content channel scheduling (i.e. selecting encoding rates at the server side), to optimize bandwidth usage.

3   A Model for IEEE 802.11b Mobile Video Services

3.1   IEEE 802.11b

IEEE 802.11 [11,12] is a WLAN standard. There are two different ways to configure an IEEE 802.11 network: *ad-hoc* and *infrastructure*. In the first one, mobile nodes form a network "on the fly". The second configuration is based on an infrastructure of fixed APs that support communications between mobile nodes. Obviously, the second configuration imposes less constraints on user terminals.

---

[2] E.g. when placing several single-band APs at the same location.

For this reason, and since our application is generally oriented to closed areas where AP installation is not a problem, we will follow the infrastructure configuration.

IEEE 802.11b physical layer supports dynamic rate shifting up to 11 Mbps: IEEE 802.11b devices transmit at lower rates (5.5 Mbps, 2 Mbps or 1 Mbps) if necessary. When devices move back to places where higher-rate transmissions are possible, they switch back to them.

Remark 1: since there is a single transmission for all the terminals in a multicast group, it is necessary to set the same AP data rate for them all. Thus, the clients of a IEEE 802.11 multicast transmission do not benefit from dynamic rate shifting.

3.2   Multicast Content Channel Scheduler

Our model is based on some basic assumptions: user behaviors are independent. Elapsed time between two consecutive user requests is exponentially distributed with parameter λ. Content channel-watching times are exponentially distributed with parameter μ.

Let p denote the probability of a user to be *active*. Then:

$$p = \frac{\lambda}{\lambda + \mu} \tag{1}$$

If μ is lower than λ there will be too much activity and the system will eventually collapse when there is no room for the multicast content channels required to serve all requests.

Requests may come from any point inside AP range, and the transmission rate triggered by a specific request will depend on the location it comes from. In ideal conditions, IEEE 802.11b transmission rate only depends on the distance to the AP. Table 1 shows the transmission probabilities used in this paper. We assume that requests are uniformly distributed within AP range. Consequently, the probabilities are proportional to the coverage of the corresponding rates. Rate range (radius interval) was determined with a D-Link DWL-1000 AP and D-Link DWL-650 wireless cards.

Not all video content channels are equally popular, and thus some will have more simultaneous users. Content channel requests follow a *preference distribution*. We use the Zipf distribution for this purpose, as suggested in [13].

Table 1. AP range

Rate	Radius (m)	Area (m²)	Probability
11 Mbps	125	49,087.38	0.54
5.5 Mbps	125 - 140	12,487.83	0.14
2 Mbps	140 - 150	9,110.62	0.10
1 Mbps	150 - 170	20,106.19	0.22

Let I be the number of content channels available. Then, the *point probability* of the i-th content channel is:

$$a_i = \frac{i^{-\alpha}}{\sum_{j=1}^{I} j^{-\alpha}}, \tag{2}$$

where parameter α determines content channel popularity. The larger the value of α, the more popular the top channels are compared to the remaining ones. In this paper we set $\alpha = 0.6$ [13].

New requests of a content channel that is already being transmitted at the current user position are always successful. However, a request is *blocked* if there is no transmission bandwidth available to serve it. If we denote multicast blocking probability as B_{mc}, blocking probability of content channel i as B_c^i and blocking probability of content channel i in the X-Mbps region as $B_c^{i,X}$, then:

$$B_{mc} = \sum_{i=1}^{I} a_i B_c^i, \tag{3}$$

$$\begin{aligned} B_c^i = p(r = 1)B_c^{i,1} + p(r = 2)B_c^{i,2} + \\ + p(r = 5.5)B_c^{i,5.5} + p(r = 11)B_c^{i,11}, \end{aligned} \tag{4}$$

where $p(r = X)$ is the probability of user location in the X-Mbps range in Table 1. Let $n_{Blocked}^{i,X}$, $n_{Expelled}^{i,X}$ and $n_{Total}^{i,X}$ be the number of blocked requests, expelled users and total content channel i requests in the X-Mbps region. Then, $B_c^{i,X}$ can be obtained by simulation as:

$$B_c^{i,X} = \frac{n_{Blocked}^{i,X}}{n_{Total}^{i,X}} \tag{5}$$

User *expulsion* from the system depends on the content scheduling algorithm, the rates of the content channels being transmitted and the space available for new allocations. A user is expelled when the system optimizes transmission bandwidth as a result, in case of pending requests. Our approach is as follows:

– If there is no room for an incoming request, the system blocks it if it belongs to the minimum-bitrate range. Otherwise, it stops transmission of a content channel in the minimum-bitrate range. As a result, all users receiving that channel are expelled from the system. By doing so, available bandwidth is maximized. For example, if a 1-Mbps content channel transmission is terminated due to an incoming 2-Mbps content channel request a, the scheduler creates room for a plus an additional 2-Mbps content channel request b or several additional higher-rate requests. User blocking probability is lower in any scenario if expulsion is allowed.
– Consequently, a cost-effective solution is reached if the number of content channels is large enough (10 content channels may transmit the most popular

open TV channels in most European cities), AP geographical density is low (and, as a result, more different bitrates are used) and the number of IEEE 802.11b channels per location is low.

Remark 2: obviously, we plan the system (maximum number of content channels transmitted, geographical density of uniformly distributed AP locations and number of IEEE 802.11b channels per AP location) **for zero blocking and expulsion probabilities**.

Let $E_c^{i,X}$ be the probability of user expulsion from an ongoing transmission of channel i at rate X. Then:

$$E_c^{i,X} = \frac{n_{Expelled}^{i,X}}{n_{Total}^{i,X}}, \tag{6}$$

and we can obtain the multicast expulsion probability E_{mc} in a similar way as we obtained B_{mc} from (4) and (5).

There are two possible strategies to achieve zero blocking and expulsion probabilities. The first one avoids lowest transmission bitrates by installing closer APs. It is important to notice that this strategy decreases the number of request arrivals, since the area serviced by a given AP is smaller. The second strategy consists of deploying multi-band APs (transmitting in several IEEE 802.11b channels) or several single-band APs per location, so that network capacity grows with the number of bands. Any of these strategies (specially the second one) requires IEEE 802.11b channel planning to minimize inter-channel interference. However, it is possible to plan IEEE 802.11b channels for up to three single-band APs per AP location. Finally, a combination of the two strategies is also possible.

It is also important to remark that, when using multiple-band APs, the maximum number of content channels grows *near* linearly with the number of bands, because the transmission of a given content channel cannot be fragmented between different bands.

The **content channel scheduling algorithm** in this paper seeks to maximize the number of multicast content channels transmitted. It consists of the following steps:

1. If a user requests a content channel that is being transmitted at a rate X that can be received at the user location, the user joins the multicast group of the content channel.
2. If the content channel is not being transmitted and there exists free bandwidth space, the server starts a new multicast group for that content channel. Let n_{AP}^i be the number of content channels served by the i-th AP (as explained above, there could be several single-band APs at the same location). Let K be content channel rate (set for subjective quality, including UDP, IP, MAC and PCLP overheads). Let β be the percentage of PCF-mode time $(CFPMaxDuration/CFPRate)$ [14]. When a user in the X-Mbps region requests the content channel, there exists free space in the i-th AP if:

$$\frac{\beta \cdot X}{1 + n_{AP}^i} \geq K. \tag{7}$$

3. If there is no free space available, the server looks for an active content channel transmitted at the lowest rate $Y < X$ with lowest audience, sends a warning message to the users receiving that content channel and assigns it to the incoming request.
4. Finally, the incoming request could be blocked and leave the system, if it were not possible to find a content channel to terminate. As previously said, a careful system planning avoids this.

4   Results

We performed a large number of simulations to determine valid system layouts. However, only the most relevant results are presented graphically. Table 2 summarizes all results.

We considered scenarios with 10, 20, 30 and 40 content channels, following a Zipf request distribution with $\alpha = 0.6$. At each AP location there are 1, 2 or 3 single-band APs. There are three possible AP location densities, corresponding to minimum bitrates per AP of 1 Mbps, 2 Mbps and 5.5 Mbps. Load p in (1) varies in $[0.1, 0.9]$. Content channel rate K is 400 Kbps, including protocol overheads. Finally, $\beta = 0.8$.

Figure 1 shows request blocking probabilities for the possible minimum bitrates (depending on AP location density), for a single AP per location and 40 content channels. We can observe that, when allowing a 1-Mbps minimum bitrate, the system performs poorly. However, if this modulation is eliminated (by AP proximity), blocking probability is practically zero for $p \leq 0.8$. If we only allow a minimum bitrate of 5.5 Mbps, blocking is negligible regardless of load p. We obtained similar results for scenarios with 10-30 content channels.

Figure 2 also shows blocking probability, for one to three APs per location, and for an AP location density corresponding to a minimum bitrate of 1 Mbps.

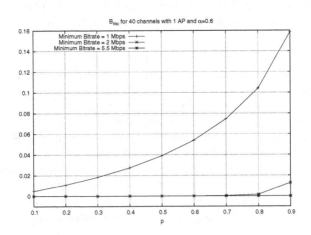

Fig. 1. B_{mc} for 40 content channels with 1 AP and $\alpha = 0.6$

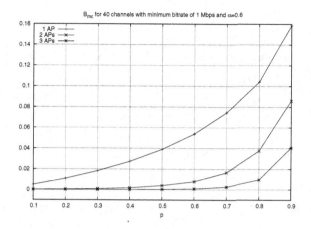

Fig. 2. B_{mc} for 40 content channels with 1-Mbps minimum bitrate and $\alpha = 0.6$

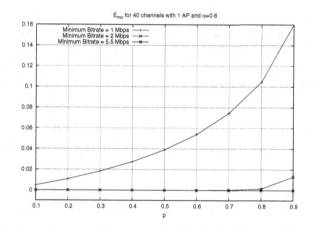

Fig. 3. E_{mc} for 40 content channels with 1 AP and $\alpha = 0.6$

We observe that increasing the number of APs per location is worse than eliminating the lowest bitrates, in terms of blocking probability. Again, we obtained similar results for 10-30 content channels.

Figure 3 shows expulsion probabilities for the AP configurations in Figure 1. The results indicate that the behaviors of expulsion probability and blocking probability are similar.

In our experiments, we considered all possible combinations of APs per location, minimum bitrates and number of content channels. Table 2 shows the configurations that meet a planning goal of zero blocking and expulsion probabilities for $p \leq 0.8$. Note that this goal cannot be attained when allowing the 1-Mbps minimum bitrate and, in the 2-Mbps case, it is necessary to install at least two APs per location (except for the scenario with 10 content channels).

Table 2. Configurations with zero B_{mc} and E_{mc} (number of content channels), $\alpha = 0.6$, $p \leq 0.8$

Minimum Bitrate	1 AP	2 APs	3 APs
1 Mbps			
2 Mbps	10	10,20,30,40	10,20,30,40
5.5 Mbps	10,20,30,40	10,20,30,40	10,20,30,40

Table 3. AP density

Minimum Bitrate	1 AP	2 APs	3 APs
1 Mbps	$1.10 \cdot 10^{-5} APs/m^2$	$2.20 \cdot 10^{-5} APs/m^2$	$3.30 \cdot 10^{-5} APs/m^2$
2 Mbps	$1.41 \cdot 10^{-5} APs/m^2$	$2.83 \cdot 10^{-5} APs/m^2$	$4.24 \cdot 10^{-5} APs/m^2$
5.5 Mbps	$1.62 \cdot 10^{-5} APs/m^2$	$3.25 \cdot 10^{-5} APs/m^2$	$4.87 \cdot 10^{-5} APs/m^2$

In order to determine the best configuration (minimizing AP density), we must compare Table 2 with AP density in Table 3: in most cases, the best choice is a single AP per location and a minimum bitrate of 5.5 Mbps. However, for 10 content channels, a single AP per location and a minimum bitrate of 2 Mbps is a better solution. These results are interesting because (*i*) IEEE 802.11b channel planning is more difficult in a multi-band AP layout and (*ii*) if 10 content channels are enough, inter-channel interference is easier to avoid with longer inter-AP separations.

5   Conclusions and Future Work

In this paper, we have evaluated the feasibility of a mobile video system for IEEE 802.11b multicast networks. Our results indicate that it is possible to serve user requests with zero blocking and expulsion probabilities using video scheduling. Our simulations show that a configuration with a single AP per location works fine if the minimum bitrate is 2-5.5 Mbps (depending on the number of content channels).

Acknowledgments

This research has been supported by project WIPv6 (CESGA, Spain).

References

1. R. Asorey-Cacheda and F.J. González-Castaño, "Real-Time Transcoding and Video Distribution in IEEE 802.11b Multicast Networks," in *Proc. IEEE International Symposium on Computers & Communications 2003*, Kemer - Antalya, Turkey, July 2003.

2. R. Asorey-Cacheda, F.J. González-Castaño et al, "Position-Aware IEEE 802.11b Mobile Video Services," *Lecture Notes in Computer Science* 3166, 2004.
3. *Status of Project IEEE 802.11h.* [Online]. Available: http://grouper.ieee.org/ groups/802/11/Reports/tgh_update.htm, Sept. 2002.
4. F.J. González-Castaño, R. Asorey-Cacheda *et al.*, "QoS provisioning in mobile video services with satellite sources," in *Proc. International Workshop of Cost Actions 272 and 280*, ESTEC, The Netherlands, May 2003.
5. A. Majundar *et al.*, "Multicast and unicast real-time video streaming over wireless LANs," *IEEE Trans. on Circuits and Systems for Video Technology*, June 2002.
6. J. Karvo, *A study of teletraffic problems in multicast networks.* Technical Report, Networking Laboratory / Helsinki University of Technology, Oct. 2002.
7. W. Li, "Overview of fine granularity scalability in MPEG-4 video standard," *IEEE Trans. on Circuits and Systems for Video Technology*, Mar. 2001.
8. J. Chen *et al.*, "Dynamic service negotiation protocol and wireless diffserv," in *Proc. IEEE International Conference on Communications*, 2000.
9. A. Campbell, "Mobiware: QoS aware middleware for mobile multimedia communications," in *Proc. 7th IFIP Intl. Conf. on High Performance Networking (HPN)*, White Plains, New York, USA, Apr. 1997.
10. T. Stockhammer, "Is fine-granular scalable video coding beneficial for wireless video applications?", in *Proc. IEEE International Conference on Multimedia & Expo ICME 2003*, Baltimore-Maryland, USA, July 2003.
11. IEEE 802.11. [Online]. Available: http://grouper.ieee.org/groups/802/11/.
12. C. Chow and V. Leung, "Performance of IEEE 802.11 Medium Access Control Protocol over a Wireless Local Area Network with Distributed Radio Bridges," in *Proc. WCNC'99*, New Orleans, USA, Sept. 1999.
13. L. Breslau, P. Cao, L. Fan, G. Phillips and S. Shenker, "Web caching and Zipf-like distributions: Evidence and implications," in *Proc. INFOCOM'1999*, New York, USA, Mar. 1999.
14. X.J. Dong, M. Ergen, P. Varaiya and A. Puri, "Improving the Aggregate Throughput of Access Points in IEEE 802.11 Wireless LANs," in *Proc. 28th Annual IEEE Conf. on Local Computer Networks*, 2003.

An Analytical Model for Throughput
of IEEE 802.11e EDCA[*]

Sunghak Jeong, Minsu Kim, Jungpil Ryu, Donghun Jo, and Kijun Han[**]

LG Electronics-MOBILE HANDSET R&D CENTER – KOREA
Department of Computer Engineering, Kyungpook National University, Korea
sh_jeong@lge.com, {kiunsen,goldmunt,firecar}@netopia.knu.ac.kr,
kjhan@bh.knu.ac.kr

Abstract. In this paper, we present an analytical model using the bi-dimensional discrete-time Markov chain for the saturated throughput of the IEEE 802.11e EDCA MAC protocol. To validate the proposed analytical model, we carried out a simulation study. The simulation results are in sound agreement with the analytical results. It is shown that differentiating the initial window size is better than differentiating the inter-frame space to support the prioritized QoS.

1 Introduction

In the IEEE 802.11 protocol, the contention-based channel access function, which is called Distributed Coordination Function (DCF), is a fundamental mechanism used to access the wireless medium. The DCF is used for asynchronous data transmission on a best effort basis [1]. The DCF is based on the Carrier Sense Multiple Access with Collision Avoidance (CSMA/CA) protocol with a binary exponential backoff. Recently, the IEEE 802.11 Working Group has been studying a new supplement, IEEE 802.11e MAC, to support QoS. It has a single coordination function, called a hybrid coordination function (HCF), for the QoS provisioning [2]. The HCF combines functions from the DCF and PCF (Point Coordination Function) with some enhanced QoS-specific mechanisms. The HCF uses both a contention-based channel access method, called the enhanced distributed channel access (EDCA) mechanism, for a contention-based transfer, and a controlled based channel access (HCCA) mechanism for a contention-free transfer [2].

In this paper, we present a saturation throughput model of the EDCA using the Markov chain model introduced in [3, 5, 7, 8]. The Markov process has been used in [5, 7, 8] to analyze the saturated throughput of the legacy IEEE 802.11 DCF. The Markov model used in [5, 8] can be regarded as an extension of the model in [6] and it took into account the maximum allowable number of retransmission attempts of MAC frames.

An analytical model for IEEE 802.11e EDCA was also built in [3]. This model, however, assumed infinite retransmission attempts. Therefore, the results overestimated the throughput in saturated conditions. Our work is based on [3], but is somewhat different from [3] in the sense that we consider a finite number of retransmission attempts.

---

[*] University Fundamental Research Program supported by Ministry of Information & Communication in Republic of Korea

[**] Correspondent author.

A. Karmouch, L. Korba, and E. Madeira (Eds.): MATA 2004, LNCS 3284, pp. 304–312, 2004.

The rest of this paper is organized as follows: Section 2 briefly describes the EDCA of the IEEE 802.11e MAC protocol, section 3 describes the system model, which is based on a discrete time Markov chain and computes its stationary probability distribution. Section 4 validates the accuracy of the proposed model via simulation study. Finally, Section 5 presents some conclusions.

2   HCF Contention Based Channel Access

The EDCA mechanism provides differentiated and distributed access to the Wireless Medium (WM) for eight UPs for QSTAs. The EDCA mechanism defines access categories (ACs) that provide support for the delivery of traffic with UPs at the QSTAs[2]. Each frame from the higher layer arrives at the MAC along with a specific user priority value. Each QoS data frame also carries its user priority value in the MAC frame header. Each queue behaves as a single enhanced DCF contending entity. In other words, each queue has its own arbitration inter-frame space (AIFS) and maintains its own backoff counter. When there are more than one AC's finishing the backoff at the same time within a QSTA, the higher-valued AC frame receives the TXOP and will be transmitted. The others, lower-valued colliding AC's behave as if there were an external collision on the WM. However, this kind of collision does not include setting retry bits in the MAC headers of MPDUs at the heads of the lower-valued AC's [2].

Different priority classes, i.e. $i=0, ..., 7$, are implemented by eight priority queues at the QSTAs. At the MAC layer, priorities are determined by *AIFS* and the contention window (CW) size, *CWmin[AC]*, *CWmax[AC]*, instead of *DIFS*, *CWmin*, *CWmax* of the DCF, respectively, to obtain TXOPs. The values of *AIFS[AC]*, *CWmin[AC]*, and *CWmax[AC]* are announced by the QoS Access Point (QAP) via a beacon, probe response and a (re)association response by the inclusion of the EDCA Parameter Set information element [2].

For the priority i class, the minimum backoff window size is *CWmin[i]*, and the AIFS is *AIFS[i]*. *AIFS[i]* is a duration derived from the value *AIFSN[i]* by the relation

$$AIFS[i] = AIFSN[i] \times aSlotTime + aSIFSTime \qquad (1)$$

where the Arbitration Inter-Frame Spacing Number in the priority i class (*AIFSN[i]*) indicates the number of slots, after an SIFS duration, a QSTA should defer before either invoking a backoff or starting transmission. The value of *AIFSN[AC]* depends on the AC. The minimum value for the AIFSN is 2 [2].

Generally, the smaller *AIFSN[AC]* and *CWmin[AC]*, the shorter the channel access delay for the UP, and hence the more bandwidth share for a given traffic condition [8]. Fig. 1 shows that higher priority traffic has a better chance to access the wireless medium earlier. We can see that *AIFS[i]*>*AIFS[j]*>*DIFS*>*PIFS*. In other words, the priority i class has a higher priority than the priority j class. Hence *AIFS[i]* has a better chance to obtain TXOP than *AIFS[j]*.

An EDCA TXOP is granted to a channel access function when the channel access function determines that it shall initiate the transmission of a frame exchange sequence. The new concept with TXOP is limiting the time interval during which a station can transmit its frames. The limit of a TXOP duration is determined by the QAP and is announced to QSTAs via the beacons using the contention-based channel access. It is called an EDCA TXOP and the corresponding QoS CF-poll frame using the controlled channel access. It is called a Polled TXOP [8].

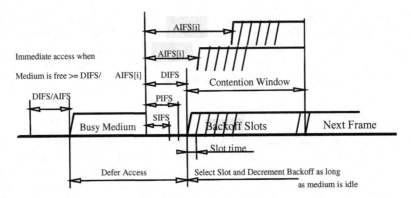

Fig. 1. 802.11e EDCA channel access

3 Analytical Model

In this section, we present an analytical model of the IEEE 802.11e EDCA using the discrete time Markov chain which has been introduced in [3, 6] to build an analytical model of IEEE 802.11e in the saturated condition. Our work is based on [3], but is somewhat different from [3] in the sense that we consider a finite number of retransmission attempts whereas infinite retransmissions are assumed in [3]. In addition, we make corrections of some mistakes made in [3] for computing the throughput of IEEE 802.11e.

3.1 The Markov Chain Model and Probability of Collision

In IEEE 802.11e, the backoff procedure shall be updated when either, 1) the transmission of a frame of an AC fails or 2) the transmission attempt collides internally with another channel access function of an AC that has higher priority [2]. If the short or long retry count for the QoS station has reached aShortRetryLimit or aLongRetryLimit, respectively, $CW[AC]$ shall be reset to $CWmin[AC]$. Otherwise, if the $CW[AC]$ is less than $CWmax[AC]$, the $CW[AC]$ shall be set to the value $(CW[AC])*2 - 1$. If the $CW[AC]$ is equal to $CWmax[AC]$, the $CW[AC]$ shall remain unchanged for the remainder of any retries. Following the update of the value of the $CW[AC]$, the backoff time counter is uniformly chosen in the range (0, $CW[AC]$).

Let $n_i(i=0, ..., 7)$ be the number of active queues in the priority i class, let $b(i, t)$ be the stochastic process representing the backoff time counter, and $s(i, t)$ be the stochastic process representing the backoff stage for a given station in the priority i class at time t. The value of the backoff time counter is uniformly chosen in the range (0, 1, ..., $W_{i,j} - 1$). The value of the $CWmin$ depends on the priority value of queue, i.e. ACs. Every unsuccessful (re)transmission attempt, either a short retry count or long retry count is increased until reaching the maximum short or long retry count [2]. On the other hand, the contention window is increased until reaching the $CWmax$.

Let 'm' mean the trial number until the contention window reaches the maximum allowable value. Let 'a' denote the number of trials up to aShortRetryLimit or aLongRetryLimit after the contention window reaches the maximum allowable value. After $m+a+1$ unsuccessful retransmission, the frame will be dropped from the queue as in [4], [7]. Therefore, the contention window size in the backoff stage j, for the priority i class, which is denoted by $W_{i,j}$, is given by

$$W_{i,j} = \begin{cases} 2^j CW_{\min}[i] & (0 \le j \le m) \\ 2^m CW_{\min}[i] & (m < j \le m+a) \end{cases} \tag{2}$$

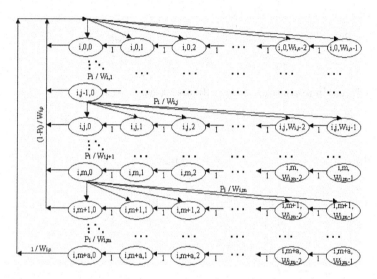

Fig. 2. Markov chain model of the backoff window size for the priority i class

As in [3], we model the EDCF as a bi-dimensional discrete-time Markov chain as depicted in Fig. 2. We denote the probability that a frame is collided by P_i. We assume that the probability P_i is independent of the backoff procedure. In this diagram, the state $\{i, j, k\}$ indicates that the priority class is i, and backoff stage is j, which can take values in the range $(0, 1, ..., m)$, and the backoff counter is k, which can take values in the range $(0, 1, ..., W_{i,j} - 1)$. The channel state, whether the channel is busy or not, is not considered to simplify the model. In the Markov chain, the only non-null one-step transition probabilities are given by

$$\begin{aligned} &\Pr\{(i,j,k) \mid (i,j,k+1)\} = 1 & &k \in [0, W_{i,j} - 2],\ j \in [0, m+a] \\ &\Pr\{(i,j,k) \mid (i,j-1,0)\} = P_i / W_{i,j} & &k \in [0, W_{i,j} - 1],\ j \in [1, m+a] \\ &\Pr\{(i,0,k) \mid (i,j,0)\} = (1-P_i)/W_{i,0} & &k \in [0, W_{i,0} - 1],\ j \in [0, m+a-1] \\ &\Pr\{(i,0,k) \mid (i,m+a,0)\} = 1/W_{i,0} & &k \in [0, W_{i,j} - 1] \end{aligned} \tag{3}$$

These four probabilities account for the following situations, respectively.

1. The backoff time counter of the station in the priority i class decrements at the beginning of each slot time.
2. The station in the priority i class selects a backoff time slot in the next stage j after an unsuccessful transmission in the stage $j - 1$.

3. The station in the priority i class uniformly selects a backoff time slot in the stage 0 if its current frame was transmitted successfully when it transmits a new frame in the queue.
4. Whether the transmission of the current frame is successful or not, the station in the priority i class enters the new backoff procedure, i.e., the contention window is reset to $CWmin[i]$, when it tries to transmit a subsequent frame.

Now, we find out the stationary distribution of the chain, which is denoted by $b_{i,j,k}$, for a given station in the priority i class.

$$b_{i,j,k} = \lim_{t \to \infty} \Pr\{s(i,t) = j, b(i,t) = k\}, \quad \text{for} \quad j \in [0, m+a], k \in [0, W_{i,j}]$$

$$b_{i,j+1,0} = p_i b_{i,j,0} \quad \text{for} \quad j \in [0, m+a-1]$$

(4)

Owing to the chain regularities, for $j \in (0, m+a)$, we have

$$b_{i,j,k} = \frac{W_{i,j} - k}{W_{i,j}} p_i b_{i,j-1,0} = \frac{W_{i,j} - k}{W_{i,j}} b_{i,j,0} \quad \text{for} \quad k \in [1, W_{i,j} - 1]$$

(5)

In addition, for $k \in [1, W_{i,j} - 1]$, it follows that

$$b_{i,0,k} = (1 - p_i) \frac{W_{i,0} - k}{W_{i,0}} \sum_{j=0}^{m+a-1} b_{i,j,0} + \frac{W_{i,0} - k}{W_{i,0}} b_{i,m+a,0}$$

$$= (1 - p_i) \frac{W_{i,0} - k}{W_{i,0}} \sum_{j=0}^{m+a-1} p_i^j b_{i,0,0} + \frac{W_{i,0} - k}{W_{i,0}} p_i^{m+a} b_{i,0,0}$$

(6)

$$= \frac{W_{i,0} - k}{W_{i,0}} b_{i,0,0}$$

From (5) and (6), we can rewrite $b_{i,j,k}$ as

$$b_{i,j,k} = \frac{W_{i,j} - k}{W_{i,j}} b_{i,j,0} \quad \text{for} \quad j \in [0, m+a]$$

(7)

Using the normalization condition and from (7), we can derive

$$\sum_{j=0}^{m+a} \sum_{k=0}^{W_{i,j}-1} b_{i,j,k} = \sum_{j=0}^{m+a} \sum_{k=0}^{W_{i,j}-1} \frac{W_{i,j} - k}{W_{i,j}} b_{i,j,0} = \sum_{j=0}^{m+a} b_{i,j,0} \frac{W_{i,j} + 1}{2} = 1$$

(8)

Substituting (1) into (7), we can figure out $b_{i,0,0}$

$$b_{i,0,0} = \frac{2(1 - 2p_i)(1 - p_i)}{CW_{\min}[i](1 - (2p_i)^{m+1})(1 - p_i) + (1 - p_i^{m+1})(1 - 2p_i)}, \text{ for } j \in [0, m]$$

(9a)

$$b_{i,0,0} = \frac{2(1-2p_i)(1-p_i)}{CW_{\min}[i](1-(2p_i)^{m+1})(1-p_i)+(1-p_i^{m+1})(1-2p_i)+p_i^{m+1}(1-p_i^a)(1+2^m CW_{\min}[i])(1-2p_i)}$$

(9b)

$$\text{for } j \in [m, m+a]$$

Let τ_i be the probability that a station in the priority i class transmits in a uniformly chosen slot time. Each station initiates transmission of a frame when the backoff counter decrements to zero, regardless of the backoff stage. In other words, transmission is triggered at one of the $b_{i,j,0}$ states for $j \in [0, m+a]$. Thus, we can get

$$\tau_i = \sum_{j=0}^{m+a} b_{i,j,0} = \sum_{j=0}^{m} b_{i,j,0} + \sum_{j=m+1}^{m+a} b_{i,j,0}$$

$$= \frac{2(1-p_i^{m+1})(1-2p_i)}{CW_{\min}[i](1-(2p_i)^{m+1})(1-p_i)+(1-p_i^{m+1})(1-2p_i)} +$$

$$\frac{2p_i^{m+1}(1-p_i^a)(1-2p_i)}{CW_{\min}[i](1-(2p_i)^{m+1})(1-p_i)+(1-p_i^{m+1})(1-2p_i)+p_i^{m+1}(1-p_i^a)(1+2^m CW_{\min}[i])(1-2p_i)}$$

(10)

When there are two or more stations in any priority class that transmit at the same time, the transmitted frames will collide. Therefore, the probability p_i that the transmitted frames collide is given by

$$p_i = 1 - \left(\prod_{h=0}^{i-1}(1-\tau_h)^{n_h}\right)(1-\tau_i)^{n_i-1}\left(\prod_{h=i+1}^{7}(1-\tau_h)^{n_h}\right)$$

(11)

From (9), (10), and (11), we can finally determine a unique solution of the unknowns τ_i and p_i using a numerical technique.

Let p_B be the probability that there is at least one transmission in the considered slot time. This means the probability that the channel is sensed as busy. Then we have

$$p_B = 1 - \prod_{h=0}^{7}(1-\tau_h)^{n_h}$$

(12)

Let $p_{X,i}(i = 0,\ldots,7)$ be the probability that transmission for the priority i class is successful. Then it follows that

$$p_{X,i} = n_i\tau_i(1-\tau_i)^{n_i-1}\prod_{h=0,h\neq i}^{7}(1-\tau_h)^{n_h} = \frac{n_i\tau_i(1-p_B)}{1-\tau_i}$$

(13)

Let $T_{s,i}$ and $T_{c,i}$ be the average times when the channel is utilized for a successful transmission for priority class i and the average time when the channel is wasted due to collision, respectively.

In the basic access mode, we have

$$T_{s,i} = T_H + T_p + SIFS + \sigma + T_{ACK} + AIFS[i] + \sigma$$
$$T_{c,i} = T_H + T_p + SIFS + \sigma + T_{ACK} + AIFS[i] + \sigma$$

(14)

where $T_H = PHY_{hdr} + MAC_{hdr}$, and it means the time to transmit the header and σ denotes the propagation delay, and T_p means the time to transmit the payload, T_{ACK} means the time to transmit the ACK.

Now, we find the system throughput for the transmitting payload of the priority i class. Let S_i be the system throughput normalized by a slot time. Then we have

$$S_i = \frac{p_{X,i}L}{(1-p_B)\delta + p_{X,i}T_{s,i} + [p_B - p_{X,i}]T_{c,i}}$$

(15)

where δ denotes the duration of a slot time, and L is the average packet payload size.

4   Simulation

To validate the proposed analytical model, we carried out a simulation study. The simulations consider three types of traffic categories as described in [9]: high priority, medium priority, and low priority. Each station generates the same mix of offered traffic of the three data type frames, which we label as high, medium and low, according to their priorities. In our simulation, we use a fixed number of stations with one station being the AP in a QBSS. We assume that all stations only transmit their packets to AP and AP does not generate its own packets except ACK packets. The system parameters used in the simulation are listed in Table 1. The frame size is fixed as 80 bytes and the ACK frame size is also fixed as 5 bytes. We do not consider the TXOP-Limit and T_H to simplify the simulation. Since *AIFS* is represented by a number instead of time, the actual *AIFS* in time is determined by *SIFS*+ *AIFS* (in number)*slot_time*.

Table 1. System parameters

PHY channel rate		24 Mbps
SIFS		16 *us*
slot_time		9 *us*
High	*AIFS*	2
	CWmin	7
	CWmax	7
Medium	*AIFS*	4
	CWmin	10
	CWmax	31
Low	*AIFS*	7
	CWmin	15
	CWmax	255

Fig. 3a ~ 3b show the saturation throughputs for the three priority classes, which denoted by PC 0, PC 1, and PC 2, obtained when the initial window size is varied while fixing the other parameters. We can see that the saturation throughput decreases as the initial window size increases. This indicates that the high priority class takes a portion of the bandwidth for the medium and low priority classes as the initial window size increases [3]. This is because a longer initial window size means a longer backoff period, and in turn, a longer waiting time and finally a lower throughput.

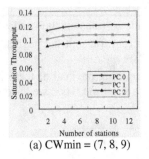
(a) CWmin = (7, 8, 9)

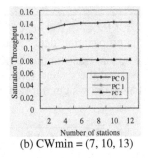
(b) CWmin = (7, 10, 13)

Fig. 3. Saturation Throughput when AIFS = (2, 2, 2)

Fig. 4a ~ 4b show the saturation throughputs for the three priority classes when we vary the AIFS while fixing the contention window size. As illustrated in these figures, differentiating the arbitration inter-frame space does not show a significant difference in the saturation throughput when compared with effects by differentiating the initial window size. This is because the initial window size has both the function for reducing collisions and for providing priorities, whereas the arbitration inter-frame space has the function of providing priorities by accessing a channel earlier or later, but not the function of reducing collisions [3].

From the simulation results, we can conclude that tuning the initial window size is a better solution to provide QoS in the IEEE802.11e wireless LANs. Differentiating the inter-frame space provides a quicker way to implement a priority mechanism for accessing the channel.

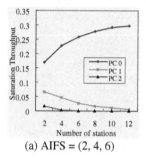

(a) AIFS = (2, 4, 6)

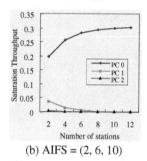

(b) AIFS = (2, 6, 10)

Fig. 4. Saturation Throughput when CW = (15, 15, 15)

5 Conclusions

In this paper, we analyzed the throughput of the IEEE 802.11e EDCA protocol under saturated conditions by using a bi-dimensional discrete time Markov chain. We also carried out a simulation study to validate the analytical model. We could see a sound agreement between the analytical and simulation results. In addition, we have shown that the IEEE 802.11e EDCA priority mechanism was very effective in terms of the saturation throughput. Our study also showed that tuning the initial window size was a better solution to provide QoS in the IEEE802.11e wireless LANs.

References

1. IEEE Std. 802.11-1999, Part11: IEEE Standard for Information technology Telecommunications and information exchange between systems Local and metropolitan area networks Specific requirements Part 11: Wireless LAN Medium Access Control (MAC) and Physical Layer (PHY) Specifications, IEEE Std. 802.11 1999 edition, 1999.
2. IEEE Std 802.11e: Draft supplement to IEEE Std 802.11, 1999 Edition: Wireless Medium Access Control (MAC) and Physical Layer (PHY) specifications: Medium Access Control (MAC) Enhancements for Quality of Service (QoS), IEEE 802.11e/D5.0, July 2003.
3. Yang Xiao, "Enhanced DCF of IEEE 802.11e to Support QoS," *Wireless Communications and Networking 2003*, Vol. 2, pp.1291–1296, March 2003.
4. Hadzi-Velkov, Z., Spasenovski, B. "Saturation Throughput-Delay Analysis of IEEE 802.11 DCF in Fading Channel," *Proc. ICC '03. IEEE International Conference on Communications*, Vol. 1, pp.121–126, Alaska, USA, May 2003.

5. E. Ziouva, T. Antonakopoulos. "CSMA/CA performance under high traffic conditions: throughput and delay analysis," *ELSEVIER Journal on Computer communications 25*, pp.313-321, 2002.
6. G. Bianchi, "Performance Analysis of the IEEE 802.11 Distributed Coordination Function," *IEEE Journal on Selected Areas in Communications*, Vol. 18, No. 3, pp. 535-547, March 2000.
7. Haitao Wu, Yong Peng, Keping Long, Shiduan Cheng, "A simple model of IEEE 802.11 Wireless LAN," *Proc. ICII 2001 - International Conferences on Info-tech & Info-net*, Vol. 2, pp.514–519, Beijing, China, October 2001.
8. Sunghyun Choi, "Emerging IEEE 802.11e WLAN for Quality-of-Service (QoS) Provisioning," *Telecommunications Review*, Vol. 12, No. 6, pp.894-906, December 2002.
9. Stefan Mangold, Sunghyun choi, Peter May, Ole Kelin, Guide Hiertz, Lothar Stibor, "IEEE 802.11e Wireless LAN for Quality of Service," *Proc. European Wireless 2002*, Florence, Italy, February 2002.

Introducing IP Domain Flexible Middleware Stacks for Multicast Multimedia Distribution in Heterogeneous Environments

Kevin Curran and Gerard Parr

Internet Technologies Research Group
University of Ulster, Northern Ireland, UK
{kj.curran,gp.parr}@ulster.ac.uk

Abstract. Extensible middleware is needed to cover small resource constrained devices to full-fledged desktop computers thus we investigate dynamic micro-protocols which enable devices to adopt specific protocol stacks at runtime in an attempt to optimise the stack to the functionality that is actually required by the application thus eliminating additional overhead functionality provided by generic stacks. Multicast media groups allow clients to subscribe to different quality of services in accordance with resource availability and move between groups according to bandwidth availability over time. Performance is increased through application specific tailored protocols & reducing protocol complexity allows stacks to fit inside the limited memory of current mobile devices. We evaluate the dynamic reconfigurability of the middleware and present some results from applications utilising runtime adaptation.

1 Introduction

Chameleon is a Middleware Framework (so named, as it adapts 'automatically' in an 'optimal' manner to a fluctuating network environment delivering streaming media), which supports reconfigurable dissemination oriented communication. Chameleon fragments various media elements of a multimedia application, prioritises them and broadcasts them over separate channels to be subscribed to at the receiver's own choice. The full range of media is not forced on any subscriber, rather a source transmits over a particular channel, and receivers, which have previously subscribed (to the channel), receive media streams (e.g. audio, text and video) with no interactions with the source. Clients are free to 'move' between differing quality multicast groups in order to receive the highest quality (or move to a lower quality group for the greater good of minimising network congestion. This is known as Primary Quality Transformation (PQT). In addition proxies offload intensive computing on behalf of clients and dynamic reconfigurable abilities allow new components to be slotted into live systems. The new components can perform additional transcoding on streams within each group. This is known as Secondary Quality Transformation (SQT). PQT and SQT provide a rich set of features for the optimal reception of multimedia flows. Chameleon is packaged with a core API and a set of Java template classes. The object-oriented design process produces a hierarchy of classes, from which a collection of objects is instantiated to build a particular application. One key idea behind our middleware is the uniform abstraction of services as well as device capabilities via proxies as the application-programming interface. Consequently, the middleware delivers requests to either device services in the middleware or transport protocols.

A. Karmouch, L. Korba, and E. Madeira (Eds.): MATA 2004, LNCS 3284, pp. 313–321, 2004.

Allowing different communication models with respect to the transactional pattern results in a middleware that provides the synchronisation independent of the underlying protocols. Our approach is inspired by micro-kernels as they were introduced into the realm of operating systems [1]. The micro-kernel accepts requests represented as so-called invocation objects, which are typically composed of a source and a target address, an operation with parameters, and additional information concerning the handling of the invocation. The micro-kernel dispatches the invocation to a local service, a local device capability or a transport plug-in, which transports the invocation to a remote micro-kernel. Transports that receive an invocation or a reply to a previous invocation – also represented by an invocation – submit them to the micro-kernel to initiate the dispatching to the corresponding local service or device capability. Invocations can be either generated by proxies, representing a service or a device capability, or manually by the application programmer, e.g. like the request object in the dynamic invocation interface in CORBA. Chameleon addresses the network congestion and heterogeneity problem by taking into account the differing nature and requirements of multimedia elements such as text, audio and video thereby creating tailored protocol stacks which distribute the information to different multicast groups allowing the receivers to decide which multicast group(s) to subscribe to according to available memory, display resolutions and network bandwidth availability. Chameleon supports dissemination of multimedia from a source to multiple destinations however end-to-end closed-loop control can be difficult and cumbersome with multiple receivers, as the slowest receiver will impede the progress of the others therefore we have adopted an alternative approach that relies on very loose coupling between the source and the receivers, i.e. an open-loop approach, more suited to real-time continuous media as shown in Figure 1. Multimedia is composed of varying types such as audio, video, text, control information, etc. Within these types, exists a multitude of formats such as PCM, JPEG, and MPEG etc. Take the example of a conference application, where control information and files need to be transmitted alongside audio and video. The control information such as who has floor control and files need reliable transport guarantees, whereas the audio and video may be transmitted with a differing QoS. Traditional transport protocols transport the media types through the same stack. If a video stream is filtered through the same stack as an audio stream, the video data will have to adopt the packet size allocated to the audio stream. Audio in general runs more efficiently with smaller packet sizes [2].

Isochronous multimedia traffic can tolerate some loss however data that misses its expected delivery time is of no use. Therefore it is more efficient to lose smaller packets than larger packets however, smaller packets demand increased header processing in routers. Small packet sizes are not optimal for video data due to the increased size of the media involved. Using an identical protocol stack to cater for all these transport types is not an ideal scenario therefore a more efficient method would construct optimised protocol stacks for each of the media e.g. audio, text and video. Maximum benefit would be achieved if this could be implemented at run-time to cater for the applications particular preferences. A traditional stack belonging to a multimedia application, for example, would send the audio and video in packets of identical size. Research shows that optimal audio packets are smaller in size than video packets [3]. Multiple multicast multimedia groups provide a finer granularity of control compared to using a single video/audio/text stream, because a receiver may subscribe to one or more layers depending on its capabilities. If a receiver experiences packet loss as a result of network congestion, moving to a lower quality multicast group will reduce congestion, and hence will reduce potential packet loss. This is known as Primary Quality Transformation (PQT).

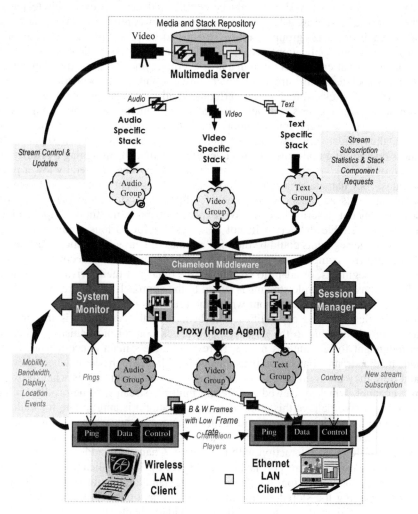

Fig. 1. Chameleon Architecture View

This technique allows media to be composed into broad bandwidth encoded qualities thus all a system needs to do to increase or decrease quality is to move between multicast groups. The Secondary Quality Transformation (SQT) technique compliments this technique by providing fine-grained control of quality within each multicast group by the insertion of transformations in the stream such as compression. The application of multiple multicast group streaming techniques to mobile devices allows the allocation of resources based on local specifications and priorities. Multicast group streaming enables receivers to change the quality of the stream they receive, independently of one another without the source being aware of the change. Considering the feedback problems of multicast, this is a useful property and fits well with an open-loop approach to congestion control of high-speed networks, as when network congestion arises, it is possible to move between quality groups without interruption in service. Service quality should only be slightly reduced however; this technique can be highly effective as a last resort for congestion control. Priorities can be assigned to each multicast group to allow streams to be protected against competing streams. This is an application level QoS scheme and can be implemented easily in Chameleon as all streams pass through a proxy. Pre-set priority levels overcome many problems associated with streaming over wireless links. Atmospheric conditions, physical obstacles, electromagnetic interference and other phenomena interfere with transmissions over wireless channels, ultimately introducing bit errors. Long lasting error bursts can severely impact upon applications, causing video frames to be dropped, thus effectively lowering the perceived quality. Chameleon supports the seamless operation of real-time streams over wireless links by assigning a priority and a portion of the link's resources, which are protected from being used by lower priority streams. As Chameleon is an open-loop system, a segment with its size defined by the application, is an independent piece of information, similar to the Application Data Unit concept described in [4]. We expect that many multimedia applications, guarantees of reliable delivery will not be necessary for various media component types, and some segments could be dropped at times of heavy congestion. Particularly for lower priority components, applications would be expected to recover gracefully from loss of segments, or adapt to changes in the delays of their arrivals. Performing transformations on multiple streams is suited to the approach of a source transmitting multiple coded media streams from which the receivers pick according to their individual specifications and capabilities. The benefit of this approach is that there is reduced complexity due to the absence of feedback control mechanisms, which are often redundant for continuous media. Here the source's main concern is to deliver various media streams onto a multicast channel, with no emphasis on where they end up and how they are used. A client's (or receiver's) main concern is what to extract from a channel, which is viewed as offering multiple streams, some or all of which are of interest. We believe this communication paradigm is appropriate for multimedia distribution services such as video-on-demand systems where a single source generates video (and associated audio) distributed to a large set of receivers who generally have little or no interaction with the source. Chameleon addresses application, application control, and transport layers (see Figure 2). The application layer consists of the multimedia application (e.g., a video-on-demand application) which is responsible for retrieving the stored audio/video file with captions/subtitles (multilingual), composition at the sending end, and the audio/video client which is responsible for decoding and displaying the video frames at the receiving end.

Application control consists of a media filter at the sending side to demultiplex each stream into several sub streams, and media filter at the receiving end to multiplex back one or more sub streams for the audio/video client. These multiplexed streams (transport layer) differ from common practice in that these streams are not logically grouped together and shipped over the wire. Instead, the media elements are divided into audio/video/text by the event filter and distributed to separate groups in accordance with application layered framing practice and then the receiving filter directs the streams to the relevant media application, thus the streams retain their distinctiveness. Media may be stored in separate files on the server and so that there is

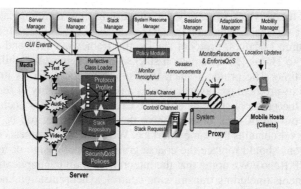

Fig. 2. Architectural overview of Chameleon components

no need to split the media in real-time. The application media filter receives events from the application which may categorised them as text, audio or video. A session manager is consulted to see how many groupings of each category are required. The normal is one for text, and three each for audio and video. The text stack is composed as a reliable stack. The audio/video stacks are both UDP differing in default packet size and header sizes. Each media is sent to separate multicast groups where the well-known addresses are obtained from the session manager. Each of the three sub-groups of audio and video will require a separate multicast address. Since the network load changes during a session, a receiver may decide to join or leave a multicast group, thereby extending or shrinking the multicast trees. Clearly, the requirement for uniform access of device capabilities as well as remote services can be easily established by our approach. The micro-kernel allows the flexible integration of new transport plug-ins and device capabilities by simply registering a new entity, which accepts an invocation. This allows the provision of access to all features available on resource-rich computer systems. The minimal functionality of the adopted protocol stacks allows the deployment of the middleware on resource-poor devices as well. The uniform reduced instruction set programming abstraction is provided by the service abstraction for remote service network access and device capabilities. When we add the extensibility of the middleware, we find that we satisfy the first and third requirement identified earlier. The middleware allows protocols to be dynamically loaded and configured through the invocation abstraction, which satisfies the second requirement. The middleware is implemented in Java allowing it to be deployed on all platforms for which a Java VM exists. The proliferation of end-systems besides classical computers capable of executing Java, such as cell-phones or PDAs, and the aforementioned embedded systems make Java a suitable starting point providing a uniform abstraction for our middleware. The benefit of our micro-protocol stack approach compared to existing middleware platforms is the minimal footprint needed for a basic configuration which qualifies it for small embedded systems as well as the extensibility providing the means to use features of more sophisticated computers.

1.1 Stack Management

Central to providing an adaptable QoS is the ability to maintain multiple protocol stacks. A protocol stack consists of a linear list of protocol objects and represents a quality of service such as reliable delivery or encrypted communication. The framework provides the services necessary for supporting new communication protocols and qualities of service. Chameleon consists of a set of Java classes for representing Uniform Resource Locators, protocol stacks, the framework API and media packet objects similar to Horus [5]. Chameleon stacks however, have the ability to be configured at run-time. The protocol stack uses micro-protocols in its implementation where each micro-protocol (or layer) enforces a part of the quality of service property guaranteed by the protocol stack as a whole. Creating a layer for each property and stacking them on top of each other achieve the properties desired by the user of a stack as each layer contains the same interface. We argue that synthesis of 'fine grain' protocol functions should replace the coarse grain protocol design of traditional protocols (e.g. TCP Reno). We argue that the integration of all the application communication requirements (including transmission control, synchronisation and presentation encoding) in a single optimised protocol graph will result in increased performance, which is in line with the ALF architecture. The protocol profiler is used to configure a protocol that satisfies the optimal protocol configuration as defined in the profiler for each media.

1.2 Adaptation Management

Chameleon adopts a centralised adaptation architecture where system monitor components are embedded in the application components and/or middleware. A centralised System Resource Decision making component periodically receives event information from these monitors and reacts according to QoS policies defined by the system administrator. The adaptation process repeats a cycle of estimating, deciding and acting with the use of observation variables, which capture relevant aspects of the system status. To address both mobility and QoS issues, two alternative but complementary architecture solutions have been identified. The first approach purely leverages existing protocols and components defined (or being defined) by the IETF, and tries to provide the necessary extensions to them. The choice of this organisation is due to the fact the Chameleon architecture is IP-centric and so therefore no modifications of existing applications are needed. The second approach presumes instead the availability of some middleware, which is providing the major functionality for dealing with mobility and QoS issues, as well as offering several Application Programming Interface (API) functionalities for to-be-developed applications. Both viewpoints are therefore synthesised in a modular fashion, indicated by different types of application classes in the architecture. There are likely to be lots of variations and developments at the lower levels, and the lower layer protocols will only provide a certain level of QoS that needs to be enhanced for many applications. Hence the need for a middleware layer to provide suitable abstraction from the networking layers and facilitate session layer QoS processing. Mobile terminals moving into regions with low signal quality or handing-off to new access points, may violate the QoS contract with the network, which can cause the frequent dropping of connections. This requires QoS adaptation and even re-negotiation. All these conditions require the applications to be adaptive in a sense that applications have to react to varying resource availability inside the network and the end systems.

In order to simplify the programming of mobile broadband applications and to allow for support of dynamic QoS changes, these active adaptation mechanisms should be hidden to application programmers. The idea of shifting adaptation mechanisms from the application level to a flexible middleware featuring QoS functions will

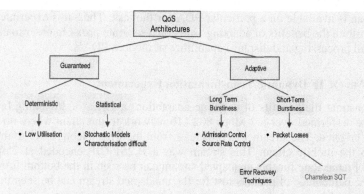

Fig. 3. Architectural view of SQT in the QoS scheme

thereby result in simplified application development for mobile environments. The goal of Chameleon is to allow any kind of application to get the desired level of support from the system in other open environments like the Internet.

Figure 3 illustrates where SQT fits in relation to common approaches to providing network QoS. For instance, the Primary Quality Transformation algorithm assumes responsibility for coarse grain adaptation decisions. This involves moving between multicast groups upon violation of group bandwidth limits. Secondary Quality Transformation assumes responsibility for responding to quality fluctuations within each group. The SQT technique works through the use of transcoder mechanisms, which transform the data as it flows through the proxy. Transformations could include downgrading a full colour 30fps AVI movie to a Black and White 15fps MPEG movie. PQT with priority relies on third party traffic being disabled (or rate controlled). This can be achieved through the technique of blocking ports. Traffic types within Chameleon are assigned port numbers to designate media type and these work alongside the well know port numbers assigned to traffic such as FTP, TCP etc. in order to bring about prioritised media traffic streams.

2   Evaluation

Distributed multimedia applications require efficient data throughput in order to serve up reasonable viewing to end users. As previously discussed, this is not always possible in mobile heterogeneous environments therefore adaptation of media under variable resource constraints is a means to maintain an optimal quality level. Chameleon utilises a proxy to perform adaptation of streams in order to provide an enhanced viewing experience for mobile clients. The expected benefits from this adaptation are to move computation from the client to the proxy and in addition to reduce the volume of data transferred to the client. This takes place by modification of the streaming media in real-time. These modifications can have a significant impact on the quality of media received. This set of experiments is an investigation into one aspect of dynamic video adaptation. Here a performance evaluation of the ability to perform dynamic runtime adaptation of multimedia is conducted. Mobile terminals differ in terms of processor and display capacities thus displaying a video encoded for a desktop machine on a PDA can be inefficient. The PDA in this case is required to resize the video on the fly in order to display it. This reconfiguration can require more CPU power than is available on a particular PDA for the task. Thus, this experiment aims to demonstrate the benefits of adapting video on a separate proxy in order to allow for the limited processing and display capabilities of modern PDA's.

2.1 CIF to QCIF Dynamic Transformation Experiment

To demonstrate the benefits of dynamic adaptation, a series of streaming broadcast tests were performed over a 2 Mbps 802.11b network to the client where no adaptation was invoked. The stream was broadcast from the Chameleon server to the proxy and onto the mobile client. This stream was a H.261 CIF encoded at 25fps. The achieved Frame Rate for this unadapted stream can be seen in the bottom line of Figure 4. The percentage of packets lost for the unadapted stream can be seen in the top line of Figure 5.

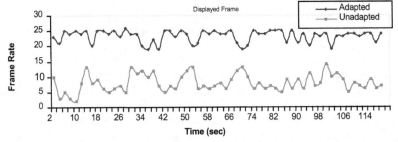

Fig. 4. Displayed Frame Rate over 802.11b

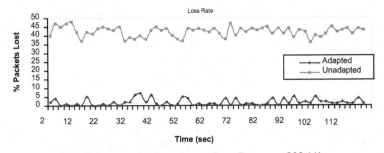

Fig. 5. Impact of Adaptation on Loss Rate over 802.11b

A series of tests were then conducted with the adaptation proxy in place. Here the H.261 CIF stream at 25 fps was forwarded over the Ethernet to the proxy who resized the video to QCIF (176x144) and reduces the quality by 20%. To demonstrate any benefits from this adaptation, measurements of the loss rate, frame rate and data rate were performed on the client. Figure 4 illustrates the displayed frame rate on the client when adaptation is performed and when adaptation is not performed. It shows that the client's reception of video is dramatically improved when the CIF stream is reduced to a QCIF stream. This is more than watchable on a PDA and most PDA's are incapable of displaying a larger picture. When the CIF stream is forwarded to the client without transformation into a QCIF screen size, the frame rate averages out at only 5-7 fps. The 22-25 fps achieved through the proxy transcoding is a more desirable experience. The transformation results in the original frame rate being achieved by the client howbeit at a reduced screen size.

Figure 5 shows the measured loss when no adaptation is invoked. Here the loss rate averages out at 40-45%. Packet losses can be caused as a result of network congestion but here the cause is due to the processor overload. Due to the limitations of the PDA screen, the original CIF stream must be resized to fit on the CIF sized screen thus valuable processing time is taken from the application thus causing high packet losses and increased processing. When adaptation is invoked, it can be seen that the percentage of packets lost averages out at about 4-6%. There can be multiple wireless clients downstream awaiting the output from the transcoding session so the transcoding operation will only need to be applied once but the filtered stream will be replicated to multiple clients. It is clear that by employing adaptation the loss rates are reduced (averaging 40%) and a more stable channel is seen by the application. As mentioned previously many handheld devices such as smart phones are incapable of displaying video beyond the QCIF format therefore it is wasteful for these clients to attempt to receive the larger original encoding streams. The role of a proxy in reducing the original stream to a more suitable reduced format should not be under-estimated. This experiment demonstrates the power of middleware which can utilise proxies to off-load re-encoding of video in order to achieve a higher satisfaction level when viewing. This re-enforces the usefulness of proxies in filtering media prior to distribution over bandwidth limited links to resource constrained clients.

3 Conclusion

This paper has presented some new results from a middleware equipped with adaptation mechanisms, which strives to achieve maximum throughput to resource-constrained devices in heterogeneous environments. Trends in system design, which support the need for Chameleon, include the increasing popularity of component architectures that reduce development time and offer freedom with choice of components. This allows alternative functionality to be deployed in various scenarios to combat differing QoS needs. The middleware presented here allows a client to request a multimedia stream from a selection of pre-encoding media residing at separate multicast group addresses.

References

1. R. Rashid, D. Julin, D. Orr, R. Sanzi, R. Baron, A. Forin, D. Golub, M. Jones: Mach: A System Software kernel. Proceedings of 34th Computer Society International Conference (COMPCON 89), February 1989
2. Eytan Modiano. An adaptive algorithm for optimizing the packet size used in wireless ARQ protocols. MIT Lincoln Laboratory, Lexington, MA 02420-9108, USA. Wireless Networks, Vol (5), No 4 (1999)
3. Society Of Cable Telecommunications Engineers, Inc. Audio codec requirements for the provision of bi-directional audio service over cable television networks. Data Standards Subcommittee Document: SCTE DSS-00-01 December 15, 2000
4. Handley, Mark. The SDR Session Directory. Tech Report: UCL, London. http://mice.ed.ac.uk/mice/archive, 1997
5. Maffeis, S. Mobile Services for Java-enabled Devices on 3G Wireless Networks, In: World market Research Report, 2002 http://www.softwired-inc.com/people/maffeis/publications.htm

Mobile Tourist Guide Services with Software Agents

Juan Pavón[1], Juan M. Corchado[2], Jorge J. Gómez-Sanz[1], and Luis F. Castillo Ossa[2]

[1] Dep. Sistemas Informáticos y Programación, Universidad Complutense Madrid
Ciudad Universitaria s/n, 28040, Madrid, Spain
{jpavon,jjgomez}@sip.ucm.es
http://grasia.fdi.ucm.es
[2] Dep. Informática y Automática, Universidad de Salamanca
Plaza de la Merced s/n, 37008, Salamanca, Spain
corchado@usal.es
http://gsii.usal.es/

Abstract. Applications for mobile devices have some restrictions because of the limited capabilities and heterogeneity of these devices. However, their communication capabilities allow the distribution of the application control and access to information in a network. If we also consider the changing environment when a user moves from one location to another, we should have software that is context-aware and able to adapt to new situations. Agent technology can support these requirements because of its distributed nature and the ability to combine flexible component architectures, some of them with planning and learning capabilities, which are appropriate for adapting to changing environments. In this paper we show one such application, a mobile tourist guide service, which has been built as a multi-agent system, where some agents are deliberative and combine the Beliefs-Desires-Intentions approach with learning capabilities of Case Base Reasoning techniques.

Keywords: Mobile Services, Tourism Application Software, Software Agents, Ambience Intelligence, INGENIAS agent-oriented methodology

1 Introduction

Applications for mobile devices have some restrictions because of the limited capabilities (battery lifetime, processor and memory capacity, small display and keyboard) and heterogeneity of these devices. However, their size, portability, and communication capabilities provide opportunities for new types of services. The telecommunication industry expects a new expansion with the development of UMTS and third generation mobile systems. New challenges of this field require a technology that facilitates the construction of more dynamic, intelligent, flexible and open applications, capable of working in a real time environment. Because of its distributed nature software agents are a promising approach for addressing these issues. Furthermore, when considering mobile services we should also be concerned about changes in the environment when a user moves from one location to another. Therefore, the software should be context-aware and able to adapt to new situations. Multiagent systems can fit in changing environments, as they are built as a combination of flexible components, some of them with planning and learning capabilities.

This paper presents a tourist guide service, which works on mobile devices, as an application of agent technology that addresses these issues. There are several types of

A. Karmouch, L. Korba, and E. Madeira (Eds.): MATA 2004, LNCS 3284, pp. 322–330, 2004.

agents in the system, some of them working in the mobile devices, essentially for interaction with the user, and others distributed in servers, which have advanced information processing and reasoning capabilities. One interesting fact concerning these second type of agents is the way they combine the Beliefs-Desires-Intentions (BDI) approach [7] with learning capabilities of Case Base Reasoning (CBR) techniques [2, 3], which facilitates context-aware behaviour, that makes use of past experiences to find the best plans to achieve goals. The whole system has been designed using an agent-oriented methodology, INGENIAS [6]. One of the motivations of this paper is to show how a real service for mobile devices can be developed using agent-related concepts and principles, and this is illustrated with this methodology.

The next section describes the mobile tourist guide service and its main components, which are organized as a multi-agent system. The system is able to program a tourist route, and modify it according to the conditions of the places to visit and the available time for the tourist. Because of its design, the services of the tourist guide agent can be easily extended (e.g. to recommend restaurants in the area of the tourist route), and support a high degree of scalability in the number of users. Section 3 describes the agents in the system. Section 4 presents the results of the validation of the system by tourists of Salamanca who have used it. Finally, section 5 highlights some of the main contributions of this kind of systems for providing new services and considers some open issues.

2   The Mobile Tourist Guide Service as a Multi-agent System

The Mobile Tourist Guide Service, called *TOURIST GUIDE-USAL*, provides a set of agents to assist potential tourists in the organization of their tourist routes and enable them to modify their schedules on the move using wireless communication systems. There is one assistant agent for each user of the system, the *Performer Agent*. Each user (tourist) willing to use the system has to register and solicit one of these agents. A *Performer Agent* can then be installed in the mobile phone of the tourist and rovide an interface such as the one depicted in Figure 1. To start using the system, the tourist has to provide a set of parameters, such as visiting period of time and a number of restrictions related to cost and tourist interest (e.g., monuments or architectonic style).

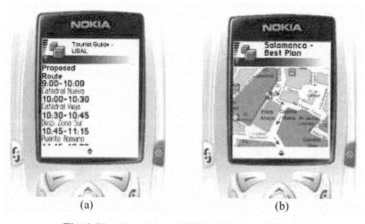

(a)   (b)

Fig. 1. User interface to TOURIST GUIDE-USAL

Once the tourist has configured the preferences for a tour, the associated *Performer Agent* will contact with the *Planner Agent*, which assesses tourists and help them to identify tourist routes in the city taking into account their preferences. *Planner Agents* reside in network servers, as they have to process a considerable amount of information, both descriptive data and cases from past experiences. *Planner Agents* are supported by *Tracker agents*, which maintain updated information about the monuments, the restaurants, public transport conditions, etc. For instance, whether a monument is open for visitors, and whether there is a waiting queue. These agents maintain horizontally and vertically compiled information on hotel accommodation, restaurants, the commercial sector and transport, in order to meet the needs of the potential visitor on an individually customized basis, and respond to requests for information, reservations and purchases in the precise moment that they are expressed.

The design of the agent system has been done following the INGENIAS methodology [6] and using its supporting tools (the INGENIAS Development Kit, available at http://ingenias.sourceforge.net). Figure 2 shows that the agent organization, TOURIST GUIDE USAL, has two groups of agents. One is the group of agents which are deployed on the mobile devices and the other consists of those agents that run on servers. A *Performer Agent* can run either on the mobile device (if it has enough capabilities, and the user authorizes its installation), or in a server (in this case the interface with the user will be simpler, by using SMS, and limited to the display of routes and schedules in text form). The user may decide whether to install the corresponding *Performer Agent* on a mobile phone or PDA, or run it on the server and interact with it via its mobile device. The first choice supposes a reduction of the cost,

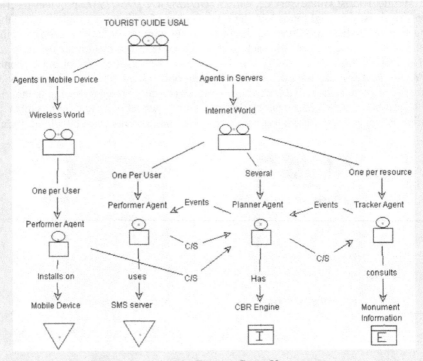

Fig. 2. Organization of the TOURIST GUIDE USAL agent system

since the tourist can interact with his agent as much as needed at no cost because it is installed in the wireless device. Nevertheless, in both cases the agent will have to contact regularly with the *Planner Agent*.

Tracker Agents consult information about monuments in the corresponding information sources (e.g., web servers when available or by an update service, which should be maintained by the city tourist department). As we do not want to limit the type of information sources, these are modelled as objects, for instance *Monument_Information* in Figure 2, which are wrapped by *Tracker Agents*. In this way we encapsulate the access to different types of information sources.

The *Performer Agents* interact with the *Planner Agent* looking for plans, and the *Tracker Agent* interacts with the *Planner Agent* to exchange information (a *Planner Agent* request for information to a *Tracker Agent* and can register for events; therefore, Client/Server and Event channel associations are established between these agents, as shown in Figure 2). The *Planner agent* is the only deliberative agent in this architecture, and has been built as a BDI agent that makes use of a CBR engine in order to be able to adapt to changing conditions by using past experience to decide which plans to propose. The *Performer Agents* can be considered assistant agents and the *Tracker Agent* is a reactive agent.

3   Agents Design

Each agent is initially described by identifying its responsibilities (what goals an agent is compromised to pursue) and capabilities (what tasks is able to perform). The three agent types in the Mobile Tourist Guide System are represented in Figure 3 (*Planner Agent*), Figure 4 (*Performer Agent*), and Figure 5 (*Tracker Agent*).

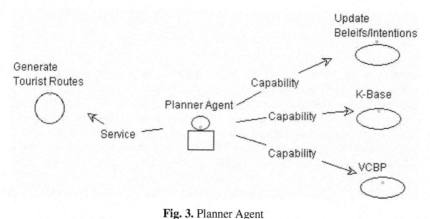

Fig. 3. Planner Agent

The behavior of each agent is defined with three components:

- Mental state, an aggregation of mental entities such as goals, beliefs, facts, and compromises.
- Mental state manager, which provides for operations to create, destroy and modify mental entities.
- Mental state processor, which determines how the mental state evolves, and it can be described in terms of rules, planning, etc.

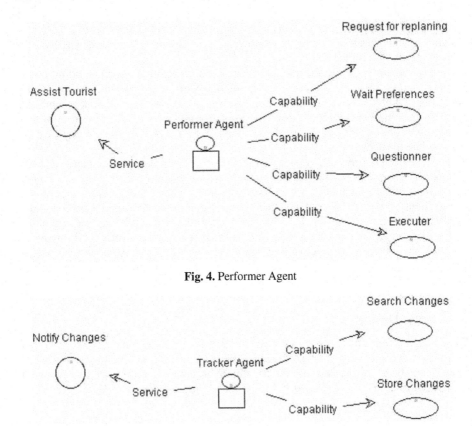

Fig. 4. Performer Agent

Fig. 5. Tracker Agent

Mental state can be seen as all the information that allows the agent to take decisions. This information is managed and processed in order to produce agent decisions and actions, by the mental state manager (M) and processor (P). The advantage of separating management and processing of mental state is the decoupling of the mechanisms that implement the autonomy and intelligence of the agent from the conceptualization of the agent. In the case of the Planner Agent, Figure 6 shows the main mental state entities and the type of Mental state manager and processor. This agent is modeled using BDI concepts but the implementation relies on the use of a CBR engine. Therefore, mental state entities are regarded as cases. This is described in detail in another paper [3].

The responsibility of the *Planner Agent* is to provide adequate plans to the Performer Agent given a number of conditions. This is represented as a goal *Generate Tourist Route*. This goal is refined in a goals/task diagram (Figure 7), which shows how the goal is broken down in sub-goals that can be achieved by execution of tasks. In this case, the goal involves the identification of those beliefs and intentions that can be used to generate a tourist route, and maintaining up-to-date those beliefs and intentions.

Some tasks require the collaboration of other agents through interactions, as the one defined in Figure 8, which shows how the Tracker Agent collaborates to keep

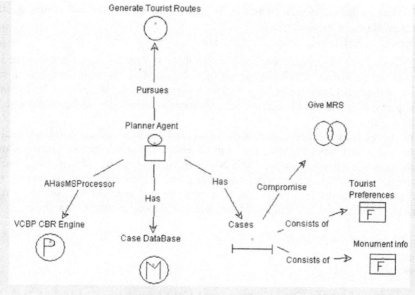

Fig. 6. Planner Agent behaviour elements

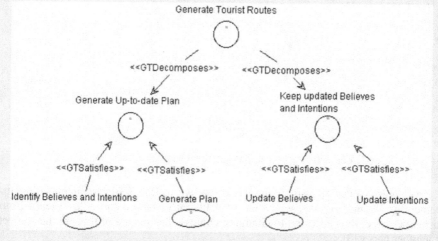

Fig. 7. Goals/Tasks diagram for the Planner Agent

track of changes in information about a monument. An interaction requires the identification of:

- Actors in the interaction: who plays the role of initiator and who are the collaborators. Which is the reason (goal) that motivates each actor to participate in the interaction.
- Definition of interaction units: messages, speech acts.
- Definition of the possible orders of interactions units: protocols.
- Which actions are performed in the interaction.

- Context of the interaction: which goal pursues the interaction and which are the mental states of its participants.
- Control model: coordination mechanisms.

The interaction diagram in Figure 8 shows that the *Tracker Agent* initiates the interaction with a FIPA INFORM to notify of a change. The reason to do this is to satisfy its goal of providing the service *NotifyChanges* to registered agents. The *Planner Agent* participates in the interaction as collaborator, as it looks to keep updated its beliefs and intentions.

The rest of the goals and capabilities are worked out in a similar way. Each goal is broken down into subgoals, until they can be associated with concrete tasks (following the activities defined in the INGENIAS methodology [6]). When they require cooperation with some other agent, the interaction is described, by considering the motivation. Interaction diagrams can be complemented with AUML sequence diagrams in order to show the temporal relationship between the interaction units.

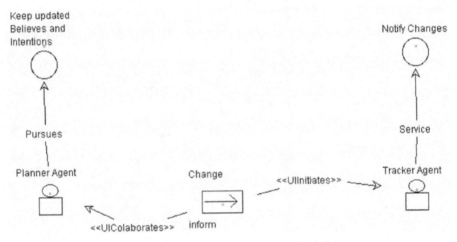

Fig. 8. Interaction of Planner Agent with Tracker Agent

An interesting design issue is the use of an hybrid BDI-CBR architecture for implementing Planner Agents, which are of deliberative nature and able to learn from past experience, thus adapting to changing context. The details of this are the subject of another paper [3].

4   Evaluation Results

The proposed system has been used to improve an agent based system developed for guiding tourists around the city of Salamanca. As mentioned before, the tourists may use a mobile device to contact their agents and to indicate their preferences (monuments to visit, visits duration, time for dinner, amount of money to spend, etc.). Planner Agents keep different types of *cases*. The cases store information about the environment, for example the opening and closing times of monument. This type of information can be seen as an agent believe, for example, The Museum of Contemporary Art opens form 9:00 to 14:00 and from to 16:30 to 20:00. Cases may also be previous successful routes (plans), which include the monuments to visit, the time to spend visiting each monument, information about the cost of the visit, the time required for going to one place to another, the characteristics of the route (museum route, family route, university route, roman route, gothic route, etc.), etc. Once a tourist contacts the system he has to describe his profile, to select the type visit in which he is interested in, to determine how much money he wants to spend and for how long, and the type of restaurants he, she or a family like more. This information is used to construct the *problem case*. Then the reasoning mechanism of the planning agent generates the plan, as described in [3].

The initial system, was tested from the 1st of May to the 15th of September 2003. The case base was initially filled with information collected from the 1st of February to the 25th of June 2003. Local tourist guides provided the agent with a number of standard routes. Three hotels of the City offered the option to their 6217 guests to use the help of the agent or a professional tourist guide, 14% of them decided to use the agent based system and 23% of them used the help of a tourist guide. The rest of the tourists visited the city by themselves. During this period the *Planner agent* stored in its case base 1630 instances of tourist circuits, which covered a wide range of all the most common options that offers the City of Salamanca. The system was tested during 135 days and the results obtained were very encouraging. In this experiment the agent intentions were related to a one-day route (a maximum of 12 hours). On the arrival to the hotel the tourists were asked to evaluate their visit and the route. Table 1 shows the responses given by the tourists after their visit. The tourists that used the help of the agent-based tourist guide provided the answer directly to the agent.

Table 1. Tourists evaluation

	%	Evaluation - degree of satisfaction				
Tourists that...		8-10	6-8	4-6	0-4	No answer
Used the help of the agent	14%	(55,9%)	(4,7%)	(2,4%)	(0,7%)	(36,3%)
Used the help of a tourist guide	23%	(62,7%)	(19,6%)	(8,9%)	(1%)	(7,8%)
Did not use any of the previous	63%	(16,7%)	(8,3%)	(1,2%)	(0,2%)	(78,8%)

Table 1 shows the degree of satisfaction of the tourists. As it can be seen, the degree of satisfaction of the tourist that used the help of a professional tourist guide is higher that in the other two cases. Nevertheless, the percentage of the tourists whose degree of satisfaction was very high (between 8 and 10) is very similar in the case of the tourists that use the help of the agent and in the case of the tourists that use the tourist guide. 38% of the tourists that used the agent based system let us know that the system did not work successfully due to technical reasons (possibly the server was down, there was a lack of coverage, the tourist did not use the wireless system adequately, etc.) If we take this into consideration, we can say that most of the tourist (92%) that used the help of the agent and did not have technical problems had a high or very high degree of satisfaction (6-10). This degree of satisfaction is higher that the one of the tourist (82,3%) that used the help of a tourist guides.

5 Conclusions

The development of mobile services can benefit from the use of agents as they can easily distribute capabilities between user terminals and servers in a network. One important feature of mobile services is that they can be context-aware. As the user moves from one location to another, new information should be taken into account. This requires some adaptation mechanisms which are normally difficult to implement in a mobile phone because of its limited computing capabilities. In this sense, the collaboration with agents in powerful servers is a solution. Furthermore, in an application as the one presented here, users are normally new to the system, so there is no past experience from them. However, collective experience from other users in the system can be combined to get this knowledge. This is the approach that has been followed by the Planner Agent.

The use of an agent development methodology (in this case, INGENIAS) has helped to build systematically the application. Agent related concepts, such as organization, goals, interactions, etc., can be useful to structure the distribution of responsibilities and capabilities of the different agents, and their collaborations.

Although distribution capabilities of agents are helpful, when dealing with mobile devices there is a need to consider failures in the connectivity. This requires caching of application data in the mobile device, which is complex task as the amount of data can be huge and vary dynamically. Performer Agents, apart of being responsible of presentation of information to users, have to manage this information cached in the mobile device in order to improve service availability and reliability.

Acknowledgements

This work has been supported by the Spanish Council for Research and Technology (MCYT) projects TEL99-0335-C04-03 and TIC2003-07369-C02-02.

References

1. Camacho D., Borrajo D. and Molina J. M. (2001) *Intelligence Travell Planning: amulti-agent planing system to solve web problems in the e-turism domain.* InternationalJournal on Autonomous agens and Multiagent systems. 4(4) 385-390.
2. Corchado J. M. and Laza R. (2003). Con*structing Deliberative Agents with CasebasedReasoning Technology*, International Journal of Intelligent Systems, 18 (12).
3. Corchado J. M. et al. (2004). *Development of CBR-BDI Agents*, submitted to the 7ᵗʰ European Conference in Case-Based Reasoning, ECCBR 2004.
4. Glez-Bedia M. and Corchado J. M. (2002) *A planning strategy based on variationalcalculus for deliberative agents.* Computing and Information Systems J, 10 (1) 2-14.
5. Glez-Bedia M., Corchado J. M., Corchado E. S. and Fyfe C. (2002) *Analytical Model for Constructing Deliberative Agents*, Engineering Intelligent Systems, Vol 3: pp. 173-185.
6. J. Pavón and J. J. Gómez-Sanz. *Agent Oriented Software Engineering with INGENIAS.* In: Multi-Agent Systems and Applications III, 3rd International Central and Eastern European Conference on Multi-Agent Systems, CEEMAS 2003. Lecture Notes in Computer Science 2691, Springer Verlag (2003) 394-403
7. Rao, A. S. and Georgeff, M. P. (1995). *BDI Agents: From Theory to Practice.* First International Conference on Multi-Agent Systems (ICMAS-95). San Franciso, USA.

Design of a Tourist Driven Bandwidth Determined MultiModal Mobile Presentation System

Anthony Solon, Paul Mc Kevitt, and Kevin Curran

Intelligent Multimedia Research Group
School of Computing and Intelligent Systems, Faculty of Engineering
University of Ulster, Magee Campus, Northland Road, Northern Ireland, BT48 7JL, UK
{aj.solon,p.mckevitt,kj.curran}@ulster.ac.uk

Abstract. TeleMorph is a tourist information system which aims to dynamically generate multimedia presentations using output modalities that are determined by the bandwidth available on a mobile device's connection. This paper
concentrates on the motivation for & issues surrounding such intelligent systems.

1 Introduction

Interfaces involving spoken or pen-based input, as well as the combination of both,
are particularly effective for supporting mobile tasks, such as communications and
personal navigation. Unlike the keyboard and mouse, both speech and pen are com-
pact and portable. When combined, people can shift these input modes from moment
to moment as environmental conditions change [1]. Implementing multimodal user
interfaces on mobile devices is not as clear-cut as doing so on ordinary desktop devices. This is due to the fact that mobile devices are limited in many respects: memory, processing power, input modes, battery power, and an unreliable wireless connection with limited bandwidth. This project researches and implements a framework
for Multimodal interaction in mobile environments taking into consideration fluctuating bandwidth. The system output is bandwidth dependent, with the result that output
from semantic representations is dynamically morphed between modalities or combinations of modalities. With the advent of 3G wireless networks and the subsequent
increased speed in data transfer available, the possibilities for applications and services that will link people throughout the world who are connected to the network
will be unprecedented. One may even anticipate a time when the applications and
services available on wireless devices will replace the original versions implemented
on ordinary desktop computers. Some projects have already investigated mobile intelligent multimedia systems, using tourism in particular as an application domain. [2] is
one such project which analysed and designed a position-aware speech-enabled handheld tourist information system for Aalborg in Denmark. This system is position and
direction aware and uses these abilities to guide a tourist on a sight seeing tour. In
TeleMorph bandwidth will primarily determine the modality/modalities utilised in the
output presentation, but also factors such as device constraints, user goal and user
situationalisation will be taken into consideration. A provision will also be integrated
which will allow users to choose their preferred modalities. The main point to note
about these systems is that current mobile intelligent multimedia systems fail to take
into consideration network constraints and especially the bandwidth available when

A. Karmouch, L. Korba, and E. Madeira (Eds.): MATA 2004, LNCS 3284, pp. 331–338, 2004.

transforming semantic representations into the multimodal output presentation. If the bandwidth available to a device is low then it's obviously inefficient to attempt to use video or animations as the output on the mobile device. This would result in an interface with depreciated quality, effectiveness and user acceptance. This is an important issue as regards the usability of the interface. Learnability, throughput, flexibility and user-attitude are the four main concerns affecting the usability of any interface. In the case of the previously mentioned scenario (reduced bandwidth => slower/inefficient output) the throughput of the interface is affected and as a result the user's attitude also. This is only a problem when the required bandwidth for the output modalities exceeds that which is available; hence, the importance of choosing the correct output modality/modalities in relation to available resources. The next section deals with related multi-modal systems. The following section presents TeleMorph while section 3 presents an overview of other Multi-modal systems. Section 4 concludes.

2 TeleMorph

The focus of the TeleMorph project is to create a system that dynamically morphs between output modalities depending on available network bandwidth. The aims entail the following objectives which include receiving and interpreting questions from the user; Mapping questions to multimodal semantic representation; matching multimodal representation to database to retrieve answer; mapping answers to multimodal semantic representation; querying bandwidth status and generating multimodal presentation based on bandwidth data. The domain chosen as a test bed for TeleMorph is eTourism. The system to be developed called TeleTuras is an interactive tourist information aid. It will incorporate route planning, maps, points of interest, spoken presentations, graphics of important objects in the area and animations. The main focus will be on the output modalities used to communicate this information and also the effectiveness of this communication. The tools that will be used to implement this system are detailed in the next section. TeleTuras will be capable of taking input queries in a variety of modalities whether they are combined or used individually. Queries can also be directly related to the user's position and movement direction enabling questions/commands such as "Where is the Leisure Center?", "Take me to the Council Offices" and "What buildings are of interest in this area?".

J2ME (Java 2 Micro Edition) is an ideal programming language for developing TeleMorph, as it is the target platform for the Java Speech API (JSAPI) [3]. The JSAPI enables the inclusion of speech technology in user interfaces for Java applets and applications. The Java Speech API Markup Language [4] and the Java Speech API Grammar Format [4] are companion specifications to the JSAPI. JSML (currently in beta) defines a standard text format for marking up text for input to a speech synthesiser. JSGF version 1.0 defines a standard text format for providing a grammar to a speech recogniser. JSAPI does not provide any speech functionality itself, but through a set of APIs and event interfaces, access to speech functionality provided by supporting speech vendors is accessible to the application. As it is inevitable that a majority of tourists will be foreigners it is necessary that TeleTuras can process multilingual speech recognition and synthesis. To support this an IBM implementation of JSAPI "speech for Java" will be utilised. It supports US&UK English, French, German, Italian, Spanish, and Japanese. To incorporate the navigation aspect of the proposed system a positioning system is required. The GPS (Global Positioning System) [2] will be employed to provide the accurate location information necessary for a LBS (Location Based Service). The User Interface (UI) defined in J2ME is logically composed of two sets of APIs, High-level UI API which emphasises portability across different devices and the Low-level UI API which emphasises flexibility and control. TeleMorph will use a dynamic combination of these in order to provide the best solution possible. Media Design takes the output information and morphs it into relevant modality/modalities depending on the information it receives from the Server Intelligent Agent regarding available bandwidth, whilst also taking into consideration the Cognitive Load Theory as described earlier. Media Analysis receives input from the Client device and analyses it to distinguish the modality types that the user utilised in their input. The Domain Model, Discourse Model, User Model, GPS and WWW are additional sources of information for the Multimodal Interaction Manager that assist it in producing an appropriate and correct output presentation. The Server Intelligent Agent is responsible for monitoring bandwidth, sending streaming media which is morphed to the appropriate modalities and receiving input from client device & mapping to multimodal interaction manager. The Client Intelligent Agent is in charge of monitoring device constraints e.g. memory available, sending multimodal information on input to the server and receiving streamed multimedia.

2.1 Data Flow of TeleMorph

The *Networking API* sends all input from the client device to the TeleMorph server. Each time this occurs, the *Device Monitoring* module will retrieve information on the client device's status and this information is also sent to the server. On input the user can make a multimodal query to the system to stream a new presentation which will consist of media pertaining to their specific query. TeleMorph will receive requests in the *Interaction Manager* and will process requests via the *Media Analysis* module which will pass semantically useful data to the *Constraint Processor* where modalities suited to the current network bandwidth (and other constraints) will be chosen to represent the information. The presentation is then designed using these modalities by the *Presentation Design* module. The media are processed by the *Media Allocation* module and following this the complete multimodal Synchronised Multimedia Integration Language (SMIL) [5] presentation is passed to the *Streaming Server* to be streamed to the client device. A user can also input particular modality/cost choices on the TeleMorph client. In this way the user can morph the current presentation they are receiving to a presentation consisting of specific modalities which may be better suited their current situation (driving/walking) or environment (work/class/pub). The Mobile Client's Output Processing module will process media being streamed to it across the wireless network and present the received modalities to the user in a synchronised fashion. The Input Processing module on the client will process input from the user in a variety of modes. This module will also be concerned with timing thresholds between different modality inputs. In order to implement this architecture for initial testing, a scenario will be set up where switches in the project code will simulate changing between a variety of bandwidths. To implement this, TeleMorph will draw on a database which will consist of a table of bandwidths ranging from those available in 1G, 2G, 2.5G (GPRS) and 3G networks. Each bandwidth value will have access to related information on the modality/combinations of modalities that can be streamed efficiently at that transmission rate.

2.2 Client Output

Output on thin client devices connected to TeleMorph will primarily utilise a SMIL media player which will present video, graphics, text and speech to the end user of the system. The J2ME Text-To-Speech (TTS) engine processes speech output to the user. An autonomous agent will be integrated into the TeleMorph client for output as they serve as an invaluable interface agent to the user as they incorporate modalities that are the natural modalities of face-to-face communication among humans. A SMIL media player will output audio on the client device. This audio will consist of audio files that are streamed to the client when the necessary bandwidth is available.

2.3 Client Input

The TeleMorph client will allow for speech recognition, text and haptic deixis (touch screen) input. A speech recognition engine will be reused to process speech input from the user. Text and haptic input will be processed by the J2ME graphics API. Speech recognition in TeleMorph resides in *Capture Input* as illustrated in Figure 1.

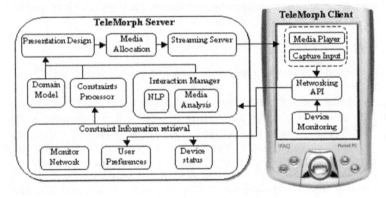

Fig. 1. Modules within TeleMorph

The Java Speech API Mark-up Language[1] defines a standard text format for marking up text for input to a speech synthesiser. As mentioned before JSAPI does not provide any speech functionality itself, but through a set of APIs and event interfaces, access to speech functionality (provided by supporting speech vendors) is accessible to the application. For this purpose IBM's implementation of JSAPI "speech for Java" is adopted for providing multilingual speech recognition functionality. This implementation of the JSAPI is based on ViaVoice, which will be positioned remotely in the *Interaction Manager* module on the server. The relationship between the JSAPI speech recogniser (in the *Capture Input* module in Figure 1) on the client and ViaVoice (in the *Interaction Manager* module in Figure 1) on the server is necessary as speech recognition is computationally too heavy to be processed on a thin client. After the ViaVoice speech recogniser has processed speech which is input to the client device, it will also need to be analysed by an *NLP* module to assess its semantic content. A reusable tool to do this is yet to be decided upon to complete this task.

---

[1] http://java.sun.com/products/java-media/speech/

Possible solutions for this include adding an additional NLP component to ViaVoice; or perhaps reusing other natural understanding tools such as PC-PATR [6] which is a natural language parser based on context-free phrase structure grammar and unifications on the feature structures associated with the constituents of the phrase structure rules.

2.4 Graphics

The User Interface (UI) defined in J2ME is logically composed of two sets of APIs, High-level UI API which emphasises portability across different devices and the Low-level UI API which emphasises flexibility and control. The portability in the high-level API is achieved by employing a high level of abstraction. The actual drawing and processing user interactions are performed by implementations. Applications that use the high-level API have little control over the visual appearance of components, and can only access high-level UI events. On the other hand, using the low-level API, an application has full control of appearance, and can directly access input devices and handle primitive events generated by user interaction. However the low-level API may be device-dependent, so applications developed using it will not be portable to other devices with a varying screen size. TeleMorph uses a combination of these to provide the best solution possible. Using these graphics APIs, TeleMorph implements a *Capture Input* module which accepts text from the user. Also using these APIs, haptic input is processed by the *Capture Input* module to keep track of the user's input via a touch screen, if one is present on the device. User preferences in relation to modalities and cost incurred are managed by the *Capture Input* module in the form of standard check boxes and text boxes available in the J2ME high level graphics API.

2.5 Networking

Networking takes place using sockets in the *J2ME Networking API* module as shown in Figure 1 to communicate data from the *Capture Input* module to the *Media Analysis* and *Constraint Information Retrieval* modules on the server. Information on client device constraints will also be received from the *Device Monitoring* module to the *Networking API* and sent to the relevant modules within the *Constraint Information Retrieval* module on the server. Networking in J2ME has to be very flexible to support a variety of wireless devices and has to be device specific at the same time. To meet this challenge, the Generic Connection Framework (GCF) is incorporated into J2ME. The idea of the GCF is to define the abstractions of the networking and file input/output as generally as possible to support a broad range of devices, and leave the actual implementations of these abstractions to the individual device manufacturers. These abstractions are defined as Java interfaces. The device manufacturers choose which one to implement based on the actual device capabilities.

2.6 TeleMorph Server-Side

SMIL is utilised to form the semantic representation language in TeleMorph and will be processed by the *Presentation Design* module in Figure 1. The HUGIN[2] develop-

---

[2] HUGIN (2003) http://www.hugin.com/

ment environment allows TeleMorph to develop its decision making process using Causal Probabilistic Networks which will form the *Constraint Processor* module as portrayed in Figure 1. The ViaVoice speech recognition software resides within the *Interaction Manager* module. On the server end of the system Darwin streaming server[3] is responsible for transmitting the output presentation from the TeleMorph server application to the client device's *Media Player*.

2.6.1 SMIL Semantic Representation

The XML based Synchronised Multimedia Integration Language (SMIL) language [5] forms the semantic representation language of TeleMorph used in the *Presentation Design* module as shown in Figure 1. TeleMorph designs SMIL content that comprises multiple modalities that exploit currently available resources fully, whilst considering various constraints that affect the presentation, but in particular, bandwidth. This output presentation is then streamed to the *Media Player* module on the mobile client for displaying to the end user. TeleMorph will constantly recycle the presentation SMIL code to adapt to continuous and unpredictable variations of physical system constraints (e.g. fluctuating bandwidth, device memory), user constraints (e.g. environment) and user choices (e.g. streaming text instead of synthesised speech). In order to present the content to the end user, a SMIL media player needs to be available on the client device. A possible contender to implement this is MPEG-7, as it describes multimedia content using XML.

2.6.2 TeleMorph Reasoning – CPNs/BBNs

Causal Probabilistic Networks aid in conducting reasoning and decision making within the *Constraints Processor* module (see Figure 1). In order to implement Bayesian Networks in TeleMorph, the HUGIN [7] development environment is used. HUGIN provides the necessary tools to construct Bayesian Networks. When a network has been constructed, one can use it for entering evidence in some of the nodes where the state is known and then retrieve the new probabilities calculated in other nodes corresponding to this evidence. A Causal Probabilistic Network (CPN)/Bayesian Belief network (BBN) is used to model a domain containing uncertainty in some manner. It consists of a set of nodes and a set of directed edges between these nodes. A Belief Network is a Directed Acyclic Graph (DAG) where each node represents a random variable. Each node contains the states of the random variable it represents and a conditional probability table (CPT) or, in more general terms, a conditional probability function (CPF). The CPT of a node contains probabilities of the node being in a specific state given the states of its parents. Edges reflect cause-effect relations within the domain. These effects are normally not completely deterministic (e.g. disease -> symptom). The strength of an effect is modelled as a probability.

2.6.3 JATLite Middleware

As TeleMorph is composed of several modules with different tasks to accomplish, the integration of the selected tools to complete each task is important. To allow for this a middleware is required within the *TeleMorph Server* as portrayed in figure 1. One such middleware is JATLite [8] which was developed by the Stanford University. JATLite provides a set of Java packages which makes it easy to build multi-agent systems using Java. As an alternative to the JATLite middleware The Open Agent

---

Architecture (OAA) [9] could be used. OAA is a framework for integrating a community of heterogeneous software agents in a distributed environment. Psyclone [10] is a flexible middleware that can be used as a blackboard server for distributed, multi-module and multi-agent systems which may also be utilised.

3 Related Work

SmartKom [11] is a multimodal dialogue system currently being developed by a consortium of several academic and industrial partners. The system combines speech, gesture and facial expressions on the input and output side. The main scientific goal of SmartKom is to design new computational methods for the integration and mutual disambiguation of different modalities on a semantic and pragmatic level. SmartKom is a prototype system for a flexible multimodal human-machine interaction in two substantially different mobile environments, namely pedestrian and car. The system enables integrated trip planning using multimodal input and output. The key idea behind SmartKom is to develop a kernel system which can be used within several application scenarios. In a tourist navigation situation a user of SmartKom could ask a question about their friends who are using the same system. E.g. "Where are Tom and Lisa?", "What are they looking at?" SmartKom is developing an XML-based mark-up language called M3L (MultiModal Markup Language) for the semantic representation of all of the information that flows between the various processing components. SmartKom is similar to TeleMorph and TeleTuras in that it strives to provide a multimodal information service to the end-user. SmartKom-Mobile is specifically related to TeleTuras in the way it provides location sensitive information of interest to the user of a thin-client device about services or facilities in their vicinity. DEEP MAP [12, 13] is a prototype of a digital personal mobile tourist guide which integrates research from various areas of computer science: geo-information systems, data bases, natural language processing, intelligent user interfaces, knowledge representation, and more. The goal of Deep Map is to develop information technologies that can handle huge heterogeneous data collections, complex functionality and a variety of technologies, but are still accessible for untrained users. DEEP MAP is an intelligent information system that may assist the user in different situations and locations providing answers to queries such as- Where am I? How do I get from A to B? What attractions are near by? Where can I find a hotel/restaurant? How do I get to the nearest Italian restaurant? DEEP MAP displays a map which includes the user's current location and their destination, which are connected graphically by a line which follows the roads/streets interconnecting the two.

4 Conclusion

We have touched upon some aspects of Mobile Intelligent Multimedia Systems. Through an analysis of these systems a unique focus has been identified – "Bandwidth determined Mobile Multimodal Presentation". This paper has presented our proposed solution in the form of a Mobile Intelligent System called TeleMorph that dynamically morphs between output modalities depending on available network bandwidth. TeleMorph will be able to dynamically generate a multimedia presentation from semantic representations using output modalities that are determined by constraints that exist on a mobile device's wireless connection, the mobile device itself and also those limitations experienced by the end user of the device. The output presentation will include Language and Vision modalities consisting of video, speech, non-speech audio and text. Input to the system will be in the form of speech, text and haptic deixis.

The objectives of TeleMorph are: (1) receive and interpret questions from the user, (2) map questions to multimodal semantic representation, (3) match multimodal representation to knowledge base to retrieve answer, (4) map answers to multimodal semantic representation, (5) monitor user preference or client side choice variations, (6) query bandwidth status, (7) detect client device constraints and limitations and (8) generate multimodal presentation based on constraint data. The architecture, data flow, and issues in the core modules of TeleMorph such as constraint determination and automatic modality selection are also given.

References

1. Holzman, T.G. (1999) Computer-human interface solutions for emergency medical care. *Interactions, 6(3)*, 13-24.
2. Koch, U.O. (2000) Position-aware Speech-enabled Hand Held Tourist Information System. Semester 9 project report, Institute of Electronic Systems, Aalborg University, Denmark.
3. JCP (2002) Java Community Process. http://www.jcp.org/en/home/index
4. JSML & JSGF (2002). Java Community Process. http://www.jcp.org/en/home/index Site visited 30/09/2003.
5. Rutledge, L. (2001) SMIL 2.0: XML For Web Multimedia. In IEEE Internet Computing, Sept-Oct, 78-84.
6. McConnel, S. (1996) KTEXT and PC-PATR: Unification based tools for computer aided adaptation. In H. A. Black, A. Buseman, D. Payne and G. F. Simons (Eds.), Proceedings of the 1996 general CARLA conference, November 14-15, 39-95. Waxhaw, NC/Dallas: JAARS and Summer Institute of Linguistics.
7. Jensen, F.V. & Jianming, L. (1995) Hugin: a system for hypothesis driven data request. In Probabilistic Reasoning and Bayesian Belief Networks, A. Gammerman (ed.), 109-124, London, UK: Alfred Waller ltd.
8. Jeon, H., C. Petrie & M.R. Cutkosky (2000) JATLite: A Java Agent Infrastructure with Message Routing. IEEE Internet Computing Vol. 4, No. 2, Mar/Apr, 87-96.
9. Cheyer, A. & Martin, D. (2001) The Open Agent Architecture. Journal of Autonomous Agents and Multi-Agent Systems, Vol. 4, No. 1, March, 143-148.
10. Psyclone (2003) http://www.mindmakers.org/architectures.html
11. Wahlster, W.N. (2001) SmartKom A Transportable and Extensible Multimodal Dialogue System. International Seminar on Coordination and Fusion in MultiModal Interaction, Schloss Dagstuhl Int Conference and Research Center for Computer Science, Wadern, Saarland, Germany, 29 Oct-2 Nov.
12. Malaka, R. & A. Zipf (2000) DEEP MAP - Challenging IT Research in the Framework of a Tourist Information System. Proceedings of ENTER 2000, 7th International Congress on Tourism and Communications Technologies in Tourism, Barcelona (Spain), Springer Computer Science, Wien, NY.
13. Malaka, R. (2001) Multi-modal Interaction in Private Environments. International Seminar on Coordination and Fusion in MultiModal Interaction, Schloss Dagstuhl International Conference and Research Center for Computer Science, Wadern, Saarland, Germany, 29 October - 2 November.

AgentViz: A Visualization System for Mobile Agents

Ken Deeter and Son Vuong

Department of Computer Science
University of British Columbia
kdeeter@cs.ubc.ca

Abstract. Although inexpensive, high performance computer graphics hardware has become commonly available, its application in the mobile agent and networking fields has thus far been limited. In this paper, we present AgentViz, a visualization tool which utilizes this technology to display and animate the parallel behavior of mobile agents over a network topology. This system provides an effective way for developers of mobile agent-based systems to understand, illustrate, and verify the operation of their systems without the need to manually process large log files. AgentViz makes use of information visualization techniques to allow users to efficiently explore large network topologies with a large number of agents. The system is built with a generic architecture to allow it to be used in a variety of situations. We also present two case studies detailing applications of the tool to visualize mobile agent-based simulations.

1 Introduction

Mobile agent technology has proven useful for building highly distributed software in which autonomous software agents navigate the network and perform their tasks in parallel. Mobile agents can move intelligently through network topologies and cooperate with other agents to carry out a collective task. The mobile agent programming paradigm offers a simple modular model to build these highly distributed and complex systems.

Along with these advantages, however, exist some disadvantages. Because of the highly distributed and parallel nature of mobile agent-based applications, the task of understanding a system's behavior can be difficult. This difficulty in turn presents a challenge when the behavior of a system must be verified against its design. For a mobile agent-based system, this involves understanding how agents are moving individually, how agents move with respect to each other, and how agents are reacting to their environment.

The conventional approach in allowing a developer to gain such an understanding of the system is to obtain a log of relevant system events. This simple approach is often inadequate for the mobile agent scenario due to the following reasons:

A. Karmouch, L. Korba, and E. Madeira (Eds.): MATA 2004, LNCS 3284, pp. 339–348, 2004.
© Springer-Verlag Berlin Heidelberg 2004

- *Parallel Events*: A log file typically provides a serial presentation of events. This forces a developer to mentally extract and reconstruct those events which occurred in parallel. Although manageable in small cases, in a large scenario this task can be time consuming and error-prone.
- *Complex Network Topology*: A developer of a mobile agent-based system must not only understand the behavior of the agents, but must also understand the network within which they operate. If this network has a nontrivial topology, this forces the developer to maintain a mental model of this topology.

In the meanwhile, advances in computer graphics algorithms and hardware rendering systems have produced inexpensive, commonly-available solutions that are capable of rendering and animating many on-screen elements rapidly and smoothly. The ability of these graphics solutions to efficiently display a large number of visual objects offers great potential for aiding the networking community. As other similar works have shown, visual displays can greatly aid the understanding and design of distributed systems.

In this paper, we present AgentViz, a tool that aims to make use of this rendering technology and apply techniques borrowed from the information visualization field to create a tool that will help developers to better understand the behavior of their mobile agent applications. It provides an off-line visualization of a network topology and an animation mobile agents moving within this topology.

2   Related Work

To our knowledge, there are no published reports directly regarding the visualization of mobile agents. However, visualization of various aspects of networking technologies has been explored. The work that is closest in spirit to that presented here is the NAM network animator [1], a visualization system for the NS network simulator. NAM reads specially formatted network trace files and displays and animates packet transmissions to enable viewers to visually comprehend complex temporal network behavior. Our work can be viewed as an extension of the NAM concept, specifically targeted toward mobile agent applications.

The distortion techniques used in AgentViz have been thoroughly elaborated upon in the information visualization community [2]. The specific application of distortion to graph drawing has also been explored [3].

Although AgentViz avoids the *graph layout* problem by requiring network nodes to specify positional coordinates, it is nonetheless a relevant problem. The problem has been explored in several approaches, including the Otter [4] and Walrus systems from CAIDA, the DynaDAG system [5], as well as the Gnutellavision system [6]. Each approach makes different assumptions about the nature of the topology being visualized and the interaction that is needed between the user and the system, resulting in a variety of layout and rendering strategies.

The usefulness of visualization as a illustration and communication tool has been explored as well [7] [8]. We recognize that the AgentViz can be used as an illustrative and educational tool, much in the same manner as the systems described in these reports.

The visualization of abstract characteristics of agents has been explored by Schroeder and Noy [9]. Their system, however, focuses on a visualization to relate similar abstract properties of agents by employing appropriate distance metrics and classification methods. Their system does not directly address the problem of understanding how the location and state of mobile agents changes over time.

3   Design Goals

The main intention for AgentViz is to be used as a debugging and verification tool. It can help a developer to understand and confirm that a system is working according to design. We assume that the user has a strong comprehension of the system they wish to visualize, and thus the goal is less to provide a tool that allows a viewer to make inferences about a system they do not know, but rather to provide a tool with which a user can match a pre-existing mental model to a visual representation.

A major goal in the design of AgentViz was to architect it in a manner that allows it to be leveraged in as many different situations as possible. In general, we believe a visualization tool should not dictate the design of a system for which it is meant to visualize. We tried to follow this principle as much as possible during the design of the tool.

As is the case with many other visualization systems, the key benefit we aim to realize is the reduction of "cognitive load" on the part of the user. Specifically, this involves reducing or removing the need for a user to maintain a mental model of a network topology, to remember absolute and relative spatial orientations in this model, or to reconstruct parallel sequences of events. By aiding in these tasks, we wish to enable a user to devote more cognitive resources to the direct goal of understanding a complex dynamic system.

AgentViz also aims to employ techniques developed in the information visualization field where they are relevant and effective. Distortion and zooming are used to allow the exploration of network topology, and *visual encoding* techniques are used to display abstract simulation state data in a user-configurable way.

4   AgentViz

4.1   Network Model

AgentViz maintains an internal network model that is designed to allow efficient rendering procedures. This model, while basic, provides a fundamental set of *entities* to simulate a mobile agents operating over a network.

Table 1. Three different entity types are available in the AgentViz network model. The table lists each type, along with their visual representations and parameters

Entity type	Visual Representation	Visual Parameters
Node	Circle	Color, Size
Link	Line	Color, Thickness
Agent	Square	Color, Size

The model supports three *entity types*: Nodes, Links, and Agents. Each entity type has a different set of visual parameters, corresponding to their varying visual representations. The visual representations and visual parameters for each entity type are summarized in Table 1.

Each node entity also records a position as a two-dimensional coordinate in a space defined by the simulation (this space is referred to as *model space*). The positions of Links and Agents are determined by the nodes that are related to them. In the case of links, their positions are defined by the positions of their two endpoint nodes. For agents, position is determined by either the position of the node at which the agent currently resides, or a location along a link if the agent is in transit.

The model also keeps track of a set of *entity states* for each entity type. An entity state is simply a named set of values for the visual parameters of an entity type. For example, a *node state* would specify one particular combination of a color and a size measure[1].

The real-world meaning of each visual state is arbitrary, and is meant to be determined by users of the system. Whereas one system might use a "large red node" to encode a significant node in a P2P overlay network, another system might use the same visual appearance to differentiate routers from ordinary hosts. The choice to leave the *visual encoding* configurable was made to meet the goal of generic design. By allowing the data source to manage the visual encoding, the tool can be adapted to display a different collection of states appropriate for each situation.

Time in the model is represented using a generic unit referred to as a *tick*. The ratio of ticks to seconds is determined by the generator of the input data, allowing different applications to define their own logical time units. The tick to time ratio can also be adjusted in the user interface to allow "slow motion" or "fast forward"-like time distortion effects.

4.2   Network Events

The input to the AgentViz tool is simply a file containing a listing of *network events*. This file is formatted using a simple syntax defined by AgentViz, and any system that is capable of generating a file in this format can be visualized using this tool.

---

[1] For nodes, the size corresponds to the radius of the node

Table 2. Listed are the types of events that can be recorded in the log file provided as input to AgentViz, along with their effects on the network model. Events with an asterisk (*) indicate those which require two timestamps to indicate when they begin and end

Event type	Event effect
create_node	Creates a new node
create_link	Creates a new link
create_agent	Creates a new mobile agent
destroy_node	Destroys a node
destroy_link	Destroys a link
destroy_agent	Destroys an agent
node_state_change	Changes state of a node
link_state_change	Changes state of a link
agent_state_change	Changes state of an agent
node_move *	Moves an node
agent_move *	Moves an agent

Each *event* has a type, which encodes its meaning in the context of the network model. Along with the type are specified arguments, which are specific to the event's type. The types of events available are summarized in Table 2.

Abstractly, each *event* is considered an operation upon the network model. When a log file is read, the initial network model is initialized to be empty. Events that express the creation of various network entities are used to create the initial topology of the network. As the system proceeds through the events, new network entities can be created and destroyed by the corresponding events, allowing the expression of non-static topologies – a common scenario in many mobile agent systems. Other events express state changes of network entities which typically result in an entity being associated with a new visual state.

Two timestamps are specified for each event, recording the time at which an event began as well as the time at which it ended. Currently, most of the supported events are instantaneous (the creation of a node, for example), in which case the second timestamp is ignored. For only two of the event types (agent_move and node_move)the system uses both timestamps to reconstruct the parallel timing of these events.

A log file can often be incorrect or inconsistent. For example, a destroy_node event may call for the destruction of a node which does not exist. Although AgentViz could have been designed to be resilient to these kinds of inconsistencies, the opposite approach is taken. The consistency of the network model is left entirely to the system generating the log file. By doing so, the system directly exposes inconsistencies, which are often indicators of bugs or incorrect design.

A log file can optionally contain headers, which are used to specify parameters for the visualization that remain static as the input is processed. The list of available header types is summarized in Table 3.

Table 3. All of the available log header types

Header type	Description
speed	The default ticks/second for playback
fixed_bounding_box	A fixed area of the model space to display
define_link_state	Defines a visual state for a link
define_agent_state	Defines a visual state for a agent
define_node_state	Defines a visual state for a node
render_link_priority	Order in which link states should be rendered
render_agent_priority	Order in which agent states should be rendered
render_node_priority	Order in which node states should be rendered

The most common usage of headers are to define entity visual states. Each entity state is associated to a string identifier, which can be used elsewhere in the file to refer to that state. Events that change the states of entities must refer to these states by name, and cannot create new states on the fly.

4.3 Rendering Pipeline

The rendering system in AgentViz is implemented as a pipeline with four stages: Layout, Zoom, Distort, and Render. A high-level view of this pipeline is provided in Fig. 1. The OpenGL API used by AgentViz is a stateful library, and causing unnecessary state changes within the library can lead to decreased performance. The pipeline design provides a clear definition of the rendering procedure, and also allows the implementation to rapidly perform clusters of similar routines without requiring costly conditional branches and state changes during the rendering process. Utilizing abstract interfaces between each stage also provides for the decoupling of their implementations, allowing for experimentation by modifying each stage individually.

In the *Layout* stage, the positions in model space for each node are determined. Currently, this stage simply uses the positions provided in the input log file. However, this stage exists as a distinct stage to allow for automatic layout mechanisms to be added later.

In the *Zoom* stage, model space coordinates are translated to screen-space coordinates. The translation can be performed in a variety of ways. One available method calculates a bounding box around all the nodes in the model, then maps the corners of this box to the corners of the available display window. Another method uses the same process except that the bounding box is calculated for a specific subset of the nodes, based on a user's "selection". Alternatively, if the simulation wishes to dictate this mapping mechanism, it can provide a fixed bounding box using a log header.

In the *Distort* stage, the screen-space coordinates of each node are modified by a distortion algorithm which creates a virtual "magnification area" whose center can be specified using the mouse. The distance from each node to this

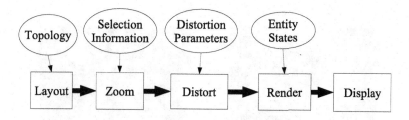

Fig. 1. This figure shows a graphical depiction of the AgentViz's rendering pipeline. Each rendering pass proceeds through the Layout, Zoom, Distort, and Render stages, and the result is sent to the display. Each oval represents the information that can affect the behavior at each stage of the process

center is scaled inversely to the distance from the magnification center. Nodes that are close to this center are spread apart, and nodes that are far away are pushed together, creating a local magnification effect.

Finally, in the *Render* stage, the screen-space coordinate of each node is used to draw all entities on to the screen. Links are rendered first, followed by nodes then agents. Within each entity type, all entities with the same state are rendered together. The order in which each state is rendered can either be specified in the log file or can be modified using the user interface. This mechanism allows particular entity types to be rendered on top of others, allowing for clarification and emphasis in dense displays. This also reduces the number of calls made to the OpenGL library to indicate a new color to be used for rendering.

4.4   Implementation Details

AgentViz is implemented using Java Standard Edition 1.4 and the Swing GUI toolkit. The rendering component uses a freely available Java binding for the OpenGL graphics library known as jogl.

5   Applications

This section describes several usage scenarios of this tool. The first was developed specifically to illustrate the usefulness of the visualization, while the latter was developed entirely independently.

As previously mentioned, AgentViz can be used as both a debugging and verification tool, as well as an illustrative tool. Below, we summarize a general methodology for using the tool from an application programmer's point of view.

1. Develop Visual Mappings: as AgentViz does not include any pre-defined mappings, a developer must first decide which system states will be mapped to which visual parameters.
2. Modify Application: Once a visual mapping has been decided, the target application needs to be modified to output an event log.

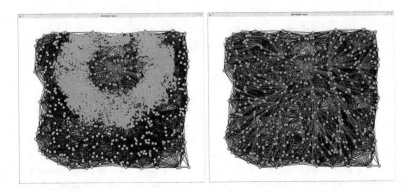

Fig. 2. Shown are two screenshots of a multi-cast tree creation algorithm in progress over a dense network of 500 nodes. Green squares show the location of mobile agents as they spread recursively from the root node. Red links show links that have been picked to form the multi-cast tree. The left image shows the algorithm in process and the right image shows the finished result. Black links and red links are represented in the log file as different link states, and the rendering priority for links is configured to render red links in front of black ones, to emphasize the overlay multi-cast tree

3. Visualize and Verify: The event log is fed into AgentViz and played back. The user interface tools can be used to control and explore the animation.

Developing a visual mapping is an iterative process, and thus several cycles of the steps enumerated above will likely be performed. AgentViz could have provided some common visual mapping presets, but this would have required more complexity in the event log format to express more detailed state changes, and could have sacrificed the system's value as a generic tool.

5.1 Multi-cast Tree Creation Using Mobile Agents

A small simulation was developed to generate a log file for a mobile agent-based multi-cast tree creation algorithm. The simulation was created using a small python program (roughly 200 lines). The program simulated a group of agents forming a multi-cast tree by beginning at a root node and replicating and spreading recursively, recording shortest paths to each node from the root. Figure 2 shows two snapshots of the animation of this process.

This example illustrates several advantages of the tool. Because the visualization has been separated from the running instance of the application, the performance characteristics of each component are also independent. A slower-than-real-time simulation can be visualized as a real-time animation.

Secondly, this example illustrates that a small program can be used to produce an involved graphical output. The details of rendering performance have been taken care of, and the application developer can concentrate on correct implementation. The efficiency of development can enable a user to quickly explore new agent interactions and system structure.

5.2   Scatternet Formation Using Mobile Agents

Our second example shows a visualization of a Bluetooth scatternet formation algorithm based on mobile agents [10]. The algorithm uses mobile agents to traverse an existing scatternet to find appropriate nodes that can accommodate a new host that wishes to join the scatternet. A screen shot of AgentViz being used to visualize this process is shown in Fig. 3.

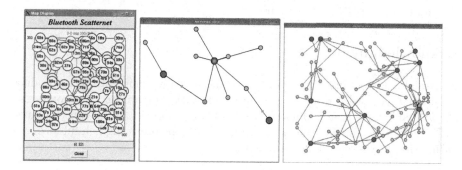

Fig. 3. The image on the left shows a screen shot from the visualization that is part of the original simulation package on which this algorithm was developed. The middle image is a view of AgentViz animating the mobile agents involved in the scatternet creation. The right image shows AgentViz displaying the finished scatternet. In the AgentViz images, Bluetooth "master" devices are shown as larger red nodes

6   Conclusions and Future Work

We have developed a visualization tool to aid developers of mobile agent-based systems to understand the parallel behavior of their mobile agent systems operating over large network topologies. The software is designed in a generic way allowing it to be adapted to different mobile agent scenarios.

The current implementation provides the most basic features. Many improvements can be incorporated, including:

– Dynamic Layout: Artificial topology generators often do not output positional coordinates for network nodes. To use these topologies in the current system, the user would have to manually derive coordinates for a potentially large number of nodes. An automatic layout mechanism would allow these types of networks to be visualized without incurring a large burden on the user.
– Increase Entities and Visual Parameters: AgentViz's network model can be extended to support a richer set of network entities, to allow the model to express a larger range of situations. The same goal can be achieved also by

increasing the dimensions for visual encodings (allowing differentiation of states using shape or texture, for example). We would also like to explore mechanisms to more directly model the characteristics of wireless hosts as the application of mobile agents in wireless scenarios becomes increasingly significant.

– Distortion and Exploration Techniques: Although the fish-eye distortion mechanism in AgentViz provides a basic tool to browse local areas of the network, further distortion techniques can be integrated to allow for new and useful types of interaction.

Acknowledgments

We would like to thank Sergio Gonzalez-Valenzuela working with us to produce a dataset to visualize from his scatternet formation algorithm. We would also like to thank Xiao Juan Cai and Christian Chita for their editing contributions, and Dr. Tamara Munzner for her inspiration and for providing helpful feedback during the early stages of development.

References

1. Estrin, D., Handley, M., Heidemann, J., McCanne, S., Xu, Y., Yu, H.: Network visualization with nam, the vint network animator. Computer **33** (2000) 63–68
2. Leung, Y., Apperley, M.: A review and taxonomy of distortion-oriented presentation techniques. ACM Transactions on Computer-Human Interaction **1** (1994) 126–160
3. Sarkar, M., Brown, M.H.: Graphical fisheye views of graphs. Technical Report 084a, Digital Systems Research Center (1992)
4. Huffaker, B., Nemeth, E., Claffy, K.: Otter: A general-purpose network visualization tool. In: Proceedings of ISOC INET'99. (1999)
5. North, S.C.: Incremental layout in dynadag. In: Proceedings of Graph Drawing '95. (1996)
6. Yee, K.P., Fisher, D., Dhamija, R., Hearst, M.A.: Animated exploration of dynamic graphs with radial layout. In: Proceedings of INFOVIS. (2001) 43–50
7. White, C.M.: Visualization tools to support data communications and computer network courses. Journal of Computing in Small Colleges **17** (2001) 81–89
8. Holliday, M.A.: Animation of computer networking concepts. ACM Journal of Educational Resources in Computing **3** (2003) 1–26
9. Schroeder, M., Noy, P.: Multi-agent visualization based on multivariate data. In: Proceedings of Autonomous Agents 2001. (2001)
10. Gonzalez-Valenzuela, S., Vuong, S.T., Leung, V.C.M.: Efficient formation of dynamic bluetooth scatternet via mobile agent processing. In: Proceedings of 5th International Workshop for Mobile Agents for Telecommunication Applications. (2003)

JavaSpace: When Agents Meet Peers

Marco Ballette, Antonio Liotta, and Carmelo Ragusa

Centre for Communication Systems Research, University of Surrey
Guildford, Surrey, GU1 7XH, UK
{M.Ballette,A.Liotta,C.Ragusa}@eim.surrey.ac.uk

Abstract. The Peer-to-Peer (P2P) model has been proven to overcome some of the main limitations of the client-server approach, including the presence of single points of failure, the appearance of bottlenecks around the server and inefficient resource utilization at the edge of the network. P2P technologies, initially fostered by the success of music file sharing applications, have now reached a widespread adoption in a range of domains. MAs are naturally geared to realize peer entities that can move and be discovered, adding an extra dimension to conventional P2P approaches. In this paper we look at how a combination of a particular P2P system (JavaSpace) and MA technologies can provide additional benefits in terms of fault-tolerance, recovery, scalability and load balancing. Through an experimental approach, we illustrate the benefits of the combined MA/P2P approach. Our initial findings indicate that a coherent merge between P2P and MA technologies have enormous potential in the context of mobile distributed computing.

1 Introduction

Peer-to-peer (P2P) computing appeared in the front-page headlines of technical Web sites in early 2000, spurred by the popularity of file sharing systems such as Napster [1] Gnutella [2] and Morpheus [3]. It can be defined as "a network-based computing model for applications where computers share resources via direct exchanges between the participant computers" [19]. P2P networks emerged as a new distributed computing paradigm for their potential to harness the computing power of the hosts composing the network and make their under-utilized resources available to others. "Sharing" and "collaboration" are the two main features that P2P technologies offer to the user. Sharing may regard files (music, video), information and storage services or, simply, computational cycles.

The P2P model is generally opposed to the Client-Server (CS) model in which a distributed system is split between one or more servers that accept requests from (distributed) clients. The drawbacks of the CS asymmetric approach are well known in the literature and are mainly related with bottlenecks (since most of the computing burden is on the server side) and inefficient utilization of resources during off-peak periods.

On the other hand, the P2P model is intrinsically more scalable given that, in many cases, performance increases with the number of collaborating peers (in the CS model performance always decrease with increasing number of clients). In addition, P2P systems tend to be more resilient to unstable and unpredictable conditions thanks to

A. Karmouch, L. Korba, and E. Madeira (Eds.): MATA 2004, LNCS 3284, pp. 349–358, 2004.
© Springer-Verlag Berlin Heidelberg 2004

dynamic, distributed discovery mechanisms. They provide an efficient way to utilize untapped resources including network, processing and storage resources. This eliminates single points of failure and bottlenecks [4]. Data and control can be distributed and requests can be load-balanced across the network.

In this paper we show how a particular P2P technology (JavaSpace) can be considered as a building block for mobile multi agent systems communication. Mobile Agents (MAs) are in fact naturally geared to realize peer entities that can move and be discovered, adding an extra dimension to conventional P2P approaches. When MAs are built on top of a P2P infrastructure, they can efficiently embody the description of the task environment, the decision-support capabilities, the collective behavior, and the interaction protocols of each peer.

We aimed at demonstrating how some of the main fundamental issues of P2P technologies (dynamic fault recovery, load balancing and scalability) can be effectively dealt with in a combined MA/JavaSpace environment. In the remainder of this paper, we first give a quick overview of P2P computing and MA-based systems (Section 2). After that, we describe the key features of JavaSpace (Section 3), illustrating our experimental framework and results in Section 4.

2   Agents and Peers in Distributed Computing

2.1   P2P Computing

P2P computing is not a new concept that originates in the first attempt of tapping into unutilized computer cycles and in the general concept of cooperative computation among different computers (distributed computing). Its roots can be traced back to the Linda project at Yale University [1]. Linda, a coordination language offering a set of primitives for coordinating and synchronizing loosely coupled processes in a distributed system, is considered to have laid the foundations for the P2P distributed computing of today.

The popular interest in P2P has been boosted by the unique publicity surrounding one particular P2P application - the music file-sharing application, Napster [1]. Furthermore, as part of its .Net initiative Microsoft is working on a large-scale P2P file-sharing system known as Farsite [7]. From the other end of the market, Sun has released JXTA, an open-source project to provide standard protocols for P2P applications and services. The JXTA platform [8][9] defines a set of XML protocols designed to address the common functionality required to enable peers to form *dynamic* networks, independently of the operating system, programming language and network transport. Thanks to these features, JXTA has the potential to attain wide applicability through a solid layer offering interoperability. The other key objective of JXTA is to promote P2P ubiquity, where a JXTA peer is meant to be "any device with a digital heartbeat".

2.2   Agent Approaches to P2P Distributed Computing

As part of our work, we investigate the benefits arising from combining the two paradigms of MAs and P2P for solving distributed computational tasks. To carry out our study, we have built and experimental framework based on JavaSpace (Section 3). JavaSpace offers fundamental P2P functionality but has not originally been designed to support MAs. However, it inherently provides mechanisms for transferring Java objects between machines in a network and can be used to implement many coordination patterns, as shown in Section 3. In accordance with Chen *et al.* [14], we argue that JavaSpace is geared to provide support for MA communication and coordination. In fact, they used it as an underlying technology for building mobile multi-agent systems. A comparison between an MA-enhanced JavaSpace system and a typical MA platform is presented in [18].

Agent systems provide ontology support for the description of peer resources and can be built on top of P2P architectures to embody the description of the task environments, the decision support capabilities, the collective behavior, and the coordination and interaction protocols of each peer. In [13] a ubiquitous agent middleware (UbiMAS) uses a JXTA P2P network as communication infrastructure. In UbiMAS agents are used to carry context information of the environment and to store "a mobile virtual reflection of the use" (the user personal information and location). Similarly in [14], Java MAs are applied to the JXTA P2P platform with minimal requirements for programming and installing the agents with an executable code and itinerary.

3   JavaSpace

JavaSpace is a framework based on Jini [16] and Java RMI for handling and managing exchange of distributed objects. It provides a compelling model for distributed P2P communication between peers. P2P services implemented on edge devices (peers) can use JavaSpace as a platform for distributed communication, coordination and rendezvous. As in Linda, a space acts as a distributed shared memory where loosely coupled processes synchronize their activities by exchanging agents called Entries. Participants in a distributed application send and receive messages and tasks in the form of objects (Entries) via the space. Each space takes care of all the details of communication, data transfer, persistence, synchronization, and security.

The following primitives are used in JavaSpace (Fig. 1):
- *write*: writes an object implementing the common interface Entry into the space;
- *read, readIfExist*: reads the object matching a certain template (Entry) from the JavaSpace;
- *notify*: sends a notification through a given event handler if entries that match a template are added to the space. There is time-out period associated with it; if a matching entry isn't added on time, the notify request fails and is dropped from the JavaSpace.
- *take, takeifExist*: reads and removes an entry from the space.

The JavaSpace technology has been shown to offer the fundamental blocks required in a mobile multi agent system such as migration of objects, message handling, and object sharing. It can be used to implement different coordination patterns, such as:

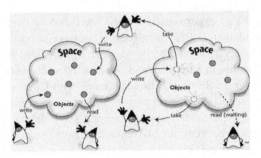

Fig. 1. JavaSpace

- *Master-Worker:* where a client (Master) executes many identical subtasks on a pool of servers:
- *Command:* where a client (Master) executes different subtasks, each on a specific server:
- *Marketplace:* where the execution task is governed by negotiation.

When building an agent platform on top of JavaSpace, patterns define the relationship between the agents. In complicated situations, different coordination patterns can be mixed together [14]. However, in the remainder, we focus on the JavaSpace implementation of the Master-Worker execution pattern, which has been proven to provide inherent support for load balancing, scalability and uncoupling in service, destination and time for distributed entities in relatively static computational environments. We then question its applicability in more dynamic and heterogeneous environments.

The Master-worker paradigm consists on the following phases:

- *Task Planning:* a MasterAgent process decomposes the application problem into subtasks. It then iterates through the application tasks, creates an agent (TaskEntry) for each task, and writes the tasks entry into the JavaSpace.
- *Computation:* WorkerAgents (peers) process retrieves these tasks from the space. If a matching task is not immediately available, the worker process can wait until the task is published.
- *Aggregation:* the MasterAgent collects the results previously published by the workers. If some results are missing, due to a WorkerAgent failure, it re-publishes the TaskEntry into the JavaSpace, after a certain WAITING TIME.

The Master and Worker roles are interchangeable in a P2P fashion and each peer can embed both the Master and Worker behavior.

4   Experiments

4.1   Experimental Framework

When a task is published, the available WorkerAgents compete to access the TaskEntry and execute the task. The first worker gaining access to the TaskEntry picks it up and executes its code. We have realized a terminal emulation system that is used to load JavaSpace in a variety of conditions (Fig.2). The execution code embedded in TaskEntries objects simply keeps the WorkerAgent in "sleeping" for a certain period of time, which is proportional to its emulated processing capabilities. Peers with different capabilities, in terms of processing power and availability, are emulated based on a configuration file set up before starting the simulations.

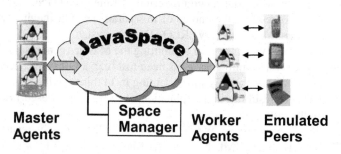

Master   Space   Worker   Emulated
Agents   Manager   Agents   Peers

Fig. 2. Experimental framework

In our system, we can set up different simulation parameters such as number of TaskEntries, number of workers (peers executing the TaskEntries), workers' properties, the load of JavaSpace and the waiting time adpoted in the case of task failure (i.e. time lapsed before that task is resubmitted by the MasterAgent to JavaSpace). In order to take into account all of these aspects we modeled for each worker different classes of connectivity, depending on the average period of network connection availability. We adopted a range going from 100% of connection availability (i.e. the case of fixed resources) to 20% (i.e. the case of extremely volatile devices). A similar approach has been adopted in order to emulate the processing power of different devices. In that case we wanted to capture the impact of the device capability on task execution time. Different classes of task have been chosen based on their duration. Internal tasks are periodically sent to each worker with a certain frequency, which is related to the JavaSpace availability class of the worker.

Connectivity and JavaSpace availability are measured in terms of percentage of time the worker is connected to the JavaSpace or is free for executing its tasks. The CPU is measured in terms of execution time requested by the worker to accomplish each task. The CPU class will inevitably affect the failure probability of each worker because the faster a worker is in executing a JavaSpace task the less is the probability that internal tasks will be submitted during the JavaSpace task execution, causing the failure of the task.

4.2 Experimental Method

When a WorkerAgent is executing the TaskEntry the peer can loose its connectivity with the JavaSpace due to a number of reasons. For instance the user may have roamed to another place; the channel may have become too noisy; shadowing areas do not allow the device to connect with the JavaSpace; or the user has simply switched off the terminal in order to preserve its battery. When connectivity is lost, the peer keeps processing the task and publishes the results back into JavaSpace as soon as the communication is re-established.

Since peers in the JavaSpace are intermittently connected, it is likely that they loose the connection with the JavaSpace during the execution of an agent. This will affect the performance of the system. A common approach is to republish the task, which may have been lost, after a certain period of time (WAITING TIME). As we will show in the next section, the choice of this parameter will inevitably affect the execution time of the task and the OVERLOAD of the system.

An overload happens when the peer submitting the MasterAgent resubmits it to the JavaSpace erroneously assuming that it has been lost (e.g. a failure has occurred in its execution) while a WorkerAgent is still executing it. In this case the task will be executed by another peer resulting in a duplication of the resources used to accomplish the execution of the task.

Upon a failure, an excessive WAITING TIME will inevitably result in a high AVERAGE EXECUTION TIME because the MasterAgent has to wait a long time before re-submitting the task lost to the JavaSpace. On the other hand, an overly short WAITING TIME will increase the overload of the peers' resources. Hence, the main factors we investigate in the experiments are:

- FAILURE PERCENTAGE = (Num. Failures * 100 / Num. Tasks);
- AVERAGE EXECUTION TIME;
- OVERLOAD PERCENTAGE = (Num. Overloads * 100 / Num. Tasks).

4.3 Results

The aim of our experiments was to show how some of the main motivations for adopting P2P technologies are fulfilled by JavaSpace through its inherent merging of classic P2P (shared distributed memory approach) and agent technologies (Entries). The experiments have been mainly focused in showing the JavaSpace inherent support to load balancing along with a way for enabling system recovery from partial failure.

In the first set of experiments we considered the FAULT TOLERANCE mechanisms that can be implemented in order to enable the system to recover from partial failure. As already mentioned, failure may be caused by the submission of an internal task to the peer while this is executing the agent downloaded from the JavaSpace. Internal tasks in each of the peer entities have a higher priority than JavaSpace tasks. Peers are in fact resource-constrained devices and the user may not want to exhaust their limited resources. Thus, we assumed that when internal tasks are executed they consume all the available resources of the peer. The common policy for providing fault recovery mechanism in the JavaSpace shared distributed memory is, for the Master, to wait for a certain period before re-submitting a task with no result published back in the JavaSpace.

Fig.3 and 4 illustrate the system performance in terms of execution time and overload for different values of the task resubmission waiting time. Both diagrams show a clear change in correspondence of the average execution time. For smaller values of WAITING TIME the systems responds better at the expense of an excessive load.

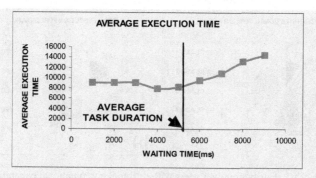

Fig. 3. Effect of waiting time on the average execution time

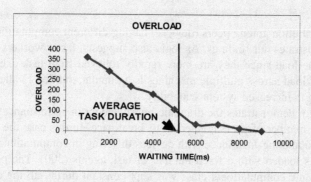

Fig. 4. Effect of waiting time on system load

Overloading results from the subsequent re-submission of tasks. For the same reason tasks tend to be served as soon as JavaSpace becomes available, hence the better response time. *Per contra*, when the WAITING TIME is larger than the average task execution time, we observe the opposite behavior.

We can draw the conclusion that, should we be able to estimate the value of the average task execution time, we would also be able to optimize the system performance by setting the WAITING TIME equal to that value. It would therefore advantageous that the Master held estimates of the loading factor associated to the agent tasks. This time will inevitably vary depending on the peers' capabilities but the uncoupled nature of JavaSpace does not allow a WorkerAgent to know which peer will execute the Agent. Predictions may be obtained for instance on the bases of historical observations (heuristics) but this aspect has been left out of the scope of our work so far.

On the other hand, the uncoupled nature of JavaSpace is a powerful tool for another important feature of P2P systems: the capability of equally distributing the load among the peers (*load balancing*). We emulated, through the use of our experimental frameworks, 5 different classes combining different devices in terms of *computational percentage* (number of task/sec of one class * 100 / total number of tasks/sec of all the classes). We sent to the JavaSpace a certain number of tasks (for a total of 300) characterized by a very high LOAD (number of task/sec) in order to assess the

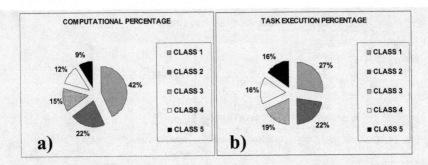

Fig. 5. Task distribution over peers with different computational capabilities

workload distribution among peers (devices) having different computational capabilities. Fig. 5 illustrates our findings. As logic also suggests, faster workers tend to take the most of the load since they are more rapidly relieved from task execution. This distribution of load across multiple machines is a popular solution to alleviate bottleneck, resulting in increased system scalability.

Finally, Fig.6 demonstrates the dramatic improvement in performance achieved by increasing the number of peers connected to JavaSpace. In this case the experiments consisted in populating JavaSpace with devices differing in computational capability. JavaSpace was loaded with a fixed number of task agents (300). The percentage of peers of the same computational class was kept constant during all the experiments. The decrease in execution time was, as expected, inversely proportional to the increase number of workers. Unexpectedly, though, the overheads that typically increases in distributed systems when the scale of the system increases, where negligible. A more in depth analysis of the system under more stressful conditions will certainly unveil other aspects relating to the limits of the system. However, as far as the purpose of our investigation is concerned, we are able to see the enormous potential of MA/P2P converged systems. JavaSpace has been chosen as a representative framework because it features both code mobility and P2P protocols.

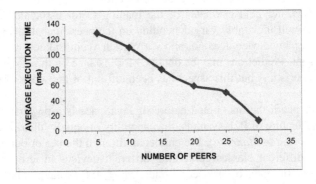

Fig. 6. System scalability

5   Conclusions

Following the widespread popularity of P2P applications, the P2P paradigm has been increasingly adopted as a means to push computation and complexity away from the network. This is in line with the principles and design choices of the Internet and, in a way, extends its ability to realise distributed systems as an alternative to simple client-server applications. Strangely enough, a similar path has been followed by a separate research community, that has been looking at Mobile Agents and code mobility as a means to pursue *distribution* but also *flexibility, programmability* and *adaptability*.

As networked systems become increasingly dynamic, with mobility being the new predominant dimension, there is a need to continue to search for computational models and paradigms that can keep the pace with changes and dynamics. In the past few years, we have been looking at P2P, Grid, and Mobile Agents from different perspectives and within separate application domain. The idea to study a converged P2P/MA paradigm is relatively recent. Hence the work will certainly spark interesting developments in the upcoming future. The achievements so far are, nevertheless, interesting and have served the purpose to provide an initial demonstration of the viability of P2P/MA systems. While some of the results were partially expected in principle, our prototype helped quantifying them more precisely. We have now evidence and confidence that the programmability and mobility features of MAs can bring enormous potential to P2P systems in terms of *fault recovery, scalability* and *load balancing*. Our immediate plan is to carry out a more in depth analysis covering all the important aspects of P2P systems. It is our intention to investigate existing P2P protocols in the context of mobile and *ad hoc* networking and unveil the full potential of MAs in this context.

Acknowledgements

The work presented in this paper has been developed in the context of POLYMICS (Policy-based Middleware for Context-aware Services), a project funded by the UK Engineering and Physical Sciences Research Council (EPSRC) - Grant GR/S09371/01.

References

1. Stefan Saroiu, P. Krishna Gummadi, Steven D. Gribble, Measuring and Analysing the Characteristics of Napster and Gnutella Hosts, Multimedia Systems Journal, Volume 8, Issue 5, November 2002.
2. M. Ripeanu, I. Foster, and A. Iamnitchi. Mapping the gnutella network: Properties of large-scale peer-to-peer systems and implications for system design. IEEE Internet Computing Journal, 6(1), 2002.
3. The Morpheus official website: http://www.morpheussoftware.net/
4. James Walkerdine, Lee Melville, Ian Sommerville Dependability Properties of P2P Architectures. Peer-to-Peer Computing: 173-174
5. The Freenet project official website: http://freenet.sourceforge.net/

6. D. Gelernter. Generative communication in Linda. ACM Transactions on Programming Languages and Systems. 7(1:80-112), January 1985.
7. The Farsite Microsoft project official website: http://research.microsoft.com/sn/Farsite/
8. Robert Flenner et al. Java P2P Unleashed: With JXTA, Web Services, XML, Jini, JavaSpaces, and J2EE, SAMS; 1st edition (September 12, 2002).
9. Sun's JXTA official website: http://www.jxta.org/
10. The ICQ official website: http://web.icq.com/
11. W. S. Ng, B. C. Ooi, and K. L. Tan. Bestpeer: A self-configurable peer-to-peer system, ICDE, 2002.
12. Rita Yu Chen, Bill Yeager, Java Mobile Agents on Project JXTA Peer-to-Peer Platform, HICSS'03.
13. F.Bagci, J.Petzold, W. Trumler, Th. Ungerer: Ubiquitous Mobile Agent System in a P2P-Network. UbiSys-Workshop at the Fifth Annual Conference on Ubiquitous Computing, Seattle, October 12-15 2003.
14. Gang Chen, Zhonghua Yang, Hao He, Kiah Mok Goh : Coordinating Multi-Agents using JavaSpaces. Proceedings Ninth International Conference on Parallel and Distributed Systems, 2002, p 63-8.
15. Cameron Ross Dunne, Using mobile agents for network resource discovery in peer-to-peer, SIGecom Exch. Vol. 2, num. 3.
16. Jan Newmarch, A Programmer's Guide to Jini Technology, APress 2001.
17. Wang A. I.:Using JavaSpaces to Implement a Mobile Multi-Agent system. AIC2002.
18. Alf Inge Wang, Carl-Fredrik Sørensen: A Comparison of Two Different Java Technologies to Implement a Mobile Agent System. Applied Informatics 1039-104 (2003).
19. David Barkai, Peer-to-Peer Computing, Intel Press, 2002.

Identifying and Documenting Test Patterns from Mobile Agent Design Patterns*

André Figueiredo, Antônio Almeida, and Patrícia Machado

COPIN/DSC - Universidade Federal de Campina Grande
Av. Aprígio Veloso, 882, CEP: 58.109-970, Campina Grande – PB, Brazil
{andrel,jaime,patricia}@dsc.ufcg.edu.br

Abstract. Developing and testing mobile agent-based applications are
complex tasks that demand appropriate support to cope with mobility
as well as usual distributed applications issues. Development approaches
have already been proposed, and the use of design patterns has proved
to be essential to increase productivity and feasibility. However, testing
of mobile agent-based applications has not been extensively investigated.
The use of test patterns seems to be a promising approach to test these
applications in a cost-effective way. Aiming to promote the use of design
patterns together with test patterns, we present an approach to identifying test patterns related to mobile agent design patterns. We also
propose a documentation template and an implementation strategy.

1 Introduction

Testing has been extensively applied to verify computing systems. In order to
improve the quality of test suites, productivity and promote reuse, test patterns
have been proposed [1, 2]. A test pattern is a kind of test which can be applied
in a recurrent context with the purpose of revealing certain defects.

Among the systems which can take advantage of using test patterns, we are
interested in mobile agent-based ones. Mobile agents are autonomous programs
that can migrate between computers during their execution, carrying their state.
Developing and testing mobile agent-based applications are complex tasks that
demand appropriate support to cope with agent mobility as well as usual features
of distributed applications [3, 4]. Currently, there is a growing interest in the use
of mobile agent design patterns to improve feasibility, productivity and reuse
[5–7]. However, testing mobile agent-based applications has not been extensively
investigated and there is a lack of adequate techniques and support.

Structure and expected behaviour of mobile agent design patterns are usually specified in some notation such as UML [6, 7]. Thus, test patterns can be
defined from test cases that are generated from these specifications. Besides, it
can be proper to associate test patterns with design patterns, since for a test case
to be considered a test pattern it needs to be recurrently required and design

---

* Supported by CNPq - Brazilian Research Council, Mobile Project, Process 552190/
2002-0 and MCT/Motorola/UFCG. First author is supported by CAPES.

A. Karmouch, L. Korba, and E. Madeira (Eds.): MATA 2004, LNCS 3284, pp. 359–368, 2004.

patterns are recurrent solutions. For each design pattern, a well-founded set of test patterns can be defined to verify applications that use the design pattern.

We present an approach to identifying and documenting test patterns from design patterns. Test cases are derived from UML models and run in different applications. The ones that prove to recurrently reveal important defects can be turned into test patterns. For documenting them, we propose a pattern template, and to illustrate these ideas, a test pattern is presented.

This paper is structured as follows. Section 2 presents related works. Section 3 introduces a test pattern template. Section 4 presents an approach to identifying test cases. Section 5 discusses test implementation and execution issues. Section 6 illustrates a test pattern in the template proposed and Section 7 presents conclusions. We assume the reader is familiar with mobile agents basic concepts.

2   Background

Mobile Agent Design Patterns. Development approaches based on the use of mobile agent design patterns have been proposed [6, 8, 7]. Particularly, Lima *et al* [7, 9] presents an approach to modelling and analysing patterns and combining them in a systematic way to produce applications. This is based on the use of a catalogue, where patterns are described according to a template that includes UML design models and is similar to the template presented in [10], with some additional issues regarding the mobile agent paradigm. As proposed in [11], the template considers two kinds of design models. The first one is platform independent, with the objective of producing a specification of a logical design independently of any specific mobile agent platform. The other one is platform dependent, considering specific platform details. This division is motivated to promote reuse and also because applications may run on different platforms.

Test Patterns. Terminology on test patterns is still vague. A test pattern is commonly defined as a solution to a recurrent problem of testing software [1, 2, 12]. We are interested in patterns that are effective in finding particular types of defects. Also, their documentation should present ways of implementing them in any system that uses a related design pattern. Test patterns have been proposed and used in the testing community. In [2], we can find patterns to design testing infrastructures. In [12], a pattern language is presented along with patterns to user interface validation. In [1], several patterns for test design of objected-oriented systems are proposed. However, some problems need to be overcome: (1) patterns are usually documented in a ad-hoc way and also they are usually not related to other patterns, (2) either they are too general or too specific in a way that can make it difficult to use them in practice, (3) there is not a standard categorisation, and (4) there is not a common accepted pattern template.

3   Test Pattern Template

In this section, we introduce our proposal for a pattern template. This template is based on those proposed by Lima *et al* [9] and, mainly, by Binder [1].

Binder proposes a test pattern template based on the one presented by Gamma et al for design patterns [10]. In our work, some elements proposed by him are discarded and others are redefined in order to contemplate some new issues, like mobility and design pattern. Regarding the elements that were redefined, we highlight *Context* that, in our proposal, also contains the information about which design pattern is related to the test pattern under description. To contemplate mobile agent issues, the *Strategy* element presented in Binder's pattern template was turned into two others: *Structure* and *Implementation*. This characteristic refers to the fact that each mobile agent-based system usually contains two kinds of models: a platform independent one (*Structure*); and a platform dependent one (*Implementation*), as mentioned in Section 2. In Table 1, we present the elements of our pattern definition template. We propose that the elements *Name, Intent, Context, Structure, Implementation,* and *Forces* (if exists) be essential, whereas the other elements can be used as complements.

Table 1. Test Pattern Template Elements.

Element	*Description*
Name	The pattern should have a name composed of a word or a short phrase. Conceptual abstractions are interesting.
Context	The context must specify the design pattern(s) which the test pattern is useful to. It also describes the applicability and the preconditions necessary to make it feasible and advantageous.
Intent	Short description of what kind of test suit this pattern produces.
Structure	Presents the test suite's design and implementation regardless of any platform. This is composed of test models of responsibilities and implementation, the procedure describing how the pattern should be applied at the implementation, and the oracle.
Implementation	Describes the solution presented in *Structure* with special attention to implementation issues, that is, considering different platforms.
Forces	This element provides constraints and *trade-offs* which the pattern should take into account.
Examples	Provides a simple use of the pattern. It is commonly used to ease the understanding of the elements *Structure* and *Implementation*.
Fault Model	Describes the kind of faults which are reached, triggered, and propagated. It can be formally or heuristically described.
Known Uses	Provides applications where the pattern has been used.
Related Patterns	Shows other pattern which are similar or complementary.
Reference	If there are other references, this element will provide the author reference and where one can find more information about it.

4 Test Case Identification

In this section, we show how we have identified test cases to check an application composed of a given mobile agent design pattern. We adopt test case as a set of inputs, execution preconditions, and expected outcomes developed to exercise a particular program in order to verify compliance with a specific requirement (IEEE terminology). Firstly, we present the design pattern which we work with. Then, a brief presentation of a methodology from which the test cases are obtained and, finally, the test cases.

For the lack of space, we consider just one design pattern: the Itinerary [9]. We have chosen a migration pattern due to its mobility issues and, specifically the Itinerary one, on account of the applications on hand that implement it, allowing test case experimentation (see Section 5). The pattern provide a way in which an agent can migrate and execute a task in remote computers. The solution is: in a source agency, the agent (called Itinerary) receives an itinerary (list of agencies) and migrates sequentially through it executing a job. In the end, the agent returns to the source agency bringing with it the obtained results.

As we are working with a pattern, our goal is to determine some test cases which any implementation that uses that pattern could be tested with. Namely, we are interested in selecting test cases from the design pattern specification that could run under any implementation that uses it. In [9], the author models and specifies patterns using UML diagrams: class diagram and sequence diagrams. Sequence diagrams, even though restricted, are a good manner to specify different scenarios of execution of a system. It is important to remark that the diagrams used in [9] are constructed based on a notation to represent agents and agencies as objects and mobility as message passing.

To identify test cases, we consider the following: (1) From each sequence diagram, a test case is be obtained; (2) Test case inputs cause the execution of the respective sequence diagram; and (3) Oracles are the necessary statements that verify if the application has executed as described in the diagrams. Note that class diagrams are used to generate an initial state, inputs, and the oracle, since they represent properties on agents and relations among the objects.

We have chosen three test cases that are presented as follows.
Test Case 1: Test case for an empty itinerary. This test case intends to check whether the implementation copes with an empty itinerary. Implementations may tend to forget to deal with empty agencies' list and ends in a null reference.
Test Case 2: Test case for an itinerary with duplicated agencies. This test case try to verify whether an implementation copes with an itinerary that contains repeated agencies. Most platforms do not allow a migration when the target is the same agency, throwing an exception. Therefore, the implementation should expect this and deal with it properly.
Test Case 3: Test case for an itinerary with an unavailable agency. This test case aims to checking whether agent implementation copes with an unavailable agency in its itinerary. In general, implementations do not expect to receive an itinerary with agencies that are not ready to work with. This usually raises exceptions and, thus, applications break.

Oracles are the components of test cases which are responsible for giving a verdict about their execution. The oracles of our test cases are very similar, since the test cases come from the same design pattern. The oracles verify three main properties: 1) whether the itinerary agent has passed through every agency; 2) whether the itinerary agent has done the desired task on each agency; and 3) whether the itinerary agent has returned to the source agency with the results.

5   Test Case Implementation and Execution

In this section, we show an implementation and execution of Test Case 3 identified in Section 4 and present the results of the execution (faults found).

In order to implement and execute the test case, we have chosen there applications that uses the Itinerary pattern. The first one provides a sample of Itinerary execution and is presented in [9]. The second one is called *Monitoring Changing Conditions* – a flight ticket sale application – presented in [13]. And, as the third application, we have the system presented in [11] – a reviewing system to manage a virtual program committee meeting for conference. These applications were developed using the Java language and the Grasshopper platform.

In the next subsections, we show how we have designed and implemented the test case, by firstly presenting our platform independent solution and, then, describing the solution for the Grasshopper platform. We also show our approach to allowing interaction between agents and test driver. Notice that the platform independent solution can be reused to implement the tests in different platforms. Also, it provides a global understanding of the problem of implementing the test case, even if only one platform is considered.

5.1   Platform Independent Solution

We are interested in determining how and when the agent under test (AUT for short) communicate with the test driver, that is, how the test driver will be informed about agents behaviour. The test architecture design must take this into account. The decision about when the agent will send information to the test driver can be done regardless of platform execution details, but how this communication will happen and the necessary infrastructure to support it should be chosen taking into account the platform where it will execute. Here, we show our proposal of when the agent should communicate with the test driver.

There are some ways to make the AUT communicate with a test driver: (1) The AUT collects the information required by the test driver during its execution and, at the end, send this information to the test driver; (2) Information is collected during the migration, namely, the agent will send the information to the test drive as soon as possible: *on-the-fly*.

Note that we are mainly interested in collecting information about an agent execution regarding its itinerary, i.e., we do not want to loose information during migration. Therefore, we have chosen the second alternative above, because we can have information required by the test driver at any point of execution. This solution is better explained in Figure 1. There, you can see an AUT migrating between different agencies and, in each of them, it sends information about its behaviour to the test driver, that can follow the execution at any point, even if the agent has not finished its itinerary.

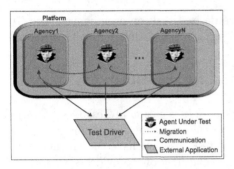

Fig. 1. Platform independent test design.

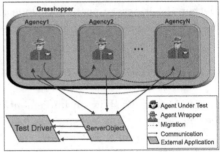

Fig. 2. Grasshopper test design.

5.2   Platform Dependent Solution

Considering platform execution, we need to define how the AUT communicate with the test driver. For this, implementation issues should be take into account as well as the platform independence of test drivers. Since the applications we want to test are implemented in the Grasshopper platform, this subsection focus on this platform. However, we expect the general approach can be used when considering other platforms.

As we have mentioned above, we expect the test driver to be an external application. So, firstly, we need to find an effective way of performing communication between the Grasshopper application and an external application (test driver). We have chosen the way proposed by platform developers in [14] (see Figure 2). This solution is based on a producer-consumer system where the AUT "produces" information and the test driver "consumes" it. The main idea is to put a *ServerObject* between the applications accessed via a proxy object.

Note that we need to turn the AUT into an agent that can send information to the test driver, namely, it need to do tasks that are beyond its responsibility. In the testing community, this is called instrumentation, because we need to put into the AUT code just for test purposes. Few works have dealt with this subject in the mobile agents area and, between them, we highlight Delamaro's work [15]. His goal is to do structural tests in mobile agents instrumenting both the agent and the platform using a tool called Jabuti/MA [16]. As we expect to use this approach in different platforms, we cannot guarantee we can instrument them, even in an automatic way (as you can see in [15]).

Thus, the possibilities are: (1) Instrumenting the platform in order to enable it to send information; (2) Instrumenting the AUT class in order to enable it to send its information; and, (3) Instrumenting the AUT via inheritance or composition producing a kind of wrapper agent which will be responsible for sending messages containing information about the AUT.

The third solution appears to be the best one, inasmuch we intend to be able to apply it in any platform and it is a safe solution (we are not inserting any new code within the agent class). This approach is proposed by McGregor in [17] and is widely used by the object-oriented development community. As you can also see in Figure 2, a wrapper agent will execute instead of the AUT. It will delegate to the AUT responsibilities regarding pattern execution and it will be responsible for sending information to the test driver. This way, the instrumentation will be as separated as possible from the agent code.

Figure 3 shows the wrapper agent structure. The wrapper is an agent that contains the AUT with two interfaces. The first one is the AUT interface, which will make the agent wrapper able to behave as the AUT during test case execution. The other one is a test interface, which will interact with the test driver. The agent wrapper will interact with the AUT through relay methods.

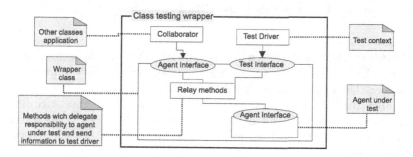

Fig. 3. Class testing wrapper.

5.3   Test Case Execution Results

Now we comment on the execution of Test case 3 in the chosen applications, mostly about faults we have uncovered when we executed the test case using the structure presented above. The first application [9] is a sample of the pattern, that is, the itinerary agent migrate between agencies sending messages to the display. As we executed the test case, we detected an application break, that is, when the agent tried to migrate to the unavailable agency the application crashed due to an uncaught exception. This is a common fault, due to the fact that applications usually do not treat these kind of unexpected behaviour. The second application [13] uses the Itinerary pattern in a context where an user intend to get information about flight ticket prices of some flight companies. Each platform agency is a flight company and the itinerary agent migrates between them in order to obtain their ticket charges. This application also has a fault. When the itinerary agent tries to go to the unavailable agency, it turn back to the source agency, leaving the following agencies unvisited. As we can see, the application treat the possibility of having an unavailable agency, but in a wrong way. Finally, in [18], the author shows a conference reviewing system where the Itinerary pattern is used when a paper (itinerary agent) is submitted to reviewing by committee members (located on different platform agencies). In this context, the fault found is more critical then other ones. When the itinerary agent tries to migrate to the unavailable agency, that is, when a paper is sent to an off-line reviewer, it gets lost carrying with it early review information (if there is any), and the other reviewers do not become aware of the problem. This is critical as the application do not crash and it can be hard to find out what happened.

6   Test Pattern Identification

As mentioned before, using test cases obtained from design patterns can be an interesting way to identify test patterns. For instance, the test case considered in Section 5 really works when we want to identify some kinds of faults. Moreover, as this test case was identified from a design pattern, we can say that it is recurring since the design pattern is recurring. Furthermore, the test case was successfully (it has identified faults) applied at three applications that uses Itinerary pattern.

After we have identified a test pattern, we need to write it using a properly pattern template. Below, we show the "Black Hole" test pattern.

- **Name:** Black Hole
- **Context:** Implementations which use the Itinerary mobile agent design pattern. This pattern is useful within a context that agencies are unstable, namely, they can be unavailable at any time.
- **Intent:** Testing an implementation aiming to verify whether it copes with agencies that are available or not. It is desirable to check if the agents do not fall in a "black hole" when there is off-line agencies in its itinerary.
- **Structure**
  - **Test Model:** Figure 4 shows the sequence diagram for a basic execution of the test (a platform independent model).
  - **Procedure:**
    - Construct an agent wrapper for the Itinerary agent using inheritance;
    - Override the methods *doJob* and *nextDestination* allowing them to call their respective superclass methods, and adding a sending message to the test driver in order to make it known about what happens;
    - Put on the test driver a code to start a certain number of agencies where one of them will be unavailable;
    - Execute the application setting the agents itinerary with those agencies.
  - **Oracle:** Using the received messages, the oracle should verify if:
    - Test drive received a message informing agent arrival for each available agencies and no one for unavailable agencies;
    - Test drive received a message informing job done for each available agencies and no one for unavailable agencies;
    - Test drive received a message informing agent arrival for source agency.
- **Implementation:**
  - **Grasshopper platform:**
  The sequence diagram for the Grasshopper platform is close to the independent one shown in Figure 4. The difference is in the way the test driver communicates with the AUT. In order to implement the exchange message between agents and test driver, the solution is to implement as the Grasshopper manual recommends [14]. The main idea is to put a *ServerObject* between them which will be accessed via a proxy object by both of them. This *ServerObject* will receive messages from agents and turn them available to test driver.

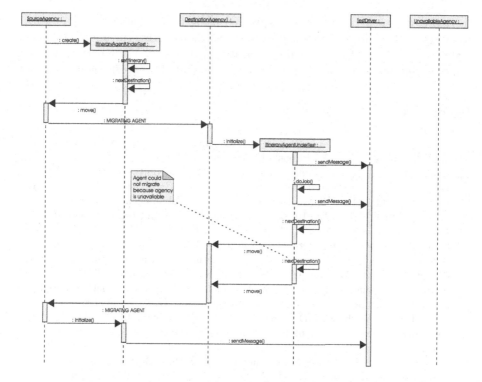

Fig. 4. Independent Black Hole's Sequence Diagram (Basic Execution).

– **Forces:** (1) Automatically starting of unavailable agencies is not a easy task in most platform. (2) In general, platforms throw exception when an agent ask for a migrate operation to a unavailable agency, what usually is not properly treated by the code.
– **Fault Model:**
  – Uncaught exception thrown because of unavailable agency – system crash;
  – Not handling agencies which come after an unavailable agency;
  – Loosing an itinerary agent after it try to go to an unavailable agency.

7   Conclusions

In this work, we intended to narrow the distance between mobile agent design patterns and test patterns. For this, we have proposed a way of obtaining test patterns from design pattern models and specifications, and to document them using a test pattern template. We also presented test cases generated from design patterns as possible test patterns. As an example, a test case has been considered and experimented by applying it to three applications. With that, we have demonstrated the corresponding test pattern efficiency and also its reliability.

Test patterns, although a promising approach, need to be widely proposed and validated by the community before we can reach definite conclusions. Furthermore, design patterns are also specified using formal languages. So, an interesting work could be to define test patterns that address the automatic generation of test cases from formal specifications, that is, the test pattern would contain solutions of automatic procedures to generate those test cases.

References

1. Binder, R.V.: Testing object-oriented systems: models, patterns, and tools. Addison-Wesley Longman Publishing Co., Inc. (1999)
2. Lange, M.: It's Testing Time! - Patterns for Testing Software. In: Proc. of XI European Conf. on Pattern Languages of Programs, Bad Irsee, Germany (2001)
3. Harrison, C.G., Chess, D.M., Kershenbaum, A.: Mobile agents: are they a good idea? Technical Report RC 19887, IBM Thomas J. Watson Research Center (1995)
4. Fuggeta, A., Picco, G., Vigna, G.: Understanding code mobility. In: IEEE Transactions on Software Engineering. Volume 24. (1998)
5. Aridor, Y., Lange, D.B.: Agent design patterns: Elements of agent application design. In: II Int. Conf. on Autonomous Agents, ACM Press (1998) 108–115
6. Tahara, Y., Ohsuga, A., Honiden, S.: Agent system development method based on agent patterns. In: 21st Int. Conf. on Software. Eng., IEEE Press (1999) 356–367
7. Lima, E.F.A., Machado, P.D.L., Sampaio, F.R., Figueiredo, J.C.A.: An approach to modelling and applying mobile agent design patterns. SIGSOFT Softw. Eng. Notes **29** (2004) 1–8
8. Kendall, E.A., Krishna, P.V.M., Pathak, C.V., Suresh, C.B.: Patterns of intelligent and mobile agents. In Sycara, K.P., Wooldridge, M., eds.: Proc. of the 2nd Int. Conf. on Autonomous Agents, New York, ACM Press (1998) 92–99
9. Lima, E.F.A.: Formalização e análise de padrões de projeto para agentes móveis. Master's thesis, Universidade Federal de Campina Grande (2004)
10. Gamma, E., Helm, R., Johnson, R., Vlissides, J.: Design patterns: elements of reusable object-oriented software. Addison-Wesley Longman Pub. Co., Inc. (1995)
11. Guedes, F.P., Machado, P.D.L., Medeiros, V.N.: Developing mobile agent-based applications. In: 29th Conferencia Latino Americana de Informática, La Paz (2003)
12. Singh, A.: Test patterns. Master's thesis, Florida Institute Technology (2001)
13. Medeiros, V.N., Machado, P.D.L., Guedes, F.P.: Desenvolvimento de aplicações baseadas em agentes móveis. In: X ENIC, João Pessoa - Brazil (2002)
14. GmbH, I.: Grasshopper Programmer's Guide, http://www.grasshopper.de. (2001)
15. Delamaro, M.E., Vincenzi, A.M.R.: Structural Testing of Mobile Agents. In Guelfi, N., ed.: Int Workshop on Scientific Eng. of Java Dist. Ap.. LNCS. Springer (2003)
16. Vincenzi, A.M.R., Wong, W.E., Delamaro, M.E., Maldonado, J.C.: Jabuti: A coverage analysis tool for java programs. In: 17th SBES, Manaus - Brazil (2003)
17. McGregor, J.D., Sykes, D.A.: A Practical Guide to Testing Object-Oriented Software. Addison-Wesley (2001)
18. Guedes, F.P.: Um modelo para o desenvolvimento de aplicações baseadas em agentes móveis. Master's thesis, Universidade Federal de Campina Grande (2002)

A Pattern Oriented Mobile Agent Framework for Mobile Computing

Nobukazu Yoshioka[1] and Shinichi Honiden[1,2]

[1] National Institute of Informatics,
2-1-2 Hitotsubashi, Chiyoda-ku, Tokyo 101-8431, Japan
{nobukazu,honiden}@nii.ac.jp
[2] The University of Tokyo

Abstract. As a consequence of the increasing role of computers through-out society, computers, especially mobile devices, are used in diverse situations. Additionally, the computing environment is becoming more changeable. A network application coordinating mobile devices needs to be able to adapt to changes in the environments. In this paper, we pro-pose a new architecture for mobile computing, which uses a mobile agent technology and adapts to changes flexibly. The framework splits the spec-ification of an application into network environments, coordination logic and patterns. Patterns are applied to the coordination logic in order to derive appropriate behaviors automatically.

1 Introduction

Owing to the growth in mobile computing and network environments, it is pos-sible to communicate with other parties through networks by using portable computing devices at almost any time and any place. Consequently, applica-tions coordinating devices to integrate information or services, namely network applications, play an important role in mobile computing. Examples of network applications are data sharing, information searches, and schedule coordination among devices. Network applications may access heterogeneous devices with var-ious performance, e.g. PDAs, portable PCs, workstations, etc. Mobile agents are useful techniques for efficient coordination of such devices. For example, when a coordination application in PDA tries to search databases in a workstation, migration of the application may be efficient rather than remote access from PDA. So, we should design the application as a mobile agent. However, devices also may move physically to other networks with a different security policy, so that mobile agents, that need to migrate logically to these devices, must adapt to changes of new network environments. In this situation, two kinds of issues have to be considered: (1) access protocol selection (logical migration or remote messaging) and (2) security issues (authentication / encryption of messages). The efficiency of access protocols depends on the ability of devices. On the other hand, security depends on application domains and the properties of the net-works through which agents communicate with others. Furthermore, depending

A. Karmouch, L. Korba, and E. Madeira (Eds.): MATA 2004, LNCS 3284, pp. 369–380, 2004.
© Springer-Verlag Berlin Heidelberg 2004

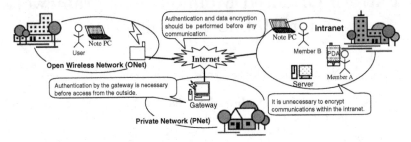

Fig. 1. A typical network environment and security policies

on security overheads, the efficiency of access protocols may change. Therefore, it is a key issue to design suitable mobile agents capable of adapting dynamically.

In this paper, we propose a new mobile agent architecture for easy design of agents capable of adapting to network changes at run time. Our architecture distinguishes dynamic aspects of agents as patterns and the definition of network environments from static aspects as coordination logic.

First, we describe a typical scenario of mobile computing in section 2 as an illustration in the remainder of this paper. Section 3 summarizes the problems of mobile computing, and section 4 describes our solution. In section 5, we discuss our architecture by comparing it with traditional approaches and from the viewpoint of adaptability. Section 6 presents related work. Finally, section 7 consists of concluding remarks.

2   A Network Application

In mobile computing, one may access various networks with portable devices while moving from one place to another. In addition, one can use public machines for computing in some cases. Network applications must coordinate not only desktop PCs but also mobile devices using public resources. In such contexts, network security policies differ.

Figure 1 illustrates an overview of our scenario. In this scenario, we consider information distribution software, such as images or music data, as a typical network application and four kinds of networks: a private network (PNet), the Internet, an open wireless network (ONet), and an intranet. All networks are connected via the Internet. The details of the **network environment** are as follows.

- **PNet**, a network in ■■■■'s house, is accessed only by people permitted to enter the house. It is connected to the Internet via the home gateway, which works as a firewall.
- **ONet** is a hot-spot public service provided at stations or shops.
- **Intranet** is a network in a company to which all group members belong. Authentication is required before accessing the network.

This scenario features three persons for a group: ■■■■, ■■■■■■ ■ and ■■■■■■ ■, and each person uses a portable PC or PDA. They can use a server machine in the intranet for their mobile computing. For simplicity, we consider only ■■■■'s

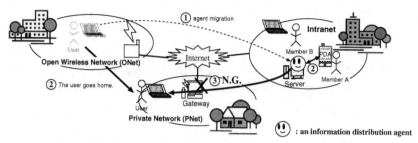

Fig. 2. An Example of Network Environment Change

information to be distributed over other members' machines. Mobile agents can be used for the distribution and created in the ▯▯▯▯'s device to bring his data.

3   Problems of Mobile Computing

To design network applications, we need to address the following concerns due to the terminal mobility.

Efficiency of resource use: In some cases, shared resources can be used. For example, a server machine can be used for mobile computing in the intranet in our scenario. In some cases, local access after migration may be more efficient than remote messaging. Agents should migrate to appropriate resources, when the agents access poor devices such as PDAs. For example, in figure 2, an information distribution agent first migrates to the intranet server before accessing to ▯▯▯▯▯▯ ▯'s PDA.

Security measures: Security considerations differ among networks. In figure 1, PNet is protected by a gateway, and so authentication by the gateway is necessary before access from the outside. In the case of the intranet, authentication of the other party should be performed before any communication through the Internet, and private data should be encrypted to prevent masquerading and wiretappings.

In addition, security policies depend on applications. In the case of our scenario, data shared in the group is private and cannot be accessible by non-members. In other words, we must prevent wiretappings of shared data.

Depending on the above measures, the efficiency of agent behavior may change. In the case of figure 1, an agent in ONet should migrate to the intranet to access both ▯▯▯▯▯▯ ▯ and ▯'s private data, if security costs for two remote messaging through the Internet are higher than the migration costs. Therefore, when we select the access protocols of agents, we must consider security measures from the viewpoint of efficiency.

Environment Changes: Most of the time, network environment changes when devices move physically to other networks or agents logically migrate to other devices in other networks. The change may lead to variation of security policies with which agents must comply. An example of network environment change is shown in Figure 2. This figure shows that ▯▯▯▯'s device is moved from ONet to PNet while the agent is searching ▯▯▯▯▯▯ ▯'s shared files. In this case,

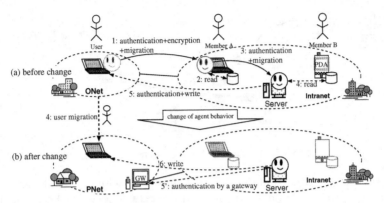

Fig. 3. Solution of Our Framework

the agent cannot return to the ▣▣▣▣'s device, because the agent assumes that the terminal is in ONet. So, the agent tries accessing the ▣▣▣▣'s device directly, but it is denied by the home gateway of PNet. [3] We need to design a system that can respond to such changes in the environment.

Difficulty of the design: It is difficult to design an efficient agent complying with suitable security even if the network environment changes due to physical migration.

4   Approach

In this section, we describe an architecture that can adapt to the changes described in section 3. Figure 3 is an adaptation example. In this case, the architecture checks the new network environment in order to apply proper security measures and re-derives the agent's behavior when it detects network errors. Finally, authentication at the gateway is added to the behavior.

In this architecture, an agent embodies three models: **coordination logic**, **network environment model** and **patterns**. Coordination logic is a definition of the agent's functions, and patterns denote the behavior. In our example, a series of device accesses is described as coordination logic.

The **network environment model** indicates runtime network environment of the agent. In the case of figure 3, the network environment model (a) explains that ▣▣▣▣'s device is in ONet, and two member's devices are in the intranet. In contrast, in the case of (b), the model explains that ▣▣▣▣'s device is in PNet.

Access protocols and security policies are implemented as **patterns**. Therefore, authentication procedures and encryption protocol are specified in patterns. In addition, access protocols, such as remote messaging and agent migration, are included in the patterns.

These three models are inputs of the architecture. In other words, the architecture derives an agent behavior from those models when the agent is created

---

[3] In this paper, we assume that agents can know new IP addresses of terminals after its physical migration using a directory service.

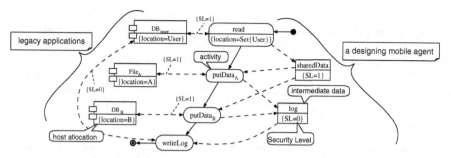

Fig. 4. An Example of coordination logic

or when the architecture detects changes of external network environments, and executes the behavior.

4.1 Coordination Logic

Coordination logic, which can be represented as a UML activity chart, defines a coordination procedure of network application. The logic is implemented using an agent, and denotes a functional aspect of the agent.

The activities in coordination logic are interpreted by the architecture as agent actions. Additionally, data flow, host allocations, and security levels are added to the chart. Figure 4 illustrates an example of coordination logic in our scenario. The broken arrows and quadrangles indicate data flow and intermediate data of an agent, respectively. A data flow between an activity and an application[4] indicates a message between the agent and the application.

Host allocation indicates the host where the cooperating applications and agent activities can be performed. The information is expressed by a property named "location". Absence of the property means the activity can be allocated to any host. In our example, there are three devices and a public server machine in the intranet. The devices of ▯▯▯▯ and ▯▯▯▯▯▯ ▯ and ▯ are named for *User*, *A* and *B*, respectively. The public machine is labeled *serv*. Thus, the "read" activity should be executed on host *User*.

"SL" is a variable that takes several values (security level). The security level expresses how to consider security for each data. This information is an application-dependent aspect of security policies. In our example, we consider the following two levels: 0 and 1. Former level indicates we need no data protection, and the latter level indicates we need to encrypt the data.

4.2 Network Environment Model

Network environment models express the runtime environment of agents. The information is described using two tables: a host information and a network information table. Table 1 is an example of a network environment model. The table shows the state at the beginning of our system illustrated in figure 1. In

---

[4] In this paper, "application" denotes any software except the mobile agent we are designing.

Table 1. An Example of a Network Environment Model

A host information table			A network information table	
Host	Type	Network domain	Networks	Network domains
Current host	NotePC	ONet	network($User$,A)	ONet,intranet,Internet
$User$	NotePC	ONet	network($User$,B)	ONet,intranet,Internet
A	PDA	intranet	network(A,B)	intranet
B	NotePC	intranet		
$serv$	DesktopPC	intranet		

our example, there are three sorts of devices: portable PCs, PDAs and desktop PCs. These are labeled as NotePC, PDA and DesktopPC, respectively. Network domains are network names to which hosts belong. A function named "network" in network information tables returns network domain names between two hosts corresponding to the second column. This function is used in patterns.

Tables in network environment models are updated when the network address of a device changes due to its migration. This information is used when an agent communicates with others.

4.3   Pattern

Patterns are rewriting rules of part of activity diagrams. Figure 5 shows some examples of patterns. The rules are expressed using two boxes named "point-cut" and "advice", similar to Aspect-Oriented programming, and the transition labeled "≪rewrite≫" between the boxes. Pointcut boxes indicate pattern conditions and applicable templates in application coordination logic. In the case of $P_{MesAuthEnc}$, the pattern is applied when the security level of a message between an activity named s and an application named app is 1. Annotation boxes of pointcut indicate the context of pattern application. Thus, in the case of $P_{MesAuthEnc}$, the current host src must be a element of a set $hosts$, networks between the agent and the application app must include the Internet, and app must be in ONet or the intranet. The context is evaluated using a network environment model of agents described in section 4.2 at run-time.

Advice boxes illustrate access protocols and security procedures. There are two types of protocols: remote messaging protocols and migration protocols. Security procedures are implementation of security policies. Thus, an advice may include encryption and decryption for preventing data leakage, signature generation and verification for preventing tampering, and authentication for preventing masquerading. The advice of $P_{MesAuthEnc}$ indicates a remote messaging protocol that includes authentication activity named "Auth" and key exchange activity named "KeyExchange" for encryption of messages between s and app. Similarly, $P_{MesGWAuthEnc}$ includes authentication by a gateway, key exchange activity for intermediate data encryption of the agent. $P_{MigServAuthEnc}$ is for the use of a public server machine in the intranet.

Annotations written in italic are parts of program code written in Java. Annotations attached to advice boxes are evaluation programs of the pattern costs and priorities of pattern application. A function "hostType" in the annotation indicates a host type of devices. This function refers to the host information table in a network environment model. Constant values in program codes, such as

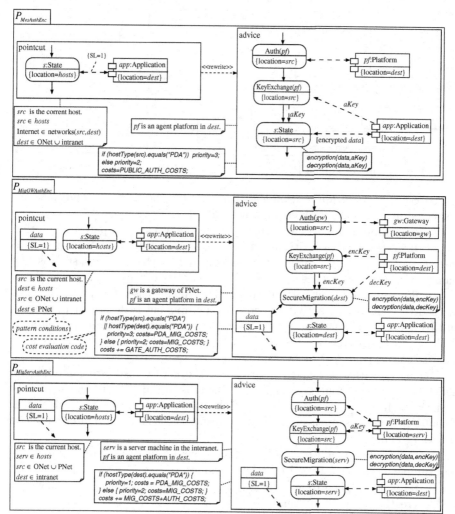

Fig. 5. Pattern Examples

PDA_MIG_COSTS or $AUTH\_COSTS$, indicate numbers of costs. For example, PDA_MIG_COSTS is the cost of an agent migration to/from PDA. These values are defined for each network environment.

4.4   Pattern Application Mechanism

Our architecture decides agent behavior using the above models. The algorithm of pattern selection and rewriting of application logic is as follows. Our architecture first extracts a sequence of activities, ▭▭▭▭▭, which starts a current activity in application logic followed by the next activities to be executed. Secondly, activities in ▭▭▭▭▭ are compared sequentially from a head with pointcuts of patterns. The structure is checked, and then the context is examined. In detail, location conditions of activities and security levels of messages and intermediate

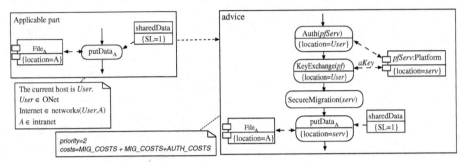

Fig. 6. An Example of Pattern Application and Calculation of its Costs

data are tested using application logic. In addition, the network conditions are inspected using the network environment model.

Thirdly, applicable parts are replaced with the advice of a pattern. In other words, migration and security activities are added to application logic, while instances of the pattern properties are substituted for the variables, such as host names of location properties. Next, costs and priority of patterns are calculated. Figure 6 is an example of pattern application. In this case, $P_{MigServAuthEnc}$ is applied to "putData$_A$" activity where the environment is described in table 1. In this figure, "s", "app" and "$data$" in figure 5 are replaced with "putData$_A$", "File$_A$" and "sharedData", respectively. In addition, host $User$ and A are substituted for src and $dest$ of location properties, respectively.

Sequences with the highest priority and the lowest costs are candidates of agent behavior. So, fourthly, applicable patterns are applied to the sequences with the highest priority recursively, and the sum total of the costs is calculated. Finally, one of the sequences with the lowest costs is selected and executed as the agent behavior.

Pattern costs depend on implementation overheads of a system. Table 2 is an example of costs expressed by relative values.

Patterns are applied to application logic at the time of any of the following.
 – At creation time of an agent.
 – When all planned activities are executed.
 – When messaging or migration fails.

Figure 7 shows adaptation steps in response to change described in Figure 2. In this scenario, an agent detects a messaging error when it tries to authenticate the $User$ host. In this case, the new behavior is derived by our architecture after updating the network environment model. The right-hand diagram in the figure depicts new derived behavior of the agent. In this diagram, the authentication of $User$ terminal is replaced by authentication of the ▮▮▮▮▮▮▮ of PNet. This mechanism is the implementation detail for Figure 3.

4.5   Implementation

We implement our architecture in a multi-agent framework, Bee-gent[1]. This section describes how to implement our architecture by extending Bee-gent.

Table 2. An example of costs

Constant name	Value	Description
MIG_COSTS	3	migration costs from/to PC
PDA_MIG_COSTS	10	migration costs from/to PDA
AUTH_COSTS	5	authentication costs using shared keys
GATE_AUTH_COSTS	10	authentication costs at a gateway
PUBLIC_AUTH_COSTS	20	authentication costs using RSA keys
ENCRYPTION_COSTS	0	encryption and decryption costs of data

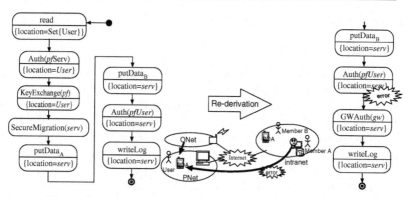

Fig. 7. Re-derivation of Behavior for Change of Environment

The Bee-gent framework features two types of agents: **agent wrappers** and **mediation agents**. An agent wrapper wraps legacy applications (i.e. stand-alone applications, distributed objects, DBs or Web services) to communicate with other agents, while a mediation agent supports inter-application coordination by handling all communications.

The mediation agents incorporate three mechanisms: a coordination mechanism, a communication mechanism and a migration mechanism. The agents move from the site of an application to another site where they interact with another agent through the network or locally. Because behavior of all agents is based on state transition as coordination mechanism, we can use this for the coordination logic of our architecture.

For our architecture, we need to execute the following rewrite of the Bee-gent framework.

- Modification of state manager class
- Preparation of abstract classes for a pattern and network configuration
- Sending methods in a state class are extended to support automatic data encryption.
- Creation of new classes for derivation of behavior: The classes are invoked from state manager
- A detection mechanism of IP address changes

By using the above facilities, we can use the usual Bee-gent agent classes with additional information: patterns with cost and network configuration.

Table 3. An Example of Rule Based Programming

```
-- definition of logic
share_data_from(PSEQ, T) :- calc_cost(PSEQ, [M1|M2|M3|M4]), read_exec(X,T, M1),
   search_A_exec(X, Y, Z,T2, M2), search_B_exec(Y, ZZ,T3,M3), write_exec(Z, ZZ,T4,M4).
-- definition of stubs
read_exec(X,T, migrate) :- network(T) = onet, network(user) = pnet,
   auth_gateway, key_exchange(user, K), migrate(user, K), read(X,nil).
read_exec(X,T, message) :- network(T) = onet, network(user) = pnet,
   auth_gateway, key_exchange(user, K), read(X,K).
-- definition of external environment
network(user) :- private.
network(user,member_A) :- internet.
```

5   Discussion

5.1   Evaluation of Our Framework

In section 3, we enumerated the problems of mobile computing. Those problems can be solved by our architecture.

From the viewpoint of efficiency, this architecture has a cost in patterns, and it can derive the most efficient behavior by selecting a candidate with the lowest cost. In this paper, we consider communication cost, migration overheads and security overheads.

In terms of security issues, we deal with security policy in addition to security overheads. In detail, application-dependent security policies are defined at the security level in application coordination logic. On the other hand, application-independent security policies are implemented in patterns. In other words, patterns are collections of proper behavior components of the agent from the viewpoint of security policy. By re-applying the patterns, the agent can behave properly even when the network environment changes.

Regarding the difficulty of agent design, the architecture distinguishes the dynamic aspects of an agent as patterns and the definition of network environment from the static aspects as the coordination logic. By distinguishing between these definitions, we can analyze the functional aspect and changeable environment easily. In addition, application independent behaviors can be implemented as patterns for library components.

Pattern libraries are extended or changed when available hosts or new types of devices are added to runtime environments. In this case, the contexts of patterns or calculation programs of priorities and costs are changed without the changes of pattern structure. Otherwise, only few activities for access protocols are added. When new network domains are available, only contexts of pattern pointcuts must be changed.

In contrast, when network security policies are changed, structure of pattern advice must be changed. However, activities for security procedures can be used in any application domain, so these are one of the CASE tool libraries. In addition, patterns are similar in structure, so the CASE tool can include templates or abstract classes of patterns.

5.2   Comparison with Other Approaches

Rule-Based Approach: In this approach, all logic, network environment and behavior are defined as rules to develop a flexible agent. The agent behavior is derived by reasoning based on the rules. This approach may be appropriate, when all aspects, such as logic and external environment, cannot be defined statically. However, in the case of our application domain, the reasoning may not be necessary. In this case, faster routine work agents should be developed rather than such intelligent agents.

Table 3 shows part of a rule-based program. The program is an example of an implementation of our scenario described in section 2. For the rule-based program, a stub or wrapping function is needed to adapt to the dynamic change, because it cannot be decided statically whether the activity is executed after migration or using remote messaging. The ▭▭▭▭_▭▭▭▭ predicate is a stub of ▭▭▭▭ activity which decides dynamically whether the migration is necessary or not. After all, static logic cannot be separated from description of dynamic aspects.

Moreover, rule-based expression is incompatible with Object-Oriented Development. Our approach only uses a rule as pattern for dynamic aspects. In addition, an inference engine is unsuitable for mobile devices, because it needs CPU and memory resources. In our approach, a pattern is just a rewrite rule of static aspect, namely coordination logic, which requires no inference other than pattern matching.

Traditional Agent Approach: If an agent is designed using traditional (OO) programming, many "if statement"s or exceptions must be inserted in the coordination logic. The implication is that it is difficult to change coordination logic, to append a new network configuration, or to modify security policies, because various aspects are jumbled and depend on each others.

6   Related Work

Cabri has proposed a context-dependent coordination mechanism based on programmable interaction space[2]. Using this mechanism, one can define environment-dependent behaviors without changes of agent behaviors. In addition, agents can program application-dependent behaviors to interact with other agents implicitly using programmable tuple space. The main difference between our patterns and programmable tuple space is that patterns can use application and environment information simultaneously. In contrast, tuple space is programmed using environment information or application by agents. Consequently, tuple space cannot control agent migration properly, because it not only needs environment information but also application logic. Similarly, tuple space cannot consider both application level securities and network security policies, although it can protect hosts against malicious agents. Patterns can be defined using both data.

Brandt has proposed a mobile agent framework that is considered to be adaptable in heterogeneous environments[3]. The framework provides a transparent access environment for agents on various OSs and machine architectures. The mechanism is that the framework separates access interface of resource from implementation of the access, so that the framework can dynamically load a proper access code corresponding to the environment. Using this framework, static aspects can be separated from dynamic ones. However, the framework cannot check overall efficiency of agent behavior. In other words, this framework can only consider the efficiency of each access. In contrast, our approach can consider the efficiency from the viewpoint of the agent behavior in its entirety.

Also, a great deal of research has been done on description languages for Security Policy[5][6][7][8]. Security policy changes can be specified by updating the policy specifications described in these languages. However, the research provides neither methods nor guidelines to deal with changes. On the other hand, our approach provides a method that can deal with security policy and its guidelines by meaning of security patterns and security levels.

7   Conclusions and Future Work

In this paper, we proposed a framework for adaptive mobile agents. In the architecture, the description of logic, patterns and environment of a system can be separated. Consequently, a prospect of system design has been improved markedly. In addition, the architecture decides appropriate behavior dynamically by applying patterns and calculating their costs. This mechanism allows the system to adapt dynamically to environmental changes.

Future work includes soundness and completeness of patterns. The soundness means that we guarantee application of patterns does not violate security policies. It can be checked by dynamic policy check mechanisms. The completeness indicates any agent behavior satisfying security policies can be derived using defined patterns for all contexts. We can verify it statically using formal methods.

References

1. Bee-gent: Muti-agent framework, http://www.toshiba.co.jp/beegent/index.html.
2. G. Cabri, L. Leonardi, and F. Zambonelli, "Engineering Mobile-Agent Applications via Context-Dependent Coordination", In Proc. of ICSE-2001, pp.371–380, 2001.
3. R. Brandt and H. Reiser. Dynamic Adaptation of Mobile Agents in Heterogenous Environments. LNCS 2240, pp.70-87,2001.
4. Giovanni Vigna, editor. *Mobile Agents and Security*, LNCS 1419. Springer Verlag, 1998.
5. N. Damianou, N. Duray, E.Lupu, and M. Sloman. The Ponder policy specification language. LNCS 1995, pp. 17–28,2001
6. J. Lobo, R.Bhatia, and S. Naqvi, A policy description laguage, In Proc. of AAAI, pp. 291-298, 1999.
7. S. Jajodia, P. Samarati, and V.S.Subrahmanian. A logical language for expression authorisations, In Proc. of IEEE, Symp. on Security and Privacy, pp. 31–42, 1997.
8. R.Ortalo. A flexible method for information system security policy specification. In Proc. of ESORICS'98, pp 67–84,1998.

Author Index

Lecture Notes in Computer Science

For information about Vols. 1–3182

please contact your bookseller or Springer